Verbal Behavior Analysis

Inducing and Expanding New Verbal Capabilities in Children with Language Delays

R. Douglas Greer
Columbia University Teachers College
Graduate School of Arts and Science

Denise E. Ross
Columbia University Teachers College

PEARSON

Boston   New York   San Francisco
Mexico City   Montreal   Toronto   London   Madrid   Munich   Paris
Hong Kong   Singapore   Tokyo   Cape Town   Sydney

Executive Editor: *Virginia Lanigan*
Marketing Manager: *Danae April*
Production Editor: *Mary Beth Finch*
Editorial Production Service: *Pine Tree Composition*
Composition Buyer: *Linda Cox*
Manufacturing Buyer: *Linda Morris*
Electronic Composition: *Pine Tree Composition*
Cover Administrator: *Elena Sidorova*

For related titles and support materials, visit our online catalog at www.ablongman.com.

Between the time website information is gathered and then published, it is not unusual for some sites to have closed. Also, the transcription of URLs can result in typographical errors. The publisher would appreciate notification where these errors occur so that they may be corrected in subsequent editions.

ISBN 10: 0-205-45837-8
ISBN 13: 978-0-205-45837-0

Library of Congress Cataloging-in-Publication Data

Greer, Robert Douglas
  Verbal behavior analysis : inducing and expanding new verbal capabilities in children
with language delays / R. Douglas Greer, Denise E. Ross.
      p. cm.
  Includes bibliographical references and index.
  ISBN-13: 978-0-205-45837-0
  ISBN-10: 0-205-45837-8
  1. Verbal behavior. 2. Children—Language. I. Ross, Denise E. II. Title.
  BF455.G742 2008
  155.4'13—dc22

                                                        2007011360

Printed in the United States of America

3 4 5 6 7 8 9 10 V0CR 17 16 15 14 13

Photo credits: p. 95: Photo by Mapy Chavez-Brown. Used with permission; p. 115: FOXTROT © 2004 Bill Amend. Reprinted with permission of Universal Press Syndicate. All rights reserved; p. 194: Photo by Lauren Stolfi. Used with permission; p. 229: Photo by Laura Dorow. Used with permission.

We dedicate this book to the memory of B. F. Skinner
and to the many children with language delays
who have taught us about verbal functions and development.
We hope that all children will benefit.
Royalties for this book are dedicated to the Fred S. Keller School.

ABOUT THE AUTHORS

R. Douglas Greer is Professor of Education and Psychology and Coordinator of the Program in Behavior Analysis at Columbia University Teachers College and the Graduate School of Arts and Sciences, where he has taught for 37 years. He is the author of over 120 research reports (27 on verbal behavior analysis) and conceptual publications in 25 different journals, 12 books, and he has sponsored 130 doctoral dissertations. Greer is a *Fellow of the Association for Behavior Analysis* and is the recipient of the American Psychology Association's *Fred S. Keller Award for Distinguished Contributions to Education*, The Association for Behavior Analysis award for *Distinguished Contributions to the International Dissemination of Behavior Analysis*, the designation of May 5 as the *R. Douglas Greer day for Westchester County* by the Westchester Legislature, and *Distinguished Contributions to the Fred S. Keller School* by The Fred S. Keller School. He is CABAS® Board certified as a Senior Behavior Analyst and a Senior Research Scientist and has assisted in the development of CABAS® School in the United States, Ireland, England, and Italy. His research interests have included verbal behavior analysis, the development of verbal behavior, a learner-driven science of teaching and the organizational behavior analytic procedures to support that system, pediatric behavioral medicine, a behavioral psychology of music, and the induction of and applications of observational learning. He has served on the editorial boards of *Journal of Applied Behavior Analysis, Journal of Behavioral Education, In Segnare all' Handicappato, Journal of Early and Intensive Behavioral Interventions* (Associate Editor), *European Journal of Behavior Analysis, The American Psychologist, Verplanck's Glossary and Thesaurus of The Science of Behavior, The Behavior Analyst, American Journal of Mental Deficiency, Bulletin of the Council for Research in Music Education*, and the *Journal of Music Therapy*. Greer has served as distinguished visiting professor at five universities in Spain (Cadiz, Almeria, Oviedo, Grenada, and Salamanca), a higher education program in applied behavior analysis in Norway, and has lectured at the University of Wales at Bangor. He has presented keynote addresses at conferences on behavior analysis in Canada, Israel, Nigeria, Japan, Spain, Ireland, England, Brazil, Norway, Italy, Taiwan, and Korea.

Denise E. Ross is an Associate Professor of Psychology and Education in the Program for Applied Behavior Analysis at Columbia University, Teachers College. She completed her doctoral degree at Columbia University in 1998 and taught at Florida Atlantic University before joining Teachers College in 2002. Her research on verbal behavior and children with autism and other developmental disabilities has been published in several journals including *Education and Training in Developmental Disabilities, Research in Developmental Disabilities*, the *Journal of Behavioral Education*, the *Analysis of Verbal Behavior*, and the *Journal of Early Intensive Behavioral Interventions*.

CONTENTS

PREFACE

It is an interesting coincidence that this book is being published on the fiftieth anniversary of the publication of Skinner's (1957) *Verbal Behavior*. His book and this one were many years in the making. We used early versions of research in verbal behavior in The Fred S. Keller School and other CABAS® Schools in the United States, Ireland, Italy, and England. Each time we set out to write the book, new sets of findings acted to postpone publishing. However, the amount of evidence that we now have, and the pressing need for it in the field, requires that we disseminate what we have learned to date. Over the last five years, we have had a watershed of findings that extended the role of the listener and the *joining of the listener and speaker* repertoires in a dramatic fashion. Some of the work we describe in the book is so recent that it is still in press or available only in dissertation form; however, a substantial amount is now published. All of the work has been replicated in both research and practice in our schools, and new findings are occurring on a regular basis in both our laboratory and others. We are confident in the findings, as least as much as is possible in any scientific endeavor.

On several occasions Skinner proposed to the first author that verbal behavior was his most important contribution. It took several readings and the initiation of a program of research with children with language delays for us to appreciate the real magnitude of the importance of Skinner's treatment of language as behavior. First, we found out that it simply worked better in terms of what we would teach. As the findings grew, it became apparent that we had happened on a purely Skinnerian account of verbal behavioral development. Our verbal development scheme eliminated the need for a psychological agency or faculty. Here was a purely behavior-selection account of verbal development tied to experience rather than age. Here was an environmental account of productive or "generative" verbal behavior. Despite the criticism of those who said that productive verbal behavior could not be accounted for in terms of reinforcement history, the evidence is now overwhelming that Skinner's *Verbal Behavior* lay the grounds for an account of the source of productive verbal behavior. While much remains to be done, there is a strong foundation for future research and current practice.

This book does not address the basic principles of applied behavior analysis—there simply was not space for doing so; readers will need to have a background in applied behavior analysis to use this text, or they can rely on one of the many excellent, currently published introductory applied behavior analysis textbooks. Instead, this book provides professionals with new and needed interventions to establish verbal developmental capabilities for children who need them. As the children acquire these new capabilities or developmental cusps, they can learn from their environment in ways they could not prior to acquiring them.

We describe interventions or protocols to teach of the capabilities in detail. However, assessing existing and missing capabilities for each child is a critical part of what is needed. In most cases, children will need to have the prerequisite repertoires and verbal capabilities in order to benefit from the protocols. The process of selecting the particular protocol needed for a particular child at any given point in their learning is as important to the success of the protocol as the accurate implementation of the protocols. In the early chapters we also describe how to monitor and ensure accurate professional interactions with children and how to make accurate professional judgments about what is needed. Contemporary applied behavior analysis requires that research findings that can address the moment-to-moment needs of a client or student, and there is a large body of research that has identified how to do this.

Moreover, there is a scientifically-based decision process for when and what the responsible practitioner should do to change tactics for teaching repertoires within each child's developmental capabilities and to introduce protocols for inducing new developmental levels. We have described these developmental levels in the early chapters. They are necessary steps to the success of any applications of behavior analysis for building new operants or higher order classes.

Understanding the sequence of capabilities is a key part of providing successful interventions. A child who does not attend to the voices of others is not likely to be ready to acquire naming, and there are several difficult steps that must be achieved before inducing the components of naming. Similarly, children who are not reinforced by social attention will need particular protocols if their tact repertoire is to expand. We suggest that the reader learn the sequence of capabilities before proceeding to the instructional protocols. The capabilities are *what the child needs to progress in one or more realms*. The protocols, described in detail according to listener and speaker capabilities, are the *means to induce new capabilities* for children *who are ready for them*. First, follow the probe procedures to find which capabilities the child has and which capabilities are missing. Second, identify which new ones are possible for a particular child at this stage in his or her development. Third, do the protocol that is needed while ensuring that the protocol is done accurately, that learn units are present, and that new tactics are used to move the child through the various components of the protocols as determined by the decision protocol.

In many cases the emergence of a new capability is built on teaching children several component repertoires in such a way that a new capability emerges from a new relation between responses and stimuli—a higher order operant. Providing appropriate education for children within their existing repertoires must continue as you work to progress them through the verbal capabilities. For example, when children have the capability for emitting mands and tacts, or basic listener literacy, teach the various educational standards that use these capabilities. The curriculum should expand educational repertoires at each developmental cusp. When the child is ready for the next capability, as described in the text, you then introduce the relevant protocol to induce the next capability.

The book can also be read as a description of a tested and purely behavioral account of verbal development. The identification and induction of verbal capabilities and a sequence of verbal capabilities sets forth an empirical and inductively derived account of verbal development—a data-driven developmental scheme that proscribes relations between experiences and the emergence of new capabilities. Thus, the book sets forth an account of the sources of the listener and speaker capabilities and the joining of those capabilities in ever expanding and more complex behavior. As such, the book sets forth an agenda for new research as a means to expand the basic science of verbal behavior.

Thus, this book provides two contributions. First and foremost, the text provides new and necessary procedures to use to radically expand children's verbal potential—what, when, why, and how to do the procedures for children who need them. Secondly, the book expands the foundation of the science of verbal behavior. A reviewer for one of our research papers asked, "Is this research applied or basic?" The same question can be asked about the book. The answer is that the book is about both—applied issues and basic science issues. The applied problem was the source for the research and was driven by Skinner's perspective. However, addressing the applied problem simply led to basic science questions that, in turn, led to conducting research that was both basic and applied science.

While the research was conducted in applied settings, the experimental control was as rigorous as most basic science studies. School settings that are based on thoroughgoing scientific practices are new kinds of laboratories. These laboratories not only provide accurate measurement of children's responses, but also accurate measurement of procedures. Moreover, the continuous collection of data on all children's responses and their interventions provide an empirical account of instructional histories. Thus, the research that led to the identification and induction of verbal capabilities in children who were missing them shows how instructional history can be experimentally manipulated. This type of experimental manipulation provides the means to expand our understanding of the science of the behavior of the individual.

Clearly, simply because we induced verbal capabilities in children missing them does not mean that all children move up the verbal developmental scheme as a result of the kinds of experiences we provided (although some preliminary research with naming suggests that typically developing children appear to progress in a manner similar to our developmental scheme). However, much more work is needed to test whether typically developing children progress in the same way. Nevertheless, the agenda to test this possibility has been set forth. Others will add to and revise what we have described. In many cases, better procedures and other capabilities will be identified. If the book serves this function, we will be gratified. A science of behavior should improve the human condition, and we hope that we have contributed to that goal. Specifically, it is our hope that using the procedures described in the book will save a few more children.

ACKNOWLEDGMENTS

A large number of individuals have contributed to the research and theory associated with verbal behavior analysis. First there are those who kept Skinner's verbal behavior alive over the years when there was little research: Jack Michael, Ernie Vargas, Mark Sundberg, Charles Catania, David Palmer, Roy Moxley, Phil Chase, Jim Holland, Richard Malott, Joe Spradlin, Joel Greenspoon, Murray Sidman, Ogden Lindsley, Kenneth MacCorquodale, Massayo Sato, U. T. Place, Paolo Moderato, Ernesto Ribes-Inesta and Barry Lowenkron. Many of our doctoral students over the last 20 years have been key scientists and practitioners in the development and application of verbal behavior analysis: Dolleen-Day Keohane, Robin Nuzzolo, Jeanne Speckman-Collins, Jessica Singer-Dudek, Grant Gautreaux, Kathy Meincke-Matthews, Mapy Chavez-Brown, Lynn Yuan, Lauren Stolfi, Seema Lodhi, Barbara Becker, Dana Gold-Visalli, Catherine Sales, Tina Covington, Gladys Williams, Hsin-Hui Tsai, Janet Twyman, Barbara Schwartz, Ioanna Tsiouri, Joann Pereira-Delgado, Susan Mariano-Lapidus, So Young Yoon, Gina Feliciano, Hye-Suk Park Lee, Hui-Chuan Chu, Amy Davies-Lackey, Carol Fiorile, Lina Gilic, Nan McCorkle, Anjalee Nirgudkar, Tracy Reilly-Lawson, Jennifer Longano, Celestina Rivera-Valdes, Nirvana Pistoljevic, Sheila Jodlowski, Irfa Karmali, Amoy Kito-Hugh, Victor Madho, Mary Jean Marsico, Amy Albers, Kenya Clay, and the legion of masters students and CABAS® teachers who have replicated research findings. We also acknowledge the contributions of Steve Hayes, Dermot Barnes-Holmes, and Brian Roche for proposing the role of multiple exemplar experiences for one of the sources of higher-order verbal operants.

We would like to thank the reviewers who read earlier versions of this manuscript: Irfa Karmali, Shelby Residential and Vocational Services; Janet Goodman, University of West Georgia; Andrew L. Egel, University of Maryland; and Caio F. Miguel, New England Center for Children.

Finally, we thank the several generations of our graduate students who have provided feedback on various versions of this book. Shira Ackerman took a particularly active role and we thank her for her efforts. Of course only we can be responsible for any errors or omissions.

R. Douglas Greer
Denise Ross

1

Verbal Behavior Analysis and Verbal Development

The presence of verbal communities indicates that human beings may be predisposed to behave verbally. But a predisposition does not insure that the behavior will occur, and its occurrence, if it occurs, does not explain how forms of that behavior are shaped by an extant community.

Vargas, E. A., as cited in Skinner, B. F., 1992, p. xiv

When we are children, we learn to communicate by discovering how language works for us. That is, when we learn that words can be used to easily attain objects or gain attention, objects acquire names. These words become essential tools, and these tools are behaviors that affect both listeners and speakers. They are a distinctive kind of behavior that requires a distinctive treatment, and we use them to communicate to others and mediate our world through the action of others. Verbal behavior is the cornerstone of human learning. For most children, verbal behavior seems to be acquired with little apparent effort and becomes the means for them to operate their world. As their world becomes more complex, the variety and forms of verbal behavior expand to meet more complex functions.

The words of the author Gabriel Garcia Marquez (2003) might best describe the process through which young children learn to use words to control their world: "The world was so new that there were no names for many things; so all the people could do was point" (p. 7). For toddlers, the world is so new that they have no names for things; so all they can do is point and then listen for an adult's response. After pointing, they repeat the names for objects and receive adult confirmation. Soon children learn to ask, "What's that?" instead of pointing. By doing so, they can identify the things to which they could previously only point. In this fashion, as things in their world become more distinguishable, they learn about their world. Without the names of objects, they cannot share the things in their world with others who constitute their verbal community. While typically developing children seem to acquire the complex verbal behavior of speaking and listening effortlessly, this is actually a result of thousands of language interactions with their parents and caretakers (Greenwood, Hart, Walker, & Risley, 1994; Hart & Risley, 1995). As children learn verbal behavior from their parents and caretakers, they evolve into verbally and socially capable individuals.

In cases in which this development is thwarted by either native or environmental factors, critical learning opportunities and developmental steps do not occur. Native factors may include genetic causes that make learning to verbalize difficult, while environmental factors may include a lack of necessary experiences to develop verbal behavior. In some cases, we characterize a child's verbal development as "minimally delayed," while in other cases, it is described as being "severely delayed"; in the latter case it does not develop at all without extraordinary and highly intensive instructional efforts. However, the presence of deficits—whether minimal or severe—does not necessarily mean that verbal repertoires are not possible; rather, special instructional skills may be needed to establish them.

Introduction to Verbal Behavior Analysis

Verbal behavior analysis is a subfield within basic and applied behavior analysis that is devoted to identifying and researching sources and instructional procedures that produce functional verbal repertoires when they are missing. It is based on B. F. Skinner's (1957) *Verbal Behavior*, a theoretical account of the **functions** of language or the effects that a speaker has on a listener. For example, instead of pouring a cup of water, a speaker can ask for it by pointing or talking, and a listener can respond by giving it to them; this is a request function or **mand** by the speaker whose response is rein-

---

TEXTBOX 1.1
Defining Verbal Behavior

Verbal behavior is behavior whose reinforcement is mediated by another person. It is concerned with the function of language—defined as the effect that a speaker has on a listener—and is derived from the science of behavior and from its applications. Since our focus is on the application of the verbal behavior theory to research, we draw on research-based applications in both verbal behavior and applied behavior analysis as part of **verbal behavior analysis.** Verbal behavior analysis is a subfield within basic and applied behavior analysis devoted to researching and identifying sources and instructional procedures that produce functional verbal repertoires when they are missing.

forced by a listener delivering the water. The speaker behavior governs a listener who then delivers the water or other reinforcing consequence specified by the request. Skinner identified six speaker **verbal functions,** referred to as **elementary verbal operants.** We will refer to research in verbal behavior and its application as *verbal behavior analysis.*

Verbal behavior analysis is the joint application of advanced research in verbal behavior, the basic science of behavior, and applied behavior analysis to determine the environmental source of verbal behavior and the application of the combined findings to develop functional verbal repertoires. This text uses procedures and findings from experiments and applications that were conducted with several hundred children that provide guidelines for developing verbal behavior (Greer & Keohane, 2005; Greer & Ross, 2004; Sundberg, 1998). Table 1.1 defines and provides examples of the six elementary verbal functions described by Skinner, along with key terms from applied behavior analysis to which readers may refer.

The processes of analyzing language by its function are different from the processes for analyzing its structure or parts of speech, as in linguistics. To differentiate this approach from more traditional treatments, Skinner called it verbal behavior because it was a treatment of the behavior function of language per se. While he did not refer to individuals who were lacking developmentally appropriate language (although **aphasia, echolalia,** and **palilalia** occurred frequently in his examples), verbal behavior was ideally suited for identifying verbal developmental capabilities and for designing curricula for those with and without communication deficits (Skinner, 1957). In fact, the ability of educators to reduce verbal disabilities has, in part, advanced significantly because of research based on the work of Skinner, despite early criticisms of his theory by some linguists who adhered solely to an innate source (Chomsky, 1959; Chomsky & Place, 2000; MacCorquodale, 1970).

Verbal behavior analysis provides **environmental** or **teaching interventions** to establish functional verbal repertoires when they are missing. *Verbal* does not only mean vocal; rather, **verbal** includes any topography that results in a **verbal function.** Language can have many different **forms** or **topographies** such as gestures, sign-language systems, clicks, or acoustically different vocal topographies (i.e., different languages) (Culotta & Hanson, 2004; Deacon, 1997). However, the function of language or use as a tool and the sources of this function—and not its form—make many individual and cultural achievements possible.

Children typically learn verbal functions through the efforts of their parents as part of their socialization. In cases where non-verbal or vocal disabilities exist, but verbal functions are present in a person's repertoire, technology and alternative means of communication can compensate for disabilities. However, until fairly recently, when *verbal functions* were lacking, there were fewer ways to compensate for them, and the individual who was non-verbal remained very dependent on others. Such children, who often have native disabilities, may not become verbal despite efforts of even the most diligent of parents. To become verbal, they require extraordinary efforts using procedures such as those made possible by a **science of verbal behavior** or verbal behavior analysis. These procedures make it possible for many more children to become social as they learn to manage and organize the arbitrary sounds, signs, or

TABLE 1.1   Definitions of Elementary Verbal Functions

Term	Definition	Example
Echoics	Hear-say responses. Vocal verbal operants under the control of verbal stimuli. They have **point-to-point correspondence** (topographical similarity) and formal similarity (are in the same sense mode) as the verbal stimuli that control them. Maintained by reinforcement (automatic or other types of reinforcement).	A teacher says, "Cookie" and a student repeats by saying, "Cookie."
Mands	Conditions of deprivation or annoying conditions. Result in speaking in the presence of a listener who then mediates the situation. They can consist of many different response topographies (signs, gestures, Morse code, speaking devices, and pictures), which specify the reinforcer delivered by a listener.	A hungry student says, "I want the cookie, please" and a teacher gives her the cookie. A child in need of a bathroom requests assistance, or is cold and asks for a sweater or jumper.
Tacts	See-say responses. Verbal operants under the control of a prior controlling stimulus (i.e., a picture, a person, or an object). Can be of many different response topographies, and are reinforced by generalized reinforcers such as attention or confirmation.	A young child sees an airplane and says, "Airplane." A parent says, "Yes, that's an airplane. You're so smart! It's very noisy!"
Intraverbals/ Sequelics	Hear-say responses. Verbal operants under the control of verbal stimuli. They do not have point-to-point correspondence with the controlling verbal stimulus, and can occur as exchanges between two speakers or as part of a verbal chain.	One speaker says, "How are you?" and another speaker says, "I'm fine." A person says, "DEF" after saying, "ABC." "My telephone number is. . .." "Two plus two is four."
Autoclitics	See-say or hear-say responses. Verbal behavior that modifies the effects of elementary verbal operants (mands, tacts, echoics, and intraverbals) on a listener. "I wouldn't tell you this if I were not your friend." More specifically narrows or qualifies the effect of verbal behavior on an audience. Also acts to minimize aversive reactions from a listener as in saying, "*Please* pass the bread," or "I want the big cookie with the chocolate frosting."	A child says, "Big car, please" and a teacher gives her a big car instead of a little one. "Big" and "please" modify the mand for a car by affecting the teacher's response.
Textual Responding	See-print-say responses. Verbal behavior under the control of printed words. Skinner called this textual behavior.	A student sees the word *cat* and says, "cat."

symbols that affect listeners in their community. How to apply these advances is the subject of this text.

Researchers from neuroscience, linguistics, anthropology, and other disciplines study various parts of language, and verbal behavior analytic research is not in competition with these disciplines, contrary to what some may believe. For example, some neuroscientists study relations between language and the brain or other neurological processes. Such research has shown physiological correlations between the behaviors of speaking and listening and those parts of the brain that are illuminated in Magnetic Resonance Imagery (MRI) when one is speaking or listening. This research identifies relationships between **behavior outside of the skin** (behaviors such as speaking or writing that are observable to another person) and **behavior beneath the skin** (behaviors such as an electronic brain impulse or blood flow that are only detectable through an MRI or other instrumentation). However, observing the brain physiology that is correlated with speaking and listening does not explain the source of verbal functions any more than the underlying muscle movement involved in hitting a baseball explains the hitter's skill; rather, in most cases, events occurring in the individual's environment must be observed in order to identify the functions.

Clearly, there are genetic and physiological factors involved in the production of language, and without them, language would not occur. However, unless certain behavioral interactions with the environment occur and those environmental events can affect the individual's behavior, verbal functions of language are often not possible, even when the physical structure is developed. That is, one may say a word and the corresponding part of the brain may show change. However, if the word does not function to effectively affect the behavior of a listener in the interest of the speaker, the topography is present, but the function is absent. Moreover, current evidence shows that even when damaged physiological structures exist (i.e., damaged neurons), inducing verbal functions through intense environmental interventions can apparently improve them (Greenfield, 1997).

We believe that while the use and study of both physiological and environmental responses are important, studying the conditions under which verbal behavior is emitted, and how to effectively teach it, is a separate and necessary science from both linguistics and the neuroscience of language. Verbal behavior analysis is concerned with environmental interventions and, as such, provides the basis for a science of teaching that identifies relations between behavior and the environment. It is a source for how to (a) provide effective teaching interventions, (b) motivate or manage verbal behavior, and (c) provide missing **verbal capabilities.** Providing missing verbal capabilities allows students to progress in their verbal development, but to do so, we must know the function of verbal behavior, or how and why it is emitted and we must know its environmental sources (Donahoe & Palmer, 1992; Pinker, 1999).

Relation between Verbal Behavior Analysis and Basic and Applied Behavior Analysis

Early on, the work of Lovaas and other behavior analysts showed that there were extraordinary training procedures that could be successful with some children with language delays (Guess, Keogh, & Sailor, 1978; Lovaas, 1977). However, obtaining generalization of trained language to regular, everyday settings proved to be problematic. Subsequently, behavior analysts placed greater emphasis on teaching communication beyond the training setting. This movement was characterized as either **incidental language training** or **naturalistic language interventions** (Hart & Rogers-

Warren, 1978; Warren, McQuarter, & Rogers-Warren, 1984).[1] This development emphasized the importance of capturing naturally occurring motivational conditions to obtain instances of speaker behavior (e.g., children asking for toys on a shelf that are inaccessible to them).

Beginning in the late 1980s, a few behavior analysts began to incorporate Skinner's theory of verbal behavior within incidental teaching by using procedures called **establishing operations,** which increased the number of teaching opportunities in the natural environment (Michael, 1993b; Sundberg, Michael, Partington, & Sundberg, 1996). From this developed a substantial program of research in verbal behavior analysis that identified ways to join Skinner's verbal behavior to the motivational components of incidental teaching, resulting in many more teaching opportunities than were possible by incidental teaching alone (Greer & Keohane, 2005; Greer & Ross, 2004). The science that made all of these innovations possible is the **basic science of behavior** and **applied behavior analysis.**

Verbal behavior analysis is a subfield of the science of behavior and its applications to human endeavors. Application of the basic principles and procedures to all behaviors constitutes **applied behavior analysis** (Bushel & Baer, 1994; Kazdin, 1978, Sulzer-Azaroff, Drabman, Greer, Hall, Iwata & O'Leary, 1988). Applied behavior analysis is the systematic application of scientific procedures derived from principles of behavior. The procedures are then used to change socially significant problems in such a way that changes in the behavior can be attributed to the procedures that were used. It has existed since the 1960s as an application of findings from the basic science of behavior. Over the years, sophisticated applications of applied behavior analysis have made significant differences in the education, performance, and well-being of typically developing students from preschool through university levels, children and adults with a range of disabilities, parents, teachers, psychologists, employees, employers, as well as in the education of educators. The oftentimes dramatic and socially significant effectiveness of behavior analysis is based on a rigorous set of scientific procedures.

We refer to findings from applied behavior analysis as **tactics** or **environmental interventions.** Successful implementation of basic scientific principles requires that different tactics be used for different individuals, which further produces learning or new relationships between behaviors and the environment. The basic and applied scientists study the **behavior of individuals** and not of groups. The role of applied behavior analysts in education, medicine, therapy, and organizational behavior management is to select the appropriate research-based tactic needed at a given time for the child or client from the growing research base. Continuous measurement is its distinguishing characteristic along with the visual displays (graphs) and the continuous use of tested, scientific procedures. These procedures are fitted to individuals, so that if one tactic does not work, others are implemented until success is achieved. That is, research-based tactics derived from basic principles are then applied using scientific procedures to test their application to a specific child.

We based our process of fitting specific tactics to individual students on four areas of research in behavior analysis. First, research on the basic principles of behavior identified fundamental environment behavior relations. Second, individual tactics from the applied research were derived from efforts to apply the basic principles to socially and educationally significant problems. For example, applied researchers developed tactics such as token economies, praise and ignoring, simultaneous stimulus prompts, response cards, fast rate instruction or "fluency" training, picture exchange systems, learn units, class wide peer tutoring, extinction training, Personalized System of Instruction (PSI), programmed instruction via computers using learn units (Emurian, 2004), reinforcement of academic accuracy to reduce problem behavior, and group contingencies to name a few tactics. Third, educational behavior analysis developed decision protocols to identify given tactics for given students at specific stages in their learning (Greer, 2002). These tactics included, for example, decision protocols to identify the source of a learning problem (Keohane & Greer, 2005), fidelity or accuracy of instruction using the Teacher Performance Rate Accuracy Procedure (TPRA; Albers & Greer, 1991; Bahadourian, Tam, Greer, & Rosseau, 2006; Emurian, 2004; Greer & McDonough, 1999; Selinski, Greer, & Lodhi, 1992), and supervisor rate measures (Greer, Keohane, & Healy, 2002). Finally, when we applied tactics to individual children, we also tested the effectiveness of that tactic of the particular child's instruction or behavior management problem. If the tactic was not effective, the practitioner returned to the decision protocol procedure (Keohane & Greer, 2005) until success was achieved.[2]

Over the last few years, the use of these four levels of scientific application led to the identification of missing verbal developmental cusps—our verbal capabilities described throughout this text—and to the development of research-based protocols to induce many of these verbal capabilities when they are missing. This work, which grew out of verbal behavior analysis and the building of a science of teaching, led to even more sophisticated teaching procedures. This is the subject matter of this text.

There are over 200 tested tactics from the research literature that are derived from the basic principles of behavior, which well-trained professionals can apply to individual learning or behavior problems (Greer, 2002). Many of them involve changing behaviors that are not functional for the individual or society, and many involve

---

TEXTBOX 1.2

Levels of Science Used to Develop Verbal Behavior Analysis

- Step 1. Identification of the basic principles of behavior
- Step 2. Identification of tactics to individualize applications of the basic principles to specific children (the building of a science of individualized treatment)
- Step 3. The development of scientific procedures to locate the source of behavior problems or learning difficulties in order to determine those tactics that would be most effective for a given child, a system to ensure fidelity of treatment
- Step 4. Using scientific procedures in the actual teaching process to test whether the tactic selected in Step 3 works for a particular child, and if not, returning to Step 2
- Step 5. The identification of, and development of, protocols to induce verbal development capabilities (a new step contributed by verbal behavior analysis)

learning new behavior-environment relations. This process of "fitting" the best tactic to either (a) a behavior management problem or (b) a particular learning problem is the heart of individualized treatment and education. This is one of the significant advances in the applied science over the last 20 years (Greer, 2002). Research suggests that professionals who apply such scientific and tactical expertise produce better outcomes for their students, children, and other clients (Cooper, Heron & Heward, 1987, 2007; Delquadri, Greenwood, Wharton, Carta, & Hall, 1986; Emurian, 2004; Engelmann & Carnie, 1991; Goldiamond & Dyrud, 1966; Greer, 1994a,b; Greer, Keohane, & Healy, 2002; Keohane & Greer, 2005; Sulzer-Azaroff, Drabman, Greer, Hall, Iwata, & O'Leary, 1988; Ingham & Greer, 1992).[3]

Protocols for Inducing New Verbal Capabilities

Tactics developed in the literature over the last 65 years were mainly concerned with *how* to modify existing environmental influences on behavior in applied settings; determining *what* behaviors to teach was relegated to traditional curriculum or "therapy" approaches. Verbal behavior theory and research added to the "what" for teaching communicative and other complex curricular goals. This work has provided a scientific basis for *what* verbal behavior to teach and procedures for how to teach it. This contribution has dramatically increased possibilities, especially for children who cannot communicate. Research in verbal behavior also shows that those who receive *behavior analytic instruction incorporating verbal behavior tactics and strategies* will have more educationally significant outcomes and represents still another advance in teaching as a science (Chu, 1998; Donley & Greer, 1993; Greer, Yuan, & Gautreaux, 2003; Greer, Stolfi, Chavez-Brown, & Rivera-Valdez, 2005; Jadlowski, 2000; Karmali, 2000; Karmali, Greer, Nuzzolo-Gomez, Ross, & Rivera-Valdes, 2005; Lodhi & Greer, 1989; Madho, 1997; Marsico, 1998; Meincke, Keohane, Gifaldi, & Greer, 2003; Nuzzolo-Gomez & Greer, 2004; Ross, 1995; Ross & Greer, 2003; Schwartz, 1994; Spradlin, 1985; Sundberg, Michael, Partington, & Sundberg, 1996; Tsiouri & Greer, 2003; Twyman, 1996a, b; Williams & Greer, 1993; Yoon, 1998).

Behavior analytic research that examines the induction of **capabilities** has led to the advancement of a technology and science of individualized treatment and education (Gilic, 2005; Greer, Stolfi, Chavez-Brown, Rivera-Valdes, 2005; Greer & Keohane, 2005; Greer, Yuan, & Gautreaux, 2005; Nuzzolo-Gomez & Greer, 2004; Ross & Greer, 2003). This technology of individualized treatment expands the tactics identified in the entire body of applied behavior analysis that can be applied to individuals as needed. The new advances provide the necessary foundational verbal capabilities (Greer & Keohane, 2005). Providing the means to apply these protocols for inducing verbal capabilities is the objective of this text.

Some research from the applied and basic sciences of behavior is concerned with variables that affect what we have already learned (i.e., our performance), while some is concerned with building new repertoires, teaching or inducing new capabilities. Both are needed in the process of working with children or with the staff who work with children. Teachers and applied behavior analysts need to know how to manage behavior appropriately based on the science and good ethical practice. However, the portions of the basic and applied sciences that are most applicable to this text concern the development of new **verbal operants** and what we will later identify as **higher order operants** or new capabilities. Teaching new verbal operants is important because when children are missing them, then they are missing verbal capabilities. Recent work in verbal behavior analysis has developed procedures to bring about or to **induce** verbal capabilities when they are missing (Keohane & Greer, 2005). Once children who are missing them acquire these capabilities, then they can also acquire operants they were not capable of learning. In many cases, without them children cannot advance in their verbal development. Textbox 1.3 further explains the term **verbal capabilities.**

TEXTBOX 1.3
Defining Capability

A common definition of a **capability** is "a talent or ability that has potential for development or use" (American Heritage Dictionary, 2006). While *capability* is frequently used in psychology to refer to certain constructs or neural and physiological capacities, we use the word *capability* to describe the acquisition of an ability that allows one to learn components of a previously inaccessible repertoire. For example, when students lack speech, they cannot learn vocal verbal functions from their teachers or peers. However, once they acquire speech, they can learn vocal mands, tacts, and other verbal functions. In other words, when a child acquires the capability of speech, then multiple, new verbal operants can be taught.

While the term *capability* has not been traditionally used in behavior analysis, the term **behavioral cusps** has been used to describe a similar phenomenon. Novak and Pelaez (2004) write the following:

> . . .Rosales and Baer (Baer & Rosales-Ruiz, 1998; Rosales-Ruiz & Baer, 1996; Rosales-Ruiz & Baer, 1997) introduced the concept of **behavioral cusps** to describe changes in person-environment interactions that enable multiple new interactions. Cusps are behaviors that have significant and far-reaching implications for further developmental stages. That is, a behavioral cusp is a new behavior, such as walking, that because it has occurred, enables the explosive development of many new interactions, such as social behaviors, exploratory behaviors, and a host of others. Another behavioral cusp is fluency in reading because it opens pathways to an enormous number of other developments. So the fluent reader can follow directions to use a computer program; in turn, this computer program allows that person to get on the Internet; in turn, this allows him or her to buy a ticket to Tahiti; which in turn, allows the discovery of a new culture, and so forth. This is just one branch of behaviors that are enabled by the development of a behavioral cusp. Cusps also enable many other "branches" as well. This is why they are important. (pp. 68–69)

Selecting a Verbal Topography: Linguistic and Verbal Behavior Contributions

Thus far we have avoided the term **language.** Language is not behavior per se; at a rudimentary level, language is a kind of dictionary or lexicon for the verbal topographies upon which a given community agrees. Lexicons consist of the "word stocks" of a particular language, or its meaningful units (identified as morphemes in linguistics; *Oxford English Dictionary, 2ⁿᵈ Edition, VII*, pp. 876–877). Dictionaries or lexicons define words with other words. In addition, structural linguistics identifies the basic structure of language such as the morpheme or the phoneme. These are the structural components of language and are the verbal practices of a particular verbal community. Conversely, verbal behavior provides a functional analysis of language defined as how the speaker affects the listener, or how the listener is affected by the speaker. The function of language is the province of verbal behavior, but much of structural linguistics is used as a basis for the study of verbal as behavior per se (Bloomfield, 1961). In his *Contingencies of Reinforcement*, Skinner (1969) described the relationship between verbal behavior and linguistics:

> Skinner . . . attributes to Bloomfield [a linguist whose basic units were used by Skinner as a point of departure] the main effort [in the field of linguistics] in the direction of finding behavioral explanations to . . . psychological ones (as cited in Matos & De Lourdes, 2006, p. 97). Both linguistics and verbal behavior analysis are needed in the broad study of language broadly construed—each for different aspects of language. In the same way that the linguist does not possess the proper methodology to study the behavioral process responsible for installing speaker and listener repertoires . . . the behavior analyst does not master the proper methodology to analyze and describe the practices of the verbal community (p. 100). However, starting from the linguist's specification of the contents to be taught, behavior analysts are capable of using the procedures and techniques from our science for training the relations between the environment and behavior—that is, for the process of teaching. (p. 102)

Words are arbitrary, that is, there is no natural word for a given phenomenon, they are simply the practices of a given community. We could click, sign, whistle, or emit any number of behaviors for a particular communicative function and these have basic structural units. While teaching children to acquire functions of language is a major focus of verbal behavior analysis, function requires topography. As noted by Skinner (1957) and others, *verbal* does not mean *vocal;* rather "verbal" includes any topography that is used for a verbal function. By *verbal behavior,* Skinner meant communicative behavior in all of its forms, which includes speaking, sign language or gestures, pictures or symbols, Morse code, and electronic speaking devices.

Throughout the text, we will use the term *speaker* regardless of the topography with which one "speaks." Thus, **speaker** refers generically to one who uses vocal behavior, signs, pictures, or electronic vocal transducers to govern the behavior of others. Perhaps, the best way to describe our use of "speaker" is to define it as someone who can govern or direct the behavior of others using various topographies of verbal behavior or language as a tool. Hence, many of the operations for teaching described herein can be used regardless of the communicative topography taught. Moreover, since verbal behavior analysis is the study and application of verbal functions, by necessity, it must also include the **listener** role, or someone who is affected by the verbal behavior of others. Thus, verbal behavior analysis includes verbal functions for governing the behavior of others as a speaker, and for being directed or governed by the verbal behavior of others as a listener.

Although sophisticated gesturing topographies exist (e.g., sign languages used in Deaf communities), and some research shows that children who used alternative communication systems also developed speech when both are used together, our preferred topography for children with language delays who are not deaf is **vocal verbal behavior,** because it enhances our ability to more easily advance the child's verbal potential. There are several reasons why vocal behavior is our topography of first choice. First, it is the most easily generalized form of communication. That is, once children can use their voices for verbal functions, anyone in their **verbal community** can mediate between their non-verbal and verbal worlds. Communicating in a specific verbal community's language is important; consider, for example, visiting a country in which you do not speak the language, or participating in the deaf community if you do not know sign language.

Another advantage of vocal topographies compared to other topographies of verbal behavior is that the **acoustic properties** or vowel-consonant speech sounds of vocalizations provide listeners with compact and accessible bits of "information"; that is, one can hear the acoustic properties of spoken words and this allows for better comprehension (Premack, 2004). Most importantly, the properties of vocal verbal behavior make advanced verbal functions more accessible. Andrew Robinson (1995), one of the leading scholars of the history of writing points out that "Writing and reading are intimately and inextricably bound to speech, whether or not we move our lips" (p. 14). For example, if children read a sentence too slowly, they cannot comprehend its intent (i.e., the latency between spoken or textual is too prolonged for the person who is reading to comprehend or listen, so to speak, to what is said). If children read or respond to text using sign language, then they must also "listen," or in this case observe the signs to comprehend. This simply is not as efficient as using acoustic properties because more bits of information can be conveyed acoustically than visually. We moved from hieroglyphs to alphabets because one can say more with less, so to speak, and alphabets are tied to speech sounds (Robinson, 1995). One of the major substitutes for speech used with children with severe language disabilities is the use of pictures and this can be useful for children when they cannot yet speak; however, some research suggests that signing is probably more efficient than pictures (Sundberg, 1993). Signing, however, does not have the broader advantages of pictures for the community (Sundberg, 1993). In fact, research comparing the use of pictures (selection-based responding) to signing and writing (topography-based responding) suggests that topography-based responding may be more efficient for acquisition of verbal functions than selection-based (Michael, 1985; Shafer, 1993; Sundberg & Sundberg, 1990; Wraikat, Sundberg, & Michael, 1991).

Imagine having to access the meaning of a passage by matching the print to a series of pictures or signs instead of matching it to the acoustic properties of speech. The subtleties of communicative behavior are enhanced through auditory sounds such that reading and writing are made easier. The type of stimuli that our own responses produce in the process of reading appears to be critical to the efficiency of reading (Karchmer & Mitchell, 2003). More can be communicated in less time because of the properties of auditory stimuli. Our position does not detract from the utility and value of sign language in Deaf communities, or the use of sign language for those for whom vocal behavior is not possible. Indeed, there are advantages of sign language over picture exchanges for the development of reading. However, sign language does not readily translate into more advanced reading, perhaps because of the reasons we just listed (Karchmer & Mitchell, 2003). What is typically described as reading comprehension is based on the stimulus control that is produced from our own responses. Reading aloud or to ourselves involves **response-produced stimuli.** The textual responses function as stimuli for us to listen or comprehend what is said. New research is exploring the possibilities of a phonetic or alphabetic type of sign system, and this work may hold promise for improving the utility of sign language for reading purposes. It is also quite possible that advances made in computer technology will eventually result in a visual system that is as efficient as vocal behavior in the future.

Devices that speak may also be used instead of either signs or pictures. For example, electronic speaking devices as small as a Palm Pilot®, make it possible for children to produce vocal behavior electronically and thus benefit from the auditory component of speaking, thereby potentially advancing the speaker and listener repertoires more effectively than either signs or pictures. Most importantly, several procedures

---

TEXTBOX 1.4

Responses Produce Stimuli (Responses Are Stimuli, Too)

Some behavior analysts use the expression **response-produced stimuli** to refer to, for example, speaking and writing as responses which, in turn, function as stimuli that exert control over listener or reader behavior. However, stimuli produced by behavior are also responses themselves. For example, "speaking" can be a stimulus for a listener or speaker response. In some cases, speaking is not just a response to a stimulus, but is also an antecedent stimulus for other behaviors; or speaking may be a consequence stimulus (Lodhi & Greer, 1989; Lowenkron, 1984, 1997). As we shall see later, the speaker-listener distinction also occurs within a person's own skin. In such cases, their own speaker response may function as an antecedent to their own listener response, or the listener response may reinforce or punish the speaker response (i.e., the editing function). Like all behavior, verbal behavior can function as both stimulus and response. A person's environment includes responses that they emit and that function as stimuli for their own behavior. The behavior or responses of others function as stimuli for our actions. Those responses that function as stimuli are part of our acquired environment. See also the terms *speaker-as-own-listener* and *conversational unit* in the Glossary in this text for further explanation. These relations are described in detail in later chapters.

now exist that allow well-trained verbal behavior analysts to induce vocal behavior for children who would not typically have attained it. We shall describe those procedures in Chapters 3 and 4. However, speech is not always possible for some children who do not have hearing impairments; we recognize that, and provide means to employ other topographies of communication and that is one of the strengths of verbal behavior. For now, those children who are *not* hearing impaired and who have the physiological structural capacity to speak are taught vocal verbal behavior as a first course. After we have exhausted the possibilities for vocal communication, we move to other topographies for communicative functions. Our second choice is the use of electronic devices that emit speech, the third choice is signing because of its potential to advance verbal capabilities, and our fourth choice is the use of pictures.

Research in Verbal Behavior Analysis

The verbal behavior analysis research, along with data-based applications to hundreds of individual children, demonstrates that well-trained practitioners can teach children to communicate more effectively than was ever possible. One of the earlier studies was an experiment that compared the use of applied behavior analysis when teaching linguistic objectives to the use of verbal behavior analysis when teaching functional communication. This experiment showed that when students were taught using verbal behavior analysis, they learned functional and "spontaneous speech," whereas, when they were taught linguistic objectives with applied behavior analysis procedures, they learned fewer forms and functions.

In the last 10 years, research in verbal behavior has grown extensively, including expanding verbal behavior to more fully incorporate the role of the listener. At the time of writing this text, there were more than 100 experiments testing the verbal behavior tactics described herein. Table 1.2 displays a few samples of published experiments on verbal behavior from behavior analytic journals. The current text represents our effort to disseminate experimental findings in verbal behavior to practitioners with basic training in behavior analysis so that they can apply them when teaching children with language delays, autism, or other developmental disabilities. While we recognize that much more research needs to be done, the existing body of work is being disseminated now to help provide communication repertoires for children who lack them.

Developmental Milestones in Verbal Behavior

Psychologists and educators provide developmental schemes according to age. Indeed, many disability diagnoses are inferences or hypothetical constructs based on a child's behavior or test performance as compared to children of the same age (Novak & Pelaez, 2004). While these developmental measures are used for diagnoses, they are not particularly helpful for instructional purposes on a day-to-day basis. Prominent developmental psychologists who are behavior analysts have described age as an empty variable for explaining development (Bijou, 1996; Novak & Pelaez, 2004). Behavior analysts seek to identify experiences that will produce changes in children's

TABLE 1.2 Experimental Research in Verbal Behavior Analysis

Verbal Function	Citation
Autoclitic	Howard & Rice (1988)
Automatic Reinforcement	Esch, Carr, & Michael (2005); Smith, Michael, & Sundberg (1996); Sundberg, Michael, Partington, & Sundberg (1996); Yoon & Bennet (2002)
Echoic	Drash, High & Tudor (1999); Foxx, Faw, McMorrow, Kyle, & Bittle (1988)
Functional Independence of Mands and Tacts	Hall & Sundberg (1987); Lamarre & Holland (1985); Lee & Pegler (1982); Twyman (1996b)
Intraverbal	Burgeois (1990); Charlop & Milstein (1989); Dattilo & Camarata (1991); Donley & Greer (1993); Lodhi & Greer (1989); Luciano (1986); Partington & Bailey (1993); Sarokoff, Taylor, & Poulson (2001)
Language Delays in Young Children	Brasolotto, de Rose, Stoddard, & de Souza (1993); Drash & Tudor (1993)
Listener	Davis, Brady, Williams, & Hamilton (1992); Greer, Stolfi, Chavez-Brown, & Rivera-Valdez (2005); Henry & Horne (2000); Kennedy, Itkoner, & Lindquist (1995)
Mand	Arntzen & Almas (2002); Bourret, Vollmer, & Rapp (2004); Carroll & Hesse (1987); Drasgow, Halle, & Ostrosky (1998); Drash, High, & Tudor (1999); Farmer-Dougan (1994); Hall & Sundberg (1987); Ross & Greer (2003); Taylor & Harris (1995); Tiger & Hanley (2004); Williams & Greer (1993); Yamamoto & Mochizuki (1988)
Naming	Greer, Stolfi, Chavez-Brown, & Rivera-Valdes (2005); Horne, Lowe, & Randle (2004); Lowe, Horne, Harris, & Randle (2002); Lowe, Horne, & Hughes (2005)
Palilalia, Echolalia, and Stereotypy	Karmali, Greer, Nuzzolo-Gomez, Ross, & Rivera-Valdes (2005); Nuzzolo-Gomez & Greer (2004); Valleley, Shriver, & Rozema (2005)
Rule-Governed Behavior	Braam & Malott (1990); Marsico (1998); Newman, Buffington, & Hemmes (1991); Reitman (1996)
Stimulus Equivalence, Relational Frame, and Response-Produced Stimulus Control	Barnes, McCullagh, & Keenan (1990); Cullinan, Barnes-Holmes, & Smeets (2001); Greer, Yuan, & Gautreaux (2005); Halvey & Rehfeldt (2005); Lowenkron & Colvin (1995); Murphy, Barnes-Holmes, & Barnes-Holmes (2005); Rehfeldt & Root (2005)
Tact	Arntzen & Almas (2002); Barbera & Kubina (2005); Carroll & Hesse (1987); Henry & Horne (2000); Lamarre & Holland (1985); Partington, Sundberg, Newhouse, & Spengler (1994); Tsiouri & Greer (2003)
Textual Responding, Writing Functions, and Dictation	Daly (1987); Greer, Yuan, & Gautreaux (2003); Madho (1997); Tsai & Greer (2006)
Verbal Functions	Lerman, Porter, Addison, Vorndran, Vokert, & Kodak (2005)

Select citations from *The Analysis of Verbal Behavior, Journal of Applied Behavior Analysis, Journal of the Experimental Analysis of Behavior, Research in Developmental Disabilities, Journal of Behavioral Education,* and *Behaviorology*

RESEARCH BOX **1.1**

Comparing Verbal Behavior and Linguistic Curricula

"Williams and Greer (1993) compared the number of words correctly used across training trials and the accuracy of responses during maintenance probes for three adolescents diagnosed with developmental disabilities across **VB** [verbal behavior] and linguistic (similar to that found in many Lovass programs) curricula. Operant training procedures, specified as incidental and discrete-trial procedures, were held constant across conditions. In general, procedural features included the antecedent use of nonverbal and verbal discriminative stimuli, contingent consequences including praise and access to additional stimuli or events, and the contingent opportunity to mand for those stimuli or events known to have reinforcing properties for a particular participant. Different words were taught across the curriculum-specific phases, with the exception of "yes/no" responses, which were taught in both curricula. The VB curriculum consisted of target responses that were first taught as, [echoics to mands and echoics to tacts, where mands resulted in the reinforcers and tacts in generalized reinforcement.] A series of autoclitic responses was also trained [specific to each verbal function]. The linguistic curriculum included target responses derived from the program developed by Guess, Sailor, and Baer (1976) in which individuals were first taught to label novel items when asked "What's that?," and were then taught to label actions, persons, and things in a similar manner. Next, individuals were taught to state possession and color by responding to questions such as, "Is this my/your—?" and "What color?" Finally, participants were taught to describe the size, location, and relationship of relevant items to other stimuli. Williams and Greer (1993) implemented two phases of training in each curriculum using an ABAB design in which the VB curriculum was always implemented first. Although the number of correct trials for each participant was similar across training conditions, the number of words emitted during the VB training sessions exceeded the number of words emitted during the linguistic training sessions. The authors also reported that more words taught during previous VB phases were emitted in the context of subsequent training phases for 2 of 3 participants, while the overall number of appropriate words taught during previous linguistic phases that occurred during subsequent training phases was lower. During maintenance probes that occurred following the completion of the first linguistic phase, the second VB phase, and the second linguistic phase, considerably more correct trials were completed from the VB curriculum than those revisited from the linguistic curriculum. The results of multiple maintenance probes conducted at the completion of training and covering all of the words taught across all phases showed a greater percentage of correct responses for the VB curriculum. Hence, the authors demonstrated considerable support for their VB language curriculum given its comparative effectiveness over the linguistic curriculum across a number of dependent measures. The Williams and Greer (1993) investigation is noteworthy because it was the first attempt to directly compare Skinnerian and traditional linguistic language curricula and, thus, can be considered more direct evidence of support for the VB approach than studies based on single verbal operants (e.g., Braam & Poling, 1983)." (pp. 20–21)

From Carr, J., & Firth, A. (2005). The verbal behavior approach to early and intensive behavioral intervention for autism: A call for additional empirical support. *Journal of Early Intensive Behavioral Intervention, 2,* 18–27.

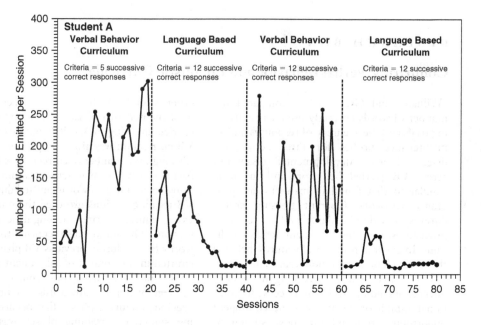

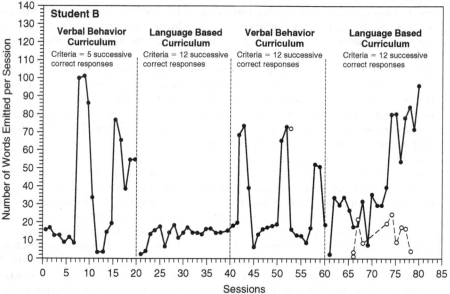

FIGURE 1.1   A comparison of verbal behavior and linguistic curricula to teach speech

Source: From Williams, G., & Greer, R. D. (1993). A comparison of verbal-behavior and linguistic-communication curricula for training developmentally delayed adolescents to acquire and maintain vocal speech. *Behaviorology, 1,* 31–46.

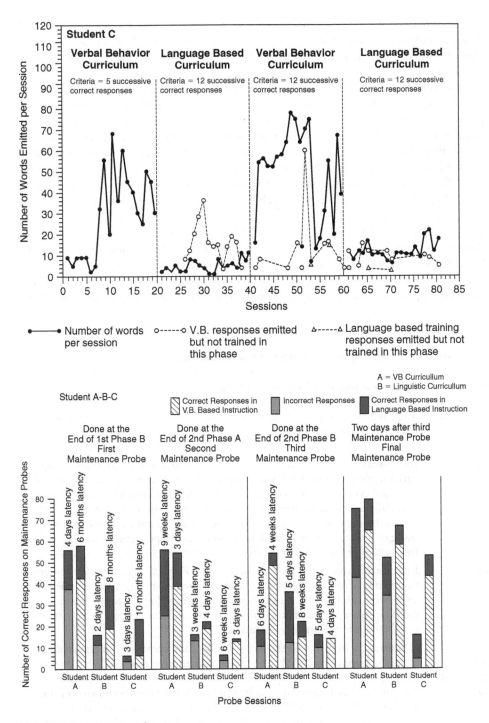

FIGURE 1.1 *(continued)*

repertoires. In that vein, current research in verbal behavior has identified verbal development schemes that can be tied to experiences (see Table 1.3). These are particularly useful for those who seek to identify ways to accelerate learning, compensate for native or environmental deficits, and use developmental stages based on critical capabilities. While much more research is needed to identify more subcomponents of major stages of verbal development, the existing stages and subcomponents have proven useful in applications with numerous children. As a result, we can organize children's progress according to **verbal developmental stages** or **verbal capabilities.** While there are many other appropriate developmental schemes, in our work with hundreds of children, these milestones have become a relatively predictable taxonomy.

These capabilities can now be established for some children who are missing them. This allows professionals to help children progress to more complex capabilities in verbal development. The continuum of developmental stages in Table 1.3 represents a progression of functional verbal capabilities that are not based on age, although they are often correlated with it; rather, they are functional capabilities that can be brought about or induced with certain intensive learning experiences.

At present, we believe that these verbal capabilities are likely derived from the kinds of experiences that typically developing children gain through their caretakers'

TABLE 1.3   Evolution of Verbal Capacity Milestones and Independence

Verbal Milestones	Effects on Independent Functioning
1. Pre-Listener Status	Total dependency. Individuals without listener repertoires are entirely dependent on others. Interdependency and entrance to the social community are not possible.
2. Listener Status	Individuals can perform **verbally governed behavior** (e.g., come here, stop, eat). Individuals can comply with instructions, track tasks (e.g., do this, now do this), and avoid deleterious consequences while gaining habilitative responses. The individual is still dependent, but direct dependent physical contact can be replaced somewhat by indirect verbal governance. Contributions to the well-being of society become possible since some interdependency is feasible and they can enter the social community.
3. Speaker Status	Individuals in the presence of a listener can govern consequences in their environment by using another *to mediate their environment* (e.g., eat now, toilet, coat, help). This is a significant step toward controlling events by the individual. The culture benefits proportionately too, and the capacity to be part of the social community is greatly expanded.
4. Speaker-Listener Exchanges with Others (Sequelics and Conversational Units)	a) **Sequelics.** Individuals respond as listeners and speakers to **intraverbals** including **impure tacts** ("What is that?") and **impure mands** ("What do you want?"). Individuals can respond to questions in mand, tact, or intraverbal functions. They respond as speakers to verbal antecedents and answer the queries of others such as "What hurts? What do you want? What's that? What do you see, hear, or feel?" As a listener, they are reinforced by speaker responses. b) **Conversational Units.** An individual emits conversational

TABLE 1.3   *(Continued)*

Verbal Milestones	Effects on Independent Functioning
	units when they are reinforced as both a speaker and listener. The individual engages in interlocking verbal operants as a speaker and listener by alternating listener and speaker functions with another. The individual is reinforced as a listener by **sensory extensions** and as a speaker by the behavior of the listener.
5. Speaker-as-Own-Listener Status, Say-Do, Conversational Units, and Naming	Three types of speaker-as-own-listener are identified in the research. a) **Say and Do.** Individuals can function as a listener to their own verbal behavior (e.g., First I do this, then I do this). At this stage, the person achieves correspondence between what they say they will do and what they do. b) **Self-talk.** Self-talk involves the child functioning as both speaker and listener. For example, while playing, the child rotates between speaker and listener responding in what some refer to as *imaginative play.* c) **Naming.** Simply by hearing others tact objects or stimuli, the individual can learn words as a listener and then use them as a speaker, or learn words as a speaker and then use them as a listener. This stage, or functional verbal capability, provides the means to expand form and function with minimal and incidental exposure.
6. Reader Status	Individuals who have reading repertoires can use written text to supply themselves with useful, entertaining, and necessary responses to setting events and environmental contingencies that extend their sensory experiences. The reader may use the verbal material without the time constraints that control a speaker-listener relationship. The writer's advice is under the reader's control without the writer (who functions as a verbal governor) being present. Reader behavior can occur despite time, distance, or accessibility to the writer, unlike listener behavior that requires that a speaker is accessible to a listener.
7. Writer Status	A competent writer may control environmental contingencies through the mediation of a reader across seconds or centuries, in the immediate vicinity of a reader or on a remote continent. This stage represents an expansion of speaker repertoires, but a listener need not be present at the time or at the same location as the writer.
8. Writer as Own Reader: Self-Editing Status	As writers can read their own writing from the perspective of an eventual audience, they grow increasingly independent of reliance on substitute or teaching audiences (e.g., teachers, supervisors, and colleagues). A more finished and effective behavior-evoking repertoire provides the writer with wide-ranging control over environmental contingencies such that time and distance spaces can be virtually eliminated. Writing can be geared to different audiences without immediate responses from the target audience.
9. Verbal Mediation for Solving Problems	A sophisticated self-editor whose behavior is governed by the verbal expertise derived from formal approaches to problem-solving (e.g., verbal communities that use the methods of science, logic, and authority); they can solve complex and new problems in a progressively independent fashion. Problems are characterized with precise verbal descriptions. Verbal descriptions occasion other verbal behavior that can, in turn, direct the person's actions to solve a particular problem. The verbal community that uses methods of problem solving bases their verbal expertise on methods that result in effective operations.

> ## TEXTBOX 1.5
> ### Benefits of Verbal Capability Milestones
>
> Verbal capability milestones provide:
>
> - Broad descriptions of children's listener, reader, speaker, and writer capabilities
> - Means for determining the ratio of instructors to students for best outcomes
> - How and what children can be taught at their present stage of learning
> - Functional approaches to cognitive or complex human behavior involving advanced academic repertoires
> - Markers of learner independence
> - Valid measures of socialization
> - Scientifically identified prerequisites for each milestone that need to be present in order to move a child to more advanced stages or milestones of verbal capacities

and teachers' actions. While we do not know this to be the case for all children, we can say that for many children from our schools or research programs, providing the specific, intense experiences described in this text has been necessary, if not sufficient, for them to acquire new verbal capabilities. Moreover, our research suggests that these stages of functional verbal capabilities are critical obstacles that must be surmounted in the education of children, particularly those with language deficits. Table 1.3 provides an introduction to the stages/functional verbal capabilities that will guide the interventions we introduce throughout the text. In addition to teaching educational standards or expanding existing verbal repertoires, we can now provide the means to progress up the verbal development scale. Unless children advance through these verbal capabilities certain educational standards cannot be learned.

The components or building blocks needed to achieve these broad capabilities have been identified recently in verbal behavior analysis and the procedures identified in that work are described in this text. They are the prerequisites for achieving the broad developmental capabilities. Table 1.4 identifies a few of these and some of the seminal research citations.

Verbal functions related to speaking or writing provide children with the means to affect or *govern* the behaviors of others, and verbal functions related to listening or reading provide children with the means *to be governed by* the vocal behavior or print of others. If the educational standards and curricula that are being taught require these functions, the child cannot learn them until they have the prerequisite capabilities. Each progressive stage shown in Table 1.3 and their components in Table 1.4 corresponds with an increase in the capacity to learn repertoires that were not possible before. The verbal capability stages are building blocks for complex cognitive behaviors and steps toward independence. For instance, those who are **pre-listeners** are highly dependent on others to meet their needs, and their progress in verbal and cognitive repertoires and in attaining certain educational standards is not possible without first acquiring the listener repertoire. Pre-listeners must be closely monitored and

TABLE 1.4   Seminal Citations for Verbal Capabilities

Verbal Capabilities and Prerequisites	Some Seminal Citations
Capacity for Sameness and Accelerated Learning	Keohane, Greer, & Ackerman, 2006a
Conditioned Reinforcement for Visual Observing and Accelerated Learning	Keohane, Greer, & Ackerman, 2006b; Longano & Greer, 2006; Tsai & Greer, 2006
Conditioned Reinforcement for Listening and Accelerated Learning	Greer, Dorow, Wachhaus, & White, 1973; Keohane & Greer, 2006
Acquisition of Basic Listener Literacy and Accelerated Learning	Chavez-Brown, 2005; Greer, Chavez-Brown, Nirgudkar, Stolfi, & Rivera-Valdes, 2005; Harapiak, Martin, & Yu, 1999
See-Do and Hear-Say Join the Duplic Frame	Ross & Greer, 2003; Tsiouri & Greer, 2003
Induction of Echoics	Sundberg, Michael, Partington, & Sundberg, 1996; Williams & Greer, 1993; also see Lowenkron, 1984, 1988, 1996 for how sign substitutes for the "echoic"
Mand and Tact Functions and Autoclitic Functions	Lowenkron, 1984, 1996, 1997 as joint stimulus control for tacts; Ross & Greer, 2003; Sundberg & Partington, 1998; Tsiouri & Greer, 2003; Twyman, 1996a, 1996b
Speaker-as-Own-Listener	Horne & Lowe, 1996, 1997; Horne, Lowe, & Randle, 2004; Lodhi & Greer, 1989; Lowe, Horne, Harris, & Randle, 2002; Lowenkron, 1984, 1988, 1991, 1996, 1997
Naming (The Phenomenon and Its Induction)	Fiorile & Greer, in press; Gilic, 2005; Greer, Stolfi, Chavez-Brown, & Rivera-Valdes, 2005; Horne & Lowe, 1996, 1997; 2004; Lowe, Horne, Harris, & Randle, 2002
Transformation of Stimulus Function, Establishing Operation Function, and Joint Control	Gautreaux, Keohane, & Greer, 2003; Greer, Yuan, & Gautreaux, 2005; Hayes, Barnes-Holmes, & Roche, 2001; Lowenkron 1984, 1988, 1991, 1996, 1997; Lowenkron & Colvin, 1992, 1995; Nuzzolo & Greer, 2004; Tu, 2006
Listener Reinforcement	Greer, Reilly-Lawson, & Walsh, 2006
Induction of Tact Repertoire and Emission of Novel Usage of Tacts	Schauffler & Greer, 2006; Pistoljevic & Greer, 2006
Metaphoric Extension from Exemplar Experiences	Matthews, 2005
Writer as Own Listener and Effective Self-editing	Jadlowski, 2000; Madho, 1997; Reilly-Lawson & Greer, 2006
Verbally Mediated Problem Solving	Keohane & Greer, 2005; Marsico, 1998

cannot be warned of harm verbally. They cannot be told what is going on and what will happen to them next; nor can the verbal community at large comfort them. They cannot communicate all of their needs, discomfort, or feelings; nor can they attain the social reinforcement and benefits implicit in conversational exchanges with others. As a frequent result, pre-speakers often resort to tantrums, stereotypy, or self-injurious behaviors as a means of relieving discomfort, annoyance, or fear. Similarly, children lacking the capacity for sameness will have difficulty matching and discriminating.

However, when children become **listeners,** they can respond to the vocal verbal speech of others and gain a measure of independence, they do not require the close supervision needed by pre-listeners, and they can be warned, instructed, comforted, and praised. Similarly, when children become **speakers** in any of the various speaker forms (vocal, sign, picture, and symbol), they can convey their feelings, affect others' behavior, and change their own circumstances; as a result their speaker behavior can have an effect on a listener. Thus, both listener and speaker functions are critical steps in attaining one of the foremost goals in education—independence.

The milestones of verbal capabilities that we have identified have a research base showing not only their importance for independence, but also the importance of mastering each milestone before the successful emergence of later milestones and the related cognitive repertoires these demonstrate. For instance, until children move from the pre-listener stage, successive milestones are not achievable or are achieved with much difficulty, the lack of mastery of prerequisites eventually leads to a learning plateau. When they achieve the listener stage, they can be verbally governed, that is, they can do as others say. Within this stage there are different levels of sophistication; however, once the child achieves the basic components that we describe in the chapter on learning to listen (Chapter 3), the foundations are in place to expand the listener's sophistication. While complete mastery of the beginning stages of listening does not necessarily preclude children's acquisition of speaker behavior (or the teaching of speaker functions), more advanced stages require that they master the components on learning to listen that are outlined in Chapter 3 so that the listener and speaker functions are joined together for the individual. The speaker stage incorporates the development of basic speaker functions such as mands, tacts, autoclitics, and intraverbal operants. In the speaker stage, the student learns to govern or direct the behavior of others such that listeners can serve the interests of the speaker.

When children can rotate **speaker-listener** verbal episodes such as talking to others, then they can have conversational units with others. This means that they are reinforced both as a listener and a speaker in an alternating fashion, resulting in conversational episodes. The child is now truly social. In the **speaker-as-own-listener** stage, children engage in self-talk by emitting both speaker and listener functions in imaginative play. Self-talk is not probable, if either listener or speaker functions are not fluent and reasonably congruent.

Another key component of the **speaker-as-own-listener** stage is a phenomenon identified in the research literature as **naming.** Achievement of the naming repertoire means that children can respond to a stimulus as a listener and then use it immediately as a speaker without instruction, or respond to a stimulus as a speaker and then use it as a listener without instruction. At this stage children can also direct their own activities with their speaker and listener behaviors; they can say what they will do, and then do it. We call this the **correspondence between saying and doing**—one of the early steps toward self-management. Achievement of the speaker-as-own-listener function allows children to edit their speaker repertoires for the different audiences they encounter (i.e., some things you just don't say in front of Mom). In effect, in the speaker-as-own-listener stage, the two repertoires of speaking and listening are joined within the individual. Each of these repertoires, speaking and listening, can proceed at different paces. Providing the means to equate or join the repertoires appears critical to the advancement of more complex human behavior. Throughout the text we treat each such that the ultimate goal of joining the two is made possible.

When the child is learning to be an effective reader, the naming and other speaker-as-own-listener functions are joined to print control. At the **reader** stage, students can follow verbal directions that are not restricted by time or distance—the reader as a speaker also listens to what is said and responds to what is said as a listener. For example, readers can prepare meals by reading a recipe's directions; speakers do not need to be present for them to do so—they respond as a listener to their own speech. In some ways the reader stage is an expansion of the listener stage and the **speaker-as-own-listener** stage. The reader stage includes **textually responding,** which is when the student says the printed word. The reader function also requires that a reader listen to the textual response they are emitting, which involves joint stimulus control for saying and doing such that the reader is verbally governed from the text. Moreover, the joining of the naming function with the textual response means that if the child has the tact for the stimulus that is said in the textual response then comprehension occurs.

At the **writer** stage one can verbally govern the behavior of a reader by producing aesthetic or technical outcomes. That is, the writer in the technical function can provide directions to a reader and in the aesthetic function the writer can affect the emotions of the reader. The writer function is an expansion of both the speaker and speaker-as-own-listener stages. When individuals function at the **writer-as-own-reader** or self-editing stage, they expand their **speaker-as-own-listener** behavior because they can effectively write and edit their own work without immediate consequences from an audience, allowing them to overcome time and distance constraints.

As each of these capabilities advance and combine, they become the foundations of verbally mediated repertoires that are part of complex problem-solving processes across all disciplines involving response produced stimuli. Such repertoires serve as the bases of science, our legal systems, philosophical inquiry, technological applications, aesthetic applications of language, and complex communication of all types. In this text, we concentrate on the very basic foundations of verbal behavior—those concerning the development of listener, speaker, conversation, speaker-as-own-listener, and early reader milestones. However, the subsequent complex stages of writing, self-editing, and verbal mediation are dependent on the mastery of all of these foundational repertoires. Furthermore, the stages we cover in this text are the necessary building blocks for more advanced stages of verbal behavior. Competence in the advanced stages appears, at present, to be traceable to a lack of competence in foundational listener-speaker, and speaker-as-own-listener stages as identified in the verbal development work (Greer & Keohane, 2005).

Summary

- Typically developing children's seemingly effortless acquisition of complex verbal behavior can be attributed to thousands of language interactions with their caregivers (Hart & Risley, 1995). However, many children with native or environmental disabilities are missing verbal repertoires because of the lack of language opportunities or the lack of verbal capabilities to benefit from language opportunities.

- Verbal behavior analysis is the application of findings from research in verbal behavior and the basic and applied science of behavior to develop verbal repertoires for individuals who are missing them. Verbal behavior analysis is a subfield of the basic and applied sciences of behavior.

- The primary subject matter of verbal behavior analysis is the function of language in a given verbal community, and not neurological correlates of that behavior beneath the skin, or the identification of the linguistic or structural practices of a language. The latter two subjects belong to other disciplines. Verbal behavior analysts study the verbal function of language.

- "Verbal behavior" was Skinner's (1957) theoretical, functional account of communication and the effect that speaker behavior has on a listener who mediates the environment for the speaker. As part of that analysis, he drew on the structural linguistic categories of Bloomfield (1961) to identify basic structural units (Matos & Lourdes, 2006).

- Skinner identified and described six elementary verbal speaker functions: (1) echoics (a duplicating function); (2) mands (the request function); (3) tacts (the labeling function); (4) intraverbals (the conversational function); (5) autoclitics (the adjective-object, basic operant modifying functions); and (6) textual behavior (the see print and say function). These are speaker operants defined by antecedent conditions and the consequences that select out the antecedent and behavior. Subsequent research and expansion of the theory by Skinner have identified key listener components of verbal behavior (Greer & Keohane, 2005; Hayes, Barnes-Holmes, & Roche, 2000; Skinner, 1989). Contemporary verbal behavior analysis includes an expanded treatment of the listener.

- The term *verbal* is not restricted to vocal responding. Rather, vocal is one type of response topography and any number of response topographies can be emitted by a speaker, including sign, gestures, and electronic devices. However, there are important advantages to the vocal topography, and much more is known now about how to induce vocal verbal behavior in children who are missing that capability. When speech is unobtainable, verbal behavior analysis provides substitute topographies to teach children verbal functions.

- Teaching verbal functions is the main objective of verbal behavior analysis, and teaching verbal forms is the sub-objective. Both are necessary, but verbal behavior analysis has the tools to install the repertoires or functions of speaking and listening.

- Verbal capabilities are higher-order operants or higher classes (Catania, 1998) that allow students to learn new skills or repertoires, in many cases without direct instruction. Inducing a given capability allows for the emission of new verbal responses without direct instruction because the untaught function has become part of a higher-order operant or class.

- Research on verbal behavior analysis has shown that the use of procedures from the science produces more speaker behavior for learners with missing verbal repertoires than linguistic-based curricula that do not employ the procedures from verbal behavior analysis (Williams & Greer, 1993).
- Verbal stages include pre-listener, listener, speaker, speaker-listener exchanges, speaker-as-own-listener, reader, writer, reader-as-own-writer, and verbal mediation for solving problems. Research in verbal behavior analysis has contributed to the identification of these stages as well as to the developmental milestones detailed in subsequent chapters and identified in Table 1.3. Each stage provides a functional description of a learner's current level of functioning, and can help direct the instructional interventions and objectives for a particular student.

ENDNOTES

1. The incidental, *milieu*, or naturalistic approach to teaching language emphasizes the role of capturing establishing operations as they naturally occur. Clearly this represented an important step toward captured opportunities. However, learning requires frequent opportunities; research in verbal behavior over the last few years has identified ways to create establishing operations such that teachers need not wait for opportunities to teach an operant. For the seminal naturalistic language references and explanations of that work see Hart & Rogers-Warren (1978) and Warren, McQuarter, & Rogers-Warren (1984).

2. The theory of verbal behavior and its research applications have been the central thread of the CABAS® curriculum for several hundred children and adolescents who attended CABAS schools in the United States, England, Ireland, Italy, and Argentina. CABAS is the acronym for the Comprehensive Application of Behavior Analysis to Schooling. It is an approach to education based on teaching as a science using a learner-driven curriculum that embraces educational standards from various countries in the Western Hemisphere. See Greer, Keohane, & Healy (2002) for an introduction to CABAS. The instructional operations and curriculum derived from research in verbal behavior, together with the verbal developmental scheme, have been applied in CABAS schools for over 25 years. However, the applications were driven by the research findings and thus the depth of the applications grew as the evidence mounted. See Greer & Ross (2004) for a program of verbal behavior research from Teachers College Columbia University and CABAS schools together with other research published in *The Analysis of Verbal Behavior,* the *Journal of the Experimental Analysis of Behavior, Research in Developmental Disabilities,* the *Journal of Behavioral Education,* the *Journal of Early and Intensive Behavioral Interventions,* and the *Journal of Positive Behavioral Procedures.* Other behavior analysts such as Sundberg and his colleagues pioneered applications of verbal behavior to the treatment of individuals with disabilities via psychological services. For procedures and assessments tools, see Sundberg & Partington (1998).

3. See Chapters 7 and 8 in Greer (2002) for a description of the role of verbal behavior analysis in the design of curricula for the teaching of complex repertoires beyond the topics covered in this text. For a description of how research in verbal behavior led to the identification of verbal developmental stages and capabilities, see Greer & Keohane (2005).

2

Teaching and Learning Verbal Operants and Verbal Developmental Capabilities: Definitions and Measurement

Two facts emerge for our survey of the basic functional relations in verbal behavior: (1) the strength of a single response may be, and usually is, a function of more than one variable and (2) a single variable usually affects more than one response.

Skinner, 1957, p. 227

Education requires a measure that contacts the natural fractures of instruction—*one that includes both the behaviors of the teacher or teaching device and the behaviors of the student.*

Greer, 2002, p. 18

Selecting Verbal Forms and Functions for Instruction

The objective of a verbal behavior approach is to teach the function of verbal behavior; teaching the form is a sub-objective. Verbal functions are **verbal operants** or learned relationships between antecedents and consequences that speakers emit to affect a listener. The form or topography of a verbal response is its shape or the targeted response from a student. This also includes the form of communication a student uses, including speech, pictures, gestures (sign language), or electronic communication.

One form of a verbal response may have different functions. For example, the vocal form or the picture or signed form of "milk" may function as a mand (request for milk) or a tact (naming the presence of milk), depending on the consequence that reinforces it. Since a form may have different functions, separate instructional operations are required for each function.[1] In effect, each function has different antecedents and consequences, although the forms are the same. In early verbal development for many children, it is unusual for one form to serve both mand and tact functions without appropriate instruction or experience with each one (Lamarre & Holland, 1985; Twyman 1996a, 1996b).

Select forms of verbal behavior by first choosing target words based on reinforcing items. Initially, observing a student's selection of reinforcing items in home or school settings can do this. Alternatively, one may use reinforcer sampling to identify reinforcing items (see Northup, George, Jones, Broussard, & Volmer, 1996 for more information about reinforcer sampling). Items such as toys, edibles, or objects; events such as hugs or play; and other activities that the student seeks out frequently or that serve as reinforcers for other behaviors are candidates for teaching **mands.** Other activities, items, or events that are not potential reinforcers can be used to teach tacts initially.

In the process of selecting forms, we identify those that are attainable and functional for the student. Select forms and items that will be useful or functional in the foreseeable future for the student, which are typically reinforcing to obtain for mands, or in the case of tacts, are useful for obtaining generalized reinforcers such as praise, tokens, hugs, or smiles. Next, choose a gestural, pictorial, or vocal response topography to teach. As described in Chapter 1, the preferred response topography is vocal verbal behavior. To obtain vocal responses, modify forms if emitting the terminal form is too complex for a child. For example, some students may not be able to echo the word *cookie*, but since the mand function is the main objective, approximations may be accepted initially. In other cases, simultaneous topographies for two different items can be taught (i.e., both sign and vocal approximations). However, when efforts to produce a vocal topography are not successful, an alternative topography may need to be selected. Textbox 2.1 provides guidelines from research for doing so.

Two lists of verbal behavior forms are developed—one for mands and another for tacts. These lists are continuously updated with new forms as students master targeted forms and as their reinforcers change or expand. The mand list contains items, individuals, or activities desired by the student, but available only through a teacher's mediation, since preventing accessibility often provides the necessary condition to

---

TEXTBOX **2.1**

Selecting a Verbal Topography

When instructing individuals who do not have speech, teachers and parents may need to choose non-vocal response topographies to teach verbal behavior. Here are some guidelines based on conceptual and empirical analyses of **selection-based** (pointing) and **topography-based** (speech, sign, and writing) verbal responses:

- Speech is preferred because it is the response topography most readily supported by verbal communities and will produce a number of vocal models for early speakers (Schaefer, 1993; Sundberg, 1993; Sundberg & Sundberg, 1990; Wraikat, Sundberg, & Michael, 1991).
- In cases where a person can physically emit vocal response topographies but does not do so, the problem is often echoic behavior (Sundberg, 1993), which can be obtained if prerequisites for learning speech (described throughout this text and in the verbal behavior literature) are taught effectively.
- When prerequisite repertoires to obtain echoics are present, or when it is not functional to wait on them before acquiring speech, sign language is preferred. This is because signs are closer to speech, and in some cases, are easier for students to acquire than pointing at stimuli (Hodges & Schwethelm, 1984; Sundberg, 1993; Sundberg & Sundberg, 1990; Wraikat, Sundberg & Michael, 1991).
- While pointing at pictures may be easier for a listener because they can look at the picture to know what the speaker is saying, they may not be easier for the speaker because they require discrimination skills that some students with developmental disabilities do not have. Learners may also have difficulties with selection-based responding as a response topography for the following reasons: 1) pictures are not always available to a speaker, can be time-consuming, and can result in errors because of difficulties scanning an array of stimuli; 2) they depend on environmental support; 3) the stimuli and responses involved can be complex; 4) there is a lack of a natural verbal community; and 5) it may be difficult to portray complex words in symbol or picture form (Hodges & Schwethelm, 1984; Sundberg, 1993; Sundberg & Sundberg, 1990; Wraikat, Sundberg, & Michael, 1991).
- However, some speech substitutes such as sign language and pointing topographies have produced increases in vocal verbal behavior (Bondy & Frost, 2001; Charlop-Christy, Carpenter, Le, LeBlanc, & Kellet, 2002).
- For adult learners or for those who have physical limitations to producing signs and speech, pointing topographies are appropriate.

---

learn the mand form. The tact list contains other items, individuals, or activities that are not potential reinforcers for mands and that may be useful for the student in the near future. Forms from each list will eventually be taught such that they are interchangeable for mands and tacts. However, initially, they are taught as the function that will be most useful in the near future. An example of a list of verbal behavior forms is in Figure 2.1. A sample form for a verbal behavior list is found in Appendix B.

Function Item	Mand Form	Date Mastered	Tact Form	Date Mastered
Cookies	Cookie, please	9/1/05		
Books	I want book	1/3/05		2/4/05
Action pictures			Running	
Classroom items			Table	

FIGURE 2.1   Sample List of Verbal Behavior Forms

Conducting and Recording Probes

To measure the presence or absence of verbal repertoires, we conduct probes before teaching a specific skill. **Probes** are test trials comprised of the antecedents, opportunities-to-respond, and reinforcement associated with a long-term objective. Generally, during probes, teachers observe and record the following: 1) antecedent stimuli such as a teacher's instructions and **setting events or establishing operations** (i.e., deprivation conditions, for example, which occur at certain times of day) that evoke a response; 2) occurrence or non-occurrence of the target behavior; and 3) reinforcers that maintain the response (i.e., **prosthetic, generalized,** or **natural reinforcers**). In some cases, responses to probes are reinforced while in other cases, responses are not conse-quated at all. However, in all cases, incorrect responses are not corrected.

Throughout this text for each protocol that calls for a probe, we specify whether or not the teacher provides consequences. That is, the probe measures that should be reinforced and those that should not be consequated are specified. For example, during probes, many listener behaviors are only recorded as being present if they are rein-forced by **generalized reinforcement** (i.e., non-specific, conditioned reinforcers such as tokens, attention, or praise that affect a wide number of behaviors) or **natural rein-forcement** (i.e., the likely consequence for a behavior as in reading a book because the content of the book reinforces continued reading) instead of **prosthetic reinforce-ment** control (i.e., reinforcers such as activities, edibles, or objects that are not natural consequences for a behavior). In all cases, incorrect responses to probes are not corrected.

Present probes by first saying the antecedent associated with the long-term objective for a repertoire or a specific program (see protocols within each chapter for a list of long-term objectives), waiting three seconds for a response, and providing consequences as specified by a particular protocol. For example, when probing for a motor imitation repertoire, say "Do this," present one motor action, and wait three seconds for a response. If students correctly perform an action, give them generalized reinforcement such as praise or a token, and record the response with a plus (+) on a data collection sheet. If they incorrectly perform the action, ignore the response, record it with a minus (−), and present a new antecedent for the same program. To maintain motivation during probes, present opportunities-to-respond to known and unknown items; responses to known items are not recorded because they are simply used to maintain attention.

Probe Mastery Criterion, Data Collection, and Graphing

During a probe session, record each response on a data collection form (see Appendix A for a sample form). After a probe session, record the presence or absence of the repertoire on a long-term objective form such as the one in Figure 2.2. Write the long-term objectives that are to be assessed during probe measures on the form. If a child emits criterion-level responding during a probe (the level to which students must respond is a **mastery criterion** and differs according to the target repertoire), then record the presence of that repertoire in the following manner next to the long-term objective: 1) use a plus (+) to indicate that target behaviors were emitted at criterion-level; 2) to indicate the reinforcer that maintained the behavior, use GR for generalized reinforcers, P for prosthetic reinforcers, or NR for natural reinforcers; 3) record the date of the probe; and 4) record the initials of the person who conducted the probe

LISTENER BEHAVIOR			
*(Prosthetic or **P** and Generalized Reinforcers or **GR** are the target reinforcement goals unless otherwise specified for the repertoire)*			
Repertoire	Mastery Criteria	Code	Comments
1) Sits still for 10 seconds when told "Sit Still"	20/20	+ 9/6/05 GR RDG	
2) Maintains eye contact for 10 seconds when told "Look at me"	20/20	+ 9/6/05 GR RDG	
3) Imitates non-verbal gestures ("Do this")	20/20	- 9/8/05	

FIGURE 2.2 Sample Probe Record.
Probe records such as this one are used throughout the text to display the repertoires that should be probed for each protocol. In this example, mastery criterion-level responding is recorded with a plus, the date of the probe (i.e., 9/6/05), the consequences that reinforced the behavior (GR for generalized reinforcer and P for prosthetic reinforcer), and the tester's initials (i.e., RDG). Missing repertoires are recorded with a minus and the probe date.

(i.e., + 6/22/05 RDG). A repertoire is recorded as being absent if the student does not emit the correct response 1) under target reinforcement conditions, 2) to criterion level, 3) in multiple probe settings (when applicable), or 4) within the first five response opportunities. Record the missing repertoire with a minus and the date of the probe (i.e., − 6/22/05). Next to each long-term objective, leave space to record comments about the number of correct responses the student emitted or the motivational conditions that evoked the response.

Instructional objectives can then be written for each student by using their probe data. Start at the beginning of the running record for a particular repertoire and choose the first behavior that was absent. Write a long-term objective for that repertoire. Use the student's current performance level to determine the short-term objectives. In some cases, particularly when a repertoire is absent within the first five probe trials or if some time has passed since the initial probes, you may have to probe for the student's response to obtain their current level of performance. Set criterion for the first short-term objective that the student must meet at a level that is only slightly higher than their current level of performance. For example, if a student can sit still for 3 seconds during a probe session, then the next short-term objectives might be that they sit still for 4 seconds, 6 seconds, 8 seconds, and then the long-term objective of 10 seconds. When the student can sit still for 10 seconds with 100% accuracy for one session, the repertoire is recorded as being present.

Presenting and Measuring Learn Units

Teaching verbal behavior to children with missing speaker or listener repertoires requires careful implementation of tactics and strategies in order for learning to occur. To do so, we must first ensure that teaching is **faultless** or "unflawed" (Engelmann & Carnine, 1991). That is, when teaching is inaccurate, students are more likely to learn incorrectly, which potentially confounds the identification and remediation of a learning problem. To ensure that instructional presentations are correct, we use **learn units** to measure the accuracy or fidelity of our teaching operations.

Learn units consist of potential three-term contingencies for students and at least two interlocking three-term contingencies for teachers (refer to Figure 2.3 for a more detailed description of learn units). They measure the occurrence of antecedents, behaviors, and consequences for both teachers and students during instruction. The term *learn unit* is used because both teachers and students "learn" as students respond to teachers' behaviors (i.e., instructions) and teachers in turn respond to students' behaviors. Learn units permit the isolation of teaching and learning from moment-to-moment as measures of the teacher's behaviors; the student's responses to the presentation are measures of the student's learning. More specifically, teachers' behaviors are measured by the accuracy of learn unit presentations and students' behaviors are measured by their responses to learn units. Additionally, both form and function are taught through learn units.

Research on learn units suggests that the following must be present in order for them to be effective: 1) unambiguous antecedent presentations (Albers & Greer, 1991;

TEXTBOX **2.2**

The Importance of Faultless Instruction

Engelmann and Carnine (1991) discuss the importance of faultless instruction:

> If the learner fails to generalize, the problem may lie with the learner or with the communication the learner receives. We can rule out one of these possibilities by assuming that the communication is responsible for the observed problem. The remedy is to identify faults in the communication the learner is receiving and correct them so that the communication is faultless. If the faultless instruction fails, we know that the problem is with the learner and not with the communication. If the faultless instruction succeeds, we know that the initial problem was indeed with the communication. (pp. 15–16)

Learn Unit: Learn units are interlocking three-term contingencies—two or more for the teacher and one for the student—that measure teachers' and students' behaviors. Teachers' behaviors are measured by the accuracy of their learn unit presentations and students' behaviors are measured by their responses to learn unit presentations. Learn units differ from operants in that learn units are used to teach operants.

Ingham & Greer, 1992); 2) opportunities for the student to respond (Greenwood, Hart, Walker, & Risley, 1994; Heward, 1994); 3) the consequence component of the potential three-term contingency for the student (Albers & Greer, 1991; Greenwood, Hart, Walker, & Risley, 1994; Greer, 1996b); 4) corrections and reinforcement operations (Albers & Greer, 1991; Greer, Keohane, Meincke, Gautreaux, Pereira, Chavez-Brown, & Yuan, 2004; Ingham & Greer, 1992); 5) students' observation of discriminative stimuli presented during correction procedures (Hogin, 1996); and 6) fast and frequent learn unit presentation rates that result in increased correct responses and objectives achieved (Ingham & Greer, 1992; Kelly & Greer, 1997; Greer McCorkle, & Williams, 1989; Selinski, Greer, & Lodhi, 1991). Learn units have been used to identify and change learning problems (Greer, 2002; Keohane & Greer, 2005), and to measure preschool, school-age, and university classroom instruction presented by teachers or computers (Bahadourian, Tam, Greer, & Rousseau, 2006; Emurian, 2004).

Both form and function of verbal behavior are taught through learn units. By presenting learn units that include motivational variables (called **establishing operations**) that occasion a response, we reproduce the **natural fractures** of verbal behavior repertoires in an instructional setting, while simultaneously and significantly increasing the number of verbal behavior opportunities that children have in a natural setting. Children who have not learned because of infrequent natural opportunities will benefit when opportunities increase through direct instructional learn units that incorporate the establishing operations as part of the verbal function being taught (Hart & Risley, 1995). Figure 2.3 displays a learn unit example.

Learn units are basic measures of student-teacher interactions and are based on research on **academic engaged time** and **opportunities-to-respond.** Specifically,

Teacher's learn unit (two interlocking three-term contingencies)	Instructional Components	Student's response to learn unit (one three-term contingency)
Teacher's first antecedent	Teacher obtains student's attention	
Teacher's first behavior	Teacher holds up a piece of cracker (that is under deprivation for the student) and waits three seconds for a response	*Student's first antecedent*
Teacher's first consequence (positive reinforcement)/ Teacher's second antecedent	Student says, "I want cracker, please" within the three second response opportunity.	*Student's first behavior*
Teacher's second behavior	Teacher gives student a small piece of the cracker.	*Student's first consequence (positive reinforcement)*
Teacher's second consequence	Teacher records student's response and learn unit is complete.	

FIGURE 2.3   Learn Unit Example

research showed positive correlations between high rates of academic achievement, academic engagement, and opportunities-to-respond (Greenwood, Hart, Risley, & Walker, 1994; Greenwood, Horton, & Utley, 2002). However, opportunities-to-respond did not include the teachers' presentation of a consequence (Heward, 1994), which is important because operants are acquired through consequences (Skinner, 1938, 1968). Subsequently, the learn unit incorporated interlocking three-term contingencies to measure the antecedents that evoke responses, the accuracy of responses, and the consequences that maintain them (Cooper, Heron, & Heward, 1984). The **learn unit context** was subsequently developed to analyze not only the student's responses to the learn unit, but other variables that affect learning, including teachers' behaviors, motivational conditions, and the **phylogenic** and **ontogenetic** history of individual students. Procedures for analyzing the learn unit context in order to identify learning problems are described in detail in this chapter.

Presenting Learn Units

We begin learn units with accurate antecedent presentations. Antecedents are accurate if the teacher's vocal and/or nonvocal antecedent stimulus is unambiguous, is consistent with the lesson plan or script, and in the case of curricular materials, the target stimuli were flawless (i.e., targeted stimulus features were salient). For example, a correct antecedent for an opportunity to echo a teacher's vocal model in a **mand** function might be to present a piece of a cookie for which the student is under **deprivation** (i.e., the student has not had the cookie in a while and, as such, the value of the cookie as a reinforcer increases), say, "cookie," and wait for a three-second opportunity-to-respond. If any of these components is omitted (i.e., the student is not under deprivation for the cookie, the teacher does not clearly say, "Cookie," or does not wait three seconds for a response), then the antecedent presentation is incorrect. Further more, other undesirable setting events can affect the student's response to the antecedent such as the teacher's body movements (i.e., unwitting cues such as leaning forward or nodding the head when presenting antecedents), or stimuli that are unintentionally presented with a visual stimulus (i.e., additional marks on pictures). Thus, it is important is to present antecedents that are clear, salient, and flawless such that students come under control, or learn to respond to, the essential properties of an antecedent stimulus and the deprivation conditions.

Next, teachers measure the accuracy of a student's response. A response is measured as correct or incorrect by both its form and function, as identified before an instructional session. In the previous example, for instance, a correct echoic form may occur when a student says *"cookie"* with point-to-point correspondence to the vocal model of a teacher (i.e., exactly matching the consonant vowel vocalization of the teacher) instead of approximating the teacher's model (i.e., saying "Cook"). A correct mand function would occur if the student said "cookie" and their response was reinforced by receiving a cookie; a correct tact function would occur if the student said "cookie" and their response was reinforced by generalized reinforcers such as praise or a token. Responses are incorrect if students emit an incorrect response form, an incorrect function, or do not initiate or emit a response within the target intraresponse time. Incorrect responses also occur if students self-correct before a teacher can give a consequence. In those instances, we provide a correction because we do not want to reinforce the sequence of responding incorrectly before a correct response. Textbox 2.3 describes the rationale for our correction procedure based on Skinner's Programmed Instruction.

The teachers' contingent presentation of a consequence (either a correction or reinforcement) forms the final component of the student's potential three-term contingency. Reinforcement occurs when a teacher presents a known reinforcer to a student for a correct response. It is most effective when it occurs on a specified reinforcement schedule and is accessible for only a few seconds immediately after a correct response. Whenever possible after a correct response, students receive an **opportunity to mand** during which teachers present known reinforcers and wait three seconds for students to mand. The opportunity to mand serves as generalized reinforcement operation along with praise.

For some verbal behavior, reinforcement is specific to the student's response. For example, when reinforcing a mand, students receive the specified reinforcer (i.e., a piece of a cookie) without praise. It is acceptable to say, "You can have the cookie" or a similar phrase, but you should avoid praise because the cookie, and not praise, was specified by the student. For a tact, generalized reinforcers such as praise, tokens, or the opportunity to mand are used. In most cases, correction procedures include the

---

TEXTBOX **2.3**

Learn Units and Skinner's Programmed Instruction

When Skinner (1968) developed programmed instruction, he introduced instructional frames that in hindsight we can identify as learn units. That is, faultless presentations were followed by the student constructing a response. Accurate responses were reinforced (i.e., the student could proceed or tokens were dispensed), and inaccurate responses required students to correct their response before the program allowed them to proceed. However, reinforcement was not given for a corrected response. Thus, when presenting learn units, self-corrections are not reinforced. Instead, inaccurate responses require students to observe the antecedent stimuli and emit the correct response. The corrected responses are not reinforced; rather, students receive the next learn unit (Holland & Skinner, 1961).

---

teacher's presentation of the verbal antecedent with an accompanying prompt or model for the target behavior. Corrections are not reinforced and the student is required to emit the corrected response. For example, if a student incorrectly tacts an item, then the teacher presents it again, models the correct vocal response, waits for the student to echo it, and provides no reinforcement. If a student does not emit a correct response during the correction procedure, the correction may be presented up to three times or until the student emits the corrected response. Note: if generalized attention does not reinforce the student's responding, the student must acquire the capability to be reinforced by attention and other generalized reinforcers. Using the opportunity to mand is a useful way to enlarge tacts until praise or attention functions a generalized reinforcer. Chapter 3 prescribes what needs to be done in cases where generalized reinforcers are not part of the student's community of reinforcers.

If during the course of instruction, students begin to independently emit response forms that are more complex or advanced than those being targeted (i.e., saying a word with point-to-point correspondence instead of approximating a response), teachers should immediately change the definition of the target form in order to progress the student. Also, in most cases, students learn from the consequences of the learn unit (from correction or reinforcement) without additional prompts; however, in some cases they require additional tactics (i.e., **simultaneous stimulus prompts** or **zero second-time delay** in which correct answers are provided and reinforced before the actual opportunity-to-respond is given; Halle, Marshall, & Spradlin, 1979). To maintain consistency during instruction, it is important to ensure that the additional tactic is recorded on the graph and data collection form. Later in this chapter, we provide procedures to identify additional tactics.

Since learn units are a measure of the teacher's behavior, then the teacher's learn unit occurs as you are presenting the student's three-term contingency. It begins by obtaining the student's attention before presenting the first direction to them (i.e., a vocal or written stimulus). That is, the teacher may have to reinforce attention before instructing the student by presenting a separate three-term contingency. Presenting the direction (the antecedent stimulus) is the teacher's behavior and the second part of their three-term contingency. The last part of the teacher's three-term contingency is the student's correct or incorrect response to the antecedent. That is, if the student responds correctly, then their response reinforces the teacher's presentation of the antecedent stimulus, thus increasing the likelihood that the teacher will present it again in a similar manner. If the student responds incorrectly, then their response functions to negatively reinforce the teacher's response and they present a correction. Another interlocked three-term contingency for the teacher begins after they reinforce or correct the student's behavior. The reinforcement and correction operation is the antecedent for the teacher to present another direction, response opportunity, and contingent consequence to the student. This sequence is repeated until a predetermined number of learn units is presented. In this way, the learn unit is used to measure or ensure the accuracy or fidelity of the teacher's presentation per the learn unit protocol. This accuracy is a necessary, if not sufficient, condition for student learning.

For most programs, instruction is presented in 20-learn unit sessions. We typically use 20 learn units to ensure sufficient opportunities for students to come into contact with the contingencies when we are teaching educational standards. However, the predetermined number of learn units for each session is specified for each protocol and varies for the different curricula that are used. Additionally, the "size" or number of responses in a single learn unit changes based on both the topography of the response and when a consequence is given. For example, during initial training programs, learn units can be as small as single, topographical responses such as clapping hands, phonemes, echoic one-word utterances, or one-word mands. However, once students master several early or single responses, topographical responses may expand to include clapping hands, stomping the feet, and tapping the head, echoing a phrase (e.g., "That's a big car.") emitting mands with several autoclitics (e.g., "May I have the big chocolate cookie with the cherry on top?") before a consequence is given by a teacher. A single learn unit is complete when a teacher corrects or reinforces a student's response(s). The number of responses is dependent on the level of responding being taught. When a child can emit a single word mand such as *cookie*, the response may expand to include autoclitics such as, "May I have the chocolate chip cookie, please?" before obtaining reinforcement. Textbox 2.4 summarizes the learn unit and the procedures for using it during instruction. The observation procedure used by a supervisor to measure and teach teachers to use learn units is the **Teacher Performance Rate and Accuracy Scale.** Its use is described in Textbox 2.5 and Figure 2.4.

Recording and Graphing Verbal Behavior

Data are collected with pencil and paper or a mechanical counter. Record data *immediately* after delivering the consequence for the student at the end of a learn unit. Use pluses and minuses to indicate correct and incorrect responses. When a prompt is used as an intervention and students begin to respond without it, record unprompted responses with a circled plus sign. When using echoic-to-mand or echoic-to-tact

TEXTBOX 2.4
Presenting Learn Units

Basic student-teacher interactions are called learn units and consist of the following steps:

1. Obtain the student's attention before presenting the antecedent.
2. Present flawless antecedents, including written or vocal stimuli.
3. Wait three seconds for the student to initiate a response.
4. For correct responses, immediately present reinforcement.
5. For incorrect responses, immediately give a correction by presenting the antecedent again, modeling the correct response, and ensuring that students emit the correct response. Do not reinforce the corrected response; rather, introduce the next learn unit.
6. Move quickly to the next learn unit. Continue this sequence until a predetermined number of learn units (usually 20 for each response) is presented.

TEXTBOX 2.5
Teacher Performance Rate and Accuracy Scale

1. *Preparing for an Observation:* The *Teacher Performance Rate and Accuracy (TPRA) Scale* is conducted by a supervisor. Before instruction, identify the following target components: 1) Student(s), 2) instructional program, 3) operational definition of behavior, 4) schedules of reinforcement, 5) antecedents, and postcedents, and 6) prerequisite skills for students. Also, locate instructional materials, data collection forms, reinforcers, and curricular supplies. Review the student's graphs to determine trends, appropriateness of the target program, and the student's expected level of responding.
2. *Conducting the Observation:* Time the teacher's instructional behaviors beginning with the first antecedent and ending with the final consequence. Record the student's correct and incorrect responses to learn units. If students respond within the intraresponse time and are consistent with the operational definition of a target behavior, the response is correct. If students do not respond within the intraresponse time, emit responses that are not in the operational definition, omit a response, or "self-correct," the response is incorrect.
3. Measure each component of the learn unit, including the accuracy of antecedents (recorded in the antecedent column with A or ✓ when correct and with circled marks when incorrect) and consequences (recorded in the consequence column with R when reinforcement is contingent and appropriate C when corrections are appropriate and contingent, and with circled marks when consequences are incorrect).
4. Each column is totaled and divided by the converted time (in minutes) to measure the teachers' number of correct and incorrect learn unit presentations per minute, and the students' number of correct and incorrect responses to learn units per minute.

Teacher Performance Rate and Accuracy Scale

Date:	1/14/03	School:	Kennedy Middle
Teacher:	L.H.	Observer:	K. Smith
Student:	T. Washington	Student:	Mand for cookie - "Cookie, please".

Teacher Antecedent	Student Behavior	Teacher Consequence
1. ⓥ	−	C
2. √	−	C
3. √	+	R
4. √	+	R
5. √	+	Ⓡ
6. √	−	C
7. √	+	R
8. √	+	R
9. √	+	R
10. √	+	R
Correct/Incorrect: 9/1	7/3	9/1

Teacher Number Per Minute Correct:	8 correct learn units = 2.25 learn units/minute
Teacher Number Per Minute Incorrect:	2 incorrect learn units = .56 learn units/minute
Student Number Per Minute Correct:	7 correct learn units = 1.97 learn units/minute
Student Number Per Minute Incorrect:	3 incorrect learn units = .85 learn units/minute
Converted Time : 3.55 min	Actual Time: 3 min 33 sec

FIGURE 2.4   Teacher Performance and Rate Accuracy Scale

procedures, record echoic responses in a column marked "E" and mand or tact responses in a column marked "M" or "T."

The maintenance of reliable and continuous data on the student's progress is critical. Data from probes and instructional sessions must be immediately plotted neatly on fully labeled graphs. We graph prompted responses, including echoics, as

Student: J.Taylor   STO: Autoclitic mands (mand plus please)

Form /	Car			Truck ("tuck")			Juice								
	E	M	T	E	M	T	E	M	T	E	M	T	E	M	T
	+			+			+								
	+			+			(+)								
	+			+											
	+			+			(+)								
	+			+											
		+		−											
		+		−											

FIGURE 2.5   Sample Data Collection Form

open circles (○) and unprompted or independent responses as closed circles (●). Also, for all listener programs, record and graph echoics (even if the target behavior is not an echoic response) and look for increases as they occur. Data should show a descending trend in open circles and an ascending trend in closed circles. That is, echoic responses should decrease while independent responses increase.

Some programs measure only a single response while others measure multiple responses, and the measurement and graphing procedures for each differ. Teaching motor imitation, for example, initially involves a single response from the student for each learn unit. Thus, each response is recorded as plus or minus, summed after the completion of one session, and graphed as a single data point. However, during programs that involve more than one response (i.e., learn units during which matching, pointing, and speaking responses are rotated), mastered responses are no longer plotted, even if you are still providing response opportunities for them (i.e., as an antecedent for non-mastered responses or interspersed to maintain the child's attention). On the graph, plot prompted or less complex responses with open circles and the unprompted, complex, or **generative responses** with a closed circle. Do not graph responses until you have completed an instructional session, which is typically 20 learn units for each behavior. Incorrect responses do not need to be graphed since they are reflected in the difference between the correct responses and the total number of responses possible.

Total learn units are blocked together for each session and graphed. The completion of a predetermined number of learn unit opportunities for a form or function constitutes a single instructional session—whether new and mastered learn units were interspersed, **massed** learn units for one objective were presented, or learn units were **captured** in natural or generalization settings. Immediately plot the correct number of responses on the appropriate graph line. Similarly, plot the achievement of mastery criterion for an instructional objective on the graph.

Teaching Graphs

There should be one graph for each repertoire—echoics-to-mands and echoics-to-tacts. Figure 2.6 shows a sample echoic-to-mand graph. Number the left ordinate or vertical axis from 0 to 20 and label it as the "number of correct responses and total learn unit opportunities." Number the abscissa or horizontal axis with the dates of each session and label it as "dates." Numerous sessions may be conducted on the same day. Number the right axis from 1 to 50 and label it as the "cumulative number of criteria achieved."

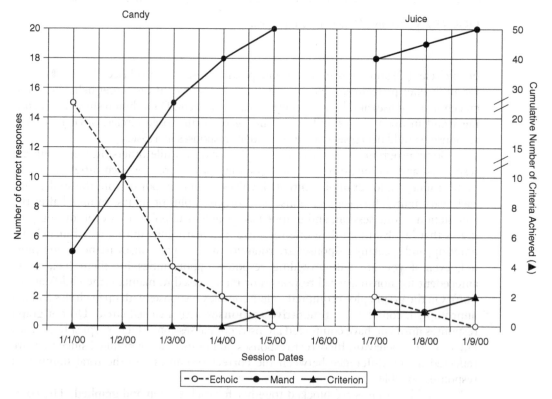

FIGURE 2.6   Sample Echoic-to-Mand Graph

TEXTBOX 2.6

Guidelines for Graphing Verbal Responses

Creating Teaching Graphs

1. Create separate graphs for responses during echoic-to-mand and echoic-to-tact instructional programs.
2. Use computer generated graphs, or graph paper with 4 squares per inch (Precision Teachers may choose to use standard acceleration charts).
3. Number the left ordinate (vertical axis) 0 to 20 consecutively and label as *"Number of correct responses and total learn unit opportunities."*
4. Write the date for each session on abscissa (horizontal axis).
5. Number the right ordinate (vertical axis) 0 to 50 and label as *"Cumulative number of criteria achieved."*
6. Graph prompted or echoic responses with open circles, unprompted or independent responses with closed circles, and criteria achieved with closed triangles.
7. Connect open circles with broken lines and closed circles and triangles with solid lines. Use phase change lines and labels to indicate new tactics and short-term objectives.

Creating Generalization Graphs

1. Generalization criteria are achieved when students emit at least two correct and unprompted tacts or mands in a non-instructional setting.
2. Mand and tact graphs may be separate but on the same page, separate graphs on different pages, or plotted as two points for the same day.
3. On the left ordinate, write numbers 1 to 50 on graph paper with 8 squares to the inch.
4. On the horizontal axis, write the date for each school day.
5. On the first school day, use two separate data points (preferably open and closed triangles) to plot the cumulative number of generalized criteria achieved for all tacts and mands.
6. For all subsequent days, plot the number from the first day *plus* the number from the second day. Continue this for each successive day by adding the current numbers to the prior day's total.
7. Connect data for mands and tacts with two separate lines (one solid and one broken).

When graphing, correct response data are plotted with closed circles and criteria achieved are plotted with closed triangles (▲). Connect the closed points with a solid line (–) and the triangles with broken lines (– –). Write the word/phrase being trained above the phase. Use vertical, broken phase change lines to indicate a new phase after a short-term objective is achieved or when a new tactic is introduced.

Generalization Graphs

Generalization is the development of essential stimulus control or responses controlled by stimuli found in the terminal or ultimate environment. We typically say that a response is generalized when a student emits it twice in a non-instructional setting, although for some students this may need modification. Make separate graphs for tact, mand, or other generalization responses. They may be individual panels on a single page or two data points per day. On the left ordinate, write the numbers from 1 to 50. On the abscissa, write the date for each school day. On the first day of instruction, plot the cumulative number of generalized criteria with a closed circle. On the second day, plot the cumulative number of criteria by adding the number from the first day to the second day. Each successive day, plot the cumulative sum of responses by adding the current numbers to the prior day's total. Connect data points with a solid line.

Providing and Measuring Accurate Instructional Decisions

Individualizing instruction based on research is an important part of verbal behavior analysis. The key to this evidence-based individualization of instruction is the use of a tested scientific algorithm for identifying the best alternative tactics. The algorithm for selecting potential sources for the problem and tactics that are likely to be effective can be used, provided that the teacher is using learn units reliably as identified by the *Teacher Performance Rate and Accuracy Scale (TPRA)* observation procedure and as described previously. When the existing science of teaching does not solve learning problems for children, procedures in this text and in other advanced applied behavior analysis texts can be used to address them. However, we have found that practitioners make more accurate instructional decisions when they have the basic capabilities of teaching as applied behavior analysis, which allows them to teach new operants and to locate alternative tactics for teaching new operants when initial tactics are not effective (Keohane & Greer, 2005). Some readers may find it helpful to review *Designing Teaching Strategies. An Applied Behavior Analysis Systems Approach* (Greer, 2002) where the procedures for finding and using alternative strategies are described in detail. However, many of these are also described here.

The analytic repertoire for addressing learning problems draws on *the learn unit context.* Used by those who do the actual teaching and their mentors, its use is critical to the advancement of each child's verbal capabilities and repertoires. The field of applied behavior analysis, including verbal behavior analysis, requires that the practitioner function as a *strategic scientist, and not just as a technician.* By this we mean that the teacher must continuously be in contact with the moment-to-moment outcome of instruction and use graphic displays of the results of instruction to make session-by-session decisions about what each child requires at any given point of teaching. Initial applications by those who function as technicians (the instructors) can result in momentary beneficial outcomes, but unless the person (usually the supervisor) who continuously monitors the technician can function as a strategic scientist, the child's progress may be slower than necessary.

Addressing the complexity of students' learning problems would be great if all we had to do was provide simple instructions for teachers to follow with little analysis. However, this is simply no more the case than a medical doctor can give everyone the

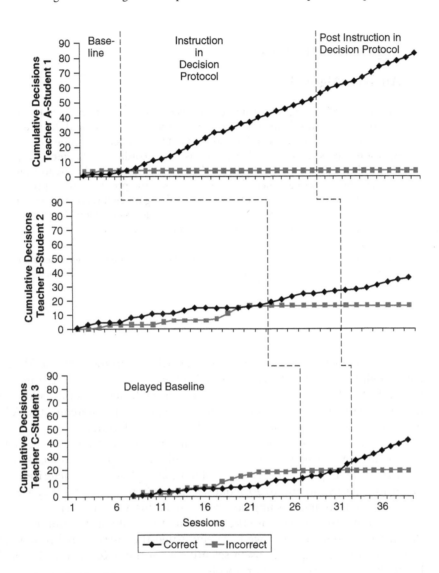

FIGURE 2.7   Analytic Algorithm

From Keohane, D. D., & Greer, R. D. (2005). Teachers' use of a verbally governed algorithm and student learning. *International Journal of Behavioral and Consultation Therapy, 1,* 249-268. http://www.behavior_analyst_today.com

same medication. The evidence for the importance of the teacher functioning as a strategic scientist is clear in research that we have conducted (Gardner, Sainato, Cooper, Heron, Heward, Eshleman; & Grossi, 1994; Greer, Keohane, & Healey, 2002; Ingham & Greer, 1992; Keohane & Greer, 2005; Lamm & Greer, 1991; Ross, Singer-Dudek, & Greer, 2005; Selinske, Greer, & Lodhi, 1991). The summary for some of this research is described in Research Box 2.1.

RESEARCH BOX 2.1

Analytic Algorithm

Keohane and Greer (2005) examined effects of teaching instructors to use a verbally governed problem-solving procedure to solve students' learning difficulties. Participants were three teachers and six students. The number of accurate decisions and **decision errors** teachers made were measured according to the **decision protocol** specified in this study. Results showed that students attained a greater number of instructional objectives when their teachers used the problem-solving procedure to solve instructional problems. The problem-solving procedure, or analytic algorithm, provided a means for teachers to systematically address students' learning problems under the control of students' data, research tactics, and rules.

From Keohane, D. D., & Greer, R. D. (2005). Teachers' use of a verbally governed algorithm and student learning. *International Journal of Behavioral and Consultation Therapy*, *1*, 249–268. http://www.behavior_analyst_today.com

Throughout the text we will describe particular protocols for building new verbal capabilities. We identify basic tactics that are used as a first step. We also emphasize that each child brings different repertoires to the table; hence, some children will need different tactics and others will need to be taught certain prerequisites. All children will require individualization in the use of instructional tactics.

Continuous measurement and graphing are the core features of behavior analysis, providing moment-to-moment pictures of a child's progress or lack of progress. Once these are in place, the professional must know how to characterize the problem in scientific terms and how to go about selecting different tactics as they are needed for particular students and learning problems. To do this, we must first eliminate errors in instruction in order to decrease the possibility that faulty instruction is the source of the learning problem. Once we have eliminated the instructional process itself as a source, we can subsequently use a scientific algorithm (Keohane & Greer, 2005) to locate alternative strategies or protocols.

First, we review some distinctions between *different aspects of the science of behavior* and how they apply to the components of either teaching or managing behavior. Portions of our science are concerned with *existing operants or performance*, which involves, for example, schedules of reinforcement and related tactics such as differential reinforcement of other behaviors, functional analyses of the reinforcers for "inappropriate behavior," vicarious reinforcement in which a peer's behavior changes as a function of observing another receiving reinforcement, the use of unconditioned or conditioned reinforcers, or the use of differential reinforcement. These are relevant to instruction when we are managing or motivating behavior that children or staff already have in their repertoires.

TEXTBOX **2.7**

Review of Components of the Learn Unit

1. Is the antecedent of the potential operant presented such that it is not ambiguous? Is the stimulus faultless; that is, if the stimulus is a shape such as a square, is it a true square and not a possible rectangle?
2. Is the student attending to the antecedent when you begin the learn unit? If not, the presentation is not a learn unit; begin again and discard the response of the presentation that was not a learn unit.
3. Once the presentation of the antecedent is done, the student must have an *opportunity-to-respond.* In most cases this intraresponse time is about 3 seconds, but this may need to be individualized for some students.
4. Once the student responds, the teacher must, in turn, respond to the student's response immediately. If the response is *accurate, the student receives a reinforcement operation* using a consequence that is relevant. For example, in a mand response, deliver the item requested with no praise. If it is tact, the response is reinforced with praise or another generalized reinforce-

ment. Other curricular programs will call for the use of tokens or unconditioned reinforcers.
5. When the response is inaccurate or no response is forthcoming, you must conduct a complete correction operation. This involves repeating the correct response and having the student emit the response while attending to the antecedent that will become the S^D for the operant you are teaching. In most cases, this corrected response is not reinforced. There are exceptions to this such as simultaneous stimulus prompts, or when the student is not yet able to tolerate corrections. In the latter case, use the tactics from Chapters 2 and 7 for teaching the student to tolerate corrections.
6. The accuracy of the response is immediately recorded before proceeding to the next learn unit presentation.
7. At the end of the session, plot the data and determine if an instructional decision is needed.

A second component of our science concerns the *induction or the establishment of new operants or higher order operants* that constitute new capabilities for our children. This component applies to children who do not have all of the components of the operant. The procedures for teaching new operants are different than those needed to manage behavior. Thus, when we manage behavior or maximize performance, we use some components of our science, and when we induce new operants or higher order operants we draw on other components of the science of behavior.

When we are building new operants or teaching, we require components of our science that involve learn units or the observation of learn units. As a first course of action, we must establish that the child is receiving learn units. In this case, we need to ensure that the basic parts of the learn unit are in place. In many cases, the difficulties children are having in acquiring new operants is traceable to missing components of the learn unit. If learn units are in place we can more reliably eliminate instructional errors of the teacher or teaching device as the source of the problem. Review the description of the components of the learn unit given earlier in this chapter. A brief and generic review follows.

The learn unit is one of the basic best practice procedures to use as a first step. One must ensure that the learn unit is present before considering alternative tactics. There are also several basic tactics that should be in place during most of the instruction. These include the following generic procedures. These are described in detail in most basic applied behavior analysis texts and in the Glossary of this text.

Research-based Tactics for Intervention

Generic Tactics

- *Learn units* (Review Textboxes 2.4 and 2.7 for descriptions of the learn unit).
- *Simultaneous stimulus prompt* (zero second-time delay, constant, or progressive time delay) related to train-test trials and programmed instruction frames. This procedure is used to avoid corrections and is sometimes described as errorless teaching. In this procedure, the teacher presents the instruction and immediately gives the student the answer as a prompt, which the student repeats and then receives reinforcement. The teacher presents instruction in this fashion for two instructional sessions (i.e., 20 learn units each). After those two sessions, the teacher provides the student with 1 second to respond (i.e., count 1001) and if the student emits the correct response, their response is reinforced. If not, the teacher provides the correct answer and the student's response is reinforced when they repeat it. If this is not successful, per the decision protocol described in Chapters 2 and 7, one may progressively increase the interval to 3 seconds or 5 seconds. If this does not result in the achievement of criterion, use standard learn unit instruction (Wolery, Holcombe, Billings, & Vassilaros, 1993). This procedure is particularly useful for students who have difficulty with corrections.
- *General case instruction* for teaching stimulus abstractions or concepts. In the general case procedure you ensure that the target aspect of the stimulus is present, and you present it in a range of irrelevant presentations. For example, if you are teaching colors, present the color in different or multiple exemplars varying in shapes, sizes, textures, and slightly different hues. The non-exemplar or foil— the *not correct response*—should be rotated. Thus, in the case of colors, different non-target colors should be presented as the foil or inaccurate exemplar. This increases the likelihood that you will teach the essential stimulus control.
- *Token reinforcement* for academic and social responding (generalized reinforcers). If necessary, tokens may need to be conditioned as reinforcers.
- *Conditioning praise* as a reinforcer for academic and social responding.
- *Vicarious reinforcement* for classroom management, or the reinforcement of students that results in a change in the behavior of other, observing students. After the initial vicarious effect, the teacher must directly reinforce the observing children for correct responding if the appropriate classroom behavior is to be maintained.
- *Interspersal of known items* when a child is having difficulty (task results in too little reinforcement, or when you are probing without reinforcement and want to

avoid extinction). In this procedure, the teacher inserts previously mastered material when teaching new material, thus increasing the likelihood that the child will respond correctly and that their responses will be reinforced. The interspersed item is not counted as a learn unit; it is rather treated as an establishing operation for maintaining the child's attention.

- *Stimulus delay.* When the student is not attending to the stimulus, you cover it before they respond. When the student is attending, you uncover the stimulus.
- *Response delay.* A similar procedure to Stimulus delay; but in this case rather than covering the stimulus, you teach the student to wait and then to respond. This is used when the student responds too quickly.
- *Rules, praise, and ignoring* to teach children to follow classroom rules (Madsen, Becker, & Thomas, 1968). This involves frequent reinforcement of appropriate behavior, ignoring inappropriate behavior, and providing reinforcement to peers who are behaving appropriately.
- *Accurate learn unit performance by teachers* (Albers & Greer, 1992). Teachers are taught to present accurate learn units, and then they are monitored by their supervisors (using the TPRA observational protocol described earlier in this chapter) in order to maintain accurate learn unit presentations.
- *Captured or incidental learn units* in which the teacher captures the natural establishing operations, as in occasioning a mand for water on a warm day after a child has been physically active.
- *Increased numbers of learn unit presentations* to decrease inattention or inappropriate behavior and to maximize learning (Kelly, 1996; Martinez & Greer, in press). While this is a behavior management tactic, it also results in better learning outcomes. That is, efficient and effective instruction replaces other procedures that are often used to deal with inattention or "bad" behavior.
- *Rapid presentations of learn units* such that there is little inter-response time between learn units.

Generic Pre-Listener-to-Speaker Tactics (Described in Chapters 3 and 4 of this text)

- *Basic echoic-mand and echoic-tact procedure.*
- *Rapid imitation to* induce mands and tacts (Ross & Greer, 2003; Tsiouri & Greer, 2003). This is a verbal capability intervention.
- *Stimulus-stimulus pairing to condition parroting as automatic reinforcer.* This is a vocal capability intervention (Miguel, Carr, & Michaels, 2001/2002).
- *Multiple-exemplar training* to induce transformation of establishing operations across mand and tact functions (Nuzzolo-Gomez & Greer, 2004).
- *Conditioning reinforcers* to replace stereotypy (Greer, Becker, Saxe, & Mirabella, 1985; Nuzzolo-Gomez & Greer, 2004).
- *Conditioning reinforcement for voices.* This is a verbal capability intervention.
- *Visual tracking protocol* (Keohane, Ackerman, & Greer, 2006b).
- *Tact procedure to decrease palilalia* (Karmali, Greer, Nuzzolo-Gomez, Ross, & Rivera-Valdes, 2005).

Generic Tactics for Children with Reader-Writer Capabilities (Described in Chapters 5 and 6 of this text)

- *Tutoring for tutor and tutee benefits* (Greer, Keohane, Meincke, Gautreaux, Chavez-Brown, & Yuan, 2004).
- *Use of textual antecedent stimuli to replace echolalia* for children who can textually respond (Greer & Bruno, 1997).
- *Response cards* to increase learn units in "group instruction" (Heward, 1994).
- *Token economy to teach self-management* (Greer, 2002).
- *Self-monitoring to teach observational learning* and accuracy in observation (Gautreaux, 2005).
- *Good Behavior* watch or bracelet.
- *Multiple exemplar instruction* to teach transformation of stimulus control across spoken and written spelling and selection to production. This is a verbal capability intervention (Greer, Yuan, & Gautreaux, 2005).
- *Writer immersion* to teach functional writing (Madho, 1997).
- *Personalized System of Instruction* or PSI tactics for teaching students self-management and the use of learn units to teach themselves (Keller, 1968).

Generic Tactics for Teaching Teachers, Parents, and Behavior Analysts (see Greer, 2002 for detailed descriptions of these tactics)

- *Personalized system of instruction* or PSI for teaching 3 components of teaching to teachers (accurate and automatic correct instruction; precise use of the terminology of the science as a writer or speaker, and as a listener or reader; and the use of scientific decision-making to solve learning problems) (Keohane & Greer, 2005; Selinski, Greer, & Lodhi, 1991).
- *Teacher Performance Rate and Accuracy* observations (TPRA) for teaching contingency-shaped responding by teachers and parents (Ingham & Greer, 1992).
- *CABAS Decision Protocol* for teaching teacher analytic repertoires (Keohane & Greer, 2005).
- *Pyramid training.*
- *Response cards* for teaching staff verbal behavior about the science of behavior.
- *Observational learning of verbal behavior about the science* (Nuzzolo-Gomez, 2002).

Learn Unit Context and Learn Unit Components

These are only the basic tactics. The reader is referred to Cooper, Heron, & Heward (1987) for a treatment of the basic tactics in applied behavior analysis; Sulzer-Azaroff, Drabman, Greer, Hall, Iwata, & O'Leary (1988) for basic tactics in education; and Chapters 5 and 6 in Greer (2002) for a more complete list. The Glossary in this text also provides details on tactics. This list does not include many of the protocols we will outline for teaching higher order operants, since they are covered in detail in the text. However, the tactics presented in this chapter are used to teach the components of the protocols for establishing higher order operants. Figure 2.8 depicting the learn unit and its context follows. We use this to set the stage for a discussion about how to use

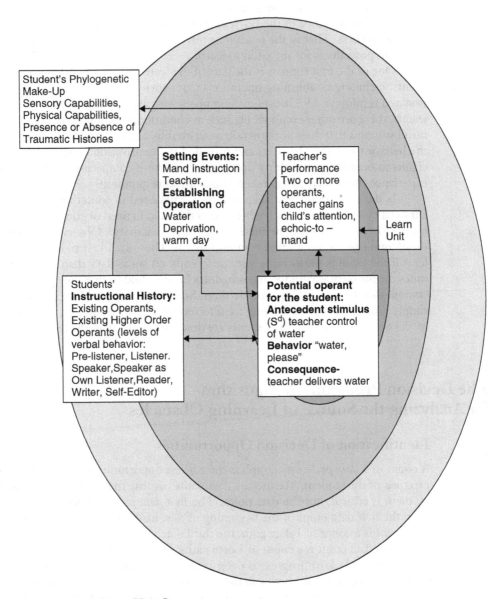

FIGURE 2.8   Learn Unit Context

the decision protocol or the scientific algorithm for searching for alternative instructional tactics.

In Figure 2.8, you will note that the teacher's and the student's behaviors occupy the center of the context. The learn unit includes the operations of the teacher or teaching device, as in the case of a computer presentation. It also includes the components of the potential operant for the student. In our decision process, first we need to ensure that the learn unit is present. Once we are sure that the learn unit is present and the student is still not learning, we can search the context for possible sources of the problem. The presence of the learn unit ensures that the problem is not in the actual teaching process. That is, the teacher or teaching device is performing necessary if not sufficient procedures for the child to learn.

One of the first sources is the part of the learn unit context that involves setting events, including establishing operations that provide the means for an item to function as a reinforcer. While establishing operations are a critical component of setting events, there are other components such as conditional stimuli (as in the presence of a novel stimulus that does not function as an establishing operation). Is the need to emit the behavior present? Teachers can provide brief deprivation or interrupted behavior chains to occasion establishing operations. Are there competing conditions based on experiences the child has had recently that affect responding?

Is the child upset, ill, sleep deprived, interested in something a peer is doing, annoyed by another peer, or frightened? Is the child in need of going to the bathroom, hungry, tired, or restless because of enforced inactivity? Observing and rectifying these conditions is often a first course of action. These are likely to be sources of problems if the child is performing very differently on some days than on others. Sometimes the problem is working out schedules for the child so that they get enough sleep, enough to eat, or more appropriate diets. Sometimes the problem is that the child is simply satiated on the item being used to reinforce their responses. Numerous tested tactics for dealing with setting events are described in detail in the texts cited earlier.

The Decision Protocol: An Algorithm for Analyzing the Source of Learning Obstacles

Identification of Decision Opportunities

A count of 3 *data paths* on a graph is the earliest opportunity for a decision about the progress of the student. We use the data paths because the angle or trend established by them is critical, not the data point. The first *data point* is a point of origin. Thus, from the first data point of the beginning of new instruction in a phase to the second data point is a count of 1 data path, the third data point is a count of 2 data paths, and the fourth data point is a count of 3 data paths. We count data paths because the trend of progress or lack of progress is determined by the angle of the data paths. At four data points we can determine whether the trend of the 3 data paths is descending or ascending. If a trend is present, or if the criterion for an instructional objective is achieved, the decision is made whether to continue, change tactics, teach prerequisites, or move to a new objective. If the direction changes for 1 or more data paths, a judgment of trend across 5 data paths should be made. If no trend is apparent at 5 data paths, a decision opportunity is at hand.

Of course, the achievement of the criterion involves only the number of consecutive sessions and data points per the program under review. If the criterion for your school or curriculum is two consecutive sessions with a program or lesson at 90% correct, then two data points at 90% constitute the decision point. A broken vertical line should appear after each decision point and a brief written statement of any tactic chosen should appear on the graph. New objectives should be set following the achievement of an objective at the criterion level. Next, we also describe how the accuracy of teacher decisions can be measured by those responsible for teaching and monitoring the teacher's analytic repertoire.

Trend Determination

Ascending trends should result in *continuation* of the present procedures in most cases, unless a procedural component of instruction is faulty or erroneous, such as the instructional procedures, the particular objective being taught, or the curricular material being used. *A descending trend or no trend* (i.e., the data paths are flat and neither descending nor ascending) should result in a decision to *analyze the source of the problem* and a broken line should be drawn to indicate this. Each *decision opportunity* that is consistent with these definitions is a correct decision for the teacher, while a decision that is not correct or the lack of a decision is an error in the teacher's analytic response to the visual display. *Each instructional session run without a decision change is another error for the teacher.* The rationale for this is that every instructional session in which the student is subjected to inappropriate pedagogy/curricula is a waste of educational time, and may indeed act to compound the student's difficulty with the instruction in progress. When a decision is made after a decision error, it is not counted as a correct decision because it is, at this point, a correction of the error. Of course, the sessions should all have been run with learn units and supervisors need to conduct frequent Teacher Performance Rate and Accuracy observations of the teachers working with the child to see that this is the case.[2]

Learn Unit Context Analysis

Once a decision for change is made, the next step is to ask a series of strategic questions about the probable source of the problem drawing, on the components of *learn unit context* shown in Figure 2.6. Once it is determined that the learn unit presentations are accurate, the problem may reside in the potential three-term contingency being taught the student. It is *a potential three-term contingency or operant* for the student until the operant is mastered. The sources for errors may be in the student's potential operant (i.e., something is wrong with the configuration of the antecedent, behavior, and consequence), the setting events in the instructional history of the student, or phylogenic or injury-based conditions (e.g., hearing or visual difficulties requiring adaptation of procedures or curriculum). If the teacher's description of the potential problem includes *a reasonably viable reference* to the learn unit, the three-term contingency, the instructional history, or the setting events, this strategic choice is counted as a correct decision. If the analysis of the potential problem draws on pre-scientific rationales or hunches not grounded in the science, the strategy analysis is counted as an error. At this point, another correct decision might be to do a correlation (AB design) or functional analysis drawing on these components as the basis for the analysis. Of course, each correct or incorrect decision for doing the instruction constitutes a decision point, for which correct or incorrect tallies may be made. *Before the teacher makes a decision about changing the pedagogical tactic, they should first consider if the student has the necessary prerequisite verbal capabilities and prerequisite component repertoires as outlined later in this chapter.* However, when you are involved in teaching the various components of new verbal capabilities, you will need to draw on research-based tactics in order to ensure that your student learns the components of the new verbal capabilities. For example, when you are using listener emersion, auditory matching, visual tracking, naming, or any of the other protocols, you will need to use different tactics for different students in order to ensure that they master the subcomponents of the new higher order operant. Also, as you are teaching educational standards that are within the child's level of verbal capability, you will need the range of tactics that essentially constitute the body of scientific tactics of pedagogy, as listed earlier in this chapter.

Selection of the Tactic

Providing that the problem is identified as a need for a new tactic, the teacher should choose a tactic from those tested in the behavior analysis or in other scientific literature that is related to the likely source of the problem. If the tactic selected for the solution to the student's problem is derived from the literature and is related to a principle of behavior or component of the learn unit analysis, another correct decision is counted.[3] If the tactic is not from the literature, then the decision is counted as an error. The teacher may skip the experimental strategic analysis and jump directly to the tactic decision without an error or an incorrect count if the evidence for the need of the tactic is compelling, and if the teacher has prior experience with this particular type of decision. This usually occurs in those instances when a teacher is experienced with the problem at hand or the student's history, and immediately recognizes a needed tactic.

Implementation of the Tactic

If the tactic is implemented correctly, the teacher receives a count of correct. If the tactic is not implemented accurately, the count is an error. The supervisor or teacher should check to ensure that the operations associated with the tactic are the actual operations being used by the teacher. It is often the case that teachers will ask colleagues rather than check the written description, and this can often result in faulty implementations of the tactic. Following the determination that the tactic was implemented accurately, we once again return to the steps in the trend determination spelled out in the preceding section.

Thus, we have described the steps for deciding when there is a problem, how to analyze the potential sources of the problem, how to determine a tactic or new intervention based on the analysis, and how the decision is recorded on the graph. At the same time we have described the measurement of the teacher's analytic expertise. The operational definitions prescribe the steps that the teacher is to follow when analyzing the visual display of instruction. The measurement provides the means for the teacher or their supervisor to use in monitoring the decisions and, therefore, provides the means to improve the repertoire.

Details of the Analytic Algorithm

We are now ready to describe the strategic analysis in more detail. We shall suggest some of the strategic questions for you to use in your analysis of the instructional problem consistent with the learn unit and its context outlined in the flow chart found in Figure 2.8.

Strategic Questions to Ask about Motivational Conditions and Setting Events

In the science of the behavior of the individual, motivation is viewed as the current and prior environmental events (setting and setting events) which act to affect the reinforcing and punishing effects of the existing consequences of behavior and, therefore, the antecedent control (Michael, 1993b). That is, the motivational setting affects the rate and strength of the behavior associated with the post-behavior effect of the reinforcement operation, which in turn affects the strength of the antecedent control. Establishing operations are part of settings that affect the existing operant or the teaching of a new operant on a momentary basis, and are the results of deprivation or satiation of food, water, attention, activities, competing activities, and their reinforcers/punishers. In cases where the setting event is a conditional stimulus and not an establishing operation, the stimulus does not have a motivational effect, but rather affects the control of the target S^d for the potential operant. In the latter case the component of the setting event that is controlling the teaching operation is a discriminative stimulus that affects another discriminative stimulus.

Teachers need to recognize the control of these variables and design or redesign classroom settings or sequences of experiences to enhance instruction rather than to allow them to compete with instruction. There are a few tactics from the applied literature that suggest ways to use establishing operations to enhance instructional effectiveness or to compensate for ways in which motivational settings interfere with instruction. A few of the tactics from the existing research findings for establishing operations are listed in Textbox 2.8.

Reinforcers and the preference of one activity over another are relative and they change from moment to moment. Whether or not an event, activity, or item functions as a reinforcer is affected by prior, simultaneous, and subsequent events (i.e., setting events, see Figure 2.8). Good strategic analyses will take these conditions into account

---

TEXTBOX **2.8**

Motivational Tactics

- Setting up situations that deprive a stimulus in a chain of operations (e.g., withhold a needed item to enhance its reinforcement effect)
- Alternating learn units between peer and target students
- Changing the sequence of activities contingent on student behavior
- Using slightly preferred activities to reinforce low preference activities
- Alternating instruction requiring much movement with activities requiring little movement or providing brief quiet periods prior to instructional presentations
- Eliminating or *using* competing stimuli, briefly eliminating access to an object associated with low preference activity or instruction. For example, use the competing stimuli as brief reinforcers for the new response/stimulus control

---

as potential variables that may affect instruction. While much more needs to be known about how to compensate for or ameliorate deprivation or satiation conditions through momentary operations in the classroom, much can be done by using what is known or seeking out new tactics through in situ research when the existing research-based tactics do not work.

Of course, one can simply wait until the competing stimuli or motivational conditions are ideal. Certainly, these ideal moments should result in *captured learn units* by the teacher (e.g., incidental teaching), but delays between natural moments result in drastic reductions in learn units and an unwitting increase in inter-learn unit latency time. It is best to both manipulate the natural conditions that will result in the immediate resumption of successful learn units and capture instructional learn units when the opportunities are there as we described earlier. A short enforced quiet period with no activity, or the reinforcement of mastered operants for sitting still or eye contact for students functioning at these levels, may be all that is needed. Alternately, teachings of learn units for a preferred subject creates a momentum or macro-reinforcement that will allow the teacher to insert the new program learn unit with success.

Strategic Questions to Ask about Instructional Histories and Prerequisite Repertoires

One of the possible sources of a student's difficulties with a particular curriculum concerns the prerequisite stimulus control of the student's behavior and the possible relationship of this history of instruction to his current difficulties. At this point, we do not go into detail about an analysis of the prerequisite verbal capabilities because this is the subject of this text and we will review that sequence later in the chapter. Presuming that the student's verbal capabilities are not the problem, the following section outlines a few of the strategic questions that provide directions for locating a likely solution to an instructional history problem when it is not a verbal capability problem.

Prerequisite Stimulus Control

Are the prerequisite stimulus control and corresponding responses presently in the student's repertoire such that they can respond adequately to the current learn unit presentations? Comparing various antecedent or setting event controls and observing differences in responding can isolate this. Are the prerequisites scientifically identified—that is, is there evidence suggesting that the presumed prerequisites are necessary, or are the prerequisites assumed on a logical basis? If the necessary prerequisites for the new response are known, what is the student's history with regard to the prerequisites (e.g., has she mastered the prerequisites)?

If the answers to the above questions suggest that it is necessary to teach prerequisite repertoires, which component(s) of the prerequisites(s) need(s) training (or retraining) in order to ease the student into the new target objective?

New prerequisites, or in some cases a set of prerequisites, may need to be identified and these are described in detail later in the section on sequencing instruction for teaching verbal capabilities. It is important to keep in mind the fact that behaviors *are often independent, even though they may be associated with the same stimuli.* Assumptions that a central concept (e.g., color concepts) has been learned simply because a student can point to colors when asked to do so may result in no instruction in naming the color. This is, of course, the lack of a **naming** repertoire or an inadequate **transformation of stimulus control** because an assumption was made that the two responses are equivalent when, in fact, they were independent repertoires that could be related only through instruction. The first response of *pointing* to colors involved a *listener* response while the latter of *saying* the colors' name involved *speaker responding.* Thus, both repertoires must be taught. Of course, the astute reader will see that the real problem is that the student is presumed to have naming, when, in fact, she does not. So until the

---

TEXTBOX **2.9**

Questions to Ask about Instructional History

- How recently were the repertoires found to be present?
- Did the student achieve both mastery and fluency?
- What was (were) the setting(s) in which the objectives were achieved and how similar or different are the current setting(s)?
- What reinforcers or corrections were used during the prior instruction for the prerequisite repertoire and how were they presented?
- Was the recording of the achievement of the objective reliably done by a teacher calibrated to a standard?
- What was the scripted or programmed instructional methodology and how reliably was it implemented?
- In what ways were the instructional operations similar or different from the operations used to teach the new objective?

student has mastered the full naming repertoire, the independent repertoires need to be taught in a multiple exemplar fashion as described in the naming protocol.

By instructional control, we mean that the behavior of the student's attention is guided reliably by the behavior or presence of the teacher as described in Chapter 3. When the teacher instructs the student to do something, can the teacher expect that the student will follow the instruction immediately and reliably (e.g., the child is looking elsewhere and the teacher says "look at me," the student immediately looks at the teacher and is ready for a learn unit presentation)? Is the difficulty that the student is having with a particular program really due to incomplete or weak instructional control by the teacher for the student? Is the instructional control problem based on the teacher's inadequate or incomplete teaching skills; is the teacher using and reinforcing the incorrect attention signals? This question must be resolved before proceeding with subsequent analyses by using the TPRA observation procedure. If the student is not compliant and attentive, additional questions cannot be answered. You must gain basic instructional control.

These questions and the questions associated with the sources of difficulty (e.g., antecedent, response, consequence, and motivational settings) are answered by reviewing the existing data for the student and by systematically observing the student under controlled instructional conditions. If the existing data record helps eliminate

---

TEXTBOX **2.10**

Questions to Ask about the Prerequisites that Need Teaching

Were there requisite responses (or stimulus controls) that were not considered when assigning the student to the new target objective?

1. Is there a chaining sequence of behaviors necessary for the new target instruction that was presumed but not actually tested or trained?
2. Is a more detailed task analysis that includes instruction in the additional prerequisite steps needed prior to reintroducing the student to the new objective?
3. Are the formerly learned stimulus controls consistent with the new ones introduced (e.g., "point to" vs. "touch the. . . ."; vs. "give me the. . . .")? Is there some intervening stimulus control that needs to be taught (e.g., before training vowel sounds, can the student discriminate between word or letter formations and nonwords on pages)?
4. Was the prerequisite stimulus control adequately trained (e.g., is the student under adequate instructional control)? For example, were the procedures of general case training used such that the ranges of exemplars of the target SD were programmed adequately against rotated non-exemplars?
5. Were irrelevant components of the stimulus rotated across the exemplar such that the response came under the control of relevant stimuli rather than irrelevant stimuli?

many or some sources of difficulty, much time is saved. Some of the possible difficulties may need to be identified by experimentally manipulating the variable(s) associated with the potential problem. The strategies of applying the experimental method through single-case experimental design (i.e., reversal, multiple baseline, and multitreatment designs) may be done rapidly to isolate the locus of the problem. Typically, this is done through *probe sessions* that are rotated with current instructional procedures isolating one variable at a time (see the design chapters in texts concerned with introductions to applied behavior analysis). However, the tactics already identified in the literature provide likely and immediate solutions that *obviate the need for prolonged experimentation in most cases.* This fact emphasizes the necessity for continuous expansion of the teacher's repertoire of verbal behavior about the science under conditions that reinforce verbally mediated tests with students.

A probe session is a teaching session in which one tests for the presence or absence of the prerequisite response/stimulus control under various environmental changes and may involve the range of controlling variables including the (a) setting (motivational conditions), (b) the response, (c) the consequence for the prerequisite behavior, and (d) the antecedents for the response (both teacher and target stimulus). If the response was already present, then one of these conditions may have been different in the student's instructional history. However, if the prerequisite is emitted under the same conditions as used in the present instruction (e.g., the same contingencies and motivational settings), the prerequisite is not necessary for this student. The prerequisite may actually belong to another repertoire (e.g., when *pointing to* is not a prerequisite for naming but actually a different repertoire). Simply because someone can identify an exemplar in a multiple-choice setting is not equivalent to naming or constructing an exemplar.

The result of this analysis will be the identification of deficits in the student's repertoire within a given verbal capability, or deficits in the teacher's presentation vis-à-vis the prior instructional history and the existing verbal capabilities of the student. Thus, the necessary prerequisites can be taught or the instructional presentation corrected before resuming the new instructional objective. When the instruction is adequate per learn unit presentations (i.e., the learn unit is intact), consistent with the student's history, and the student has the necessary prerequisites, then *the student will learn.*

Figure 2.9 is a flow chart that summarizes the analytic steps you need to take in performing the analysis of the source of learn unit problems in the learn unit context. In effect, this is a set of printed stimuli that should serve to govern your verbal tacts that constitute the analysis. It represents the verbal stimuli that constitute part of the verbal behavior of a scientist of behavior—in this case the repertoires that constitute the analytic components of verbal behavior analysis. It is the last step that we illustrated on our figure on the evolution of verbal behavior.

Now that we have identified the components of the teacher's analytic repertoires for ensuring that the relevant tactics for teaching are identified for individual learning problems, it is time to return to solutions to learning problems that are identified as stemming from the missing verbal capabilities. That is, once we have ensured that the teaching is faultless and the student achieves objectives easily within the constraints of

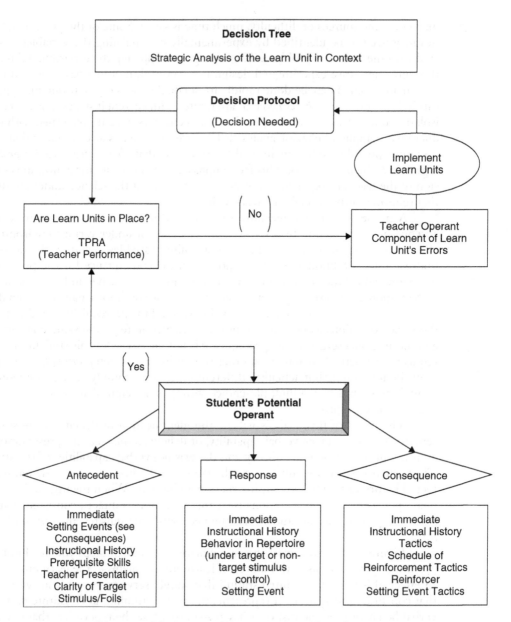

FIGURE 2.9   Diagram of the Decision Tree or Analytic Algorithm

her verbal capability per the verbal developmental stages, we are ready to determine if the student is ready for interventions leading to a more advanced verbal stage.

Once we have established that the student's learning problem is not traceable to (a) a lack of accurate presentations or learn units; (b) use of the decision protocol, resulting in the adequate use of likely tactics to teach, and (c) the lack of a verbal capability or developmental cusp, the next step involves the use of protocols for inducing new verbal capabilities. The measurement procedures for the verbal capabilities are outlined next.

Measuring and Recording Developmental Milestones

We use verbal milestones to determine the attainment of verbal capabilities (see Figures 2.10 and 2.11). Each of the repertoires listed in Table 2.1 is a subcomponent of the verbal milestones listed earlier in Table 1.3, and the teaching of these milestones and their subcomponents requires scientifically-tested procedures for children who do not acquire them without specialized interventions. The research in verbal behavior adds to existing procedures to increase children's verbal capabilities when those capabilities are missing. We also introduce the specialized terms associated with identifying and teaching the verbal milestones that will be defined and described in detail in subsequent chapters. In Figures 2.10 and 2.11, a **capabilities chart** that can be used to record the current status of verbal capabilities, is available for pre-reader and reader categories. We describe the procedures and probes for each of these capabilities in subsequent chapters.

Defining Verbal Milestones

Pre-Listener Components

- Visual Tracking: The capacity to follow visual stimuli by moving one's eyes (called tracking) is usually established during early infancy and is a prerequisite for attending behaviors. When this capacity is missing for learners, the visual tracking program is designed to teach it by conditioning tracking responses as children follow and then select a preferred object that was hidden under a container prior to being rotated among other, identical containers.
- Capacity for sameness across senses: The capacity for sameness is a prerequisite for stimulus discrimination (Engelmann & Carnine, 1991). Typically developing children seem to acquire this matching capacity early, possibly because they have multiple opportunities to match their own sensory stimuli with multiple exemplars in their environment. When pre-listeners are not obtaining basic auditory or visual discrimination during instruction, we teach the capacity for sameness across visual, auditory, gustatory (taste), olfactory (smell), and tactile (touch) stimuli by using a match-to-sample protocol.
- Basic compliance based on visual contexts and on the teacher as a source of reinforcement: The capacity to attend to another person's simple directions or actions is another early capability that may be missing for pre-listeners. Children have basic compliance when they can sit down or stand up when told to do so, sit still for a period of time, look at a teacher to receive instruction, and can imitate the actions of another person. When we teach these skills, they are often taught

TABLE 2.1   Does the Child Have These Verbal Milestone Subcomponents?

Pre-Listener Components
- Visual Tracking
- Capacity for sameness across senses
- Basic compliance based on visual contexts and on the teacher as a source of reinforcement

Listener
- Conditioned reinforcement for voices
- Discrimination between positive and negative exemplars of words
- Auditory matching of words
- Generalized auditory matching of words
- Basic listener literacy with non-speaker responses
- Visual matching to occasion naming
- Naming
- Observational naming and observational learning prerequisites
- Reinforcement as a listener
- Listening to one's own speaking
- Listening to one's own textual responses
- Listening and changing perspectives

Speaker
- Parroting
- Basic echoic-to-mand (visible or not)
- Echoic-to-tact
- Mands and tacts with basic adjective-object pairs
- Faulty echoics and palilalia are not present
- Transformation of establishing operations across mands and tacts
- Intraverbal mands
- Intraverbal tacts
- Tacts and mands from incidental experiences (naming and speaker repertoires)
- Comparatives (smaller/longer)
- Specificity

Speaker-Listener Exchanges with Others
- Sequelics as speaker
- Sequelics as listener-speaker
- Conversational units

Speaker-as-Own-Listener
- Basic naming from the speaker perspective
- Observational naming from the speaker perspective
- Verbal governance of speaker responses
- Conversational units in self-talk

Early Reader Repertoires
- Textual responses: see word-say word at adequate rate improved by prior conditioning of print stimuli as conditioned reinforcement for observing

individually and, as such, do not demonstrate the capacity for auditory discrimination, but rather, non-auditory stimulus control based on another's actions.

Listener Components

- Conditioned reinforcement for voices: Developmental scales suggest that during early infancy, children discriminate voices as they attend to those of their parents or caregivers. For children with missing verbal repertoires, the capacity to attend to the voice of a teacher or parent may be missing because such voices are not conditioned reinforcers. We teach this by pairing reinforcers with an instructors' voice and tape recordings of a parent until attending occurs. See the protocol for conditioning attention to voices in Chapter 3.
- Discrimination between positive and negative exemplars of words. Auditory matching of words: The capacity for sameness with words builds on early matching capacities and, for some listeners must be taught as a prerequisite for speaking. We teach this capacity, which has led to emerging echoic repertoires, by using a match-to-sample protocol for sounds and then words. See the protocol for auditory matching in Chapter 3.
- Generalized auditory matching of words or the matching of novel words on the first attempts. Individuals who have generalized auditory matching can match novel auditory stimuli during probes. When this is missing, we use the auditory matching protocol described in Chapter 3 to teach it.
- Basic listener literacy with non-speaker responses: The capacity for auditory discrimination is demonstrated when listeners differentially respond to a series of interspersed commands or a speaker's vowel-consonant combinations. When this capacity is missing, we teach it by establishing auditory discrimination across mastered and nonsense commands at a rate criterion.
- Visual matching to occasion naming (student can tact item from hearing the teacher tact it during matching instruction): The capacity to acquire tacts and mands without direct instruction—called naming—is significant for speakers (Horne & Lowe, 1996). One of the first steps for naming is visual matching during which an instructor says the name of a stimulus as part of the instructional antecedent. As the capacity for naming is later acquired, learners should acquire tacts and mands from hearing the name of the stimulus during a listener response such as matching.
- Naming: The listener component of naming is the first stage of naming, and involves both matching and selection (or point) responses without direct instruction during which the name of the stimulus is presented as part of the antecedent (i.e., match (stimulus) to (stimulus) and point to [stimulus]). When students master these responses, the responses will eventually become discriminative stimuli for tacts without direct instruction on the tact.
- Observational naming and observational learning prerequisites: This is the capacity to learn verbal or non-verbal response without direct instruction by observing the consequences received by a peer. Prerequisite skills for this capacity include:

- Listening to one's own speaking: This is say-do correspondence, which occurs when speakers can follow their own verbal behavior by complying with it.
- Listening to one's own textual responses: Reading comprehension, or following directions that one has read.
- Listening and changing perspectives: Diectic. Changing from "I" or "my" as a speaker to "you" or "your" as a listener during intraverbals, or as a listener in response to a speaker's tacts or mands.

Speaker Components

- Parroting: Skinner's (1957) term to describe an early stage in a child's verbal development during which they produce vocal patterns that are self-reinforcing because the patterns match sounds in their environment and not because they are imitating any muscular actions that produce them. He noted that these sounds will, eventually, become a part of the child's verbal behavior. We believe that parroting is an early form of copying that leads to echoic behavior. It is taught by using stimulus-stimulus pairing protocols (Sundberg, Michael, Partington, & Sundberg, 1996) for some children who are missing echoic behavior.
- Basic echoic-to-mand (visible or not): Skinner (1957) observed that echoic behavior initially has an educational function because parents use it to teach their children new forms for other verbal functions. When children cannot learn new forms for verbal functions from verbal models, we teach this capacity by using echoic-to-mand instructional protocols.
- Echoic-to-tact: The educational utility of the echoic as Skinner (1957) described is also useful for teaching tacts. Since tacts have a different function than mands, echoic-to-tact protocols must be used to teach students to learn new forms and the tact functions from echoics.
- Mands and tacts with basic adjective-object pairs: A type of autoclitic, the specificity of mands and tacts for a speaker is expanded by bringing adjective-object pairs (i.e., the blue car, the big cookie) into the mand and tact operants.
- Faulty echoics and palilalia: Faulty echoics (often called immediate echolalia) or palilalia (often called delayed echolalia) can occur as a function of not discriminating contexts when echoing should occur and as a type of vocal stereotypy. We reduce both by replacing them with another verbal function or form. We also reduce palilalia by conditioning other activities such as books or toys.
- Transformation of establishing operations across mands and tacts: Mands and tacts are initially functionally independent of one another and each function must be separately trained in order to occur (Lamarre & Holland, 1985). When multiple exemplar instruction is used to present establishing operations across both mands and tacts (Nuzzolo-Gomez & Greer, 2004), students can learn a form in one function and use it in another. When this is present, the child has transformation of establishing operations across mand and tact functions.
- Intraverbal mands: Verbal forms with the mand function that occur under verbal stimulus control (i.e., "What do you want?"). Unlike pure mands, they are preceded by a verbal antecedent. They are typically acquired separately from pure

mands and tacts in early speakers, and a specialized instructional tactic such as multiple exemplar instruction is used to help speakers acquire pure and impure mand responses to a single stimulus.

- Intraverbal tacts: Verbal forms with the tact function that occur under verbal stimulus control (i.e., "What is it?"). Unlike pure tacts, they are preceded by a verbal antecedent. They are also typically acquired separately from pure tacts and mands in early speakers, and multiple exemplar instruction to induce naming is used to help speakers acquire pure and impure tact responses to a single stimulus.

- Tacts and mands from incidental experiences (naming and speaker repertoires): Children who can acquire tacts without direct instruction will probably learn more tacts than those who cannot because they can learn from incidental experiences. *Naming* is the capacity to learn tacts from instruction as a listener (listening to the name of an item when matching it or pointing to it) and to learn listener behavior (matching or pointing) from instruction as a speaker (tact instruction). When students do not have the naming capability, we teach it by using multiple exemplar instruction across speaker and listener instruction (Fiorile & Greer, 2006; Gilic, 2005; Greer, Stolfi, Chavez, Brown, & Rivera-Valdes, 2005).

- Comparatives (smaller/longer): If comparative autoclitics are not in a student's repertoire, then they are taught with mand and tact functions using mand or tact protocols.

- Specificity (in/on/under/beside): If autoclitics of specificity are not in a student's repertoire as part of their mand and tact functions, then they are taught along with mand and tact functions.

Speaker-Listener Exchanges with Others

- Sequelics as speaker: These are intraverbals during which one verbal response is controlled by a prior verbal stimulus. The two verbal stimuli do not have point-to-point correspondence with one another.

- Sequelics as listener-speaker: These are present in a speaker's repertoire if they can emit verbal responses to another person's verbal stimulus (intraverbal behavior). An individual responds intraverbally as a listener.

- Conversational units: These are present in a speaker's repertoire if they can emit verbal responses to another person's verbal stimulus (they are first a listener and then a speaker), and then respond with their own intraverbal during which they are the first speaker who, after speaking, responds as a listener to the other person's response.

Speaker-as-Own-Listener

- Basic naming from the speaker perspective: This is present in a speaker's repertoire if they can tact stimuli after hearing another person tact them.

- Observational naming from the speaker perspective: This is present in a speaker's repertoire if they can tact stimuli after observing a peer receive listener or speaker instruction for the stimuli. See the protocols in Chapters 3 and 5.
- Verbal governance of speaker responses: This is present in a speaker's repertoire if they can do what they say they will do. For example, if a child says, "I will play with blocks" and then plays with blocks, they have verbal governance of their own speaker responses. This is often referred to as a *say and do repertoire*. See the protocol in Chapter 5.
- Conversational units in self-talk: Also called self-talk, this is present in a speaker's repertoire if they can first speak, then listen, and then respond as a speaker to themselves. This occurs during play with toys or other stimuli in which the child treats the toys as characters and has the toys exchange speaker listener roles and is a precursor to thinking as Skinner (1957) defined it. See the protocol in Chapter 5.

Early Reader Repertoires

- Textual responses: Responding to textual stimuli by seeing a word and then saying it. The acquisition of textual responding is accelerated by conditioning print stimuli as a reinforcer for observing before textual instruction. See the protocol in Chapter 6.

Figures 2.10 and 2.11 represent ways to graphically or visually summarize the child's progress through the developmental capabilities. The student's progress proceeds from the bottom of the pyramid to the top. In the following chapters, each of these steps will be described along with protocols to induce them when they are missing. They are presented here as examples of visually summarizing children's progress in verbal development.

Summary

- This chapter described ways to measure and create visual displays for all verbal functions, capabilities, and milestones.
- Choose items for instruction that will be functional for a student in the foreseeable future. Target items for mands may include toys, edibles, or objects; events such as hugs or play, and other activities that the student seeks. For tacts, choose common items that are not potential reinforcers. List mand and tact items separately on a running record and update it with new forms as students achieve criteria.
- Before instruction, conduct probes by presenting the antecedent and motivational conditions for the long-term objective associated with the repertoire you are targeting. Responses during probes are never corrected, but may be reinforced depending on the repertoire. Record the antecedent conditions that evoke a response, the occurrence or non-occurrence of the response, and the reinforcers that maintain it (generalized, prosthetic, and natural).

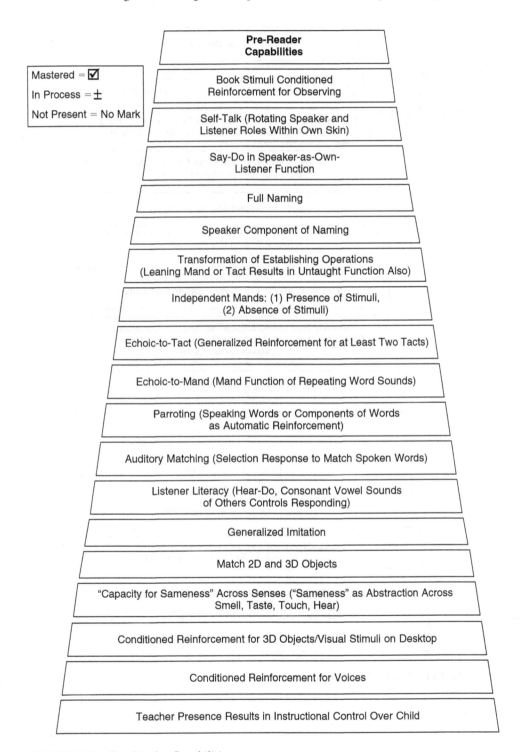

FIGURE 2.10   Pre-Reader Capabilities

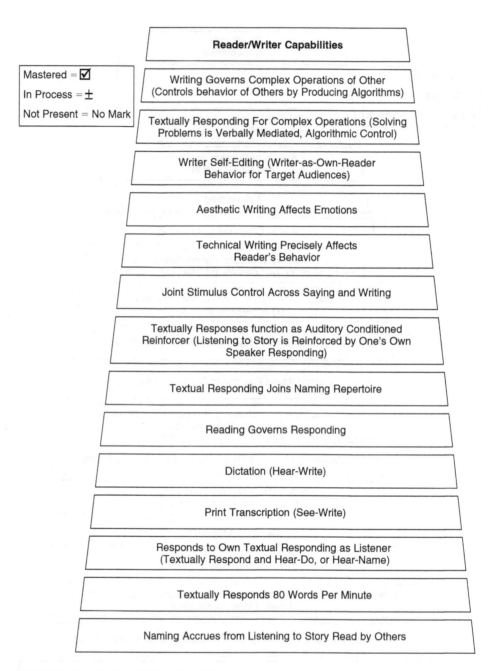

FIGURE 2.11 Reader/Writer Capabilities

- Only teach repertoires that were not occurring at criterion-level responding during probes. Teach missing repertoires by using learn units, which are interlocking three-term contingencies for teachers and students. First, obtain the student's attention, then present a flawless antecedent, wait three seconds for a response, and then contingently reinforce or correct it. Corrections for incorrect responses involve presenting the antecedent again and waiting for a response, but not reinforcing it.
- The *Teacher Performance Rate and Accuracy (TPRA) scale* is used to measure the rate of teachers' accurate learn unit presentations. At the end of a session and a day, summarize learn units into total learn units, and correct learn units and number of learn units to criterion.
- During instruction, standard mastery criterion for obtaining short-term objectives is 90% correct responding across two consecutive sessions or 100% correct responding for one instructional session. Write instructional objectives based on a student's probe data.
- On a data collection form, use pluses and minuses for correct and incorrect responses. For prompted responses, circle the plus sign. For echoics, mands, and tacts, record pluses and minuses in columns marked E, M, and T.
- Training graphs are numbered 1 to 20 on the left axis for responses, and 1 to 50 on the right axis for cumulative number of criteria achieved. Plot correct responses with a closed circle and criteria achieved with closed triangles. Use phase change lines to indicate the attainment of an objective or the use of a new tactic. The slope and direction of data paths and data points tell the learning rate for new verbal behavior forms—steeper slopes show rapid learning; flatter slopes show slower learning.

ENDNOTES

1. See the following references for research on the functional independence of mands and tacts: Lamarre & Holland (1985); Nuzzolo-Gomez, Leonard, Ortiz, Rivera-Valdes, & Greer (2002); Twyman (1996b).
2. See Ingham & Greer (1991), and Ross, Singer-Dudek, & Greer (2005) for descriptions of the Teacher Performance Rate and Accuracy scale observation procedures.
3. The research-based instructional tactics described in this chapter are also described in detail in several applied behavior analysis texts; see Greer (2002) and the *Journal of Applied Behavior Analysis* and other behavioral journals.

Learning to Listen: Induction of the Listener Repertoire of Verbal Development

We need separate but interlocking accounts *[italics added] of the behaviors of both speaker and listener if our explanation of verbal behavior is to be complete . . . in many important instances the listener is also behaving at the same time as a speaker.*

Skinner, 1957, p. 34

The Listener Role in Verbal Behavior

The **listener function,** or the ability to be governed by the speaker behavior of others, is key to the development of verbal functions. As we saw in Chapter 1, the listener role is important because a child who is not a listener is totally dependent on the assistance of caretakers. In addition, the early stages of "thinking" are dependent on the listener function, as we shall describe. While Skinner's theory of verbal behavior dealt primarily with speaker behavior and only indirectly with listener behavior, all verbal functions were based on the presumption of a listener capability.[1] Thus, when the listener capability is missing, it must be induced.

Several examples illustrate the problem that some children have in acquiring the listener function. For instance, it is not unusual to observe that vocal instructions do not control a learner's response because during instruction they simply repeat their own responses, follow visual cues provided unwittingly by teachers, respond to the sequence of instruction, or respond to the exclusion of an instruction. During a matching program (e.g., "Match red with red," which is frequently used to teach visual discriminations), students might only respond correctly to visual prompts to point to the correct stimulus and not to the teacher's spoken words. We can test for "true" auditory stimulus control by interspersing instructions such as "Point to red" with nonsense phrases such as "blah, blah, blah" or non-target antecedents such as pointing to our nose. In response to non-target antecedents, children who are not under true auditory stimulus control may continue to emit the previously targeted response of matching. In other words, the student begins to respond to the visual cues and not to the teacher's spoken words because the **auditory properties of speech** have no directive function or stimulus control over the child's behavior. They do not have the **basic listener capability.**

Children with autism or other speech-delayed diagnoses become very good at picking up visual cues simply because they do not discriminate vocal instructions. They often respond by watching the teacher's eyes, by depending on position prompts, and by utilizing other means of obtaining reinforcement. However, they do not come under the control of vocal instructions. In effect, repeatedly reinforced instructional units simply teach them better use of visual cues. The result is that without visual cues (intentional or unintentional) by the teacher, they cannot perform a listener task. Until the auditory properties of speech—that is, the consonant-vowel properties of speech or phonemic combinations—govern or direct children's behavior, their worlds are limited to a visual and non-verbal environment.

Listener instruction is important because for some students it is essential for the development of other verbal repertoires such as first instances of speaker behavior, the echoic response, and social behavior (Novak & Pelaez, 2004). Thus, for some students it may be necessary to develop basic listener repertoires before, or as speaker responses emerge (Chavez-Brown, 2005; Chavez-Brown & Greer, 2003; Greer, Chavez-Brown, Nirgudkar, Stolfi, & Rivera-Valdes, 2005). Furthermore, certain key listener repertoires are the foundation of complex verbal communication and are necessary for the more advanced stages of verbal behavior identified in Chapter 1. Specifically, the listener repertoire is essential to stages of verbal behavior involving

a. conversational episodes between individuals (**conversational units**)
b. a special milestone called **naming**
c. **self-talk** episodes during which a child takes on the role of both speaker and listener in their self-talk (conversational units)
d. "say and do" correspondence of self-management in which children do what they say they will do

e. reading comprehension that involves responding as a listener to what one has read
f. problem-solving, which is guided by listening to one's own instructions
g. listener reinforcement in social interactions

· Some behavior analytic instructional guides often emphasize the importance of gaining compliance or "instructional control" when teaching early forms of communication, but it is not simply compliance that is needed; rather, children need correspondence between their non-verbal responses and the speech of others (i.e., teachers say, "Come here" and children respond to the auditory properties of their speech). Learning this correspondence is fundamental in order for students to acquire listener and speaker functions; basic discriminations such as matching or discriminating colors, shapes, events, and activities; and other building blocks for more advanced learning.

In the earliest stage of listening, children must have the **capacity for sameness** (Engelmann & Carnine, 1991), which is the ability to identify attributes of sameness, in non-vocal sounds (e.g., animal calls and environmental sounds) and vocally produced words (identical consonant-phoneme combinations). Quite early, children acquire the capability to distinguish between words and other sounds in a very basic step similar to the process whereby they learn to discriminate between printed words, pictures, or figures. Moreover, matching the "same" stimuli is a basic step before discriminating "not same" stimuli. These basic steps are sometimes taken for granted during discussions of development because typically developing children seem to acquire them in a seamless manner; the acquisition of which many developmental psychologists attribute to innate ability (although parents and caretakers actually continuously, incidentally, and inadvertently reinforce this capacity). However, when establishing verbal repertoires in children who are missing them, teaching these basic steps requires careful attention.[2]

The reader will by now have noticed that we have not used the terms *receptive* and *expressive* speech. We may describe a child as a *receiver* (i.e., receptive language) as in a radio *receiver* receiving electronic transmissions or an electric signal, but the role of the listener (and the role of the speaker) is very different and much more complex because the function of the "signal" must be learned. Therefore, the child is not simply a *receiver;* rather the child is a complex organism that must make sense out of essentially arbitrary sounds. The child is a locus of experiences and genetic capacities; new experiences or instructions must use the existing repertoires of the child to develop complex verbal functions. Similarly, the term *expressive* suggests that an individual is *expressing* something that comes from inside. As such, expressive is a metaphoric construct, whereas the terms *listener* and *speaker* denote the activities that humans engage in by describing how they affect another person. Moreover, since research based on Skinner's use of the listener and speaker has empirical bases for both functions, these terms also become the basis for educational interventions. For example, research shows that speaker and listener functions, like mand and tact functions, are initially independent, but at some point have an interrelation that allows complex human behavior to be possible (Greer, Stolfi, Chavez-Brown, & Rivera-Valdes, 2005; Lamarre & Holland, 1985; Twyman, 1996b). This research suggests that children must acquire both speaker and listener repertoires in order to develop an interrelation between them. In another example, research shows that difficulties with advanced stages of verbal development are sometimes tied to deficits in listener repertoires (Chavez-Brown, 2005). From this research we know that basic listener repertoires must be taught to ensure acquisition of more complex repertoires such as social exchanges, reading comprehension, and problem-solving.

In summary, the listener repertoire is important because: 1) acquiring listener repertoires requires learning correspondence between non-verbal behaviors and the auditory properties of vocal production; 2) acquiring listener and echoic repertoires requires that listeners have the capacity for sameness with speech (i.e., producing new vocal words requires listening to auditory stimuli and then matching them by producing identical or similar vocal sounds and also recognizing that one's speech is the same or different as the stimuli); 3) verbal behavior is social behavior that requires the listener role—without it socialization is incomplete; 4) listener repertoires are key to more advanced verbal milestones.

The Instructional Sequence for Teaching Listener Repertoires

The research evidence for establishing and inducing listener capabilities suggests a developmental scheme or listener sequence that progresses from pre-listener to advanced speaker and reader-writer functions. In this chapter we describe the listener sequence and the research-based protocols for obtaining missing capabilities. Each protocol is based on experiments and applications with numerous children. The progression that we describe is derived from our research findings and from those of other psychologists and educators who have identified prerequisites or co-requisites necessary for obtaining advanced verbal behavior functions (Greer, Chavez-Brown, Nirgudkar, Stolfi, & Rivera-Valdes, 2005; Greer & Keohane, 2005).

We begin with the prerequisites for **basic listener literacy** as a first step. For many children these procedures alone are sufficient to form the foundation for more advanced capabilities. For children who do not gain basic listener literacy through these procedures, we subsequently describe procedures for teaching prerequisites that lead to basic listener repertoires. These include the mastery of **visual tracking** and **instructional control.** We also ensure that children have the capacity for sameness across the senses. For others, neither familiar nor unfamiliar voices are reinforcers for attention, and may need to be **conditioned as reinforcers** for attending to speech. For still others, the **auditory matching** of spoken words may need to be taught. More advanced listener repertoires of **sequelic responding** (i.e., intraverbals) and naming (bidirectional listener and speaker repertoires) require the mastery of basic listener literacy along with speaker repertoires that are described in Chapters 4, 5, and 6. We approach the listener repertoire by outlining procedures that will work for many children including the basic attention training and fundamental listener responding, or what we shall refer to as basic listener literacy.[3] Figure 3.1 outlines the listener sequence described in this section.

Sequence of Interventions to Induce Basic Listener Capabilities

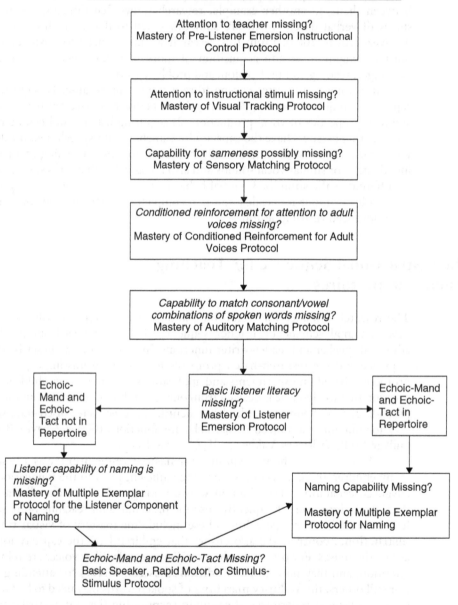

FIGURE 3.1   Basic Listener Sequence

Basic Listener Literacy

The first cluster of listener goals involves responding correctly to simple commands from teachers, parents, and other significant adults in the child's life. We typically teach our children to respond to commands during instructional sessions consisting of 20 learn units because doing so provides larger numbers of instructional presentations, response opportunities, and more reliable and valid measurement. Teaching sessions that include 20 learn units also result in children receiving more learn units, and hence achieving more instructional goals.

Developing Initial Instructional Control: Five Basic Attentional Programs

There are several basic commands with which we begin, and often the first is "Sit" as a discriminative stimulus for sitting. That is, we want the acoustic properties of the word *sit* to evoke a sitting response. In the first stage of instruction, children may come under non-speech control (i.e., other stimuli control responses to "Sit"); however, for many students this is still a necessary first step that we can build on. While some children simply learn to observe what they are to do rather than to follow the auditory properties of the command "Sit " (or any other initial command), they need to be able to attend to the instructor so that true listener responding can be taught. In other words, these programs may simply be functioning as a means to develop attentional control rather than true auditory stimulus control, but this step is necessary for the later mastery of auditory stimulus control. While some characterize this as "discrete trial instruction" and even as "discrete trial therapy" we identify them as rudimentary learn units when the instruction has all of the components of the learn unit. Most instruction involves the presentation of antecedents, the opportunity to respond, and consequences that correct or reinforce. We are building new operants, but the operants that we think we are building are often not what is learned, as in the case when the child learns to "sit" because of visual or sequential cues.

Simply speaking, prior to instruction we must have children's attention before we can teach them. The child needs to have a history with the teacher such that the presence of the teacher evokes attention. This pre-listener/listener attention repertoire is the first step toward introducing children to learn a verbal world that they do not know. Efforts to teach children to follow commands, either as a true listener or from visual cues, should teach correspondence between the behavior of the teacher and the ensuing response of attending to the teacher. Each completed learn unit, regardless of whether children respond correctly or incorrectly, is followed by another learn unit. Review the learn unit procedures described in Chapter 2 if needed. All of the steps we describe herein presume that learn units are being conducted.[4]

There are five simple programs designed to teach the child attentional *prerequisites* to learning true listener responding: sitting, sitting still, eye contact, generalized imitation, and imitation. These are standard procedures in effect since Lovaas (1977) introduced them in his seminal program of research on teaching children with autism. The goal is that children learn to do what the teacher asks even if their responses are based on non-speech cues. With some students this process may actually induce or lead to true auditory stimulus control, but we can only be certain of this when we implement the listener emersion procedure. These attentional responses are the most basic repertoires that the child will need if she is to benefit from instruction that will help her achieve educational standards and from interventions devoted to verbal development.

Protocol Description for the Five Basic Attentional Programs

The Five Attention Programs: Attentional Control to Teacher

1. *Sit:* The teacher says, "Sit," and the child comes to a chair and sits within 3 or fewer seconds. Present instruction in different settings and from different places in the classroom or at home. Also, intersperse learn units from other attentional programs to avoid teaching the same command across consecutive learn units and to make the auditory properties of speech the discriminative stimuli; this will ensure that the child does not respond to irrelevant cues or discriminative stimuli such as our presence, location, or the availability of items for reinforcement. If you do teach a single command, intersperse it with nonsense words that should not evoke any response from the child if he or she has listener literacy, such as "blah, blah, blah." However, if the child does not respond immediately by distinguishing between relevant and irrelevant spoken commands, add visual prompts such as eye or hand positioning for the target response (i.e., pointing to the chair), while still interspersing target commands with nonsense words. In certain situations, call the child's name before saying, "Sit."

Our goal at this point is to gain enough instructional control to teach so it is acceptable for students to depend on non-vocal properties of instruction to respond. Later we teach discrimination of auditory properties through the listener emersion program. For now, we simply want learners to be under positive reinforcement control. That is, they learn that "fun things" happen when they do what the teacher directs them to do. In other words, they do not respond because they have to do so (i.e., negative reinforcement), but because they want to do so (positive reinforcement). Learn units are typically rotated across these programs rather than running them consecutively by response type. Doing this increases the possibility that the auditory properties may gain stimulus control.

2. *Sit still:* The teacher says, "Sit still," and the child sits still (no movement, feet on the floor, and bottom on the seat) for progressively longer periods of time before receiving reinforcement. Begin instruction with the longest time period that the child can sit (typically the first short-term objective requires only momentary stillness), then, gradually increase the amount of time from 1 to 10 seconds for all subsequent short-term objectives. To achieve an objective, children must sit for a prescribed time period during 19 or 20 learn units across two successive 20 learn unit sessions. Corrections involve prompting the child (i.e., positioning them with a physical prompt) for the prescribed time period immediately after the incorrect response. Reinforcement is not given for a corrected response.

3. *Look at me:* The teacher says, "Look at me," and the child immediately looks into the teacher's eyes for a prescribed time period before receiving reinforcement. As is the case in the sit still protocol, arrange short-term objectives such that students make eye contact for progressively longer time periods leading up to 10 seconds before receiving reinforcement. Correct a student's incorrect responses by obvious ignoring for a brief period. If contact with others is neither aversive nor reinforcing to the student, initially gain the attention by using a small tangible or edible reinforcer (if appropriate) and then gently holding the student's head so that he or she looks at you for the prescribed period of time. Quickly fade the reinforcer as a prompt. We are not really teaching the child to look at someone for 10 seconds; that would not be particularly useful. Really our goal is to ensure that the child is under the reinforcement control of the teacher. It is also the goal of the teacher to provide that reinforcement control.

Typically, we use existing preferred items as a prompt during instruction by moving them up to the teacher's eyes and fading their use within the session as rapidly as possible. Another tactic to prompt the student is called **zero-second time delay** (or **simultaneous stimulus prompt**). In this tactic, prompt correct responses immediately after presenting the antecedent (zero seconds of intraresponse time), and then reinforce the prompted response. If the child performs the correct response before the prompt is presented, omit it and reinforce the child immediately. After two sessions of zero-second time delay, provide a one-second delay before prompting. All prompted responses are recorded with a minus (−) and correct responses are recorded with a plus (+). Graph the total number of prompted responses as open circles and the number of unprompted ones as closed circles.

For many children, zero-second time delay is a good first step because it avoids their dependence on a prompt. However, if they do not achieve criterion with zero-second time delay, increase the intraresponse time (i.e., 3 seconds), or use other tactics such as standard learn units (where a correction follows an incorrect response) or least-to-most intrusive response prompts. For some children, teachers can place a small mask over their own eyes (e.g., a Batman mask), and when children begin to look, quickly fade it by cutting away portions until it is no longer present. Refer to the decision protocol outlined in Chapter 2 when other tactics are needed.

4. *Do this:* The teacher says, "Do this," followed by the presentation of an action that the child imitates with point-to-point correspondence. These actions include, but are not limited to, clapping hands, imitatively pointing to body parts and objects (the point should be fairly accurate with an extended index finger and the other fingers closed because students will need the pointing response later), standing up, turning around, sitting down, rubbing the hair, opening a book, touching the mouth, and so on. Remember the teacher's command is "Do this" and not the tact for the activity (i.e., not "Point to nose"). Learn units are used or the zero-second time delay procedure can be used as a prompt unless the student's instructional history suggests other tactics. In each 20-learn unit session, present two to four different responses for the child to imitate, ensuring that there are equal numbers of each target response (i.e., five learn units for each of four different actions). Vary the order of actions within a session so that the child does not respond to a particular sequence. For students who do not acquire auditory speech control of their responding, they will simply respond from visual cues or from the sequence of presentation. For our purposes at this stage, such responding is acceptable.

Sometimes children can imitate most actions, but have difficulty pointing to their own body parts, often pointing to the teacher's body parts instead. If this happens, suspend these responses until they master the listener emersion program. Once they can imitate four or more specific actions, begin the generalized imitation program for "Do this" as described next.

5. *Do this as generalized imitation:* This is an extension of the prior program. After children acquire four or more responses in the initial imitation program described earlier, you will want to see if the student has generalized imitation. When children have generalized imitation, they can do what a teacher does, even if imitation of a particular action has not been taught.

During instruction, the teacher says, "Do this" and the child imitates novel responses that have not been taught. Reserve some untaught actions from the earlier imitation program to be used only during the generalized imitation program (e.g., hop, shake your head, put your head on the desk, or stack blocks). When the child performs one session of accurate responses (19 or 20 correct responses), and has achieved criterion on the other pre-listener instructional control programs, move to the listener emersion program, which teaches them to solely follow the vocal auditory properties of commands. If they have difficulty with generalized imitation, teach other sets of specific imitations until they can imitate untaught responses to mastery criterion (see "Do this" protocol). The presence of generalized imitation indicates that children have a see-do capability as a response class; a key stage in the acquisition of observational learning because they are beginning to learn by watching others. The child can perform new behaviors that they have seen for the first time as an instructional response. The response can simply be demonstrated and the child will do it; hence, the components of the behavior no longer have to be shaped. Once these are mastered we are ready to test for, and if necessary, teach basic listener literacy using the listener emersion protocol. Basic listener literacy is a key verbal developmental capability.

The Listener Emersion Protocol to Develop Vowel-Consonant Control for Listener Responses[5]

For children with basic listener literacy, listener emersion serves as a test of the auditory control of responding; for those who do not have basic listener literacy, the protocol provides a means to induce it. Research shows that mastering the listener emersion sequence results in a drastically improved rate of learning, moving children to more advanced listener stages in the developmental scheme. During listener emersion, the child needs to follow instructions quickly and without error. Students must learn correspondence between spoken auditory instructions and performing the requested actions. They must depend solely on the spoken vowel-consonant blends as discriminative stimuli for their behavior and not on any visual cues. Figure 3.2 illustrates the effect of mastering listener emersion on subsequent learning during one study. Participants in the study were tested for their responses to listener emersion before and after the procedure on sets of the following responses: eye contact, motor imitation, sitting still, following one-step directions, matching objects, mands, tacts, pointing to objects and body parts, block structure imitation, visual tracking, looking at books, playing with play-dough and puzzles, textual responses to letters/numbers/words, two-step directions, coloring, reciprocating social greetings, and matching textual stimuli. Their rate of learning was accelerated from four to ten times that of their pre-listener

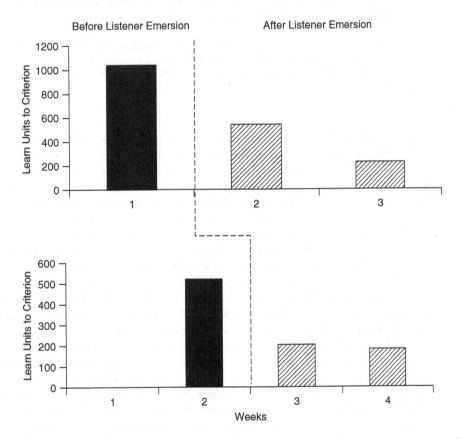

FIGURE 3.2   Listener Emersion

From Greer, R. D., Chavez-Brown, M., Nirgudkar, A. S., Stolfi, L., & Rivera-Valdes, C. L. (2005). Acquisition of fluent listener responses and the educational advancement of young children with autism and severe language delays. *European Journal of Behavior Analysis, 6 (2),* 88-126.

RESEARCH BOX **3.1**

Listener Emersion

This experiment tested the effects of the listener emersion procedure on participants' pre and post numbers of weekly learn units to criterion. Participants were eight 3- and 4 year-old children with autism who had few verbal operants and who could not meet instructional objectives for matching, basic discriminations, and instructional control programs. Results showed that listener emersion procedures reduced the number of learn units to criterion for all participants and they were able to attain more complex behaviors. Findings suggested that the rate of learning is improved by teaching students to discriminate between auditory stimuli, which reduces the amount of instruction required to teach them listener repertoires and forms the foundation for more advanced verbal repertoires.

From Greer, R. D., Chavez-Brown, M., Nirgudkar, A. S., Stolfi, L., & Rivera-Valdes, C. L. (2005). Acquisition of fluent listener responses and the educational advancement of young children with autism and severe language delays. *European Journal of Behavior Analysis, 6 (2)*, 88–126.

---

emersion rates of learning. These effects show that the children have acquired a critical verbal developmental stage—they are responding as beginning listeners.

To teach listener emersion, select 16 target commands from the basic attentional programs described earlier and 4 nonsense commands that should not be responded to (i.e., "touch the sky" or "blah, blah, blah"). Target commands include, but are not limited to, the following instructions: come here; stand up; turn around; get your book bag; sit; look at me, and sit still (increasing the target time from 1 to 10 seconds); look here (in response to a pointing gesture by the teacher); touch your nose (or ear, mouth, hair, shoe, leg, chair, desk, or stomach); and point to objects (toys, books, crayons, pencil, etc.). These include all of the commands from these programs plus others. The nonsense commands can be repetitive sounds such as "blah, blah, blah" or "yada/yada," or impossible commands such as "Fly a kite" or "Touch the sky," and should be presented with the same number of syllables and intonation as target commands.

Do not make extensive use of visually based programs such as generalized imitation; rather, intersperse a few generalized imitation instructions with non-visually based responses (e.g., point to body parts). In the sets, include some previously mastered point or match responses, and present all of the commands in such a way that the student cannot predict the order of presentation, intonation, visual cues, or number of syllables. If needed, reduce the number of commands in a set to two or three (always including the nonsense commands), but quickly move to four commands as soon as possible to avoid visual control of responding, making sure that you always include the nonsense commands.

Divide commands into four instructional sets comprised of five responses each— four "true" responses (sit down, come here, etc.) and one nonsense command (every command within a set will be presented four times during a 20-learn unit session. Teach each set as a separate program and instructional session. In an unpredictable or counterbalanced sequence, present each command and wait three seconds for a response. If students respond correctly, reinforce their response with praise and a preferred item. Continue to use praise, but gradually decrease the use of preferred items as students acquire more correct responses. For nonsense or impossible commands, reinforce the absence of a response since the student should not respond to the instruction. Correct errors (i.e., the student responds to an impossible command) by presenting an obvious ignoring response such as looking away and pausing. Teach all of the sets at the same time; do not teach one to mastery before you teach the next.

Instructional sets are taught until students achieve both mastery and rate of responding criteria. Children will progress through this sequence differently for different sets. Rate of responding refers to the number of correct responses in a unit of time, (in this case the number in a minute). Thus, *12 responses per minute* means that at least 12 correct responses and 0 incorrect responses were emitted in one minute. Teach responses to mastery until students can perform all of the responses in each set for two successive 20-learn unit sessions with 90% or 100% accuracy. Next, teach responses to a rate criterion until students can emit 30 responses in one minute or one response every 2 seconds. This means that the child will emit 20 responses in 40 seconds without error.

Children who respond in a slow fashion may need a slower rate criterion. We have had success with rates as slow as 12 per minute, but if the rate of 30 per minute is feasible, use that as the goal. It is possible that some students may require even faster rates, but the data and general responding speed for each child drive such decisions. Of course the teacher needs to be adept at presenting learn units because if the presentations are inaccurate, desired outcomes are not possible. As students respond more accurately, use praise after each response and distribute other reinforcers on a variable schedule; or if praise reinforces their responses, present it on a variable ratio schedule. If edibles or tokens reinforce correct responding, place those in a separate location (i.e., in a cup for edibles or place tokens on a board for tokens) for each correct response, and allow consumption or exchange at the end of the program.

The long-term objective for listener emersion is for students to immediately follow instructions, demonstrating that they are responding under the auditory properties of the vocal antecedent only. To ensure that the listener is responding only to the vocal antecedent, be careful to avoid any vocal or visual cues that are not the target auditory stimuli. Until students meet the listener emersion objective, suspend all other instruction, except for opportunities to emit mastered mands or tacts at the end of a session. Use a recording device such as a digital dictation instrument or computer to present at least one set of commands. The student should first meet a percentage mastery criterion for a set presented by the teacher, and then a rate criterion with the teacher and a recording device presenting the commands for the same set. Use voices of different teachers for different learn units on the recording device so that the student attends to the command regardless of the voice. Teach all of the sets simultaneously, so that the child is working on a rate of responding to one set while still working on percentage mastery to one or more sets. We want to move the student rapidly through these programs and then move on with other instruction. Until the child has mastered basic listener literacy, instruction will be tied to visual prompts.

When students have mastered two sets, create new sets by rearranging mastered responses. Assign different sets to mastery and rate instruction and teach them simultaneously, so that the child is working to achieve both mastery and rate short-term objectives for different sets. Use zero second-time delay or learn units for commands that are not in the student's repertoire.

During listener emersion, the student is *immersed* in listener programs until the *emersion* of basic listener literacy. Record correct responses with a plus (+) and incorrect responses with a minus (−). If students echo antecedents during instruction, circle the plus or minus because the occurrence of echoics may be important for the naming repertoire, which we will describe later. Graph correct and incorrect responses along with echoics and look for increases if they occur as described in Chapter 2. That is, look for the possibility that tacts may be emerging because of the listener emersion procedure (see the basic teaching operations for the speaker repertoire in Chapter 4).

The actual response components of a single learn unit increase when teaching rate objectives. That is, a single learn unit may have 4 responses instead of 1. When children can emit 20 responses at the target rate, they are actually receiving one learn unit for all 20 responses and criterion is achieved. That is, a student may have to emit 4, 8, 10, or 15 responses at a target rate before the consequence is given; this number of target responses must be emitted again for the next learn unit. Corrections are done after each subunit of responding so that the rate of responding is not interrupted.

If the child was receiving instruction in basic attentional programs and stimulus discrimination prior to listener emersion, determine the mean number of learn units-to-criterion that they required during one or more weeks of instruction before and after implementing the program. This is done to evaluate the effect of listener emersion on learn units-to-criterion to test if the rate of learning has accelerated. Of course, if basic attentional programs are the first cluster of instructions introduced to the child, you cannot use this as a measure because there are no other prior instructional programs.

Research Box 3.1 shows how to graph these data to determine if the child's listener emersion instruction resulted in the *attainment of basic listener literacy*. Once listener literacy is achieved, determine the numbers of learn units-to-criterion for one or more weeks following listener emersion on all of the student's instructional programs as was done prior to introducing listener emersion. If basic listener literacy was achieved, then data should show a drastic reduction in the number of learn units required to achieve instructional objectives. If learn units-to-criterion are low before listener emersion, it is likely that students have basic listener literacy. If they have low numbers of learn units-to-criterion, they will complete listener emersion quickly, documenting that they have basic listener literacy. However, you cannot reliably determine their listener literacy status without running the child through the program. Once this basic literacy capability is attained, teachers can build a repertoire to develop the advanced components of listening that are necessary for progressing to more complex verbal development capabilities.

TEXTBOX **3.1**

Listener Emersion Instructional Sequence

1. Identify sixteen listener commands (i.e., come here, stand up, point to your nose, and touch your shoe) and four nonsense commands (phrases such as "blah, blah" or "touch the sky" that cannot be followed) to teach. These should include some previously mastered pointing or matching responses; try to avoid use of visually based commands from generalized imitation.

2. Arrange commands into sets of five (four listener and one nonsense command each) such that students cannot predict the order of presentation. Suspend all other instruction except for mand opportunities, which can be presented after a listener emersion session. Tape different voices saying the commands. All of your instruction should be devoted to the listener emersion until the objective of the protocol or basic listener literacy is achieved. Continuing other instruction before the child has listener literacy is counterproductive.

3. Using zero-second time delay learn units, say a command, prompt the student to perform it, and then reinforce their correct response. If needed, use other tactics to teach the correct response. Nonsense commands should not evoke a response (reinforce the absence of a response); if they do, briefly ignore it before presenting the next learn unit. Continue until each command is presented four times during a session; rotate the order of presentation for each set of five learn units that is presented.

4. When students can respond independently (100% accuracy) for two consecutive sessions to one set of commands, set a rate criterion of one correct response every two seconds (30 per minute). Slower rates as low as 12 correct responses per minute can be used if needed. When a rate is used, the learn unit changes; responses are reinforced after a certain number of responses are emitted at a target rate. That is, a student may have to emit 4, 8, 10, or 15 responses at a target rate before the consequence is given; this number of target responses must be emitted again for the next learn unit.

5. While a rate criterion is being learned for one or more instructional sets, teach other instructional sets to mastery criterion. Mastery criterion is 90% accuracy for two consecutive sessions or 100% accuracy for one session. Rate criterion is 30 correct responses per minute (1 correct response every two seconds). Slower rates may be needed for children who respond slowly in general. When students achieve rate mastery criterion for all target sets and one set that is presented with a recording device using different voices, return to or begin their regular instructional program.

6. Children who have basic listener literacy can achieve the objectives of the protocol in one or two days. In this case you have identified that the child has the capability. Do not assume that the capability is present without using the protocol.

Other Prerequisites to Basic Listener Literacy

If students do not meet the basic attention long-term objective (see basic attentional protocols), which is the prerequisite for the listener emersion programs, then other prerequisites need to be taught. Some children have difficulty achieving the prerequisites for listener emersion, or indeed achieve them, but cannot attain listener emersion. In our research, we have found that the following programs—conditioning visual tracking and establishing sameness across senses—are useful prerequisites for meeting the listener emersion long-term objective if the prerequisites for listener emersion are present or if the child cannot meet the prerequisite attentional programs objectives. However, if the child achieves the listener emersion goal, you do not need to do these programs. They are for those children who do not meet the attentional instructional control, or in some cases meet the attentional control objective but cannot meet the component programs of listener literacy, even with the use of various tactics.

Establishing Visual Tracking through Conditioning Eye Contact to Stimuli

When children cannot master basic listener literacy sets after a day or two of instruction and several tactics have been used (see Chapter 2), they may be missing prerequisite repertoires. One possible missing repertoire is that they do not attend to visual stimuli on the tabletop or desk, such as matching objects. If that is a likely problem, suspend the attentional instruction and teach them to visually track stimuli. The visual-tracking procedure is really a stimulus-stimulus pairing program in which you pair reinforcers with the stimuli the students are tracking. The reinforcers that are used should be based on the student's instructional history.

When teaching visual tracking, select identical semi-opaque containers such as non-transparent cups or baskets and create sets of three containers; vary color, size, and shape between sets. Next, select preferred items that can be placed under target containers (i.e., edibles, tokens, and toys). The program is presented in 20 learn unit sessions and the number and rate of rotations increase for each short-term objective.

For the first short-term objective, place a preferred item under one of two containers on a table or desk while the student watches. If necessary, before each instructional learn unit, prompt them to look at the containers and at the preferred item under the container. Say, "Find the (*item*)" and wait two to three seconds for their response. If the student picks up the target container and takes the preferred item, a correct response has occurred. If the student does not look under the target container and/or does not take the preferred item, an incorrect response has occurred. Do not rotate the containers before presenting a new learn unit for the first short-term objective.

For the second short-term objective, proceed as before, but complete one or two rotations of the containers on the table after hiding the preferred item. The remaining short-term objectives are similar, but the number of rotations increases from two to three and so on for the third and fourth objectives. The final objective is the most complex because the teacher should add a third container to the rotations and proceed through the number of rotations as in the prior short-term objectives. While a mastery criterion of 80% across two consecutive sessions is used, it is important that decisions for progressing from one short-term objective to the next are based on analyses of the data as described in Chapter 2. The goal is for the student to continually observe by tracking the stimulus or reinforcer. Textbox 3.2 describes the steps to teaching visual tracking.

Once children have met the mastery criterion for visual tracking, return to the basic attentional programs. If they are still having difficulty matching, they may need to develop the capacity for sameness. The following sensory-matching program may be introduced to teach that capacity. Again, suspend the attention programs and teach the sameness repertoire until the child masters it. Then return to the attentional control programs as soon as possible so that they can begin the listener emersion protocol. Research Box 3.2 contains data from a visual-tracking study.

Sensory Matching or Establishing the Capacity for Sameness across Senses

The capacity for sameness is a prerequisite for discrimination learning. The long-term objective for the sensory-matching program is that given one positive exemplar and two non-exemplars, students will "match" identical exemplars of target items, across gustatory (taste), visual, olfactory (smell), and tactile (touch) senses until they achieve a standard mastery criterion. You may use stimuli that are preferred items (i.e., favorite cookies or juice); however, select items that the child can only identify through the targeted sense modality. The objective of this protocol is to have the child match "sameness" across different sensory stimuli when the stimuli are rotated. The objective is *not to teach each separately* but rather to teach sameness as an abstraction across senses. That is, a match or sameness occurs across senses establishing the basic capacity for sameness across senses.

Select two exemplars of stimuli for each sense that the student is to match across each of the five senses. These are the matching stimuli and will serve as the target stimulus to be matched and the non-matching stimuli, depending on the exemplar for matching that is presented to the child at any given learn unit presentation. Some examples of pairs of sensory stimuli are as follows: 1) auditory sense (a dog barking and water running), 2) visual sense (picture of a cow and picture of a bike), 3) tactile sense (sandpaper and velvet pasted on index cards with textured side not visible to student), 4) smelling or olfactory sense (vinegar and perfume in matching containers), and 5) tasting or gustatory sense (sweetened vs. unsweetened soda water). See Table 3.3 on page 103 for a list of possible stimuli. For auditory matching, place two sound-recording devices on the table with pre-recorded sounds of the selected auditory exemplars and non-exemplars (each device should have four or more buttons). Push your sound button, producing the exemplar that the child is to match; then, push the exemplar sounds that are in front of the student. The student is then to respond by pushing the matching exemplar sound.

Present instruction in 20-learn unit sessions; this means that there are two presentations of each sense stimulus as the target and two as the non-exemplar, or each

TEXTBOX 3.2
Protocol for Conditioning Visual Tracking

1. Use visual tracking when students do not attain the five basic attentional repertoires after two days of instructional sessions using tactics described in Chapter 2. Also use this for children who are having difficulty mastering matching instruction.

2. Select three identical semi-opaque containers such as cups or baskets. Vary the color, size, and shape of identical sets for each instructional presentation. Select a variety of a student's preferred items to place under containers (i.e., edibles, tokens, and toys).

3. On the table, place a preferred item under one of two containers while the student watches. If necessary, prompt the student to look before the first few learn units. Say, "Find the (item)" and wait 2-3 seconds for a response. The student responds correctly if they look at the stimulus during the rotations, look at the container as they pick it up, pick up the target container, and then take the item,

which is also their reinforcement. The student responds incorrectly if they do not look under the target container and/or do not take the item. Ignore incorrect responses.

4. Proceed through short-term objectives (STO) as follows: STO 1) Do not rotate containers, STO 2) rotate containers once or twice, and STO 3) increase to two or three rotations. For subsequent short-term objectives, increase the rate of rotations, and the number of rotations and containers, and proceed as in prior short-term objectives.

5. The long-term objective is achieved when students can select the correct container from three, rapidly rotated containers with 80% accuracy across two consecutive 20-trial sessions. Compare the number of learn units to criterion for instructional programs before and after the visual tracking program to identify changes in responding.

---

stimulus is presented as a target two times for each sense. Place one exemplar and its non-exemplar on a desktop in front of the child; rotate the locations of the non-exemplars between learn units. Dispense reinforcers with praise for correct responses; the correction procedure for incorrect responses is the absence of reinforcement and the teacher briefly and conspicuously ignoring the child. This procedure departs from the standard learn unit protocol because a correction procedure creates confusion for the student. Thus, rather than using the standard correction procedure, we use a differential reinforcement procedure. Repeat this process across different senses until all five senses have received an instructional presentation. Rotate or counterbalance the sequence of instruction and the non-exemplars for the senses so that the child does not learn a particular order of instruction.

In many cases, students need only match the preferred stimulus since this is an indication of identification of sameness. For example, the non-exemplar may be distasteful for the student, in which case, the student will quickly pick the preferred stimulus. Once the child has met the long-term objective, you may return to the basic attentional instruction or begin the listener emersion program. You need not necessar-

RESEARCH BOX **3.2**

Conditioning Visual Tracking

Researchers tested the effects of conditioning visual tracking and children's acquisition of visual-matching responses on the number of learn units to criterion across instructional programs. The participants included four children between the ages of four and five diagnosed with autism, educational delay, and pervasive developmental disorder. Prior to the study the children had not demonstrated mastery of visual-matching programs or achieved many other instructional objectives. Following implementation of the visual tracking protocol, learn units to criterion decreased across all instructional programs, including visual matching. This procedure established visual control of stimuli presented by the teacher. The objective was to condition students' attention to visual stimuli as a first step toward visually discriminating stimuli.

From Keohane, D. D., Greer, R. D., & Ackerman, S. A. (2006b, May). *The effect of conditioning visual tracking on the acquisition of instructional objectives by pre-listeners and pre-speakers.* Paper presented as part of a symposium at the annual International Association for Behavior Analysis, Atlanta, Ga.

ily do the gustatory response if the child refuses. At times we find that for some children either the gustatory or the olfactory stimuli will be aversive. We have had success with children for whom one of these sensory stimuli has not been present. The objective of this program is to provide the student with the capacity for sameness across different sensory modes. That is, we rotate, smell, hear, taste, touch, and see match responses to provide a "sameness" abstraction. Because verbal behavior and other instruction requires that the learner begin with the capacity for sameness, this procedure has provided this basic capacity when other types of instruction failed to do so. If the students master this program, we may establish the foundation for the abstraction of sameness across sensory stimuli. Textbox 3.3 describes this procedure.

Conditioning Voices as Reinforcers

Still another foundation for listening is the presence of conditioned reinforcement for voices as a reinforcer for orienting to, or attending to, the voice or voice source. See Chapter 7 for the role of this capability in the evolution of verbal behavior. Typically developing infants rapidly orient to both familiar and unfamiliar voices. That is, the children respond to adult voices as conditioned reinforcers for observing (in this case, observing is an auditory observation often accompanied with looking at the source). We can provide this foundational stimulus control with the **conditioned reinforcement** protocol described next. This is a generic procedure that can and should also be used to condition new reinforcers for a variety of observational and leisure activities; it has been successful in reducing stereotypy, sometimes referred to as "self-stimulation," so it is

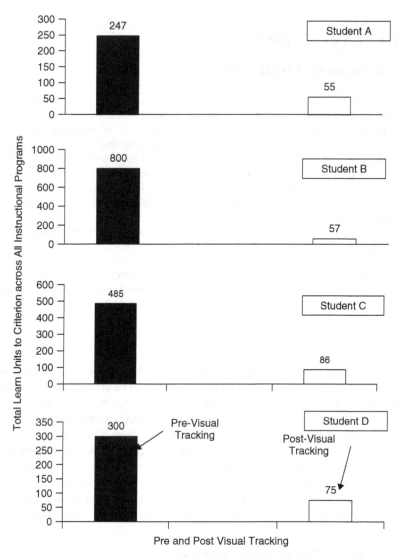

FIGURE 3.3   Conditioning Visual Tracking

used for that purpose as well. That is, the newly conditioned stimuli displace the reinforcement effects of stereotypy (Greer, Becker, Saxe, & Mirabella, 1985; Longano & Greer, 2006; Nuzzolo, Leonard, Ortiz, Rivera-Valdes, & Greer, 2002). This procedure is used for expanding children's community of reinforcers, and we feel that this should be one of the major goals of education. Chapter 7 describes the ways in which this early conditioning of observational responses such as attention to voices or looking at books is related to subsequent learning with similar stimuli (i.e., books or voices) across verbal capabilities.

TEXTBOX **3.3**

Sensory-Matching Procedure

1. Teach sameness across senses immediately after the student acquires visual tracking, and suspend attention programs until sensory matching is mastered.

2. Rotate learn units within a 20-learn unit program such that visual, olfactory (smell), gustatory (taste), tactile (touch), and auditory responses have five learn units each and are presented in a random manner. Use two different exemplars for each sense. For example, present one learn unit with an olfactory stimulus, followed by one with a visual stimulus, followed by one with a touch and so on, such that it is the "general case" of sameness that we are

establishing, and not just the matching of particular stimuli.

3. Place an exemplar and a non-exemplar (a distracter) on a table and give the student the sample exemplar. After the student "senses" an exemplar by touching, tasting, smelling, hearing, or observing it, wait three seconds for them to match the sample stimulus to its positive exemplar. The student responds correctly if they place the sample exemplar next to the, (positive examplar or if they touch the positive examplar. Ignore incorrect responses. The criterion is 80% accuracy across 2 consecutive 20-trial sessions.

The target behavior for the conditioning voices protocol is that students choose to listen to recordings of teacher and parent voices. Once the protocol is mastered, we expect to see that the student attends to voices, resulting in significant decreases in the numbers of learn units the student requires to master listener and, sometimes, speaker repertoires. The criterion for meeting the test of conditioned reinforcement is selecting the conditioned stimuli during 90% of the 5-second observational intervals for 2 consecutive 5-minute free play sessions in which the recording device, or another stimulus being conditioned, is available. The conditioning procedure per se, consists of trials that include both a stimulus-stimulus pairing (i.e., the conditioning training trial) followed by a test trial. In the stimulus-stimulus pairing or training component, an unconditioned or a conditioned reinforcer is paired with the stimulus being conditioned, in this case listening to adult voices. The reinforcer is paired with listening, beginning at 5 seconds, by alternating two or three reinforcer pairings. When the child meets the criterion for the 5-second stimulus-stimulus pairing trials, she immediately receives a test trial for the same period of time. Sessions consists of 20 train/test trials. In the training trial, the teacher pairs conditioned reinforcers with listening to voices on the recording devices (i.e., the unconditioned reinforcer) by giving students edible reinforcers while the student depresses a button resulting in hearing recordings of voices. The voices include short statements by significant others in the child's life such as parents, grandparents, and most importantly, the teachers, teacher assistants, speech therapists, and psychologists who are teaching the child. The statements can be greetings (e.g., "Hi Bobby"), questions such as "Bobby, are you playing now?", nursery rhymes, and children's stories. The voices should be continuous on the tape and

RESEARCH BOX **3.3**

Sensory Matching (Capacity for Sameness Across the Senses)

Researchers tested the effects of a sensory matching protocol and children's acquisition of visual matching responses on the number of learn units to criteria across instructional programs. The participants included four children between the ages of four and six who were diagnosed with autism, developmental and learning delays, and traumatic brain injury. Prior to the study, none of the children demonstrated a capacity for sameness during visual matching programs. Following implementation of the sensory matching protocol, results showed that learn units to criterion decreased across instructional programs, including visual matching, with corresponding increases in long- and short-term objectives. This was a preliminary study demonstrating that children may need to acquire the capacity for sameness across all sensory responses as a prerequisite for moving to higher levels of verbal *capability*.

From Keohane, D. D., Greer, R. D., & Ackerman, S. A. (2006a, May). *Effects of teaching sameness across the senses on acquisition of instructional objectives by pre-listeners and listeners and emergent-speakers*. Paper presented as part of a symposium at the Annual International Association for Behavior Analysis Convention, Atlanta, Ga.

should be rotated. This may be done with various recording devices. However, the child must control the continuation of the voices by keeping her finger on an object on the desktop, such as a colored circle taped to the desktop, or a switching device that, when depressed, produces the voices and, when lifted, results in the cessation of the voices. You can simulate the effect of the switching device by having the child touch a colored circle or other object on the tabletop and the teacher starts or stops the recording device contingent on the child continuing to maintain contact with the substitute "button." Each training trial should have either two or three pairings of the reinforcing stimulus with the child hearing the voices in each training interval (alternate training trials between those with two and three pairings). That is, the first training trial has two pairings and the second has three pairings. *If the student stops playing the tape*, begin the training trial again until they emit the target behavior for the entire interval—initially this is 5 seconds. A training trial is not complete until the child has completed the trial, listening to the voices with the reinforcement pairings. So, each of the 20 trials has a successful pairing trial followed by a test trial of the same duration as the training trial. The training trial functions to condition the voices, while the test trial determines whether the reinforcing effect is shifting from the reinforcement used for pairing to the voices.

After the training trial, perform a test trial for one interval—the initial interval is 5 seconds. If the student continues to select the recorded voices for the entire interval, as just described, record a plus but do not reinforce or correct. If the student stops

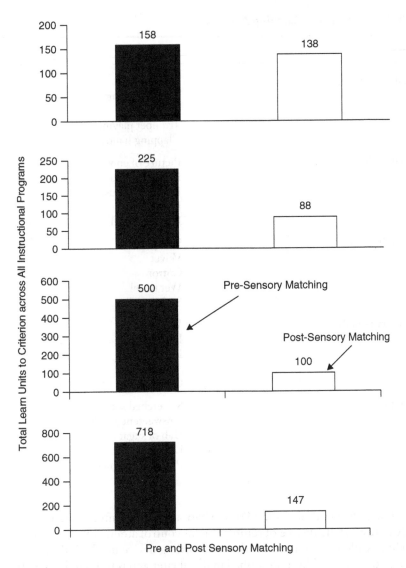

FIGURE 3.4   Sensory Matching

From Keohane, D. D., Greer, R. D., and Ackerman, S. A. (2006, May). *Effects of teaching sameness across the senses on acquisition of instructional objectives by pre-listeners and listeners and emergent-speakers.*

listening to the voices, record a minus. When the student has 19 or 20 correct intervals for the test trials in two consecutive 20 train/test trials, probe again in the free listening setting as just described and outlined in the next section. Test the child for the free play listening criterion as done originally. The criterion for the free play area is that the student selects the stimulus during 90% of 5-second intervals for two consecutive 5-minute free listening sessions.

TABLE 3.1   Sensory Matching Materials

Sense	Exemplars
Auditory (sound)	Dog barking Water running Car starting Trumpet playing Clapping hands
Visual (sight)	Picture of cow Picture of bike Picture of house Picture of tree Picture of ball
Tactile (touch)	Sandpaper Velvet Cotton Wet towel Satin or silk
Olfactory (smell)	Vinegar Perfume Lemon juice Air freshener Cinnamon or other spices
Gustatory (taste)	Sweetened soda water Unsweetened soda water Dab of sugar Dab of salt Preferred edibles

Once the child meets the 90% criterion for the train test trial sessions, you are ready to test for the degree of reinforcement control attained by the voices. To do this, the child is allowed 5 minutes with the recording device in which they may or may not listen to the voices. This is described in detail later and is termed the **free play period.**

If the child does not meet the free play listening criterion, increase each training trial session by 5 seconds (i.e., 10, 15, 20, 30, 40, and 50 seconds). However, still provide only *two or three pairings as just described.* Never reinforce test trial responses; the goal is to shift reinforcing stimulus control from the unconditioned reinforcer to the voices. Mastery of each of the time periods (i.e., 5, 10, 15, 20, and 30 seconds) results in a retest in the free play setting. If the criterion is not achieved in the free play setting, return to the conditioning trials but increase the length of intervals by 5 seconds for each short-term objective. That is, begin with 5-second intervals for the 5-minute observation period until the student emits the target behavior at the standard mastery criterion level; then use 10-second intervals, and so on, until the student selects the voices in the free play area for the entire 5 minutes. If the student does not achieve the free play long-term objective of 90% of 60 sequential 5-second interval observations (54 intervals), increase the intervals for the conditioning training settings. If the child is not increasing free play selection after 40 seconds, either the procedure is not being run correctly, the child has not met the prerequisites, or the reinforcement pairing procedure is faulty. This protocol has been extensively researched (see Tsai & Greer, 2006 for an experiment and for the related studies).

The following sections describe the generic conditioning procedure that you will use both for the voice-conditioning protocol and for other stimuli that you wish to condition. You will want to use this conditioning protocol as a way of decreasing stereotypy, so in the following section we describe the procedure generically. As just stated, data are collected in two settings: **Free play** and **train/test trials.** The free play session consists of placing the child in the free play setting (or in the case of the voice conditioning, placing the child at a desk with the recording device available). There are 60 continuous 5-second intervals in 5-minute free play sessions. In the free play setting, use continuous 5-second whole-interval observation for playing with, selecting voices, or looking at the stimuli and for passivity (these are the intervals during which the student does not engage the stimuli, but engages in stereotypy, if relevant). Also, simultaneously use partial-interval recording to record stereotypy for the 5-minute sessions; that is, any incident of stereotypy results in a minus, even if the child selects or observes the stimulus being conditioned. If neither listening (or play for other stimuli) nor stereotypy occurs, the interval is recorded as passivity (p). An audiotape or countdown timer must be used to prompt each "observe and record" interval in order for the observer to avoid looking away from the student to record. Obtain point-by-point interobserver agreement between an independent, calibrated observer and the data collector to ensure measurement accuracy.

For the **train/test trials,** use a countdown timer to measure intervals for training and testing trials; record the student's response during test trials as a plus for an engaged interval and a minus for an interval during which the student was passive or emitted stereotypy. In the case of the voice-conditioning protocol or related types of observed stimuli, if the child is observing or selecting at the end of the training trial simply continue the period without a pairing also using the countdown timer. At the end of the test trial record the child's performance and begin a new training trial using the stimulus-stimulus pairing procedure.

Auditory Matching of Words

The following protocol has been found to be effective in evoking first instances of echoics and significantly improved pronunciation for children whose pronunciation is poor. It is a listener program because it targets the echoic and the matching of vowel-consonant blends. It is also a useful procedure to help children achieve the goals of listener literacy when they are having difficulty with it; and when the prerequisite programs for the capacity for sameness, visual tracking, and conditioned reinforcement for voices have not been totally successful in obtaining the listener emersion criteria. This protocol may be used before the voice-conditioning protocol, but, if the

---

TEXTBOX 3.4

Instructional Program for Conditioning Voices

1. On different recordings, record teachers and a parent reading children's stories and nursery rhymes using an audio recorder. Each recording should be 5 or more minutes in length. The taped voices are to be conditioned as reinforcers for listening. The students' selection or depression responses are direct measures of listening.

2. There are two conditions in which the taped voices will be used. One of the conditions will be the training setting, and the other will be a free-choice listening opportunity. The free-choice listening condition involves having the child sit at a desk or table with the tape recorder in front of them and no toys or other distracting stimuli on the table. Typically the child wears headphones. While wearing the earphones the child can touch a piece of colored paper (about the size of a half-dollar) that is taped to the table to indicate that the tape should be played. As long as the child is touching the paper, the teacher ensures that the tape continues. When the child stops touching the paper, the teacher stops the tape, and it's restarted when the child touches the paper. Preferably use a device that allows the child to control the voices. These are available from companies that provide products to speech therapists and educators.

3. Data consist of the number of whole interval 5-second intervals in a 5-minute session the child touches the paper or selects the voices. Whole interval means that the child has to touch the paper or depress the button that controls the voices for the entire 5 seconds for the response to be correct. Use continuous measurement recording to collect data. That is, each new interval directly follows the previous interval. When the child meets the criterion just specified, this indicates that the voices have acquired conditioned reinforcement for listening. This condition is done before training sessions begin and after the criterion is met. Obviously if the child meets the criterion for listening in the pretest, the child has conditioned reinforcement for listening to voices.

4. The tapes are used in the training setting and different voices are used from session to session or within sessions. During the training sessions, there are training trials and testing trials. During the training trial, two or three adult approvals and two or three edible reinforcers are paired in one interval. Alternate training trials with two pairings or three pairings. That is, rotate the trials such that one involves two pairings and one involves three pairings. Have the child touch the paper and start the tape. Reinforcement pairing occurs when the student is touching the paper. If the child removes their finger, start the pairing trial again. After a single training trial in which the child has listened to the entire interval with the pairing in effect, if the child is listening, continue a testing trial for the same interval as the pairing trial. If the child stops after the pairing trial and has met the pairing trial criterion, have them touch the paper again and start the tape. If they continue to listen for the 5-second interval this constitutes a plus (+) interval. If they stop it is a minus (−). Proceed to the next train/test trial. A single session consists of 20 train/test trials until the criterion is achieved as specified under the procedure just described.

5. When the child meets the training criterion, do the free-listening probe. If the criterion for the free-listening probe is not met go back to the train/test trials and increase the interval by an additional 5 seconds but maintaining the two and three reinforcer pairing. See the description for the interval progression.

RESEARCH BOX **3.4**

Conditioning Books and Toys to Replace Stereotypy

In two experiments, researchers tested the effects of conditioning stimuli (toys and books) as reinforcers on stereotypy and passivity. Participants were one preschooler and three elementary school children with autism who showed passivity or stereotypy when in the free play area. Results showed that passivity and stereotypy decreased, and play interactions increased as a function of the book-conditioning procedure. Results suggested that stereotypy may have a play function, which can be replaced with appropriate play behavior. Also see Tsai and Greer (2006); Greer, Becker, et al. (1985); Greer, Dorow, Wachhaus, & White (1973); Sundberg, Michael, Partington, & Sundberg (1996).

From Nuzzolo-Gomez, R., Leonard, M. A., Ortiz, E., Rivera-Valdes, C. L., & Greer, R. D. (2002). Teaching children with autism to prefer books or toys over stereotypy or passivity. *Journal of Positive Behavior Interventions, 4*, 80-87.

child has difficulty with this auditory-matching protocol, consider doing the voice-conditioning procedure and then returning to the auditory-matching protocol that we describe in this section. The capacity to be governed by spoken consonant-vowel combinations (words, phonemes, and morphemes) emitted by a speaker is a critical verbal capability, and it is a major achievement when a child first responds to speech. The auditory-matching protocol is useful in inducing that capability for children when it is missing.

Before teaching students the auditory matching of words, you can also probe for the **listener component of naming** and for echoic-to-mand responses or echoics (the procedures for doing so are in subsequent sections of the current chapter as well as in Chapters 2 and 4). This is useful because in some cases mastering the auditory-matching protocol has resulted in the emergence of some components of naming.

The listener component of naming is present when, without instruction, a child can point to a stimulus after receiving instruction on matching it. For example, a teacher says the name of stimuli during matching instruction (i.e., "Match red with red"), and a child can later point to the stimulus upon hearing the teacher say, "Point to *(name of stimulus)*." If the child has the listener component of naming, they will point to the correct stimulus simply because they heard the word during the matching instruction and not because they received direct instruction for the pointing response. If the child does not have the listener component of naming, is having difficulty with the listener emersion protocol, or has poor or nonexistent echoic responses, then they will need instruction in the auditory-matching protocol.

To begin, obtain sound reproduction devices such as BigMack® Buttons that can be quickly recorded and manipulated (a computer program for doing this protocol is in the process of being developed). Identify sets of words and sounds to be recorded on the device. *Since it is important that the procedure move along quickly*, it is advantageous if

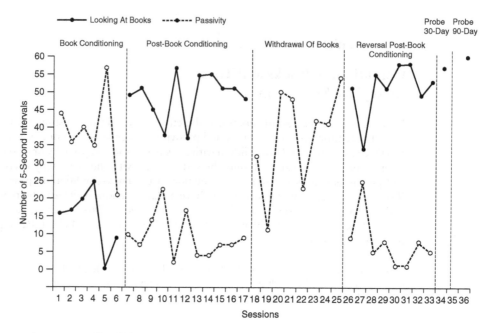

FIGURE 3.5   Conditioning Toys as Reinforcers

you have several pre-recorded buttons so that target words and sounds can be quickly alternated between learn unit presentations. In our applications, we have found that 12 buttons are sufficient. Select words that are preferred items for potential use as mands; as potential tacts, select pictures of common objects that are not preferred items. One device (e.g., one BigMack® Button) is in front of the teacher, and the child has two of the devices (e.g., two BigMack Buttons) in front of them. Sounds may include a baby crying, cats meowing, cars starting, or dogs barking paired with the non-exemplars of no sound, white sound, or water running/trumpets playing, brushing teeth, and clapping. Words may include *juice, bus, pen,* or *book* paired with non-exemplars of water running/trumpets playing/brushing teeth, or clapping; nonsensical phonemes such as "baba, ehe, tete, or aca," or words such as *house, clock, door, chair, swimming, three, jack,* and *bed.* It is important that the sounds be clear sounds that are readily distinguishable. See Table 3.3 for auditory matching materials.

In auditory matching, the stimuli change for each short-term objective, but the teaching procedure remains the same. Three buttons are on the table; the teacher has one and the student has two. The teacher's button is always the positive exemplar or the exemplar or sample that the child is to match, and the student's buttons are always one positive and one negative exemplar (see Figure 3.6). First, the teacher presses her own button and then presses each of the student's buttons. Next, the teacher presses her button again and says, "Now you do it." The student presses the positive exemplar button from the two buttons in front of them. If their response is correct, reinforce it;

FIGURE 3.6   Picture of the BigMack® Buttons used for Auditory Matching

if it is incorrect, model or physically prompt the correct "button-pressing" response as a correction. Rotate the location of the buttons for each learn unit. After a few sessions, the student will independently press all three (the teacher's and their own) before selecting the positive exemplar. If they do not, use a zero-second time delay procedure. This process of pressing the teacher's buttons, their own buttons, and then pressing the button that matches the teacher's continues for each short-term objective outlined in the next section. As is the case for most of the verbal development protocols there are several sub-objectives that are met in order to induce a new capability. Mastery criterion is 90% for two consecutive 20-learn unit sessions or a single session at 100% accuracy.

Auditory Matching Steps

STO 1. Learning to use the device.   Using the instructional procedure just outlined, teach the child to use the buttons by placing positive and negative exemplars of pictures in front of her buttons that she will then match to a target picture on the teacher's button. At this stage the buttons do not produce a sound, but you must teach them to press the button behind the target picture. Rotate the orientation of buttons between each learn unit. Once picture matching with the buttons is mastered, move on to the "sound versus no sound" step. Figure 3.6 illustrates the orientation of the devices to the child and to the teacher. Once the picture procedure is mastered, no pictures are used again. Do not use picture prompts of the sounds.

TABLE 3.2   Auditory Matching Materials

Phases	Target Items	Non-Exemplar Items
Phase 1: Match sound (i.e., dog barking) using no-sound as non-exemplar	Baby crying Cat meowing Car starting Dog barking	No-sound
Phase 2: Match sound (i.e., dog barking) using white sound as non-exemplar	Baby crying Cat meowing Car starting Dog barking	White sound
Phase 3: Match sound (i.e., dog barking) using other sounds as non-exemplar (i.e., brushing teeth)	Baby crying Cat meowing Car starting Dog barking	Water running Trumpet playing Brushing teeth Clapping hands
Phase 4: Match word (i.e., cup) using sound as non-exemplar (i.e., brushing teeth)	Juice Bus Pen Book	Water running Trumpet playing Brushing teeth Clapping hands
Phase 5: Match word (i.e., cup) using nonsense pho-nemes as non-exemplar (i.e., baba)	Juice Bus Pen Book	Baba Ehe Tete Aca
Phase 6: Match word (i.e., cup) using another word as non-exemplar (i.e., bed)	Set 1 words: Juice, bus, pen, book Set 2 words: Apple, ball, two, milk Set 3 words: Broom, running, shoes, thumb Set 4 words: Dog, cup, cook, paper	House Clock Door Chair Swimming Three Jack Bed

STO 2. Sounds and non-sound.   Teach the child to match a set of five sounds against a non-sound button. First, press your button to produce one of the five target sounds, then push the sound button or positive exemplar in front of the child and the non-sound button or negative exemplar. This establishes the comparisons. Push your button again and tell the child, "It's your turn." This is the antecedent stimulus for the student to respond. Because they may not comprehend the instructions, the procedure will teach the sequence and not the auditory control of the words. Once the child has the sequence, you need not say anything. If the child pushes the correct button, rein-force; if not, push your button again, then prompt her to push the correct button (e.g., point to the button and have the student press it). Once the child learns the sequence,

simply push your button as an antecedent for their response, but do not say anything. The learn unit correction and reinforcement process should teach the child. Alternately, you may use zero second time delay until they push the correct button before you do, after which you use the standard learn unit protocol. Present four learn units for each sound stimulus, totaling 20-learn unit sessions with four presentations of each sound stimulus.

STO 3. Sounds that are not words and consonant-vowel sounds of words. Teach the discrimination between words and sounds by having the child match recorded words (consonant-vowel combinations) as positive exemplars given sounds as negative exemplars (dog barking, sound of car, water running, car horn, and sounds of musical instruments). Rotate words from a set of five words (consonant-vowel combinations) against non-word sounds until they reliably match the entire set of words. Both words and sounds are rotated such that the essential attributes of consonant-vowel combinations evoke the correct auditory-matching response at 90% for two consecutive 20-learn unit sessions or a single session at 100% accuracy.

STO 4. Positive exemplar words with negative exemplar words. Teach a set of words with non-target words as negative exemplars. You may start with a set of negative exemplars that is very different from the five target words (i.e., if *apple* is a target word, then *zebra* might be a highly contrasting word). If the child is successful, use a second set with more closely related positive and negative exemplars, such as *fat* and

---

TEXTBOX **3.5**

Auditory-Matching Instructional Sequence

1. Pre-record target sounds on several Big-Mack® buttons. Place two buttons with an exemplar and non-exemplar sound in front of the student; place a button with an exemplar sound in front of the teacher.
2. Auditory-matching learn units begin by pressing the teacher's button and then the student's two buttons, saying, "It's your turn," and waiting three seconds for the student to press the teacher's button and then the correct exemplar. Eventually, a verbal instruction will not be needed.
3. Correct responses occur if the student matches to the positive exemplar within the intraresponse time. Incorrect responses occur if the student matches incorrectly, or does not match within the intraresponse time. Correct responses are reinforced and incorrect responses are corrected. The standard mastery criterion is 90% for two consecutive sessions or 100% for one session. Present auditory-matching instruction in 20-learn unit sessions comprised of four stimulus sets.
4. Short-term objectives should proceed as follows with the student matching to show discrimination between: (1) environmental sounds from non-sounds, (2) environmental sounds from white noise, (3) environmental sounds from other environmental sounds, (4) words from non-word sounds, (5) nonsense words from common words, and (6) common words from common words. Finally, the child must emit 100% accuracy to novel words in one session.

RESEARCH BOX 3.5

Auditory Matching

This study tested the effects of teaching an auditory match-to-sample repertoire on the acquisition of an echoic repertoire by nine preschool children who lacked an echoic repertoire or emitted inexact echoics. Results showed that the number and accuracy of echoics increased for most of the participants following the auditory matching sequence. Findings established the importance of auditory discrimination during the listener stage as a precursor to the acquisition of echoic repertoires. See also Marion, Vause, Harapiak, Martin, Yu, Sakko, & Walters (2003).

From Chavez-Brown, M. (2005). *The effects of the acquisition of a generalized auditory word match-to-sample repertoire on the echoic repertoire under mand and tact conditions.* (Doctoral dissertation, Columbia University, 2005). Abstract from UMI Proquest Digital Dissertations [on-line]. Dissertations Abstracts Item: AAT 3159725.

cat. Teach new sets of words until the student meets the generalized auditory-matching objective described next.

LTO. Generalized auditory matching of words: At this stage you need to have taught several sets of target words with different negative exemplar words as distracters. Continue doing so until the child emits correct responses to a novel word set in a single session. Once the student meets the criterion for matching a novel set of words in a single session, return to listener emersion and to echoic-to-mand or tact training (see Chapter 4). Also, probe the listener component of naming and echoic responding (see naming protocols in Chapters 3 and 4). If the listener component of naming does not emerge at 80% accuracy or better following attainment of auditory matching, use the multiple exemplar tactic described in the following section to teach mastery of that capability.

Inducing the Listener Component of Naming

One key listener repertoire is the **listener component of naming,** or learning to respond as a listener after incidentally hearing a word spoken by another person. This repertoire can be taught even before children have a fluent speaker repertoire. We can easily test for its presence or absence by teaching and probing for two different responses—matching and pointing. This procedure simulates the conditions by which typically developing children learn incidentally from others' tacts; that is, they respond as a listener after hearing a tact spoken by others. The acquisition of this capability allows one to respond as a listener without receiving direct instruction. The child who does this can acquire the listener response through a kind of observation; that is, they listen to the name that another provides as they learn the matching

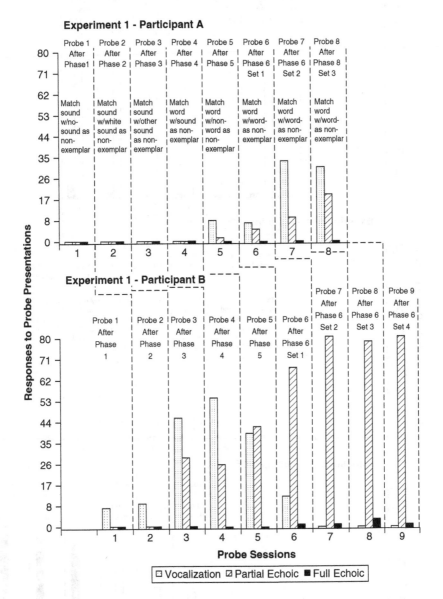

FIGURE 3.7   Auditory Matching

From Chavez-Brown, M. (2005). *The effects of the acquisition of a generalized auditory word match-to-sample repertoire on the echoic repertoire under mand and tact conditions.* (Doctoral dissertation, Columbia University, 2005). Abstract from UMI Proquest Digital Dissertations [on-line]. Dissertations Abstracts Item: AAT 3159725.

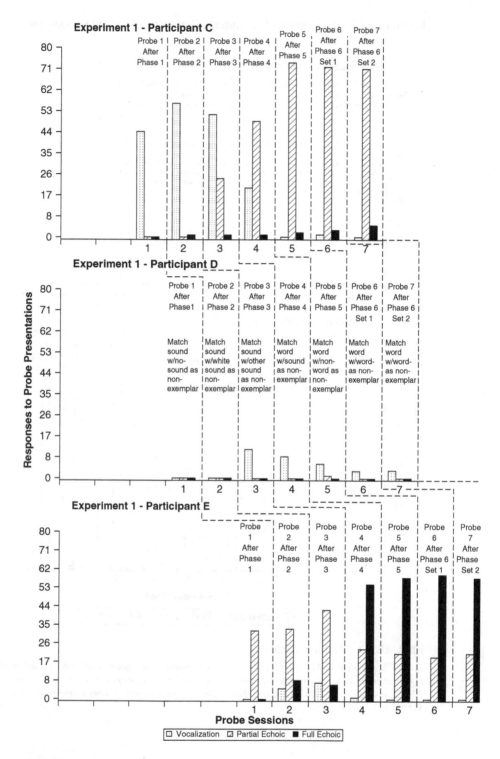

FIGURE 3.7 *(continued)*

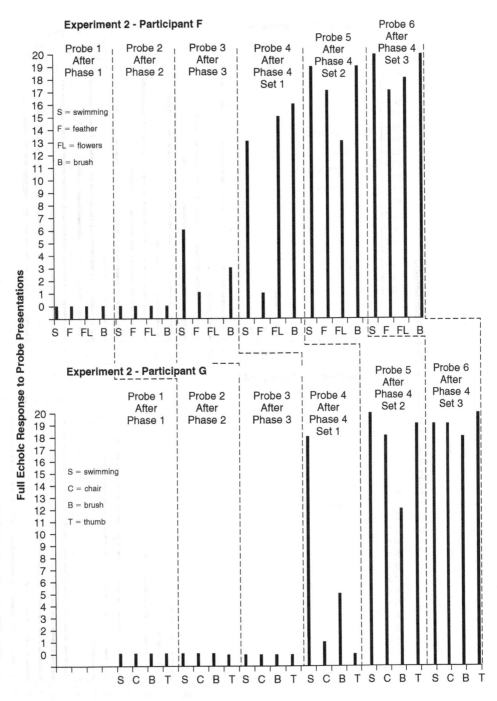

FIGURE 3.7 *(continued)*

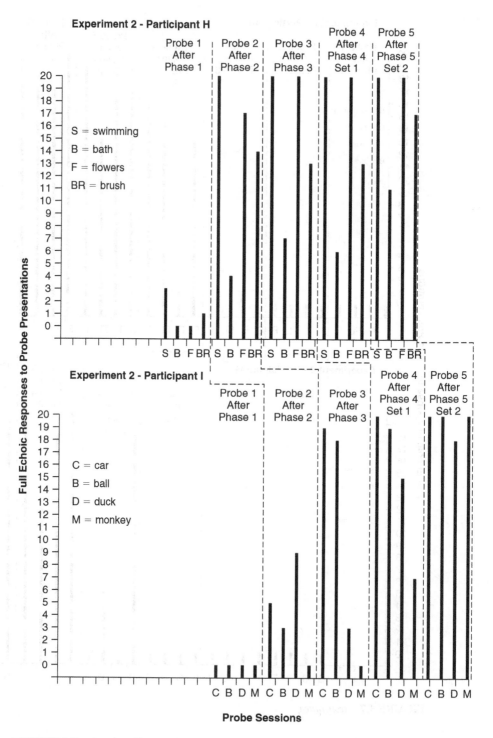

FIGURE 3.7 *(continued)*

response, and this observation results in the emission of a separate listening response (i.e., they point to a stimulus without pointing instruction). Table 3.3 lists the matching and pointing responses that we use to occasion the listener component of naming. An overview of the multiple exemplar instructional sequence is presented in Figure 3.8 for referral during naming instructional protocols throughout this text.

**TABLE 3.3   Probe Items for Matching and Pointing Responses
to Occasion the Listener Component of Naming**

Visual Discrimination: 1) Teacher Antecedent, "Match ___ with ____", 2) Pointing with antecedent "Point to _____, or 3) Components of Naming. All match or point to objectives should be taught in one response topography (i.e., match) and tested in the other response topography (i.e., point) until student can emit responses that were not taught.

Repertoire	Mastery Criteria	Code	Comments
1. Matches common 3-dimensional objects that are exact duplicates of one another; one rotating non-exemplar is used as distracter			
a. Pictures to pictures	18/20		
b. Dimensional objects to pictures	18/20		
c. Pictures to objects	18/20		
d. Pictures to objects for four untaught objects that are new to student prior to session (5 learn units per object)	18/20		
2. Matches across irrelevant dimensions while teacher tacts relevant dimension (i.e., a red truck to a red car—"Match red with red")			
a. Colors	18/20		
b. Shapes	18/20		
c. Coins	18/20		
3. Matches pictures with irrelevant dimensions varied (e.g., white dog with spotted dog)	18/20		
4. Probe for untaught pointing responses to: a. Pictures b. Basic shapes c. Colors d. Coins e. Pictures with varied irrelevant features If responses are not present, use multiple exemplar instruction to teach them and then probe again when untaught pointing responses begin to emerge.	18/20		

From Greer, R. D., & McCorkle, N. P., (2003). *CABAS® Curriculum and Inventory and Curriculum for Children from Pre-School through Kindergarten*, 3rd edition. Yonkers, NY: Fred S. Keller School. Used with permission of the CABAS Board.

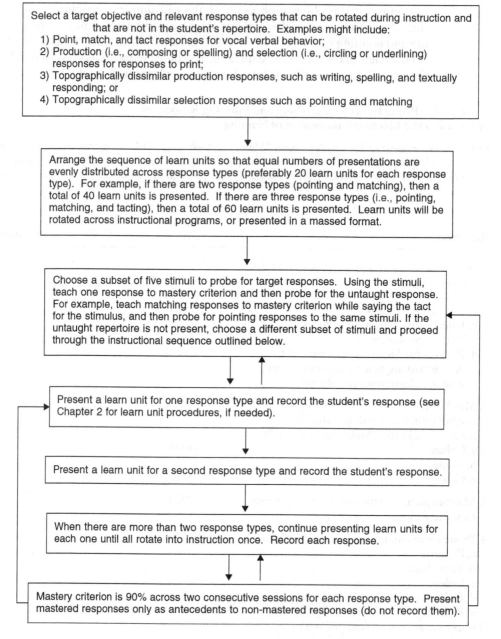

FIGURE 3.8   Generic Multiple Exemplar Instructional Sequence

Use "Point to" and not "Show me" as the verbal antecedents until the student has the repertoire of pointing. If they do not have a *point* topography, then teach it by using a "Point here" program. In this program you say, "Point here" and model by pointing to different places in the instructional area (desk, shoe, table, or objects on the table) while systematically rotating the place where the student is to point. Once the student masters this or does 20 learn units for two consecutive sessions at 90% or better accuracy, use the new topography to teach point-to discriminations. Typically, the student will need to master matching sameness as a prerequisite to pointing to stimuli. Initially, teach a program for each (i.e., a program for matching colors and a program for pointing to the colors). If this works, then continue all of the programs with both response forms, alternating the match and point responses in a multiple exemplar fashion. When you implement this instruction to occasion pointing as a result of teaching matching alone, you are teaching joint visual and auditory stimulus control. Some students will, however, require the matching repertoire to be mastered before success with the pointing response. As soon as the matching response is mastered, insert point-to programs for all discriminations in the multiple exemplar fashion of rotating point-to and match responding. Alternate the point and match instruction such that the student *cannot simply echo his prior response.* That is, one set of instructions involves pointing to red and the next involves matching green. Our goal is to teach the discriminations across the match and point responses in an alternating fashion such that the student will need to discriminate both the vocal command and the visual discrimination consistent with the multiple controls of the vocal and visual stimuli.

To teach the listener component of naming, create several sets of five pictures or objects (based on the student's educational standards) that they do not accurately point to or tact. Choose one set for pre-and post-instructional evaluation probes, one set for novel stimulus probes, and three or four sets for instruction. We use **multiple exemplar instruction (MEI)** to teach the listener component of naming. The instructional procedures are outlined in Figure 3.8.

Pre-instructional probe.   Use learn units to teach the matching response for a set of pictures, objects, or text; include the name of the stimulus in the antecedent (i.e., say, "Match the horse with the horse"). After the child masters the matching repertoire at a standard mastery criterion, then probe for pointing responses to the same stimuli (i.e., say, "Point to the horse"). If the child has the listener component of naming, they will emit the correct pointing responses without direct instruction. Conduct probe trials as just described (no reinforcement for correct responses and no corrections for incorrect responses), but intersperse them with trials on other programs that the child has mastered in order to provide reinforcement and maintain attention.

Teaching the matching response for Set 1.   In 20-learn unit sessions, teach the child to match the first set of five common objects or pictures. This set will be the set that you also use for subsequent probes. Teach matching by saying the word for each picture (i.e., "Match the horse" when selecting from five different farm animals). Thus, the child hears the name of the object as they master the matching response. Be sure to say the name of the picture in the correction. For example, if the child responds incorrectly, repeat the name of the picture during the correction (i.e., "Match the horse"). Continue teaching the matching response until the child responds with 90% or better accuracy for two consecutive sessions or 100% for a single session. After the student has achieved mastery of the matching response, probe for the pointing response as described in the next section.

Probing for the pointing response following matching instruction for Set 1.   Use 20-trial probe sessions. Do not reinforce or correct the student's responses during the probe sessions. However, between each probe trial present one trial on a previously mastered program that will result in positive reinforcement for a correct response so the student will not stop responding. We do this because providing direct reinforcement might actually teach the pointing response. Ensure that match and point response opportunities are counterbalanced across stimuli (i.e., "Match poodle, point to cocker spaniel, match collie, and point to poodle") so that the pointing response is differentiated from the matching response; thus, the child must listen to the antecedent rather than learn the sequence. We want to determine if they incidentally acquire the pointing response from the matching instruction.

If the pointing response is missing.   If the pointing responses are not present with 80% accuracy or better following mastery of the matching task, use a separate set of stimuli with multiple exemplar instruction (MEI) to teach the listener response. In the MEI procedure, provide a matching response juxtaposed with a pointing response to a

---

RESEARCH BOX 3.6

Acquisition of Naming

Researchers tested the effects of multiple exemplar instruction on the acquisition of naming (the listener to speaker component of naming) by measuring participants' responses to probe trials for untaught listener (point-to) and speaker (tact) responses. Results showed that, as a function of multiple exemplar instruction, untaught speaker responses emerged after matching responses were taught. Findings suggest that naming is an important capacity for the emergence of untaught speaker behavior. See Fiorile, C. A., & Greer, R. D. (2006). *The induction of naming in children with no echoic-to-tact responses as a function of multiple exemplar instruction.* Manuscript submitted for publication. Also see: Gilic, L. (2005). *Development of naming in two-year-old children.* (Doctoral dissertation, Columbia University, 2005). Abstract from: UMI Proquest Digital Dissertations [on-line]. Dissertations Abstract Item: AAT 3188740; Feliciano, 2006.

From: Greer, R. D., Stolfi, L., Chavez-Brown, M., & Rivera-Valdes, C. L. (2005). The emergence of the listener to speaker component of naming in children as a function of multiple exemplar instruction. *Analysis of Verbal Behavior, 21,* 121–134.

single stimulus (i.e., a "Match Poodle" learn unit followed by a "Point to Poodle" learn unit; see Figure 3.8). Choose five different pictures (i.e., dog breeds) and several sets of five stimuli (use stimuli that are tied to educational standards).

First, the child matches the pictures. In front of the student, place a positive exemplar of the target picture next to a negative exemplar (i.e., a poodle as the target and a cocker spaniel as the negative exemplar). Give the child a picture of the target exemplar (i.e., a picture of the poodle) and say, "Match *(say the tact for the stimulus)*." Contingently reinforce or correct the response per the learn unit protocol. Next, rotate the pictures in front of the child and say, "Point to *(say the tact for the stimulus)*." Contingently reinforce or correct their response and then begin a match learn unit for the next picture in the set. Continuously rotate match and point learn units for each new picture. Also, rotate the negative and positive exemplars so that they do not consistently show up in the same sequence. That is, the poodle exemplar should be presented with a different negative exemplar each time you present it. You should also have different pictures of each dog breed (or other stimulus) to promote abstract stimulus control for the particular breed (i.e., black, blond, white, standard, and toy poodles). Continue to rotate across matching and pointing learn units until you have presented all five pictures. At this point, you will have completed 10 learn units—five with each matching and pointing response.

Use the same five pictures again in a rotated fashion, but change the order in which you present them with the nontarget pictures. That is, if you used a cocker spaniel, poodle, collie, Afghan, pug, and Scottie, then change the order of presentation of the pictures (i.e., Scottie, pug, Afghan, collie, and poodle). At this point you have completed a total of 20 learn units—10 with pointing responses, and 10 with matching responses. If the child is attending, continue until you have 20 learn units with matching and 20 with pointing. If the child is tired or not responding correctly, implement a different program or activity and return to the MEI instruction later.

Do not graph the program until you have completed 20 learn units for each response. When the student meets the criterion on the matching response, which he is likely to do first, stop plotting the mastered or matching response, but continue to present it as an antecedent to the non-mastered or pointing response until the criterion is achieved. Do not reinforce correct mastered responses; rather, proceed immediately to the non-mastered response and consequate it with contingent reinforcement or corrections. On a single graph, plot the matching responses with open circles and the pointing responses with closed circles. When the child has mastered one set of five pictures in both responses, then return to a probe of the original farm animal pictures.

Probing for the "point-to" response with Set 1 (e.g., farm animals) after the multiple exemplar instruction for the MEI instructional set (e.g., dog breeds). Probe the pointing response with the original stimuli from the pre-instructional probes. If the child achieves 80% mastery or better, then the listener response has emerged.

If the listener response did not emerge. Teach two other sets of five pictures of common objects using the multiple exemplar procedure as you did before. After mastery of one set, immediately teach the next set. If at this time, pointing responses occur

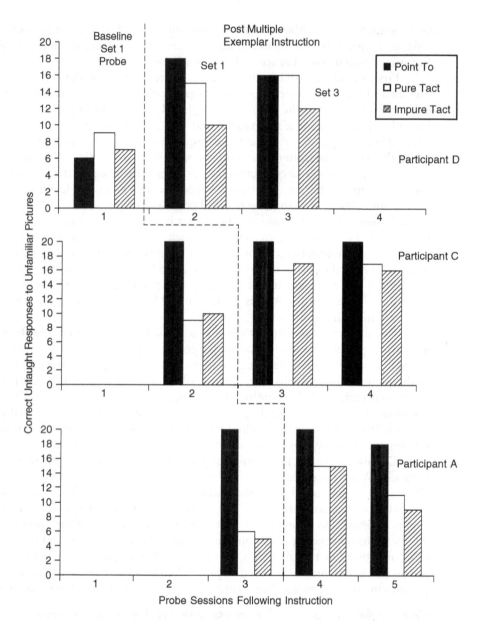

FIGURE 3.9 Naming

From Greer, R. D., Stolfi, L., Chavez-Brown, M., & Rivera-Valdez, C. L. (2005). The emergence of the listener to speaker component of naming in children as a function of multiple exemplar instruction. *Analysis of Verbal Behavior, 21,* 121–134.

within two or three sessions, probe for the pointing response to the Set 1 stimuli. If the pointing response for Set 1 (e.g., the farm animals) does not emerge, repeat the matching responses for that stimulus set until the child achieves the criterion; immediately probe for the pointing response. If the pointing response emerges to mastery criterion levels, then they have acquired the listener component of naming. If not, teach other sets until the probe shows that the child has the listener component of naming. Also, consider that a prerequisite repertoire may need to be taught (see Chapters 2 and 7).

For all subsequent discrimination programs that you teach. First teach the matching component by saying the tact of the picture or text during the matching instructions, and then probe for the pointing response. If it does not emerge, then teach it using the multiple exemplar procedure. Continue this sequence until you can teach the child to match stimuli, and the pointing response emerges at 90% or 100% accuracy. If the child has speaker behavior or begins to echo the names of the pictures, then after teaching them a match program, probe for pure and impure tact responses or full naming (see Chapter 4). That is, do 20 probe trials (not learn units) for pure tacts during which the child must tact target items without a verbal antecedent stimulus, and 20 separate probe trials for impure tacts during which the child tacts target items after a verbal antecedent stimulus of "What is this?" If the child emits pure or impure tacts at 90% to 100% accuracy, then the naming repertoire has also emerged as a bonus outcome!

Once you have induced the basic listener literacy described in this chapter, the child will have the prerequisites for moving up the verbal development capabilities. Also, the child can learn all of the basic educational goals that are possible once she is a true listener. Once the child has the listener half of naming, they learn two responses for every one you teach.[6]

Summary

- The listener function, or the ability to be governed by speaker behavior of others, is key for the acquisition of both early and advanced speaker, speaker-as-own listener, and reading and writing repertoires.
- *Basic attentional programs* include sitting, sitting still, making eye contact, imitation, and generalized imitation; they are prerequisites for teaching students fluent listener and speaker repertoires. These must be mastered such that the student is under the reinforcement control of the teacher, which is a prerequisite repertoire for students to be successful in all instructional programs and subsequent verbal development protocols.
- Children with autism and other speech-delay diagnoses become very good at relying on visual cues because they do not discriminate vocal instructions or the auditory properties of speech. They are often not under true auditory stimulus control.
- The listener capabilities include basic listener literacy obtained through the listener emersion program. The prerequisites for testing and teaching the basic listener literacy include visual tracking or reinforcement for observing visual

instructional materials, basic attentional responses, the capacity for sameness across senses, voices as conditioned reinforcers for observation, and the auditory matching of spoken words.

- *Listener emersion* serves as a test of, and a teaching protocol for, inducing basic listener literacy or the auditory spoken control of responding by the listener. During listener emersion, children need to follow instructions fluently and accurately, depending solely on the spoken vowel-consonant blends as a discriminative stimulus for their behavior. The program is designed to induce true auditory stimulus control.

- *Conditioning visual tracking* and the *sameness across senses* repertoires are prerequisites for basic listener literacy. The visual-tracking program is actually a stimulus-stimulus pairing program that conditions the behavior of tracking or observing visual instructional stimuli. The sameness across senses or the *sensory-matching* program teaches students the capacity for sameness across visual, tactile, olfactory, gustatory, and auditory responding. The capacity for sameness is a prerequisite for discrimination and may provide the basis for cross-modal stimulus control that underlies language function.

- *Conditioning voices for reinforcement* is another prerequisite repertoire that teaches the basic response of orienting or attending to adult voices. The procedure described for conditioning voices is also used to condition books and other stimuli in Chapter 5.

- *Auditory matching of words* is an instructional protocol used to teach the matching of vowel-consonant blends for the listener function in the echoic response or other listener control. We assert that echoic responding enters into a *duplic frame* with parroting and motor imitation. Thus, the auditory-matching capability is a key prerequisite for the acquisition of echoic responses, since speakers must match their response with that of another speaker.

- The *listener component of naming* is a key advanced listener repertoire that allows an individual to respond as a listener after incidentally hearing a word spoken by another person. It is also a prerequisite for the full naming repertoire described in Chapter 4. We teach this half of naming by using *multiple exemplar instruction* across pointing and matching responses.

ENDNOTES

1. While Skinner's extrapolation of basic behavior analytic research to verbal behavior was directed at the function of language from the perspective of the speaker, it was the listener, together with the speaker, who made verbal behavior social (Skinner, 1957). Thus, the listener was the mediator between the speaker and other aspects of the environment. Skinner also described how a listener and a speaker reside within the same skin. As he stated, "Of course others will add to it (verbal behavior) as the research accumulates." [Personal statement March 1984, Banff Canada]. Finally, in the Appendix to the reprint of verbal behavior, Skinner noted that any complete description of verbal behavior should incorporate the listener. Thus, the analysis of the listener side of the verbal equation became necessary when applying the science of behavior to identify specific verbal functions and to induce them in children with language delays (Greer & Ross, 2004; Greer, Stolfi, Chavez-Brown, & Riviera-Valdes, 2005; Lodhi &

Greer, 1989; Nuzzolo-Gomez & Greer, 2004). Moreover, the basic research in behavior analysis has expanded on the roles of listeners as a necessary part of locating environmental explanations for complex human behavior (Hayes, Barnes-Holmes, & Roche, 2001).

2. See Greer & Keohane (2005) for a description of the empirical basis for verbal development with specific reference to the experiences that make successive developmental stages of verbal functioning possible.

3. Using sessions of 20 learn units, instead of 5 or 10, provides more tests of learning and more learning opportunities with less downtime. Continue to group sessions in blocks of 20 even when students, for various reasons, require abbreviated instructional sessions, when using captured or incidental learn units, or when interspersing verbal behavior learn units with other instructional learn units. We avoid percentages because of the disparity that exists between, say, 50% of 4 learn units, and 50% of 20 learn units. Also, when sessions have more learn units, there is less downtime or transition time between learn unit opportunities for children. When instructional components meet all of the requirements of learn unit presentations, children maintain interest long after the teacher is fatigued. See Greer, McCorkle, & Williams (1989) and Selinski, Greer, & Lodhi (1992) for the importance of providing more learn units to increase learning opportunities and to decrease learn units-to-criterion. Also, see Greenwood, Hart, Walker, & Risley (1994) for the importance of planning increased opportunities-to-respond.

4. For more details and a list of research references on procedures for ensuring teacher accuracy in presenting learn units, see Chapters 2 and 7 in this text, and *Designing Teaching Strategies: An Applied Behavior Analysis Systems Approach* (Greer, 2002).

5. We use the terms *emersion* and *immersion* throughout this text and in research papers that we cite. We use emersion to refer to the emergence of a repertoire *that was not present* in the child's repertoire. We chose the term *listener emersion* because it seemed particularly appropriate. The *Oxford English Dictionary, 2nd Edition (OED)* describes *emersion* as "the action of coming out or issuing (from concealment or confinement)" (*OED*, 1989, p. 177). Thus, once a child has acquired the listener repertoire, they may have, in some ways, come out of the confinement of the pre-listener status. They acquired an essential component of what is necessary to progress along the verbal behavior continuum. We use the term *immersion* when the child has the repertoire, but does not emit it as often as we would like; the speaker and writer immersion programs place children in an environment where they must use it until the repertoire is adequately functional.

6. The terms *cross-modal* or *intermodal* are used to refer to "transfer of responding" across different senses. Developing the capacity for sameness across senses might be an example of cross-modal "transfer." We view this as an instance of transformation of stimulus control, or the acquisition of sameness, across different senses such as indicating the sameness of scents, tastes, colors, textures, and auditory stimuli. We do not believe that different behaviors can represent the same "understanding." That is, children do not learn the same objective when they respond in different topographies. However, certain experiences that result in higher-order operants can bring different behaviors under common or joint stimulus control; this is the case when imitation joins the echoic response as a duplic higher order operant or when naming is acquired.

4 Basic Teaching Operations for Early Speaker Functions

The form of a response is shaped by the contingencies prevailing in a verbal community. A given form is brought under the stimulus controls through differential reinforcement of our three-term contingency. The result is simply the probability that a speaker will emit a response of a given form in the presence of a stimulus having certain broad conditions of deprivations or aversive stimulation. So far as the speaker is concerned, this is the relation of reference or meaning.
Skinner, 1957, p. 115

The Behavioral Functions of the Speaker

The focus of this chapter is on teaching early speaker behavior—namely, pure verbal operants, autoclitics, the **speaker component of naming,** and impure verbal operants or intraverbals. In *Verbal Behavior,* Skinner (1957) differentiated **pure** verbal operants—those controlled by one controlling variable such as the presence of an item or a motivational condition such as hunger or thirst—from **impure** verbal operants, which are controlled by more than one controlling variable such as a motivational condition and a verbal antecedent. In this chapter, we describe teaching operations for establishing pure mand and tact repertoires, and related autoclitic functions, in order to increase the likelihood that verbal behavior instruction will result in "spontaneous" speaker behavior, which can be challenging for early speakers. When mands and tacts are taught initially with verbal antecedents, such as "What do you want?" or, "What's that?" children often learn to respond to the verbal antecedent and not to the natural motivational conditions that are the real controls for "spontaneous speech." To illustrate the problem, the first author, early in his career, spent weeks teaching a child who would only eat peanut butter and jelly sandwiches to eat a variety of foods. This instruction was done in a classroom such that before each bite the child was told, "Eat." The child eventually ate a wide variety of foods, but in the school cafeteria, the child did not eat. When told of the problem, a visit to the cafeteria did in fact show that the child did not eat. However, when the first author told the child to eat, he did so. Eating was not controlled by hunger alone. He had been taught to wait until the verbal antecedent occurred. A verbal stimulus was required for the child to eat. This illustrates the necessity of teaching under the relevant antecedent conditions. Such is the case for teaching spontaneous speech. Spontaneous speech (e.g., vocal, signing, or pictures) is speaking behavior under the control of the stimuli and motivational conditions that do not have verbal antecedents. In order to teach spontaneity, the relevant antecedents must be taught and verbal antecedents are not always relevant—they are, at times, counterproductive.

As part of the teaching operations for mands and tacts, we first describe the best practices for developing the echoic; these work for most children. However, for some children other tactics are needed to induce speaker behavior when basic teaching operations are ineffective; we describe those procedures as a second course of action. Finally, we describe the procedures that are used to induce the speaker component of naming that corresponds to the listener component of naming that was described at the end of Chapter 3. Teachers will first need to be familiar with Chapter 3 because there are prerequisites or co-requisites to teaching speaker functions. We begin by describing **duplic** responses or those that have point-to-point correspondence with the verbal stimulus that controls them; in this chapter, these include parroting and echoic responses.

Parroting and Echoics

Parroting is an early stage of speaker development during which self-reinforcing or automatically reinforcing vocal verbal patterns are produced because they match sounds in a child's environment and not because the child is imitating any muscular actions that produce them (Skinner, 1957). Parroting is essentially an early **production** response during which vocal sounds are emitted because they are **automatically reinforcing.** That is, the sounds and kinesthetic outcomes produced by saying words are the reinforcers for this response. Vocal sounds are emitted by most infants as easily as are the continuous movements that establish their motor capacities. These speech sounds eventually develop into words that function to affect the behavior of a listener who mediates the environment for the infant. But early on, this is babbling and the babbling per se, results in the reinforcement of hearing the sounds. These sounds will eventually comprise a child's verbal repertoire (Skinner, 1957) as they become part of a **duplic frame** with other members of a matching response class such as motor imitation and the echoic function, allowing speakers to gain the capability of echoing others. Once an echoic capability is established, mands and tacts can be taught by arranging instruction to place the response in the relevant establishing operation context. Procedures to induce parroting when it is missing are presented later in this chapter. It is described here because it precedes the echoic function developmentally, and as such, is differentiated from echoic responding.

An echoic is a verbal operant that has point-to-point correspondence with the verbal antecedent stimulus that controls it. For example, a student emits an echoic response when they say, "Juice" after a teacher says, "Juice." Unlike parroting, which is self-reinforced by hearing the production of sounds, echoic behavior is reinforced by parents and teachers or by the delivery of the specified item, and is used to teach new verbal forms (Skinner, 1957). In other words, the speaker emits the echoic response because a history of having echoed words led to the obtainment of reinforcement from a listener, and not because emitting the response is automatically reinforcing.

Establishing Operations and Mands

A mand (derived from *command* or *demand*) is "a verbal operant in which the response is reinforced by a characteristic consequence and is therefore under the functional control of relevant conditions of deprivation or aversive stimulation" (Skinner, 1957, pp. 35–36). For example, if a student is thirsty (deprivation of water) and receiving water from a listener reinforces their saying, "Water, please," then a mand has occurred. Rather than go through the difficulty of getting the water, the child "uses" speaker behavior to have the listener mediate their environment. "Pass the bread," Can I have a tissue?" "Can I have some candy?" Can I play with it?" "Let me sleep some more," and "No," are all mands when spoken under the relevant environmental conditions for the mand. Note that the words themselves cannot determine the response as being a mand—the conditions just stated determine whether or not the "words" or forms are, in fact, mands.

Mands are identified by the controlling variables of deprivation (or uncomfortable conditions) and specific reinforcement, not by their form. The form may be a gesture, a tantrum (not a very desirable form), or a complete sentence specifying the size of a glass of water (i.e., *a tall glass of* water; words such as these that specify mands and other verbal operants are termed **autoclitics**). However, it is the effect on a listener and the conditions under which speaker behavior occurs that determine its function.

Michael (1993) further identified the key motivational conditions that evoke mands as **motivating** or **establishing operations** (Laraway, Snycerski, Michael, &

Poling, 2003). An establishing operation is an event that momentarily alters the reinforcing effectiveness of a stimulus. For example, when cookies no longer strengthen behavior because of satiation, teachers or parents can place the cookies under deprivation by not giving them to a student for a period of time. Deprivation in this case is an establishing operation that momentarily alters the reinforcing effectiveness of the cookie. Other examples of establishing operations might include eating healthy food when deprived of preferred junk food; wearing an undesirable but warm coat in extremely cold weather; or drinking water after eating salty food. In these examples, an event involving deprivation or aversive stimulation (deprivation of junk food, the presence of cold weather, or the consumption of salty food) momentarily alters the reinforcing effectiveness of another event (eating healthy food, wearing a heavy coat, and drinking water). In Figure 4.1 free salty popcorn is an establishing operation for purchasing lemonade.

Although establishing operations can occur for non-verbal behaviors (Ahearn, 2003) or for verbal behavior (Williams & Greer, 1993), they are critical ingredients that must be taught if the real function of speaker behavior is to be learned. For children with little or no verbal behavior, establishing operations must be conspicuously in effect for teaching verbal operants. For instance, mand learn units must include deprivation of the item to be manded; that is, access to it must be limited. In the research literature, there are at least three tested teaching tactics to invoke establishing operations

FIGURE 4.1   An Illustration of an Establishing Operation

RESEARCH BOX **4.1**

A Comparison of Establishing Operations

Schwartz compared the effects of three types of establishing operations (brief deprivation, interrupted behavior chain, and incidental teaching) on the acquisition and maintenance of mands by preschool children with limited mand repertoires. Results showed that each establishing operation resulted in acquisition, generalization, and maintenance of mands, but all of the participants acquired mands at a slower rate with the interrupted behavior chain.

From Schwartz, B. S. (1994). *A comparison of establishing operations for teaching mands to children with language delays.* (Doctoral dissertation, Columbia University, 1994). Abstract from UMI Proquest Digital Dissertations [on-line]. Dissertations Abstracts Item: AAT 9424540.

(Schwartz, 1994). The first is called **brief deprivation** and involves an item being visible, but obtainable only with acceptable verbal responses. This is usually done after a short period of time when the item to be trained is not available (Williams & Greer, 1993). The second is an **interrupted chain** that involves removing items the student needs in order to complete a sequence or chain of behaviors until they mand them (e.g., puzzle pieces, sandwich parts, or schoolwork utensils; McGee, Krantz, Mason, & McClannahan, 1983; Michael, 1982). The third is an **incidental** or **captured** moment that involves placing a desired item in its natural environment such that the student cannot access it without the teacher's mediation (e.g., a toy is on a tall shelf that cannot be reached, and the teacher waits for the student to request the item; Hart & Risely, 1975). Some data suggest that it is beneficial to teach mands under all three establishing operation tactics (Schwartz, 1994). In the classroom, establishing operations may include delivering reinforcing items to other students while the target child is observing, thus enhancing the reinforcing effectiveness of the item for some children. Establishing operations (EOs) can also occur by placing target items in a child's view when teaching.

Tacts

A tact (derived from "con*tact*" with the environment) is a verbal operant under nonverbal antecedent control such as a physical stimulus, and is reinforced by generalized reinforcers such as praise or attention. While mands are important for the acquisition of early speaker behavior, the tact repertoire is even more critical when building complex verbal responses. Since the reinforcer for tacts is a generalized reinforcer, one related establishing operation is deprivation of attention, praise, or another type of generalized reinforcer. The echoic-to-tact instructional procedure used to teach the tact operant incorporates this deprivation, since the capability to be reinforced by generalized reinforcers is important when learning to emit and use tacts at a high frequency.

Tacts may be emitted for any sensory discrimination. While the visual tact has received the most attention in the literature, it is important to teach tacts across the senses. Examples of these types of stimulus control include tacts of sounds, scents, textures, tastes, as well as tacts of private events. Private events are incidences of pain or other visceral sensations beneath our skin; these are also important types of tacts. Since they are not observable by the teacher, we use corresponding observable events to teach them. That is, when a child holds her stomach and cries, we say, "You have a

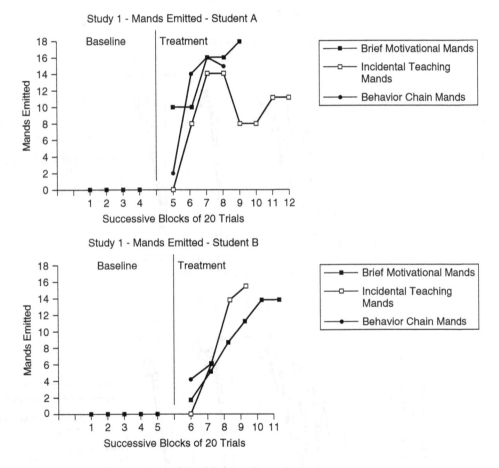

FIGURE 4.2 A Comparison of Establishing Operations

From Schwartz, B. S. (1994). *A comparison of establishing operations for teaching are mands to children with language delays.* (Doctoral dissertation, Columbia University, 1994). Abstract from UMI Proquest Digital Dissertations [on-line]. Dissertations Abstracts Item: AAT 9424540.

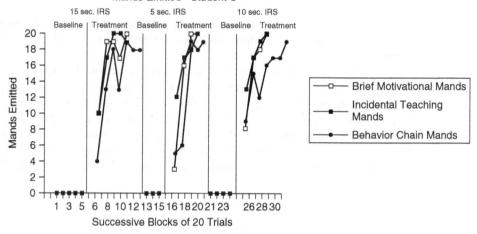

Study 2
Mands Emitted - Student C

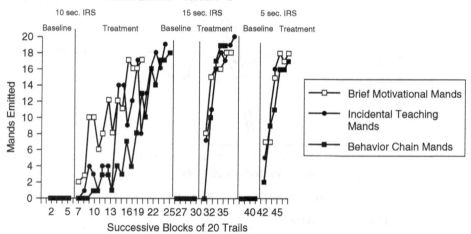

Mands Emitted - Student D

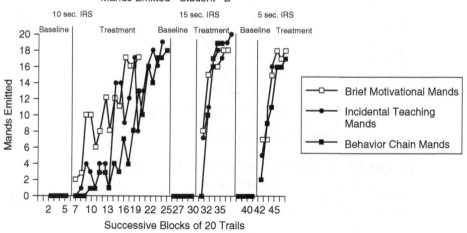

Mands Emitted - Student D

FIGURE 4.2   *(continued)*

stomach ache. We'll make it better." In fact, we do not know that the child's pain is the same as those that we experience when we tact that event, but we operate on correspondence between the child's behavior and ours as a part of our verbal community. One possible way to facilitate this repertoire for speakers is to teach tacts across the senses—smells, tastes, sounds, textures, and visual stimuli.

Similarities and Differences between Mand and Tact Instruction

The instructional procedures described herein utilize the controlling variables for the emission of verbal behavior. In the case of *pure* tacts and mands, the controlling variables include antecedent conditions (e.g., deprivation in the case of a mand) and the presence of the item or event (this variable is necessary for tacts, but mands can be emitted without the presence of the actual item). This type of verbal behavior is referred to by laypersons as *spontaneous speech* (of course, it only seems spontaneous to the person who does not know a student's learning history). Students who learn to emit tacts and mands through the training procedures we describe will be likely to have useful verbal behavior that has the benefits of what some call spontaneous speech. That is, if the child learns the forms under the relevant tact conditions, then they can use the behavior when they need it.

The controlling antecedent for both the pure tact and pure mand is a non-verbal antecedent. For tacts, the object, event, sensation, or activity to be tacted must be an observed antecedent stimulus—it needs to be in the existing environment. For mands, antecedents may consist of cues related to the availability of items to be manded (i.e., the presence of a listener), or initially the item itself. However, in both cases there are also certain setting events and motivational or establishing operations in effect. That is, students do not continuously emit mands, but rather emit them under certain brief deprivation conditions (the deprivation of a preferred item) or the presence of stimuli that provide some discomfort (e.g., a cold draft in the room or the need to void). Deprivation involves deprivation of the item to be manded (i.e., a bite of cookie or a sip of juice). The mand specifies its reinforcer. For tacts, both the item that is to be tacted and potential generalized reinforcers are present. For example, young children seem to frequently tact items in their environment, and this speaking gains attention.

Finally and critically, the consequence for the response completes the functional role of verbal behavior. That is, a mand results in the delivery of the item that is typically consumed or used immediately by the individual. A tact results in praise or attention from a teacher, and an opportunity to mand a reinforcer (this consequence is specific to teaching situations that are specially constructed to reinforce tacts with opportunities to mand). In many cases, praise will suffice as reinforcement for tacts. In fact, some students may not emit a mand during the opportunity to mand that follows a correct tact response. In our teaching procedure, we use the opportunity to mand as a step toward establishing natural conditioned reinforcers such as attention. The critical characteristics of tacts, however, are that they are under the control of generalized reinforcers and the stimulus that is tacted (whether a public or private event) is present in the child's environment.

In terms of mands, if the student has typically manded an item when it is present, but then mands it when it is not present, deliver it. The eventual control for the mand is the deprivation condition *without the presence of the reinforcer* as well as manding the item in the presence of the item. When the child emits a mand in the presence of the item, one must be certain that the response is truly a mand and not a tact. Usually the setting events and consumption provide the necessary information to the teacher.

In the event that an item trained as a tact is manded (or vice versa), then that item has acquired both mand and tact status. However, in most cases, responses will need to be taught separately for each function. To assist the student (and the teacher) in shifting between the mand and tact functions for a stimulus, it is suggested that a few standard **autoclitics** be trained to accompany the mands/tacts as soon as possible. For current purposes, autoclitics are verbal behaviors that affect other verbal behavior functions. They quantify, qualify, affirm, negate, or specify either mand or tact functions. For example, in the mand "*I want the big* cookie," or the tact "*See the big* bird," the autoclitics (in italics) specify the mand for a cookie and the tact of the bird. Students can learn autoclitic responses along with the new form trained as tacts/mands in order to facilitate shifts between mands and tacts. Table 4.1 lists the responses that should be probed prior to teaching the basic speaker repertoires just described. When repertoires are missing, use the teaching procedures described here to establish them.

TABLE 4.1   Probe Record for Speaker Behavior
*Prosthetic or **P** and generalized reinforcers or **GR** are the target reinforcement goals unless otherwise specified for the repertoire. Natural reinforcers or **NR** are specified for some repertoires.*

Repertoire	Mastery Criteria	Code	Comments
1. Uses appropriate verbal behavior (rather than crying/tantrum) a. in response to demand situations b. to mand instructions from teacher c. to gain adult attention	5 days of observation		
2. Echoes with point-to-point correspondence the vocal verbal behavior of others (label picture or sign substitutes as *imitation*) a. single words b. 2 words c. 3–5 words	18/20 for each repertoire		
3. Does not emit echolalia or palilalia NR	5 days of observation		

TABLE 4.1   *(continued)*

Repertoire	Mastery Criteria	Code	Comments
4. Under non-verbal antecedent control, mands objects, events, activities, and individuals using vocal, gestural, sign, picture, or electronic voice production (specify response topography) a. simple mands (one or two words) NR b. mands plus please NR c. several autoclitics in mands ("I want the <u>item</u>, please") NR d. autoclitics in tacts in sentences ("This is ____, that is ____, it is ____")	18/20 for each repertoire		
5. From observing another student, the speaker: a. uses mand forms learned by observing others b. uses tact forms learned by observing others c. uses autoclitics not directly taught with: (1) mands (NR) and (2) tacts	20 or more for each repertoire		
6. Mands a. "help" or assistance from others NR b. "play" with peers NR c. opportunity to see something a peer or adult has NR			
7. Mands permission to engage in activity NR			
8. Mands information from others using: a. single words b. autoclitics in phrases c. autoclitics in sentences	18/20 for each repertoire		
9. Tacts objects or pictures of objects or individuals using single words: a. 10 objects or pictures b. 20 objects or pictures c. 50 objects or pictures d. 100 objects or pictures e. autoclitics in phrases f. autoclitics in sentences	18/20 for each repertoire		

TABLE 4.1 *(continued)*

Repertoire	Mastery Criteria	Code	Comments
10. Identifies actions when asked (running, walking, singing, etc.) (impure tacts) a. using single words b. "I" am (playing or another activity) c. "You" are (coloring or other activity)	18/20		
11. Uses accurate nomination in sentences when asked a. he, she, I, they, you, it, person's name b. him, her, me, them	18/20		
12. Uses plurals as intraverbals a. regular (e.g., cat**s**, boy**s**) b. irregular (e.g., mice, feet)	18/20		
13. Uses "more/less" quantifying autoclitics: a. as a mand NR b. as a tact GR	18/20		
14. Uses "more/less" quantifying autoclitics for untaught comparison: a. as a mand NR b. as a tact GR	18/20		
15. Indicates ownership of objects using autoclitics of possession in response to questions a. possessive endings (John's shoe) b. autoclitics of possession as mands (my, your, his, her, their) NR c autoclitics of possession as tacts (my, your, his, her, their)	18/20		
16. Asks questions about objects, events, daily activities or individuals as mands ("Where is John?" "What is that?" "What are you doing?") NR			
17. Tacts activities done in school (recent events) a. single word (e.g., played) NR b. autoclitics of specification (e.g., "I played; she played; we played; they played; it played") NR	18/20		

TABLE 4.1   *(continued)*

Repertoire	Mastery Criteria	Code	Comments
c. subject/predicate/object as autoclitic of specification (e.g., "I played with ____") 1. him 2. her 3. me 4. them			
18. Tacts temporal relations when describing actions using: a. past tense b. present tense c. future tense	18/20		
19. Narrates (tacts actions and events) a. peer play (GR) b. own play	18/20		
20. Tacts pictures of common emotions or private events (happy, sad, angry, surprised, scared, tired, sleepy)	18/20		
21. Generative verbal discriminations a. Naming: When the student meets a match or point-to-program for a discrimination; they tact (under pure and impure antecedent conditions) without being taught for new discriminations GR or P 1. tact 2. intraverbal	18/20 new conditional discriminations		
b. When student can tact (under both pure and impure antecedents), they point or match new stimuli without direct instruction 1. Discrimination of ____ 2. Discrimination of ____ 3. Discrimination of ____	18/20 new discriminations		

From Greer & McCorkle (2003). *CABAS® international curriculum and inventory for kindergarten.* Yonkers, NY: CABAS® and The Fred S. Keller School. Used with permission.

Echoic-to-Mand-Procedures
(Level 1 of Mand Instruction)

The purpose of the echoic-to-mand procedure is for students to quickly acquire the vocal topography and then to shift the response from verbal to non-verbal antecedent control as soon as possible. When all of the prerequisites for vocal responding are acquired (see Chapter 3) and the echoic-to-mand teaching procedure described here is ineffective, substitute the production of echoic behavior with either sign, electronic devices, or pictures. Select words for known reinforcers (i.e., preferred activities or edibles such as cookies or candies, toy names, friends, family, or teachers). During the echoic-to-mand procedure, correct responses are reinforced with bits of the specified item or a few seconds with the specified item, event, or an individual.

Obtain the student's attention by saying their name, if necessary. The student must be under the instructional control of the teacher (see Chapter 3 on listening). That is, they will sit still and look at the teacher while the teacher's instructional antecedent, either visual or verbal, is presented. For pure mands, use a non-verbal antecedent stimulus such as the target item; do not say, "What do you want?" in order to gain the effects of "spontaneous" verbal behavior that occur with pure mands (Williams & Greer, 1993).

Begin instruction when the student looks at the teacher's mouth (or at the sign or picture for non-vocal topographies). Be sure that the item is truly under deprivation for the child, and has a history of being a preferred item that functions as a reinforcer during instruction. If necessary, prompt their attention by placing the mand item near your lips, hand, or the picture. Show them the item and say the form that is to be echoed. For example, while showing them a cookie, say (or if necessary sign and say), "Cookie." Wait three seconds for them to echo your antecedent (i.e., they say, "Cookie"). If they emit the target form (i.e., in perfect form or an approximation selected before instruction), immediately give them a small piece of the specified item (i.e., the cookie) or a few moments with the specified activity. Do not praise their response, but rather reinforce it with the item. If the student does not emit the form as a mand (indicated by refusing the specified item) or emits the wrong form, provide an echoic correction by saying the target words again and obtaining an echoic; do not deliver the item. The echoic *correction* should not result in reinforcement unless the student rarely or never emits echoic responses, in which case reinforcing an echoic may be a very short-term solution for shaping the eventual correct response.

These steps constitute a single learn unit. Record a plus (+) on the data collection form for a correct response and a minus (−) for an incorrect response. Present another echoic learn unit for the same item, but be certain that the child has finished consuming the item and is again interested in gaining it. Continue until you obtain three to five consecutive correct echoic responses, and then shift to mands without echoics. That is, show the item that is under deprivation and wait 3 seconds for a response (see Level 2 of Mand Training in the next section).

Shift items immediately into higher levels of mand training (see Figure 4.2) if students mand them twice without an echoic outside of the training setting (i.e., on the playground). We refer to these as **captured** mands if they result in reinforcement. We typically indicate that the child has achieved a criterion for a particular mand form if they emit two captured mands in a non-instructional setting. Also, during instruction if the student mands a target item twice before the teacher presents an echoic model, shift to mand training immediately. Record and graph each of these responses as a criterion achieved for echoic training. See Chapter 2 for procedures to record and graph captured mands.

Mand Function Procedures
(Level 2 of Mand Instruction)

Once the student has achieved a criterion on an echoic form targeted as a mand, shift to mand instruction immediately. Select two items that were taught to a criterion during echoic instruction. To enhance deprivation conditions, the student should not have played with or consumed the items for at least one hour prior to the mand-training session. Place the items conspicuously in view and say the student's name to obtain their attention. Gesture or point to the items and wait three seconds for the student to mand one (fade this gesture within the session as students progress and fade saying the child's name).

If students mand, deliver the item immediately. Remember, if they mand a different item that is in only at the echoic training level, deliver it as well. The student has a three-second intraresponse time. Do not praise their response. You may say, "Help yourself," "Go ahead," "Okay," or "Surely." Deliver items immediately after correct responses.

Record correct responses on a data form after delivering the items. Continue to the next mand learn unit or introduce a learn unit for another curricular area such as pointing to colors. When students respond correctly to other instructional learn units (i.e., matching instruction), praise their response and then provide them with the opportunity to mand one of their target reinforcers. This constitutes a second, intermittent mand learn unit. Record students' responses to mand learn units after delivering target items. If the student begins to mand incorrectly or does not emit a correct response on three to five consecutive opportunities with the mand item, reinstate echoic-to-mand training and then shift to mand training for that item. The student must not be satiated on the item or it will lose the necessary motivational properties to teach the mand function.

When the child has manded the reinforcer for a predetermined number of consecutive opportunities (e.g., the number varies by their instructional history, typically three to five successive occasions or 18 correct responses out of 20 opportunities), they have met the mand criterion for that item. Remove the item and replace with a new echoic mand item. If necessary, teach a new mand echoic form before proceeding (i.e., add an autoclitic such as "I want"). Continuously add to the mand repertoire as each mand is acquired. If the mand repertoire is difficult to expand, emphasize tact instruction and provide an opportunity to mand after a correct tact response. When a student's community of reinforcers expands as a part of reinforcer-conditioning pro-grams, you can return to the task of expanding mand forms. Children need only a few mands, and as soon as a few are mastered, concentrate on tacts and reinforce correct responses with opportunities to mand and praise for the tacts. Also, provide an oppor-tunity-to-mand after correct responses during others instruction.

Echoic-to-Tact Procedures
(Level 1 of Tact Instruction)

During tact instruction, the teacher should ensure that the item to be tacted is observ-able and there should be at least two reinforcers available on the side. Obtain the stu-dent's attention by using their name, if necessary. Ensure that the student can see the object to be tacted, and then raise it to your lips or point to it before pointing to your lips, allowing the student to follow the object. Say the name of the item and wait three seconds for the student to emit an echoic response. If the student echoes correctly or emits a successive approximation, immediately praise their response and gesture to a reinforcers, signaling an opportunity to mand. The student then has three seconds to mand a reinforcer.

If the student responds incorrectly or does not respond, pause briefly, look away, and proceed with the presentation as a correction. Thus, the correction is a brief ignoring response from the teacher. However, if the student needs to improve the clar-ity of the vocal response, provide up to three echoic corrections before proceeding to the next learn unit. Of course, if the student corrects their response before the three opportunities are finished, then proceed to the next learn unit.

Record the correct or incorrect response for the echoic-tact learn unit on the data collection form under the E column with a plus (+) for a correct response or a minus (−) for an incorrect response. If the mand response was correct, record a + in the M column adjacent to the tact response; if the mand response was incorrect, record a − in the M column; leave the space blank if the student did not mand. When stu-dents correctly echo the tact form for a predetermined number of successive tact learn units (usually 2 to 5), they have met the criterion. If they emit an unprompted tact two times in a non-instructional setting, they have met a generalized tact criterion. For some students, extend the number of successive sessions required for generalized cri-terion (i.e., four consecutive unprompted tacts across two non-instructional settings). If five learn unit opportunities pass without a correct response or the student emits the correct response in fewer than 4 of 10 opportunities, stop training that form (sound/gesture). Switch to a new form. If, however, three different tact forms are unsuccessful per the criterion described (0 of 5, or less than 4 of 10) refer to the alter-nate teaching tactics after following the decision protocol described in Chapter 2. Also determine whether any of the listener capabilities described in Chapter 2 are present or missing. If they are missing, use the procedures outlined in Chapter 3 and once these are in place, return to the tact instruction.

Tact Function Instruction Procedures
(Level 2 of Tact Instruction)

At this level of tact instruction, it is important to shift the antecedent stimulus control from the teacher's echoic presentation to the stimulus tacted as soon as possible. Delay the vocalization for five seconds after gesturing to the object before pointing to your mouth and saying the words. This provides opportunities to evoke the desired response. It is a good idea in some cases to prompt the student to point to the object as a cue and to ensure contact with the object tacted; this may also serve to induce the listener response, possibly bringing about components of naming. Once the student has met the echoic tact instruction criterion, shift to tact-instruction immediately (that day, that session, or the next learn unit opportunity). The tact-instructional procedure is detailed in the following section:

1. Place the object to be tacted in a conspicuous place and/or hold it up in front of the child if possible. Point to the object. Do not use vocal verbal prompts. If necessary, say the student's name to draw their attention to the object and then point to or raise the object. Wait three seconds for them to emit the target response reinforced during echoic training.

2. If they emit the correct response or an acceptable successive approximation, praise the response. Gesture to two or more reinforcing items/events/activities, giving the student an opportunity to mand. Deliver the object manded if the response is correct. Do not praise mands, but use praise for tacts. Record their tact and mand responses.

3. If the student does not tact the item correctly within three successive learn unit opportunities, revert to echoic-to-tact training. If they subsequently echo correctly, at the next echoic opportunity, do not vocalize the sound, but form the sound of the word/words with your lips (or form part of the sign while saying the word or words). If a correct response is emitted with this lip prompt, return to the tact program immediately. If the response is once again incorrect, provide an echoic antecedent. Remember to record all echoic trials in the correct column on the data form. If a lip prompt is used, the data collection must reflect the prompt. The research on these procedures is presented in Research Box 1.1 on page 15. Figure 4.3 lists the steps for echoic-to-mand and echoic-to-tact training.

Autoclitics with Mands and Tacts

The autoclitic has several functions; it may specify, locate, quantify, qualify, negate/affirm, or indicate possession for both tact and mand functions. For mands, the autoclitic functions to gain a specific reinforcer (e.g., big, chocolate, that/this/the, no/yes, and my/your cookie). For tacts, the autoclitic, which is emitted within an adjective-object pair, functions to gain generalized reinforcement (i.e., a grade, mark,

	Basic Mand Teaching Procedure	Basic Tact Teaching Procedure
Level 1	**Echoic-to-Mand**	**Echoic-to-Tact**
Establishing Operation	Student is deprived of cookie before instructional session	Student is reinforced by attention, and if necessary provide brief deprivation of attention as in reinforcing another child
Antecedent Stimulus	Teacher shows student cookie, says, "Cookie," and waits 3 seconds.	Teacher shows student picture of truck, says, "Truck," and waits 3 seconds.
Student's Response	Student says, "Cookie" within 3 seconds	Student says, "Truck" within 3 seconds.
Consequence	Teacher gives student small piece of cookie. No praise given. Waits until cookie is consumed before presenting another antecedent.	Teacher says "Good," gives student a reinforcer (not the truck) and provides an opportunity to mand when the student has a mand repertoire.
Level 2	**Mand Training**	**Tact Training**
Establishing Operation	Teacher waits until cookie is consumed before presenting it again.	Student is reinforced by attention, and if necessary provide brief deprivation of attention as in reinforcing another child
Antecedent Stimulus	Teacher shows student cookie and waits 3 seconds for response	Teacher shows student picture of truck and waits 3 seconds for a response.
Student's Response	Student says, "Cookie" within 3 seconds	Student says "truck" within 3 seconds
Consequence	Teacher gives student small piece of cookie. No praise is given. Waits until consumed before presenting another antecedent.	Teacher says, "Good," gives student a reinforcer (not a truck).
Levels 3 and 4	Repeat Levels 1 and 2 for new items. When student has two or more items in repertoire, show all reinforcers as the antecedent stimulus.	Repeat Levels 1 and 2 for each new item. When student has two or more items in repertoire, intersperse tact learn units for each item.

FIGURE 4.3   Basic Mand and Tact Teaching Procedures

or token) and often, but not always, social reinforcement (i.e., praise). For example, when a tact such as *that bird, this bird, a bird, flying bird* is emitted, a listener may respond by saying, "Yes, that's right," or "I see the one you mean," and give a smile, thumbs up, or other form of attention, which functions to reinforce the autoclitic tact.

To teach the autoclitic function, students must learn to emit accurate tacts that discriminate the different functions of each autoclitic (i.e., big/small, more/less, red/blue, this, that, on, under, and beside), and they must learn that by doing so, they avoid the withdrawal of reinforcers. In other words, for the speaker the autoclitic should function to increase the likelihood of generalized reinforcement and the possibility of avoiding punishment from a listener or audience. Thus, social attention and other generalized reinforcers (e.g., tokens as correct response indicators) must be reinforcers for the tact response.

After students achieve the generalized criterion for a mand or tact form, use the echoic-to-mand and echoic-to-tact teaching procedures described earlier to expand their autoclitic speaker repertoires. For mand responses, add phrases such as "I want the (mand item), please" or "May I have the (mand item), please?" For tact responses, add phrases such as "That is the number (tact)," "That is the color (tact)," or "This is the number (tact)." Students may use the phrases interchangeably or emit variations such as "That is the big (little, ugly, messy) _____" as long as the basic autoclitic of specification is present. Also, reinforce variations in responding that are appropriate to the setting (e.g., no foul or aggressive language).

Teach a target response until students achieve a criterion for autoclitics ("Please" and "I want a _____" with mands; "This is a _____, That is a _____, or Good _____ for tacts). Subsequently, as they achieve mand or tact criteria for a new item, the item should then be taught with the qualifying autoclitic. Thereafter, teach a new function by shifting the autoclitics. For example, when the student has learned "Cookie, please" as a mand, use "Good (tact)" or "That is a (tact)" when they are taught *cookie* in a tact function. Thereafter, the form that the student uses determines the teacher's response. That is, when the student adds *"please,"* the function is that of a mand, and the form is always to be consequated as such. Similarly, the use of "This (that) is a _____" or "Good _____" results in a generalized reinforcer such as praise and an opportunity to mand. A data based procedure for doing this is described later (Nuzzolo-Gomez & Greer, 2004).

Students may confuse autoclitic mands and tacts by saying, "(stimulus), please" or "Can I have juice, please?" for tacts. When this occurs, the student has not learned the autoclitic function. Do not provide reinforcement for the corrected response, but rather present 3 echoics to correct, as just described so that the student will learn the different adjective-object pair functions. Initially, the autoclitic functions for mands and tacts need to be directly taught. Emitting a mand for the *big* cookie is a response that is independent of using the adjective *big* in a tact function. For example, after the child learns to specify the *big* cookie in a mand function, they cannot typically use *big* to tact the *big* crayon. While these two usages are independent, we want to teach our students the different adjective-object pair functions for the same "word" or form as described earlier in this chapter.

Pure tacts and mands can continue to be taught to children who use verbal behavior infrequently. However, once children acquire a basic repertoire of mands and tacts quickly, they should be introduced to multiple control (intraverbal) training immediately. Once students can make their needs known (e.g., mand) to critical listeners in the environment or gain attention/instruction through comments on their environment (tact), they should be introduced to other repertoires of verbal behavior. Expand the tacts and expand the autoclitic functions as described next. Once the child has several mands and tacts with different autoclitic functions, you will need to determine if the mand and tact forms are independent. When they are independent, the child learns a mand but cannot use the same form in a tact function, or vice versa (Twyman, 1996b; see Research Box 4.2). If they are independent, you will need to use the **transformation of establishing operations** procedure described later in this chapter.

For all of the advanced tact capabilities described hereafter, incorporate adjective-object pair functions. If we use the transformation of establishing operation protocol (described subsequently), students have all of the components they need to emit autoclitics during tact instruction. Autoclitics might include *this is, that is, the stimulus is in/on/under, that (stimulus) there, the (stimulus) here*, among others. Teach existing tacts (i.e., colors and shapes) as autoclitics with a tact function, since autoclitics must have a specific function relative to mands and tacts. While autoclitics are often called adjectives, prepositions, or adverbs from a linguistic perspective, it is the function that determines whether the words/gestures/signs/pictures are actually joined adjective-object pairs that function as tacts. The word *big* gets the big cookie, or "that is a ____," results in generalized reinforcement—inaccuracies are not reinforced. If the child is to use "please," then simply saying," cookie" does not result in receiving the cookie.

RESEARCH BOX 4.2

Functional Independence of Mands and Tacts

This study tested for the functional independence of impure mands and tacts. Participants were four preschool children with developmental delays. They were taught both a mand response ("I want a yellow marker.") and a tact response ("That's a yellow marker."). Results showed that responses learned in one function did not shift to the other function without direct instruction, and that each function had to be directly taught in order to develop for the same stimulus.

Twyman, J. (1996b). The functional independence of mands and tacts of abstract stimulus properties. *Analysis of Verbal Behavior, 13*, 1–19.

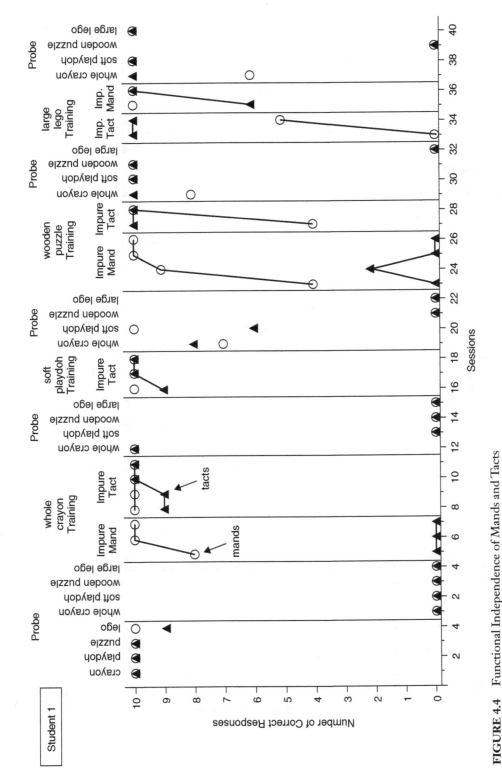

FIGURE 4.4 Functional Independence of Mands and Tacts

From Twyman, J. (1996b). The functional independence of mands and tacts of abstract stimulus properties. *Analysis of Verbal Behavior, 13*, 1–9.

FIGURE 4.4 (continued)

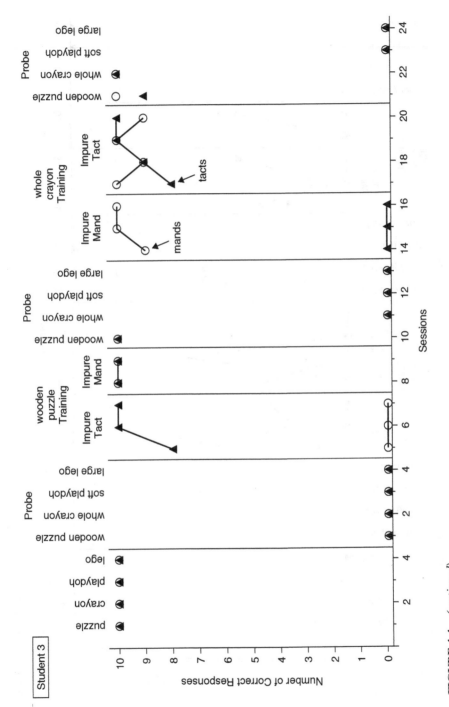

FIGURE 4.4 (*continued*)

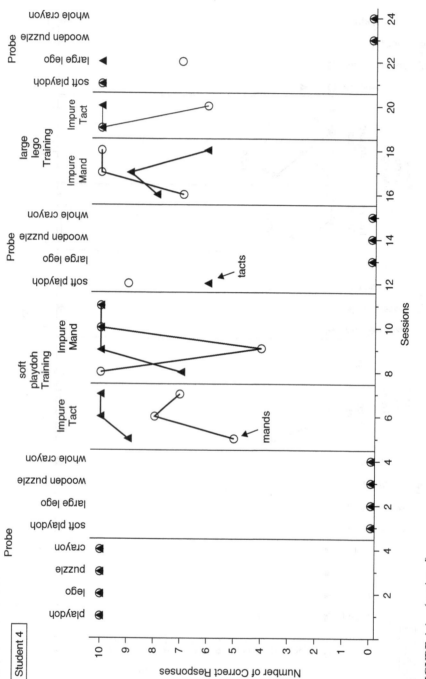

FIGURE 4.4 *(continued)*

Alternative Procedures for Teaching Echoic-to-Mand and Echoic-to-Tact Responses

A few students will easily master the basic training sequence with little or no difficulty, but most students will need the teacher to deal with difficulties by further clarifying the teaching sequence or using alternative tactics (see Chapter 2). Teachers should not continue to use ineffective procedures, since this will simply compound the difficulties for the child. Chapters 2, 3, 5, and 7 provide suggestions for surmounting major difficulties encountered by students or by the teacher by determining the presence or absence of prerequisite capabilities or repertoires. In this chapter, we now describe alternative tactics or protocols for inducing mand and tact responses when the basic echoic-to-mand and echoic-to-tact procedures are not effective, particularly if the echoic is not forthcoming.

Stimulus-Stimulus Pairing Procedure

The stimulus-stimulus pairing protocol is a procedure that uses automatic reinforcement to induce new sounds or words in children without echoic behavior by pairing the sounds or words with sensory reinforcers (i.e., tickling or hugging) (Sundberg, Michael, Partington, & Sundberg, 1996). Begin the pairing procedure by recording the sounds that a student emits in the free-play area for three 10-minute sessions and during a single 20-minute instructional session. Use those data to identify a sound that a student does not make in either setting. This sound or word becomes the target sound/word for the pairing procedure. While this procedure is based on the same

---

RESEARCH BOX **4.3**

Automatic Reinforcement of Parroting to Develop Echoics

Researchers examined the effects of pairing a reinforcing stimulus with targeted sounds, words, and phrases on the development of new sounds not previously emitted by five pre-speakers (automatic reinforcement). Post-pairing measures showed that the targeted responses were emitted by all participants following the pairing procedure. In a systematic replication, Yoon and Bennett (2002) found similar results. Findings suggested that pre-speaker children can acquire new vocal-verbal responses without shaping by pairing vocal stimuli with known reinforcers. Yoon, in an unpublished 1998 dissertation, demonstrated that placing the parroting response into the echoic-mand procedure led to mands.

Sundberg, M. L., Michael, J., Partington, J. W., & Sundberg, C. A. (1996). The role of automatic reinforcement in early language acquisition. *Analysis of Verbal Behavior, 13*, 21–37.

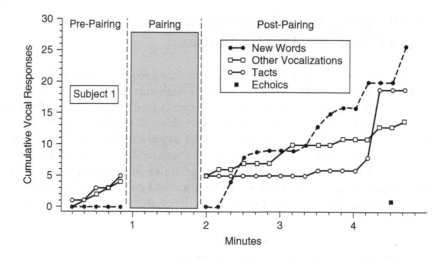

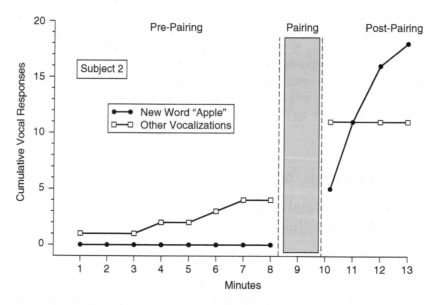

FIGURE 4.5 Stimulus-Stimulus Pairing

From Sundberg, M. L., Michael, J., Partington, J. W., & Sundberg, C. A. (1996). The role of automatic reinforcement in early language acquisition. *Analysis of Verbal Behavior, 13*, 21–37.

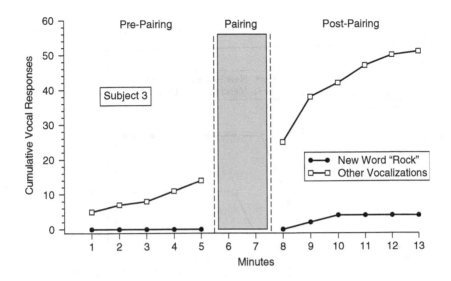

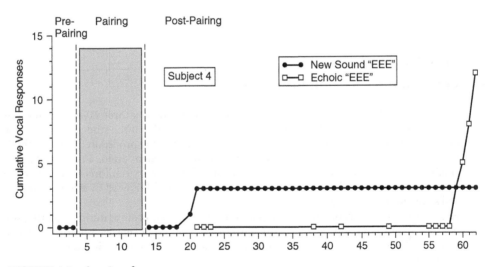

FIGURE 4.5 (*continued*)

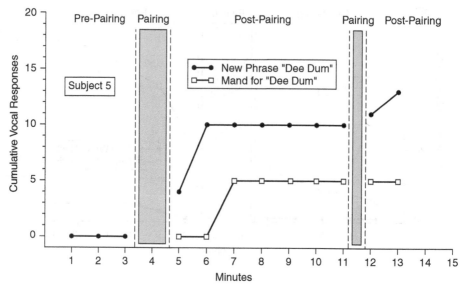

FIGURE 4.5   *(continued)*

TEXTBOX **4.1**

Stimulus-Stimulus Pairing Procedure

1. Record sounds that the student emits in the free play area during three 10-minute sessions and during one 20-minute instructional session. Identify a sound that the student does not make in either setting and use it as the target sound/word for the pairing procedure. Also, use these data to determine the number of sounds per minute that the student emits. Pre-record a series of audio prompts that cue the teacher to pair a sound with a sensory reinforcer every four seconds upon hearing "one" followed by a four-second pause, "two" followed by a four-second pause, and so on, for one minute.

2. Each pairing session is one minute. Upon hearing the audio prompt during a pairing session, say the target sound and tickle the student briefly. A different sensory reinforcer (tickling or hugging) should be used for each sound that is targeted. Repeat pairing each time an audio prompt is heard.

3. Continue until the student reliably emits the sound before you do so for 80% of pairing trials. Stop delivering the pairing trials and simply present the sound, wait for the student to emit it, and reinforce its occurrence with the sensory reinforcer.

4. Alternatively, words such as *cookie* or *chip* may be used in place of sounds for the pairing procedure and then shifted into the basic mand instructional procedure (see Table 4.1) after criterion is mastered for pairing.

RESEARCH BOX **4.4**

Inducing Echoic-Mands
and Echoic-Tacts

Tsouri and Greer tested the effects of presenting rapid motor imitations and mand opportunities on the emergence of speaker behavior for five pre-speakers with autism. The procedure effectively induced echoic mands and tacts for all participants. This study was a systematic replication of Ross and Greer (2003). Both studies demonstrated that echoic responding could be established without lengthy shaping procedures.

From Tsouri, I., & Greer, R. D. (2003). Inducing vocal verbal behavior in children with severe language delays through rapid motor imitation responding. *Journal of Behavioral Education, 12*, 185–206.

principle as the stimulus-stimulus procedure described in Chapter 3 for conditioning voices as reinforcers for observing, it differs in critically important ways.

Each pairing session is one minute. Based on the rate of the student's emission of sounds during probes, determine the number of sounds or rate per minute that the student emits. Using this rate, pre-record a series of audio prompts to tell the teacher when to deliver the pairing procedure. For example, if a student emitted approximately 15 sounds per minute during probe sessions, then the audiotape would prompt the teacher to pair a sound with a sensory reinforcer every four seconds by saying, "One (wait four seconds), two (wait four seconds), and so on" until the minute is completed. Each pairing session is one minute.

During the sessions, the teacher implements the pairing procedure when they hear the prompt. Specifically, the teacher says the target morpheme or word (i.e., "Ah" or "Cookie"; complete words are preferable) and tickles the student briefly (select a sensory reinforcer that is paired with each targeted sound or word). Pairing trials continue in this manner for approximately 15 trials until the one-minute session ends. Pairing rates will differ for each student based on their rate of emitting sounds during initial probes. Continue until the student reliably emits the sound before you provide the sensory reinforcer or does it simultaneously with the emission. After several sessions, stop delivering the pairing trials (this is the post-pairing phase) and simply present the sound, which is reinforced by delivering the sensory reinforcer. Alternatively, words that function as echoic mands such as *cookie* or *chip* may be used in place of sounds for the pairing procedure, and then shifted into echoic-to-mand training during the post-pairing phases (Yoon, 1998).

Rapid Motor Imitation

Another procedure that can be used to induce vocal verbal behavior is rapid motor imitation (Figs. 4.6 and 4.7). The student must have generalized imitation skills; that is, they can imitate any motor action that the teacher presents. After ensuring that the

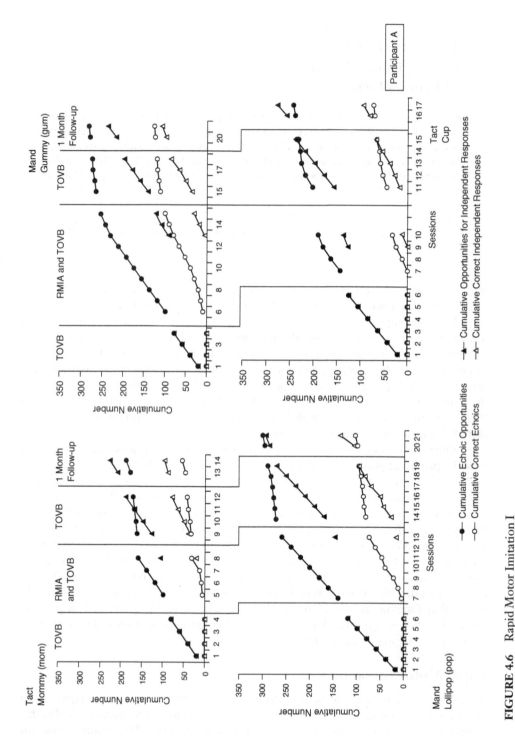

FIGURE 4.6 Rapid Motor Imitation I

From Tsiouri, I., & Greer, R. D. (2003). Inducing vocal verbal behavior in children with severe language delays through rapid motor imitation responding. *Journal of Behavioral Education, 12,* 185–206.

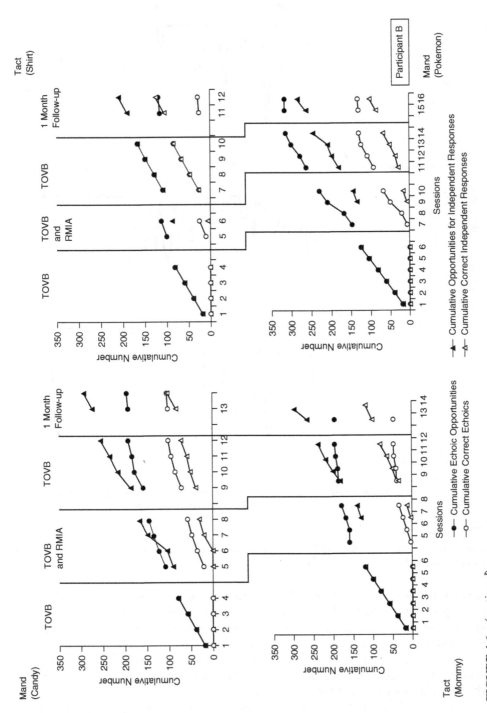

FIGURE 4.6 (*continued*)

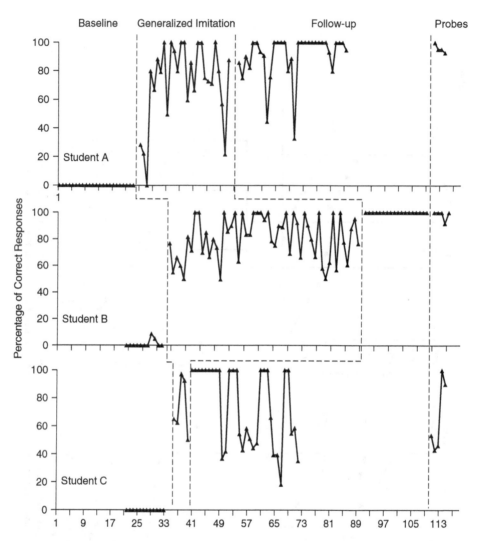

FIGURE 4.7   Rapid Motor Imitation II

From Ross, D. E., & Greer, R. D. (2003). Generalized imitation and the mand: Inducing first instances of speech in young children with autism. *Research in Developmental Disabilities, 24,* 58–74.

student will not emit echoic-mands using the echoic-to-mand or the echoic-to-tact probe procedures described in this chapter (in other words, the student does not emit speaker behavior under echoic control for the mand or tact function), identify five to six items that function as mand or tact stimuli. On your data collection sheet, create columns for each item and under each item label 3 smaller columns with an E for echoic, a GI for generalized imitation, and a M or a T for mand or tact, depending on the function that you select for this procedure.

For mands, place the item under deprivation (you will still need to do so if you are targeting tacts because it is the mand item that will reinforce the emission of

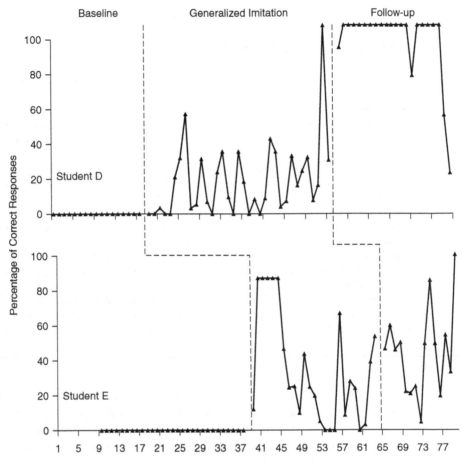

FIGURE 4.7   (*continued*)

echoic-tacts during this procedure). Show the student the mand item and then rapidly present two large motor actions (i.e., clapping your hands and then touching your head) and three small motor actions (i.e., touching your nose and then your teeth or lips). Immediately after the last action, present an echoic model for the target item while holding it up (the tact or the mand item, depending on the function that you chose). If the student emits the echoic response, then reinforce their response with the mand item, record a plus on the data form in the GI column, and present the rapid motor imitation series again. If the student does not emit the echoic response, then ignore any response, record a minus on the data sheet in the GI column, and present the rapid motor imitation series again.

After two consecutive correct responses under the rapid motor imitation antecedent, shift to an echoic antecedent without motor imitation. After two correct echoic responses, shift to a mand or tact antecedent without the echoic. If the student responds with mands or tacts, then continue until at least 10 learn units across all three types of antecedents (motor, echoic, and mand/tact) are presented.

TEXTBOX **4.2**

Rapid Motor Imitation Protocol

1. Identify five to six items to use as mand or tact stimuli. Place mand items under deprivation before an instructional session.
2. Show the student the item and then present two large motor actions such as clapping your hands or touching your head. Wait for the student to imitate each action. Repeat for two to three more actions, typically small motor actions such as touching your nose and then your teeth.
3. Immediately after the last action, present an echoic model for the target item while holding it up. For example, after the student imitates your last action by touching their mouth, hold up a piece of a cookie and say, "Cookie." Wait three seconds for a response. The motor actions and the echoic model should be presented rapidly.
4. If the student says, "Cookie," then give them a small piece of the cookie without praising them. If they do not say, "Cookie," repeat Steps 2 and 3.
5. If the student imitates your actions and echoes your antecedent twice, then shift to the echoic-to-mand or echoic-to-tact teaching procedures for two consecutive learn units (see Table 4.1). If the student echoes two consecutive times during echoic-to-mand or tact-teaching procedures, then shift to the mand and tact-training levels where you will omit the echoic model.
6. If at any level (i.e., motor imitation, echoic-to-mand, or mand training) the student does not respond correctly for two consecutive learn units, then return to the previous level.

Shift in the opposite sequence for incorrect responses. That is, after two incorrect mand or tact responses, shift to an echoic antecedent. After two incorrect echoic responses, shift to a motor imitation antecedent. After two incorrect motor imitation mands/tacts, return to generalized motor imitation to probe for fluent generalized motor imitation responding on a thin schedule of reinforcement (avoid dense or fixed schedules). Alternatively, you might shift to a different mand or tact item, change the topography of the targeted mand or tact form, or place the mand items under further deprivation to increase the likelihood that a vocal model will be correctly and reliably echoed.

Speaker Immersion

Speaker immersion (Greer, 2002; Greer & Ross, 2004; Ross, 1995; Ross, Nuzzolo, Stolfi, & Natarelli, 2006) is a tactic that increases spontaneous speaker behavior, particularly for students who have limited mand and tact repertoires (i.e., they emit very few mands, tacts, or autoclitics). The speaker immersion tactic uses intensive numbers of establishing operations, mainly during transitions within a classroom or school, to structure the environment such that rates of mands increase. During speaker immersion, a student is required to mand a number of routine events or desired items in order to engage in or use them, including standing, sitting, exiting the classroom, wearing their coat, or receiving a tangible or edible reinforcer. The opportunity to mand such routine events and/or desired items is presented until the physical response to the speaker immersion procedure requires more effort than the emission of high

TEXTBOX **4.3**

Speaker Immersion Procedures

1. Select several routine events and activities that can be manipulated throughout the school day or during a short time period (i.e., one hour). Identify the establishing operation that will be associated with the routine event; preventing the student from entering or exiting the classroom, withholding cookies during snack time, or removing crayons during coloring time. Determine the target form for the student's mands. For example, when the student wants to leave an area of the classroom, they may be required to say, "I want to leave the room" or "Can I leave the play area?" (i.e., single-word mands or autoclitic mands). The entire target time period should be taken up with establishing operations that will occasion the opportunity-to-mand.

2. During baseline, present the student with an establishing operation for an activity and wait 10 seconds for them to respond. If they emit the target form, allow them to engage in the activity. If they do not emit the target form, exaggerate the establishing operation by bringing attention to others who are engaging in it or looking expectantly at the student. Wait 10 more seconds before allowing them to engage in the activity (unless it can be replaced with a less reinforcing item, as in the case of giving a less preferred chip in place of candy). Record their responses as correct or incorrect. Do not praise correct responses; simply give them the activity or item (see mand procedures).

3. When baseline responding is low and stable, use an echoic prompt to teach the target response. As in echoic-to-mand procedures, present the establishing operation followed by an echoic model; wait 10 seconds for a response. If the student correctly echoes you, deliver the activity or item without praise. If the student does not echo you within 10 seconds or echoes incorrectly, repeat the echoic, but exaggerate the mand (see Step 2). If they still do not echo you, wait a few more seconds, and then allow them to engage in the routine event (if necessary) or withhold the target item.

4. When the student responds echoically with 90% accuracy for two consecutive sessions (i.e., two days or two hours), return to the initial condition when the echoic was not present. In other words, when the establishing operation is presented, the student must independently mand the target stimulus. When they respond correctly, deliver the item or activity. When they respond incorrectly, exaggerate the mand. Use the echoic as a correction in this phase. When the criterion of 90% accuracy during this condition is met, probe students' mands in the natural condition for the target time period.

5. During this procedure, measure the frequency of tacts and intraverbals as well. Speaker immersion can also be used to increase the diversity of autoclitics emitted for mands.

---

rates of vocal mands for the same events. In other words, vocal communicative behavior begins to obtain maximum reinforcement with less effort.

Inducing Transformation of Establishing Operations across Mand and Tact Functions

As described earlier, a form taught in one function (mand or tact) is not typically emitted in an untaught function without specific training for many children (Lamarre & Holland, 1985; Twyman, 1996b). Research suggests that this is particularly true for early speakers (regardless of their age). However, since most typically developing children eventually acquire the capability of emitting both functions for one stimulus without direct instruction for doing so, there are certain experiences that appear to make this possible (Greer & Keohane, 2005). Recent evidence also suggests that the independence of mands and tacts for typically developing children may be short lived (Petursdottir, Carr, & Michaels, 2005) particularly if the instruction involves multiple exemplar training across speaker and listener responses at the outset. When individuals can emit both mand and tact responses to the same stimulus, they have the capability we identify as the *transformation of establishing operations* across mand and tact functions (Greer & Nirgudkar, & Park, 2003; Nirgudkar, 2005; Nuzzolo-Gomez & Greer, 2004). That is, speakers can respond to the establishing operations that occasion either a mand or tact response once they have leaned the form in one function. The process through which typically developing children acquire this capability is probably similar to the process through which they acquire other advanced verbal capabilities such as *naming* (Barnes-Holmes et al., 2001). That is, parents and caregivers provide and reinforce a sufficient number of experiences with both verbal functions until multiple responses to the same stimulus occur (Novak & Pelaez, 2004). Multiple exemplar instruction with establishing operations attempts to simulate the probable experiences that work for typically developing children by rotating mand and tact opportunities for a subset of forms across the different establishing operations that control each function.

Begin this protocol by identifying several items that are functional but are not yet in the student's repertoire as mands or tacts. As with other instruction, these may include stimuli that are related to their curriculum (see Table 4.2). Divide materials into three sets of four stimuli each—one for mand probes, one for tact probes, and one for instruction.

Choose either the mand or tact function to probe for the presence of *transformation of establishing operations*. Teach one set of stimuli to mastery criterion in the target function (mand or tact) using echoic-to-tact or echoic-to-mand instructional procedures. Rotate across stimuli during instruction, such that each stimulus is

TABLE 4.2   Materials for Transformation of Establishing Operations

Participants	Set 1	Set 2	Set 3
A & B	Crayon	Pencil	Sticker
	Piece	Peg	Vehicle
	Paintbrush	Marker	Chalk
	Glue	Scissors	Board
C	Puzzle	Marker	Notebook
	Car	Button	Hole puncher
	Tape	Glue	Binder
	Eraser	Scissors	Clip

From Nirgudkar, A.S. (2005). *The relative effects of the acquisition of naming and the multiple exemplar establishing operation experience on the acquisition of the transformation of establishing operations across mands and tacts* (Doctoral dissertation, Columbia University, 2005.) Abstract from UMI Proquest—Digital Dissertations [on-line]. Dissertations Abstracts Item, AAT 3159751.

presented five times during a 20 learn unit presentation. When students can reliably respond to target stimuli in the trained function (i.e., mands), then present the same stimuli to probe for their responses in the untrained function (i.e., tacts). If they do not achieve mastery criterion during probes for the untaught function, then they do not have the transformation of establishing operations in their repertoire; proceed to multiple exemplar instruction across establishing operations to teach it as described next.

For a new set of stimuli, present a learn unit in one function using the echoic-to-tact or echoic-to-mand teaching procedures. Ensure that the relevant establishing operations are present as part of the antecedent. That is, for mands, the stimuli are

---

RESEARCH BOX 4.5

Transformation of Establishing Operations

Researchers examined effects of multiple exemplar instruction across mand and tact functions for four preschool children who did not emit an untrained function after being taught another function during baseline. Results showed that multiple exemplar instruction across mand and tact functions resulted in students emitting both mand and tact responses to a trained set, and emitting either the mand or tact function without direct instruction when a novel set was introduced and trained. This study extended research on the independence of verbal operants, establishing operations, and multiple exemplar instruction by identifying an instructional history that resulted in emergence of an untaught verbal function.

These results were replicated in:

Greer, R. D., Nirgudkar, A., & Park, H. (2003, June). *The effect of multiple exemplar instruction on the transformation of mand and tact functions.* Paper presented at the annual international conference of the Association for Behavior Analysis, San Francisco, CA.

Lee Park, H. S. (2005). *Multiple exemplar instruction and transformation of stimulus function from auditory-visual matching to visual-visual matching.* (Doctoral dissertation, Columbia University, 2005). Abstract from UMI Proquest Digital Dissertations [on-line]. Dissertations Abstracts Item: AAT 3174834.

See also:

Petursdottir, A. I., Carr, J. E., & Michaels, J. (2005). Emergence of mands and tacts among preschool children. *Analysis of Verbal Behavior, 21,* 59–74.

Nirgudkar, A. S. (2005). *The relative effects of the acquisition of naming and the multiple exemplar establishing operation across mands and tacts* (Doctoral dissertation, Columbia University, 2005). Abstract from UMI Proquest Digital Dissertations [on-line]. Dissertations Abstracts Item: AAT 3159751.

Nuzzolo-Gomez, R., & Greer, R. D. (2004). Emergence of untaught mands or tacts with novel adjective-object pairs as a function of instructional history. *Analysis of Verbal Behavior, 24,* 30–47.

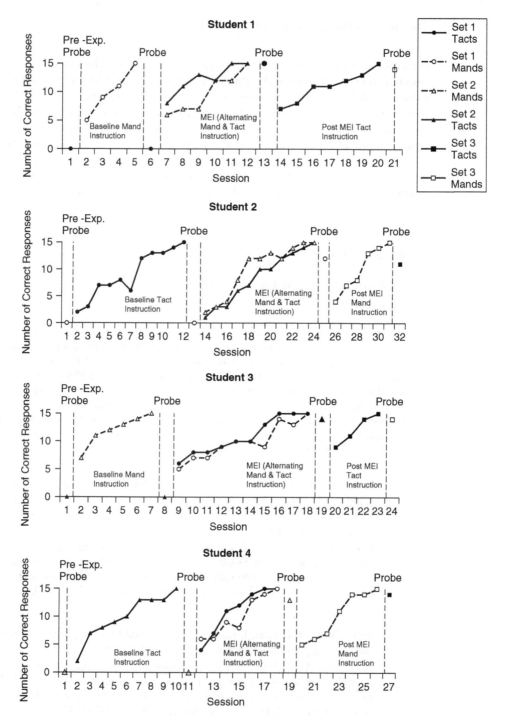

FIGURE 4.8 Transformation of Establishing Operations

From Nuzzolo-Gomez, R., & Greer, R. D. (2004). Emergence of untaught mands or tacts with novel adjective-object pairs as a function of instructional history. *Analysis of Verbal Behavior, 24*, 30–47.

under deprivation. For example, items such as pens, markers, or scissors may need to be presented in an interrupted chain in order to create an establishing operation for mands (i.e., during an arts and craft activity, the target items are unavailable to students unless they emit the appropriate mand). When the student emits a target form (echoic or non-echoic), immediately deliver the item, but do not praise their response (see echoic-to-mand teaching procedures).

In the next learn unit, make generalized reinforcers such as tokens (e.g., plastic discs) visible to the student. Show them the same stimulus that was presented in the mand learn unit and use echoic-to-tact teaching procedures to present the learn unit. For example, to teach a tact for *scissors*, say, "Scissors," wait three seconds for students to echo you, and reinforce their response with a token and praise. After two to three correct echoic learn units, shift to non-echoic learn units. Alternatively, students can learn from the learn unit correction instead of an immediate presentation of an echoic prompt. Record data on the same form used to teach mand and tacts (see Chapter 2). Rotate instruction across stimuli as well as across mand- and tact-establishing operations.

Continue multiple exemplar instruction until students can emit both mand and tact responses to all stimuli in the training set at mastery criterion. Return to the initial probe set to determine if they can emit the untaught function that they could not do before. If they cannot, teach another training set and return to the initial set that they could not do. If necessary, and if their accuracy is increasing, teach still a third set until they emit the untaught functions at 80% accuracy or better. To conduct post-instructional probes, use a novel untaught set of stimuli and a different function (i.e., set 3 stimuli for the function that was not probed before instruction), teach one function to criterion, and then probe for the untaught function. If students can emit the untaught function, then they have the transformation of establishing operations. However, if they cannot, teach additional sets until the untaught function emerges. If it does not emerge after several sets, return to the basic teaching procedures for mands and tacts; assess students' prerequisite repertoires (see Chapters 2 and 7).

Naming

In Chapter 3, we described ways to induce the listener component of naming for children who lack speaker repertoires. After children have the speaker responses described thus far in Chapter 4, they may be ready to acquire the naming capability. When they do not have the basic speaker responses, use the procedures described in Chapters 3 and 4 to teach the listener component of naming, basic listener literacy, and the mand and tact operants. Once children have a speaker repertoire and have the listener capabilities outlined in Chapter 3, proceed to establishing the naming capability.

In the current section, we concentrate on providing a particular speaker-as-own-listener repertoire that has been termed **naming** (Horne & Lowe, 1996). **Full naming** is the capacity to acquire a tact (pure or impure) and a listener response by simply hearing another person tact a stimulus. It also includes both the capacity for children to respond as listeners and speakers without direct instruction. That is, if someone points to a bird and says, "That's a blue bunting," a child can say, "That's a blue

---

TEXTBOX 4.4

Multiple Exemplar Instruction and Naming

The term *multiple exemplar* in teaching and research is used in two types of applications. The first (also called general case teaching) is related to the teaching of abstractions or essential stimulus control, as in the control of abstract properties such as colors, shapes, parts of speech, and properties of mathematics (i.e., mammals, phonetic reading, chairs, tables, and dresses). In this case, students respond to presentations of abstractions in which the irrelevant aspects of a stimulus or conglomerate of stimuli are rotated across positive exemplars. For example, in teaching children to sound out words from the "at" family of phonetic textual responding, printed "at" words (i.e., cat, fat, and sat) are presented with altering font types and sizes and different first letters. In addition, negative exemplars, sometimes called foils, are presented (cut, sun, and beg) with positive exemplars, and the student identifies the correct stimulus. Such instruction can result in correct responding to untaught stimuli that have essential characteristics of the abstractions (i.e., a child phonetically sounds out a word they have never seen before such as *saturation* without direct instruction). Direct Instruction Curricula make extensive use of multiple exemplar procedures that they refer to as *general case instruction* in order to teach a subset of a concept such that the abstraction to untaught examples occurs (Engelmann & Carnine, 1991).

The second type involves bringing responses that were initially independent under joint stimulus control. This is done by rotating different responses to a single stimulus (i.e.,

writing, spelling, and textually responding to a single word) such that students acquire the capability of learning multiple responses from instruction in only one response (e.g., after learning to spell a word vocally, a student can write and read it without direct instruction). For example, one type of multiple exemplar instruction (MEI) involves rotating match, point, pure tact, and impure tact responses to the same set of stimuli, resulting in untaught responses to novel stimuli. In still another instance, using multiple exemplar instruction across establishing operations for mands and tacts results in the emergence of untaught responses within each verbal function. These multiple exemplar experiences have induced new higher order verbal operants or verbal developmental capabilities in children for whom they were missing. This body of work suggests environmental sources for what some psychologists have referred to as *generative* or *productive language usage* that was theorized to be evidence of a language instinct. In his text on verbal behavior (Skinner, 1957) often referred to these types of verbal behavior as *emergent verbal behavior.* Thus far, the procedures that have been identified in the research have induced untaught usage of tenses, suffixes, production and selection responses naming, joint stimulus control across reading and writing, and metaphoric responding (Gilic, 2005; Lee Park, 2005; Mariano-Lapidus, 2005; Matthews, 2005; Yuan, 2005). In addition, observation of others receiving learn units in MEI fashion has resulted in the emergence of higher order operants in observers who were missing them prior to the observation.

---

bunting," or they can orient and point to a blue blunting without direct instruction when someone tacts the stimulus. In other words, after only hearing another person tact a stimulus, they can tact it in response to a verbal antecedent (an impure tact), can tact it in response to a nonverbal antecedent (a pure tact), and can point to it when asked to do so (a listener response). This is the full naming repertoire.

Naming is a **bi-directional** capability, meaning that both listener and speaker capabilities are acquired in a symmetrical relation. (Catania, 2007). That is, by acquiring the listener component of naming, learners simultaneously acquire the speaker component without instruction, and by acquiring the speaker component, learners simultaneously acquire the listener component (Hayes, Fox, Gifford, Wilson, & Barnes-Holmes, 2001). Naming is also an observational learning repertoire involving relations between visual and auditory speech stimuli. When children achieve the naming repertoire, they can expand their tacts and mands through incidental experiences such as observing others. The repertoire is basic for children to acquire the capacity to learn verbal behavior by observation. It is also a basic repertoire that allows typically developing children to expand their repertoire exponentially. We use a *multiple exemplar protocol* to induce the naming repertoire. Textbox 4.4 provides an overview of multiple exemplar instruction. See Figure 3.8 for a visual representation of the instructional sequence.

We teach the first stages of naming by combining the initially independent repertoires of matching, pointing to, and tacting stimuli. Matching and pointing responses are basic listener repertoires made feasible by a child's prior mastery of listener emersion (see Chapter 3) and the basic speaker repertoires. For many children these listener and speaker repertoires are independent. That is, a child can match stimuli, but even though they hear the tact spoken when they match them, they cannot point to them if asked to do so. In other words, hearing the tact does not result in learning to respond to the word as a listener. Moreover, even when they can match or point to a stimulus, they may not be able to tact it under pure or impure conditions. This means that they must be directly instructed in each of these separate repertoires. In contrast, once children learn naming for 3-dimensional objects, they can acquire new vocabulary indirectly (Fiorile & Greer, 2006; Gilic, 2005). They do not require direct instruction; rather, they acquire their exponentially expanding vocabulary seemingly effortlessly. It is probable that some developmental experiences similar to the kinds of experiences used to induce naming may be responsible for this learned capability. Some research indicates that children do not enter first grade with full naming for 2-dimensional stimuli such as pictures of objects, suggesting that naming for 2-dimensional stimuli requires additional experiences (Greer & O'Sullivan, 2006). Nevertheless, children as young as 2 years of age and children with language delays can be taught naming for 2-dimensional stimuli (Greer, Stolfi, & Pistoljevic, 2006).

The acquisition of the naming capability means that when children learn either a listener or a speaker response to stimuli, then they can emit the other untaught responses (matching, pointing, and speaking) without direct instruction. Of course, acquiring the naming repertoire provides the child with a giant step forward in verbal behavior since learning a single response to a stimulus will produce all of the necessary responses without direct instruction. The capability of naming increases the child's learning capacity threefold. Figure 4.9 is a representation of a child who lacks naming; Figure 4.10 depicts a child who has the listener half of naming; Figure 4.11 shows a child who has full naming. Each of these steps provides the child with new capabilities to learn incidentally. The importance of naming for the acquisition of complex "cognitive" behaviors is illustrated in the figure showing the joining of naming with print control. Figure 4.11 also identifies components of the naming capability and examples of components that can be assessed. These components can also serve as identifying capabilities that are present or that need to be induced.

When a Child Lacks Naming

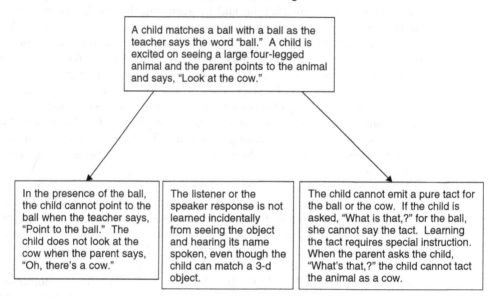

A child matches a ball with a ball as the teacher says the word "ball." A child is excited on seeing a large four-legged animal and the parent points to the animal and says, "Look at the cow."

In the presence of the ball, the child cannot point to the ball when the teacher says, "Point to the ball." The child does not look at the cow when the parent says, "Oh, there's a cow."

The listener or the speaker response is not learned incidentally from seeing the object and hearing its name spoken, even though the child can match a 3-d object.

The child cannot emit a pure tact for the ball or the cow. If the child is asked, "What is that,?" for the ball, she cannot say the tact. Learning the tact requires special instruction. When the parent asks the child, "What's that,?" the child cannot tact the animal as a cow.

FIGURE 4.9   When a Child Lacks Naming

When the Child has the Listener Half of Naming

A child matches a ball with a ball as the teacher says the word "ball." A child is excited on seeing a large four-legged animal and the parent points to the animal and says, "Look at the cow."

In the presence of the ball, the child can point to the ball when the teacher says, "Point to the ball." The child looks at the cow when the parent says, "Oh, there's a cow." The listener response was learned incidentally.

The child cannot emit a pure tact for the ball or the cow. If the child is asked, "What is that?," for the ball, she cannot say the tact. Learning the tact requires special instruction. When the parent asks the child, "What's that?," the child cannot tact the animal as a cow. Even though the listener half is present the speaker half is missing.

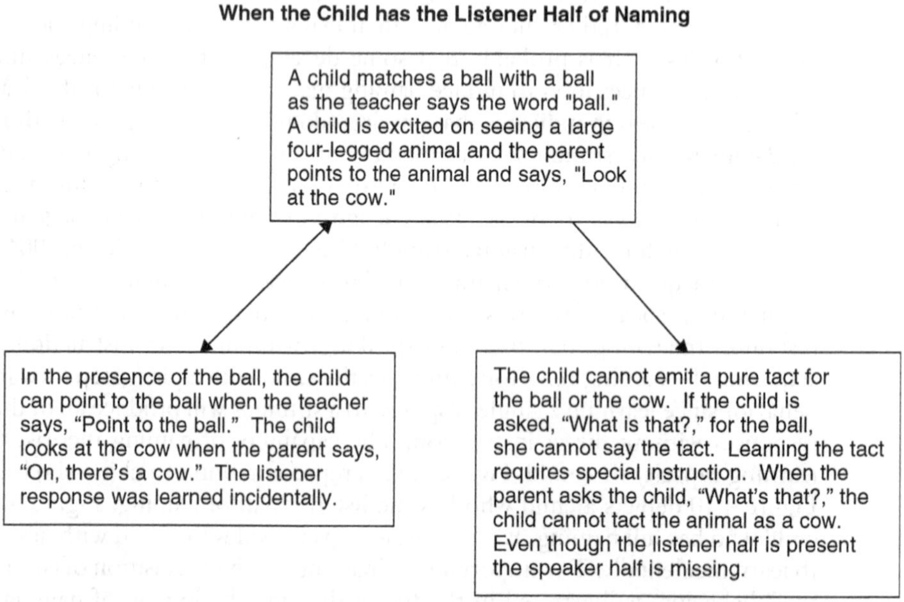

FIGURE 4.10   When a Child has the Listener Half of Naming

The Child has the Joint Stimulus or Bidirectional Control of Naming

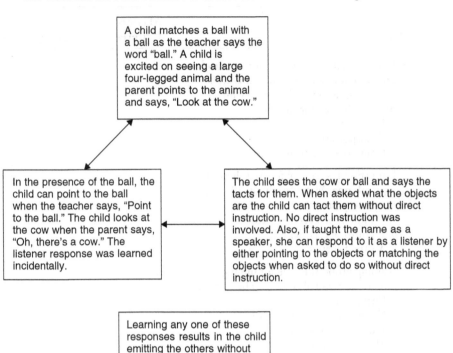

A child matches a ball with a ball as the teacher says the word "ball." A child is excited on seeing a large four-legged animal and the parent points to the animal and says, "Look at the cow."

In the presence of the ball, the child can point to the ball when the teacher says, "Point to the ball." The child looks at the cow when the parent says, "Oh, there's a cow." The listener response was learned incidentally.

The child sees the cow or ball and says the tacts for them. When asked what the objects are the child can tact them without direct instruction. No direct instruction was involved. Also, if taught the name as a speaker, she can respond to it as a listener by either pointing to the objects or matching the objects when asked to do so without direct instruction.

Learning any one of these responses results in the child emitting the others without direct instruction.

FIGURE 4.11   Child has Joint Stimulus or Bidirectional Control of Naming

Before naming can be induced the child needs to have certain matching and pointing responses in their repertoire. They will need to have basic listener literacy and all of the subcomponents needed for listener literacy described in Chapter 3. Once they have these, teach some of the basic visual discriminations that they will need in order to set the occasion for them to learn naming.

Basic Visual Discrimination to Occasion the Advancement of Speaker and Listener Repertoires

There are numerous visual discrimination programs that involve listener responses, and these set the occasion for advancing the listener repertoire. These include identifying sameness and differences for pictures, shapes, letters, words, objects, family members, classmates, modes of transportation, animals, workers, numbers, and number-object correspondence, to name a few of the foundational identifications that the student will need. These discriminations are taught so that the student will eventually respond to

TABLE 4.3   **Probe Responses for Full Naming Repertoire**

Repertoire	Mastery Criteria	Code	Comments
1. Joint stimulus control for **point-match equivalence:** Points to stimulus after being taught to match stimuli while hearing the tact for the object. a. Farm animals b. Transportation c. Common objects in home			
2. Joint stimulus control for **match-point equivalence:** Matches stimuli after being taught to point to stimuli a. Common objects in school b. Pictures of classmates c. Abstract shapes			
3. Naming probe 1: Probe for untaught impure intraverbal responses by saying, "What is this?" a. Common objects in school b. Pictures of classmates c. Abstract shapes d. Farm animals e. Transportation f. Common objects in home			
4. Naming probe 2: Probe for responses to "Give me the ____" after student receives learn units on point and matching responses for a target stimulus. Rotate an untaught non-exemplar. a. Action pictures b. Classroom objects (pencil, book)			
5. Naming probe 3: Probe for responses to "What is this?" when above are at criterion: a. Action pictures b. Classroom stimuli			

them under four different antecedent stimulus conditions involving both visual and spoken stimuli needed to induce the naming capability. The responses are

1. Matching ("Put ____ with ____") including shapes colors, pictures, letter, numbers and 3-dimensional objects and general environmental stimuli

2. Pointing to ("Point to _____"), including shapes colors, pictures, letter, numbers and 3-dimensional objects, and general environmental stimuli
3. Tacting under non-verbal antecedent conditions (the stimulus is shown and the student "tacts" the stimulus with no verbal antecedent from the teacher)
4. Intraverbal responding (responding to "What _____ is this?")

Essentially, matching and pointing responses are listener responses, while tact and intraverbal responses are speaker responses, and learn units can be used to teach each repertoire separately. However, the speaker responses discussed in the naming repertoire are ones that we wish to be obtained from listening alone and not from direct learn unit instruction. They are the basis for the child acquiring the capacity to incidentally learn speaker responses from listening.

Inducing Full Naming

To teach the full naming repertoire, combine the listener responses with the speaker responses such that joint stimulus control is developed across speaker and listener repertoires. Once the child has basic listener literacy and basic mand and tact operants, with autoclitics such as "This is _____," "I see," "That's a _____," "It's a _____," "This is a _____," "May I have _____, please?" "Can I have _____, please?" a "Please give me _____ the one on/under, in, above, beside" and other adjective-object pairs relations that specify or quantify the mand or tact operants, they are ready to begin all discrimination instruction in a manner that will lead to the naming repertoire. Instruction is arranged such that the match, point, pure tact, and impure tact responses are taught to develop joint stimulus control across the speaker and listener repertoires. We do this by presenting a match instruction, followed by a point instruction, followed by a tact instruction, followed by an impure or intraverbal instruction. These are done such that there are sets of four stimuli taught in a rotated fashion across all four responses, but not so the child *can simply echo the prior response* as a speaker. For example, the response for "Point to red," is followed by "Match blue," followed by a pure tact opportunity for green (i.e., the teacher points to or holds up the colored card and the student says the color with no verbal antecedent), followed by an impure tact opportunity for yellow (e.g., the teacher says, "What color is this?" followed by the student saying the color). In the next rotation, the colors are presented with different response forms until all possible combinations achieve 20 separate learn units. Actually, you will only present five opportunities for each response in a single 20-learn unit session, but block or group the learn units by their separate response functions across all target stimuli (20 matching, 20 pointing, 20 tacting, and 20 impure tact responses across all four colors).

To test for the presence or absence of naming and to teach naming, we have used picture sets of dog breeds, landmarks, and types of vegetables, abstract stimuli such as Greek symbols and Japanese characters, and other stimuli the child is not familiar with. You may use other stimuli, but they should be pictures or objects that are unknown to the student and that are part of the local educational standards. If children have difficulty with pictures, use three-dimensional objects until they master this capability; return to pictures later. If children do not have extensive experience with pictures and looking at pictures in books, begin with 3-dimensional objects (Greer & O'Sullivan, 2006).

The stimuli you will need for the protocol for inducing naming are arranged according to test stimuli and instructional stimuli. You will need (1) 2 sets of 5 pictures or objects unknown to the child that are to be used as *tests for the presence or absence of naming;* and (2) 2 or more sets of pictures/objects, also unknown to the child, which are *used for multiple exemplar instruction.* First, probe all of the sets to be sure that the child does not respond to the stimuli as both a listener and a speaker. Probe each stimulus one time each for each of the responses—the match, tact, impure tact, and pointing responses. Do not tact the names for the stimuli in the matching trials, but rather say, "match" without tacting the stimulus. It is likely that they will match the stimuli with close to 100% accuracy. In these probes you do not reinforce or correct. This should determine that the child does not respond to the stimuli as a listener (pointing) or as a speaker (pure and impure tacts). This tells us that the child is unfamiliar with the stimuli.

Next, we want to determine if the child has the naming capability. That is, can they learn the two types of tact and listener responses for the stimuli when they hear the name as they match them? Run 20-learn unit sessions of matching while saying the name or tact for each of the stimuli; each stimulus is presented four times. The child should have the target picture/object and a negative exemplar in front of her. If the child does not emit 80%–100% accuracy in the first session, continue running these *teaching sessions* until they match with 80% or higher accuracy. Hand her the match picture/object and say, "Match the poodle with the poodle," for example. Provide reinforcement and corrections until a criterion is achieved. At this point we have simulated the situation that naturally occurs when children learn "words" incidentally through the naming capability.

At this point, we are ready *to test for the naming capability.* From now on, the test will consist of probe trials that have no reinforcement or correction components. First, to test for the listener repertoire, run 20-probe trials asking the child to "Point to the _____," when there is an example of a poodle (e.g., the target stimulus) and a negative exemplar (a dog that is not a poodle) in front of the child. Next, run 20-probe trials in which you show the child the stimuli and wait for a tact response (the impure tact response). Finally, run 20-probe trials in which you present the stimuli and ask the child, "What is it?" If the child does not have 80% or better correct responding to each of the listener and speaker probe trials, we are ready to teach the naming capability. If the child meets the 80% criterion, we list the child as having the naming capability.

To teach the child the naming capability we use multiple exemplar instruction as described in Textbox 4.5. After we have taught at least one of the teaching sets using multiple exemplars of responding to each stimulus, we return to the initial set of stimuli that the child could not respond to accurately as a listener or as a speaker and repeat the probes for the listener or pointing responses, and the tact and impure tact responses. If naming does not emerge at 80% accuracy across the untaught responses, teach an additional set of stimuli and return to the probes until the child demonstrates naming for the initial set. After that, use a second novel set (identified at the outset) to further test for naming. Teach the child to match the unfamiliar stimuli while saying the tact or name for the stimuli using learn units, as was done with the initial test set. When this is

TEXTBOX **4.5**

**Multiple Exemplar Instructional Procedures
to Teach Naming**

1. A teacher places a red car and a blue car on a table, gives the student a matching blue car, and says, "Match blue." The student places the blue car next to the one on the table within three seconds. The teacher says, "Good" and records a plus in the "match" column of the data collection form. If incorrect, the teacher makes a correction.
2. The teacher changes the location of the stimuli on the table and then says, "Point to red." Note that *you must not present the same stimulus* that was matched following the match opportunity because the student may simply echo the prior tact. The student points to the red car within three seconds. The teacher praises the student and records a plus in the "point" column on the data collection form. If incorrect, the teacher makes a correction.
3. The teacher points to the blue car or holds it up and the student says, "Blue" within three seconds. The teacher praises the student and records a plus in the "pure tact" column of the data collection form. Finally, the teacher points to the red car, says, "What color is this?" and waits three seconds. The student immediately says, "Red," and receives a reinforcer from the teacher. A plus is recorded in the "impure tact" column of the data collection form. If either of these are incorrect, the teacher makes a correction per the learn unit protocol.
4. The teacher begins the instruction again, but presents a point learn unit first, followed by a match learn unit, an impure tact learn unit, and then a pure tact learn unit. Green and yellow pencils are used to teach discrimination of the color green during this discrimination of listener and speaker instruction.
5. Instruction continues across rotated stimuli until each response form (i.e., point, match, pure tact, and impure tact) is presented 20 times, and each stimulus (i.e., green, blue, red, and yellow) is presented 5 times within each response type. When the student makes errors, the teacher presents the antecedent again, physically (match and point) or vocally (pure and impure tacts) models the response, and waits for the student to respond. No praise or other reinforcement is given for corrected responses.
6. When instruction ends, the student has met the 100% accuracy criterion for matching responses, but not for point or pure and impure tact responses. The teacher graphs the matching response with an open circle and uses a triangle to indicate that one criterion was achieved. Hereafter, the teacher will still present the matching response opportunity during multiple exemplar instruction, but only as an antecedent for point and tact responses. It will no longer be recorded on the data collection form or graphed.
7. This procedure continues until the child has mastered all of the repertoires for the 5 stimuli in this teaching set.
8. Probes for the set of stimuli that the child could not respond to as a listener or speaker should reveal that they can now emit the untaught responses. If the child does not achieve the 80% criterion, teach another instructional set and probe the test set again. Continue teaching new sets as long as the child is making progress.

done and the child has met the matching criterion while hearing the tact for the stimuli, probe for the pointing, tact, and impure tact responses. If the child can respond at 80% accuracy to the listener and speaker probes, we can be reasonably assured that they have the naming capability. In some cases additional multiple exemplar instruction may be needed, although we have not found this to be the case in several experiments and numerous instructional applications. See Chapter 7 for ways to capitalize on the new naming capability and build independent learner repertoires.

Textbox 4.5 describes the multiple exemplar instructional procedures to teach the full naming repertoire. See Figure 3.9 for research on the use of multiple exemplar instruction to induce naming.

Once you have taught the naming capability, the child has the capability to acquire new listener responses and speaker responses by hearing others say the name of stimuli. However, before the child has naming and has been reinforced extensively for verbal functions through the naming capability, multiple listener and tact responses must be taught directly. Before children have fluent naming we need to provide intensive instruction to expand their tact repertoires so that when naming emerges, they have a large repertoire to build on.

The Importance of Tacts

Prior to the introduction of the naming protocol, we described the basic teaching sequence for tacts and mands, and the capability to do so from direct contact with teacher-presented learn units. Many children will need extensive tact instruction before they are ready to learn the naming capability. As described earlier in this chapter, the tact repertoire requires intensive attention because it is foundational to subsequent verbal developmental stages and complex communication functions. Once basic mands and a few tacts are taught, teachers must vigorously pursue expanding children's tact repertoires without decreasing other types of learn units—a daunting but necessary task. To accomplish this, we use a program of **intensive tact instruction.** That is, tact learn units are interspersed between other curricular learn units and during transitions from instruction to free time, in hallways, from transport to the school building, during lunchtime, and within indoor and outdoor play settings. For example, when a student has earned enough tokens throughout the day for an exchange or when they have earned the opportunity to mand, they must emit one or more tacts first. While such interactions may be characterized as incidental learning, they are systematically designed incidences with the goal of having the student become a perpetual talker who talks to recruit attention, confirmation, and praise.

"Awareness" follows the learning of tacts. Tacts are the basis of functional language, and both functional and structural language are the bases for responses on Intelligence Quotients or IQ tests. The acquired capabilities of fluent reading, naming, "wh" (what, when, where, and who), and observational learning repertoires replace much of the need for direct learn unit instruction to expand tacts. However, until the child has these, teachers and parents must provide the major source for building a tact repertoire. Unless we provide this intensive tact instruction prior to acquisition of later capabilities described in Chapters 5 and 6, the child has no names for things, and names are fundamental to achieving these capabilities.

As mentioned earlier, tacts should be taught across the senses. Once you teach tacts of the senses, you can build on these by playing extensions of the game, "I see" (parents play the "I see game" with their children as a means of entertainment). This is a powerful way to build tacts. When two children are present, or in instruction in which you alternate learn units, like the one we describe in Chapter 5, you can use a *yoked-contingency game* as an establishing operation. Once you add the other senses to the game, you expand the child's tacts across all of the senses. Thus, the game includes "I smell," I taste," I hear," I feel" as well as "I see." As this repertoire advances, you can add tacts of private events— "I feel full," I feel hungry," I feel excited," "I feel angry," and "I feel happy," to name only a few of the possibilities.

In the several experiments we have done using the intensive tact protocol, the results have shown that the children and adolescents that we studied did not simply emit the tacts they were taught in the intensive tact instruction; rather, they emitted numerous other tacts that they had in their repertoire. This suggests that the intensive tact procedure increases the students' ability to recruit reinforcement by talking. Once this establishing operation is salient, it may set the occasion for the student to benefit from the naming protocol just described. The intensive tact protocol may be mastered before the protocol for inducing naming is introduced.

Procedures for Rapid Expansion of Tacts through Direct Contact with Learn Units (Intensive Tact Protocol)

Select sets of five stimuli for each of four curricular short-term objectives (100 additional learn units daily or five different 20-learn unit programs) that are related to educationally significant long-term goals from curricular standards. That is, select the tact stimuli from state and national educational standards prescribed in your local school district (or in the case of other countries, use the national standards such as England's Excellence in Education Standards). Also, you want to relate the tacts to senses other than visual responses. For example, teach sets of tacts associated with the following: I see, I smell, I hear, I feel (i.e., tactile), and I taste. Of course you also want the student to tact all the people in the room and objects in the school and playground, as well as what they see out of the window.

This program teaches academic literacy and its discipline subcategories (i.e., life sciences, global studies, and tacting family members) as well as communication curricula categories that are present in all educational standards for school curricula. The following examples are only suggestive as generic objects or pictures, but the ones chosen for the children you teach should be drawn from educational standards; include all of the senses. Use sets of four different types of stimuli, including breeds of dogs, types of flowers/trees/leaves, transport, family members, shapes, colors, and types of horses or airplanes. These should be tacts associated with curricular areas such as life sciences, global studies, literature, object numbers/sets in math (actual numbers are textual responses; see Chapter 6), and other subjects that will advance the child's educational attainment. Use pictures of the stimuli, two-dimensional representations of the actual stimuli, or the actual stimuli (or multiple exemplars of both two-dimensional and actual stimuli). Also, use multiple exemplars of stimuli for each type of tact (e.g., vary irrelevant stimuli such as different types of poodles). Graph each set of five as a single program. Each time the student meets criterion on a single set, add another set of four stimuli as you continue to teach the non-mastered sets. These programs need to continue across hundreds of tacts until the student has repertoires to replace direct learn unit instruction, including 1) fluent and independent textual responding (reading), 2) fluent naming, 3) observational learning for tacts, and 4) the capability to recruit new tacts using "wh" questions. Protocols to induce these capabilities are described in Chapters 5 and 6.

The basic tactic to use during *intensive tact instruction* is echoic-to-tact learn units; when the child emits three to five consecutive echoics, then they must tact independently (see echoic-to-tact procedures). Some students may require five echoics or even more, while others will require fewer. The instructional history data for a child will guide this decision (see Chapter 2 and 7). Record the echoic prompted responses with a circled plus (for prompted), the independent correct tacts as a plus (+), and the independent incorrect tacts as a minus (−). On your graphs, plot prompted responses of the echoic-to-tact as open circles and independent as closed circles. Data should show a descending trend in open circles and an ascending trend in closed circles. That is, echoic responses should decrease while independent responses increase. Incorrect

---

TEXTBOX 4.6

Instructional Sequence for Intensive Tact Training

1. Choose four short-term objectives across curricular areas from your school's educational standards (i.e., for a first-grade life science objective, the child tacts components of plants), or use tact repertoires that are missing such as tacting classroom objects and individuals. For each objective, make a set of five tacts that include responses across all five senses (not just visual responses). Use multiple exemplars of target stimuli. This should result in 100 additional daily learn units or five different 20-learn unit programs.
2. For large or stationary objects such as desks or trash cans, walk to the object with the student. For pictures or small objects, put several exemplars of the objects in different containers and place the containers around the room for easy accessibility throughout the day.
3. Use learn units to teach each new item. Point to the item and wait 3 seconds for the student to respond. If they respond correctly, provide generalized and, if needed, prosthetic reinforcement. If they respond incorrectly or do not respond, say the name of the item and wait for them to respond. This is a correction procedure; so do not praise or correct their responses. Continue until the student tacts the item before the correction is presented.
4. The mastery criterion for each stimulus set is 19 or more independent tacts for two sessions or 100% for one session. When one set is mastered, add a new set that should be taught to mastery. Mastered stimuli should become a part of the students' regular curriculum.
5. If the learn unit is not effective for teaching tacts, then use a zero-second time delay procedure for three consecutive sessions before using one-second time delay.
6. Continue the intensive tact training protocol for new stimuli until the child has the following repertoires: 1) fluent and independent textual responding (reading), 2) fluent naming, 3) observational learning for tacts, and 4) the capability to recruit new tacts using "wh" questions.

responses are the differences between prompted and independent responses. See Appendix B for a sample graph.

If learn units alone are not effective, then use the zero-second time delay procedure, which is really another means of presenting echoic-to-tact opportunities, but increases the numbers of echoic opportunities that the student receives before having the opportunity to emit the independent tact. That is, the student receives three sessions of echoic-to-tact instruction before introducing a one-second-time delay to emit the tact independently. Subsequently, follow the standard decision protocol described in Chapters 2 and 7. Avoid response or stimulus prompts, and carefully identify possible missing prerequisites if students have difficulty. The data collection form for the programs needs to be on a single form for the entire day. It must be accessible so that the teacher can easily record data while conducting other programs (i.e., all five programs on a single form). See Appendix C for a sample data collection form.

Initially, teach three programs as pure tacts (no vocal antecedent), and two programs as impure tacts (with vocal antecedents such as "What is this?"). If there are no differences in the students' learning of pure or impure tacts, continue with the two and three distribution across programs. If the student has difficulty with an impure or a pure function, use the naming protocol or multiple exemplar instruction to induce the naming repertoire (described earlier in this chapter).

Once we have taught basic verbal operants and basic listener literacy as described previously and in Chapter 3, we must expand the tact repertoire. Our first intervention or protocol for advancing the tact repertoire is through intensive direct contact with learn units for teaching tacts. This intensive tact procedure is designed to develop new tact operants, particularly those that are needed to meet educational standards and are part of school curricula, tacts that provide the foundation for verbal episodes, and tacts that expand categorization. At this point, our students have acquired the echoic-to-tact verbal development stage, and we are simply adding new forms by teaching autoclitics. Textbox 4.7 briefly describes the process for adding autoclitics during intensive tact instruction.

RESEARCH BOX 4.6

Intensive Tact Instruction

This study examined the effects of intensive tact instruction on the number of tacts emitted by three preschool children with autism (3 to 4 years of age) in several non-instructional settings. Intensive tact training involved the presentation of 100 additional tact learn units each day. When compared to baseline, participants emitted more tacts and mands in all non-instructional settings.

See also Schauffler, G., & Greer, R. D. (2006). The effects of intensive tact instruction on audience-accurate tacts and conversational units. *Journal of Early and Intensive Behavioral Interventions, 3.1, 120–132.* http://www.behavior-analyst-online.org

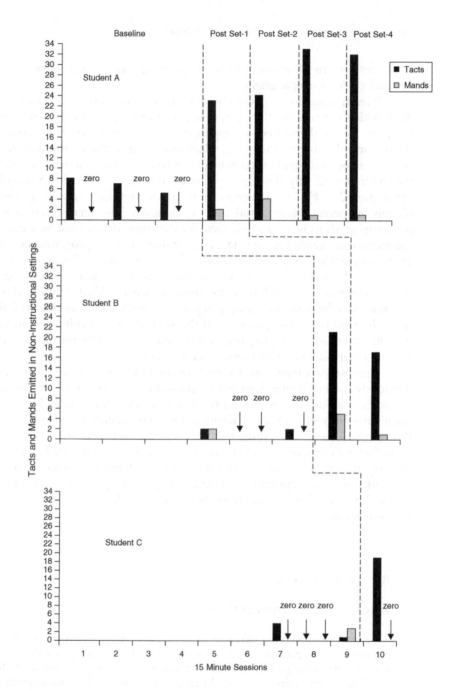

FIGURE 4.12 Intensive Tact Training

From Pistoljevic, N., & Greer, R. D. (2006). The effects of daily intensive tact instruction on preschool students' emission of pure tacts and mands in non-instructional settings. *Journal of Intensive Behavioral Intervention, 3*, 103–119. http://www.behavior-analyst-online.org

TEXTBOX **4.7**

Incorporating Autoclitics during Intensive Tact Instruction

Follow the intensive tact training protocol in Textbox 4.6 but teach autoclitics by presenting an echoic model before opportunities-to-respond for each target stimulus. When modeling a tact for a big or little car, for example, say, "The big car," and wait three seconds for the child to repeat you. Reinforce correct responses and then present the next learn unit for a new stimulus (i.e., "A small car" or "A big cup"). Train similar autoclitics for stimuli. For example, teach big/small across stimuli. Repeat for each target stimulus for two days. Do not use the echoic model for subsequent sessions on the same stimuli. Select target autoclitics from the probe record in Chapter 5.

The tested procedures we have described in this chapter have been successful in helping many children become effective speakers for the first time. The procedures also describe how to design instruction such that speaking simply becomes the easiest way to get things done. Once a few mands are learned, the child needs to learn many tacts as well as the capability for the transformation of establishing operations across mand and tact functions. At that point, learning either a mand or tact function results in an untaught function. Finally, when the child acquires the naming capability, the number of responses acquired from learning a single operant are multiplied because they have the higher order operant capability of naming. At this point, we are ready to advance to the interlocking speaker-listener capabilities, and this is the subject matter of Chapter 5.

Summary

- Speaker operants include echoics, mands, tacts, autoclitics, and intraverbals. *Pure* mands and tacts occur under nonverbal antecedent control, and *impure* mands and tacts occur under verbal antecedent control. *Multiple control* mands and tacts are those that occur under the control of physical and verbal antecedent stimuli.
- *Parroting* is an early stage of speaker development during which self-reinforcing verbal patterns are produced because of *automatic reinforcement*, and not because they are verbal operants. *Echoics* are verbal operants with *point-to-point correspondence* to the verbal antecedent stimuli that control them.
- *Mands* are verbal operants of various forms emitted under conditions of deprivation or aversive stimulation and reinforced by presentation or removal of a specified item.

- *Establishing operations*, events that momentarily alter the reinforcing effectiveness of a stimulus, can be used by teachers to increase learning opportunities. In some cases, manipulating environmental events to create establishing operations is a necessary condition for mand and other verbal and non-verbal instruction.
- *Tacts* are verbal operants that occur under non-verbal antecedent control (i.e., the presence of a stimulus evokes a tact) and are reinforced by generalized reinforcers.
- *Autoclitics* expand mand and tact repertoires by specifying, quantifying, or modifying them.
- The teaching procedures for mands and tacts are echoic-to-mand and echoic-to-tact instruction. These procedures begin with echoic functions, but quickly shift to mand and tact functions.
- Mands and tacts are functionally independent and require separate instruction. However, once the child has the *transformation of establishing operations* capability, learning one function for a mand or tact results in the other without direct instruction. When children have the prerequisites, then the protocol for inducing the transformation of establishing operations across mands and tact can result in this capability.
- When vocal speaker behavior is not present, *rapid motor imitation* and *stimulus-stimulus pairing* are alternative procedures to evoke it. When mands and tacts are present but infrequent, *speaker immersion* can be used to evoke it.
- When tacts are present but infrequent, the *intensive tact* procedures can be used to increase a tact repertoire. In fact, until the child has full naming, new tacts can be acquired primarily through direct instruction. Hence, until naming is present, the intensive tact instruction procedure needs to remain in place.
- Once the *full-naming capability* is acquired, new verbal operants can be acquired incidentally and intensive tact instruction is no longer necessary. The full-naming capability involves both listener and speaker components of naming, and is demonstrated when students can incidentally acquire speaker responses after hearing a tact from another person. It is important for the tact repertoire because it allows students to acquire tacts without direct instruction. As in the listener component of naming (see Chapter 3), multiple exemplar instruction is used to evoke this capability.

Inducing Advanced Speaker Functions and Correcting Faulty Vocal Behavior

Verbal responses are distinguished by the occasions on which they occur and the consequences they produce. They can be occasioned by either verbal or nonverbal stimuli, and they have verbal or nonverbal consequences.

Catania, 1998, p. 24

Advancing Key Verbal Capabilities

When children have acquired the basic listener literacy, speaker operants, and higher verbal capabilities outlined in previous chapters, we build on them to establish more complex communicative functions. Some of the functions that we describe in the text are new verbal developmental stages or verbal capabilities related to tact, intraverbal, and autoclitic functions. In addition to describing procedures for the acquisition of new capabilities and the expansion of existing repertoires, we also describe procedures to use with some students who need functional verbal behavior to replace non-functional vocal responding. Verbal behavior that does not have a function in the verbal community (i.e., echolalia or palilalia) must be replaced with verbal behavior that does have a function (i.e., tacts and appropriate intraverbals). It is also important to correct improperly learned echoic responses and to replace them with intraverbals. Similarly, the sources for stereotypic speaker responses need to be identified and replaced with reinforcement that accrues for tact responses. Thus, in addition to providing the means to advance verbal functions, we also provide procedures to replace faulty speaker behavior with functional verbal behavior. To assist the reader in sequencing verbal development instruction, a flowchart at the end of this chapter (Figure 5.12, p. 213) outlines the sequence of procedures from prior chapters and from the current chapter.

Inducing and Expanding Tact and Intraverbal Capabilities

Tact Capabilities

While the mand repertoire is important for the acquisition of initial speaker behavior (Sundberg, 1991), tacts become more prominent in typical verbal development because they provide the foundation for complex verbal repertoires. Unless people are in destitute situations, they typically do not spend their entire day emitting mands. Typical verbal development requires that we acquire tacts exponentially. That is, children must learn to tact, tact, and tact some more! Just as there are several ways that typically developing children acquire tacts, there are a number of procedures we can use to teach tacts and the means by which they are acquired to children who need to learn ways to acquire them. In the next section we describe four capabilities or ways by which individuals can acquire tacts, and methods to teach these capabilities if they are missing. All four are critical stages of verbal development.

Capability 1.   Initially, we acquire new tacts by direct instruction in the form of naturally occurring or instructionally designed learn units. In Chapter 4, we described procedures for teaching the capability of learning tacts by direct instruction and expanding them through intensive tact opportunities and autoclitics.

Capability 2. We need to teach our students the capability of to recruiting tact instruction by using what, when, where, who (i.e., "wh" questions), and "how," if these repertoires are missing.

Capability 3. We must teach our students to acquire tacts incidentally through **naming.** If children do not have the listener-to-speaker component of naming, we must induce it. Procedures to do so were described in the naming sections of Chapters 3 and 4.

Capability 4. Students learn new tacts through indirect contact with contingencies by observing others receive reinforcement or corrections for emitting tacts; if that repertoire is missing, we must teach it, too.

Intraverbal Capabilities

In addition to tact capabilities, we build on tacts to establish various intraverbal and related listener or speaker-listener functions. These are also critical developmental stages. They must be present if children are to advance the complexity of their verbal development.

Capability 5. Children engage in self-talk, which is a fundamental part of the speaker-as-own-listener capability. If this is missing, then we must teach it.

Capability 6. Intraverbal discourse with others is a critical component of socialization that culminates in the emission of conversational units, and if this is missing, then we must induce it.

Capability 7. Children learn perspective-taking involving I, you, my, your, here, there, then, and now—these are types of adjective-object pairs used as autoclitics in tact and mand functions. They are autoclitic listener and speaker functions that require types of observational tacts and mands.

It is likely that typically-developing children who have rich language experiences acquire these seven capabilities, or verbal development stages, through incidental experiences with their parents and caretakers. We believe that they can do so because they have acquired the necessary prerequisite capabilities described in earlier chapters. There is much debate from those of differing perspectives (both scientific and pre-scientific) about the role of experiences and heredity in the verbal development of typically-developing children. Some argue that these capabilities are not learned at all; rather, they are "hard-wired" in the form of genetic capacities.[1] Some linguists have attributed the development of these capabilities to neurological factors alone. Verbal behavior research suggests that when procedures such as those in this chapter and text are used to establish certain instructional histories, these seven capabilities can be induced for children who are missing them (see Tables 1.2 and 1.4 for a list of relevant research). Thus, verbal capabilities need not be restricted to "hardwiring" alone, but can be traced to environmental experiences which, when provided in an intensive

TEXTBOX **5.1**

Summary of Advanced Tact and Intraverbal Capabilities

Capabilities Needed to Expand the Tact Repertoire

Capability 1. Acquisition of new tacts by direct learn units (see Chapter 4 for the intensive tact protocol)

Capability 2. Acquisition of the capability to recruit tacts ("wh" questions and "how" questions)

Capability 3. Acquisition of new tacts incidentally via naming (see Chapter 4 for full naming protocol)

Capability 4. Acquisition of tacts by observing others receive learn units

Intraverbal Capabilities for Social Interaction

Capability 5. Acquisition of self-talk (speaker-listener exchanges within one's own skin; typically developing children do this aloud in solitary play)

Capability 6. Acquisition of conversational units and related speaker-listener exchanges

Capability 7. Acquisition of the capability to take the perspective of others, including empathy for others

---

fashion, give children the capabilities they were previously missing. The protocols we describe in this chapter are derived from this research.

In order to induce each of these capabilities, certain prerequisite repertoires need to be present. That is, unless we can provide the prerequisites, and in some cases join or connect them to one another, subsequent capabilities may not be possible. It is possible that these capabilities are also fundamental for children with verbal deficits who do not have native disabilities, but who lack sufficient types of specific learning experiences and opportunities. We draw this conclusion from research on language acquisition and parent-child interaction demonstrating that unless frequent parent-child language interactions occur, typically-developing children will have vocabulary deficits.[2] We suspect that such vocabulary deficits occur because of insufficient experiences and opportunities with vocabulary and multiple exemplar instruction that would produce the verbal capabilities or stages we have identified. The lack of such experiences means that at some point in later stages of verbal development, children will incur problems. For example, the "dyslexic" reader may have missed key experiences, resulting in absent listener repertoires. This chapter describes the existing tested procedures that have resulted in the acquisition of these capabilities by children for whom they were missing (Greer & Keohane, 2005).

Capability 1: Acquisition of new tacts by direct learn units.   These procedures were described in Chapter 4; refer to the intensive tact protocol if needed.

Capability 2: Recruitment of new tacts by using "wh" and "how" questions. A key capability that people use to acquire tacts is the emission of "wh" questions such as "What is that?" or "Where is it?" It is possible that the "need to know" a tact is the establishing operation for emitting "wh" questions such as "What is it?" This may be evoked by a history of using the "wh" question, obtaining the tact, and then receiving generalized reinforcement for the tact. We must teach the "need to know" function for students to ask "Wh" questions. This "need to know" is a special case of establishing operations during which the student searches for a tact because they need to have a verbal response leading to reinforcement, but they do not have the tact. At this point, one might say that the student needs a means to receive an echoic-tact exemplar, which is a way to recruit tacts. While one might refer to this as a "mand for information," the ultimate source of reinforcement is a conditioned generalized reinforcer associated with the tact. Therefore, the establishing operation associated with the tact (and not the mand) must also be the establishing operation for recruiting tacts. If students were to recruit tacts and subsequently mand the items they tacted, then the ultimate reinforcement would be that of a mand—a specific rather than generalized reinforcer. The following "wh" questions protocol is designed to induce the **conditioned-establishing operation** control for recruiting echoics for tact functions as in the echoic-to-tact sequence.

The goal of this program is for students to ask, "What is it?" during all tact instruction for any item they do not know, including textual responses (i.e., looking at a printed word or number and saying it). Thus, during instruction whenever the student does not know a tact, they should ask, "What is it?" before a correction is given (but their response should not be reinforced). Rather we want them to use the "What is it" as a means of getting a correction that will lead to the eventual production of the correct response, which then is reinforced. Using the question becomes a means to getting correct answers that are reinforced. Thus, as soon as the student masters a "wh" objective, all corrections for instruction require them to ask for the answer. We are attempting to build the **conditioned establishing operations** for asking questions that is perhaps the basis of what some refer to as *curiosity* or the *need to know*. Children are less likely to ask questions if they do not receive generalized reinforcement or are punished for asking questions and obtaining answers that are used and not reinforced. Building the conditioned establishing operation for the need to know is a critical part of education, and a science of pedagogy suggests a way.

If the criterion is not achieved, then return to the "wh" instructional procedure described in Textbox 5.2 until the child meets the mastery criterion. Continue this until they meet the criterion on tacting or until a decision point is reached (see Chapter 2) that calls for a change in instructional procedures or revisiting the possibility that a prerequisite verbal development stage may need inducing. If the criterion is not achieved at the point where a decision is needed (Chapter 2), return to teaching a new set using the tandem sequence until the criterion is achieved for the new set. After the criterion is reached for the new set, return to the initial set and proceed as you did before. If the student does not meet the criterion by the time an instructional decision must be made, teach still another set using the tandem sequence. Continue doing this

TEXTBOX **5.2**

Teaching "Wh" Questions

1. For each question type (see Table 5.1), identify 100 unknown target stimuli (visual, tactile, olfactory, gustatory, and auditory stimuli) that are part of the student's educational standards. Questions should be learned in the following order: 1) What is it? 2) Who is it? 3) Where is it? and 4) How do I do it? Sample stimuli include shapes, colors, or categories of object. Create twenty sets of five stimuli to use for instruction and reserve some sets for probe sessions.

2. Use 20-trial sessions to conduct pre-instructional probes and record the accuracy of the following target responses for each stimulus. 1) tacting the picture within three seconds of seeing it, 2) asking, "What is it?" if the tact is not emitted, 3) echoing the name of the picture when it is given (wait a few seconds and give the name of the picture even if they do not ask "What is it?"), and 4) *naming* or emitting the tact when they see the picture again during the probe. The student does not need the program if they say, "What is it?" and emit a naming response for 90% of picture presentations.

3. Begin instruction by presenting one picture and waiting three seconds for the student to emit the target responses as described in Step 2. Each picture will be presented at least two times in a session (once to provide the tact and again to probe for the acquisition of the tact). **Correct Responses:** If the student tacts the picture the first time it is shown to them, then reinforce their response. If the student says, "What is it?" instead of tacting the picture, then you should tact it, but do not reinforce their response. **Incorrect Responses:** If the student does not tact the picture or say, "What is it?" the first time it is shown, you should say, "What is it?" and wait for them to echo you, after which you should provide the tact without reinforcing their response. **Consequences:** Only reinforce responses if the student acquires a tact after asking, "What is it?" or if they tact a picture without your echoic prompt.

4. Each time a tact is acquired, replace the picture with an unknown stimulus. Only independently emitted naming and "What is it?" responses should be recorded with a plus. When an echoic is used to prompt the student to say, "What is it?" or to provide a tact, record the response with a P for prompted (essentially an incorrect response). Graph responses as 20-learn unit sessions with an open circle for prompted responses and a closed circle for correct responses. Stop when the student emits tacts without using the question for 90% of two 20-learn unit sessions, or 100% for one session. Conduct probes on untrained sets as described in Step 2 to test for this repertoire.

5. The instructional sequence can be modified with 0-second time delay instead of using the echoic prompt as a correction. Also use these procedures to teach the following: 1) "Who is it?" 2) "Where is it?" and 3) How do I do it?

until the student meets the criterion for the initial set before a decision point. Once this is done, we want to ensure that the student can meet the probe criterion for the stimuli after receiving only one session of questions resulting in the answers. Remember to do this program across different senses other than vision alone (i.e., sounds such as bird calls, smells such as flowers, and tastes such as new foods, and textures). Introduce the extensions of the "I see" game described in subsequent sections. It may be best to do two or more "wh" programs at the same time (i.e., "What is it," "Where is it," and "Who is it"). In this way we can teach the child the contextual controls for the different words to use for different kinds of questions.

Where Is It?   Do similar programs with "Where is it," in which you hide an item such as a toy or edible reinforcer while the child is not looking, and then the student asks, "Where is it?" followed by your telling them where it is. Let them retrieve it and have the hidden toy, edible, or token. Conduct sets of items as we described for teaching the "What is it?" question. Remember to do this across different senses other than vision alone (i.e., sounds such as bird calls, smells such as flowers and tastes such as new foods, and textures). Reinforcement occurs for asking, "Where is it" and then finding the item as a result of asking.

Who Is It?   Use pictures of historical figures, cartoon characters the child does not know, other children in the school the student does not know, characters in storybooks the child does not know (e.g., Spot the Dog, Ziggy Zebra, and Debbie Dolphin). Next, conduct 20 probe trials for responses to new students or to adults entering the class. Teach missing responses by using the tact recruitment procedure to ask and obtain reinforcement for repeating who the person is (see Textbox 5.2). When an adult or another student that the child does not know enters the classroom, provide echoic prompts for them to ask, "Who is it?" until they ask the question without the prompt. The goal is for the child to ask, "Who is it?" whenever someone unknown enters the classroom or other setting. If the child has acquired or been taught conditioned

TABLE 5.1   Teaching Question-Asking

	Materials	Target Responses	Consequence
What is it?	Unknown pictures and objects	Independently asks question and then acquires tact from speaker's response	Tact response and generalized reinforcement
Who is it?	Pictures of unknown story characters and historical figures, unknown people	Independently asks question and acquires tact from speaker's response	Tact response and generalized reinforcement
Where is it?	Hidden preferred items	Independently asks question and locates item from speaker's response	Tact of location and receiving hidden item
How do I do it?	Computers, puzzles, and math problems	Independently asks question and then performs operation based on speaker's response	Instructions and manipulation of item

reinforcement for observing others as described in Chapter 3, then they will be more likely to look when people enter the classroom, and the natural conditioned establishing operation will be in place for motivating the "Who is it?" response.

How Do I Do It?   The computer may serve as a convenient device to teach the "How do I do it?" question. Take children to the computer and if they do not know how to start it or use a particular program, then prompt "How do I do it?" questions in 20-learn unit sessions until they always ask, "How do I do it?" before you provide instructions. This program may also be done in conjunction with teaching daily living skills such as dressing, preparing lunch, solving three-dimensional puzzles, doing novel math problems, and any circumstances that call for the question, "How do I do it?" While this may not lead to a tact as do some of the other questions, this question leads to asking the teacher to model or provide verbal instructions to which the student can respond as a listener. It has a recruitment function for obtaining spoken instructions or imitating a model, and is likely to serve a mand function. We include it here because the instructional protocol is similar to that used for learning to recruit new tacts.

Capability 3: Acquisition of new tacts incidentally via naming.   See Chapter 4 for the full naming protocol.

Capability 4: Learning tacts from observation or indirect contact with the contingencies received by others.   Learning tacts by observing the consequences received by others differs from the learning processes involved in the acquisition of tacts as a function of the naming capability. In naming, the reinforcement for the response is not observed; rather the emission of a naming response is likely tied to the effectiveness of gaining generalized reinforcement when the relevant establishing operations are in effect. At present, it does seem that observational learning does not require naming as a prerequisite (Greer & O'Sullivan, 2006). In one study we found that children acquired observational learning even when they did not have naming. Also we found that some children acquired naming as a result of being taught observational learning (Greer, Weigand, & Kracher, 2006). At present, it appears that observational learning of tacts from observing instruction received by others occurs before the naming capability. Regardless of the relation between the two, they are different. The procedures for inducing observational learning from indirect contact with the instruction received by others is described next.

Learning Tacts from Observation

When children have the capability of learning tacts from observing the instruction of others they acquire new tact operants as a result of watching others receive both reinforcement for correct responses and corrections for incorrect response. In effect, they learn new tacts by watching others receive learn units (see Greer, Keohane, Meincke, et al., 2004). This process involves the child observing the teacher-tutor-parent provide tact instruction to a peer in the form of learn units. In observational learning of the tact, the student observes the consequences received by another for responding to the teacher's tact instruction. As a result of that observation, the student tacts stimuli that were not previously in their repertoire, and they do so without direct contact with the learn unit. In other words, they learn new naming responses as a result of *indirect contact with a learn unit—one received by the observed peer.*

This type of observational learning should be differentiated from a related but separate repertoire in which a target student tacts items after observing a peer do so, but the observed tacts are already in the target student's repertoire. That is, the target student did not learn a new tact via observation, but emitted a previously acquired tact after seeing the contingencies under which their peer did or did not receive reinforcement. At present, our objective is the acquisition of new tact operants, obtained specifically by observing another student receive tract instruction. This is a true case of observational learning through which we are inducing a new verbal stage—the learning of tacts by observation of the consequences received by others. Once this is acquired, the child has new ways of acquiring tacts (Greer, Keohane, Meincke, Gaatreaux, Rivera-Valdes, Chauez-Brown, & Yuan, 2004).

Instructional Procedure for Teaching Observational Learning of Tacts (Developing Tacts by Observing Others Receive Learn Units)

Observational learning from contact with others who receive instruction is fundamental to children's success. It is a critical verbal capability—one that allows children to advance via indirect contact with learn units received by others (Greer, 1994b). In many mainstream settings, children receive infrequent numbers of direct learn units; thus observation is a key component in learning in mainstream settings. This capability is also key to the interventions we describe later in this chapter for developing social repertoires.

Once students master the basic observational tact repertoire, you may conduct instruction with two or more students in which each one is not only taught through separate instructional programs, but is also probed for correct responses derived from the other student's instruction. This is one way to prepare children for mainstream learning, and this capability may be key to successful inclusion. It may be useful to do the **yoked contingency** procedure (described later in this chapter) in this setting as an establishing operation for building this type of advanced listener learning. When children can learn from both direct learn units and observation of their peers' learn units, then we can conduct group instruction and exponentially expand both direct and observational learn units. Also, when teachers can conduct this procedure and maintain accurate data as well as present learn units and probe for observational learning—all the while keeping students engaged—they will have mastered the repertoire of providing group instruction with learn units that are entirely individualized.

Children who do not have full naming may also need to receive observational learning instruction for listener responses as well as tacts. If this capability is missing, separate interventions for inducing this capability may be needed. However, the protocol is the same, only the nature of the response differs.

Pre- and Post-Intervention Evaluation Probes for Observational Learning of Tacts

Before and after observational tact instruction, we test for the presence or absence of this capability. If the child does not have it, then it needs to be taught. Thus, evaluation probes are both tests for the presence of the observational learning capability before teaching, and assessments of the effectiveness of instruction. Select five different stimulus sets (five tact stimuli each) to teach the peer or observed student. These need to be stimuli that are part of the local educational standards and that neither student knows. Separately probe to ensure that neither student has the tacts to be taught by using 20-trial sessions for each set of stimuli (four response opportunities for each stimulus; no reinforcement or corrections for all five sets). Neither student should have the tact responses for these stimuli. Select students for dyads based on similarities in capabilities and repertoires. When you have the sets of stimuli that neither student has in her repertoire, you are ready to probe for observational learning.

Probe and instructional procedures to teach one set of stimuli.   For observational probe trials, reinforce the target observing student for attending to you and instruct her to watch what you and the peer do. To maintain attention, you may also need to insert opportunities to respond to known items for the target student. Tell the target student that the two of you are going to play a game, and that "I (the teacher) am going to teach your peer/friend to match, and I want to see if you (the target student) can learn the pictures by watching your friend." In the teaching procedure, present the four target stimuli to the peer in four successive learn units, which will probably result in corrections since they do not know the response; learning from observing corrections of inaccurate responses is a key component of the protocol. Next, present unreinforced and uncorrected probe trials to the target student for each stimulus that you taught the peer. After probe trials, return to four learn units for each stimulus with the peer, but change the order of presentation. Probe the target student again using four learn unit presentations. Continue alternating this teach and probe procedure until you have 20-learn units for the peer and 20-probe trials for the target student. Graph the learn units for the peer and the probe trials for the target student. If the target student has not acquired at least 80% correct responses on the probes, then he is a candidate for the instructional intervention using the yoked contingencies protocol described next.

Yoked-contingency Interventions

A special game board or token path is needed for this procedure (see Figure 5.3). The "game" involves a race to see which of two figures first attains the goal at the end of their path. Arrange a path with 20 steps. One path is for the teacher and is represented by a cartoon figure such as the Incredible Hulk that is affixed with Velcro to one game board path. The two "yoked" children select another hero (i.e., Spiderman, Superman, or Shrek) and affix it to their path. They also choose a preferred toy, activity, or edible; replicas of their selection are placed at the end of both paths. This serves as an establishing operation to enhance the reinforcing effectiveness of listening.

Once the game board is in place, begin the intervention with non-probe sets of stimuli (i.e., Sets 3 and 4). Seat students next to each other and present the peer with a learn unit for one of the four target stimuli; contingently praise or correct the peer's response. Immediately probe the target student for their response to the same stimulus. If they respond correctly, praise both children and tell them to move their figure up the path; alternately allow each student to move the figure. For example say, "Mary, it's your turn." If the target student responds incorrectly to the target stimulus, say, "The (teacher's figure) gets to move up the path," and do a bit of gloating. Continue these learn unit and probe trial rotations until either you (the teacher) or the team (the yoked children) wins (20 total probe trials). Present at least one other set the same way. If the students master the game quickly, present several sets of stimuli so that the target student will have enough exemplar exposures to the yoked procedure to increase the probability that the observational repertoire has emerged.

Probe the students on the post-intervention probe stimuli using the same procedures that were used in the pre-intervention probe. That is, teach four learn units to the peer, and then probe for the target student's responses to all four stimuli. If the target student emits 80% or higher on probe trials, then the criterion is achieved; if not, conduct two mores sets with the yoked-contingency protocol, then re-probe the post-intervention stimuli. If progress is being achieved, but the criterion is not met, teach other sets until criterion is achieved. If there is not sufficient progress (see Chapter 2 for guidelines to determine this), then use the alternative joint-yoked contingency and monitoring procedure described next.

RESEARCH BOX 5.1

Observational Learning and Textual Responding

Four school-age children diagnosed with autism were each yoked with a peer model. Points during a game were only earned when the target student emitted a correct response to a stimulus previously taught to the model. Results showed that the yoked contingencies established observational learning in all participants. Findings suggested that for some children, the capacity to learn from observation must be taught. See also Greer, Singer-Dudek, & Gautreaux (2006), Deguchi (1984), Stolfi (2005), Gautreaux (2005).

From Davies-Lackey, A. (2005). *Yoked peer contingencies and the acquisition of observational learning repertoires*. (Doctoral dissertation, Columbia University, 2005). Abstract from UMI Proquest Digital Dissertations [on-line]. Dissertations Abstracts Item: AAT 3159730.

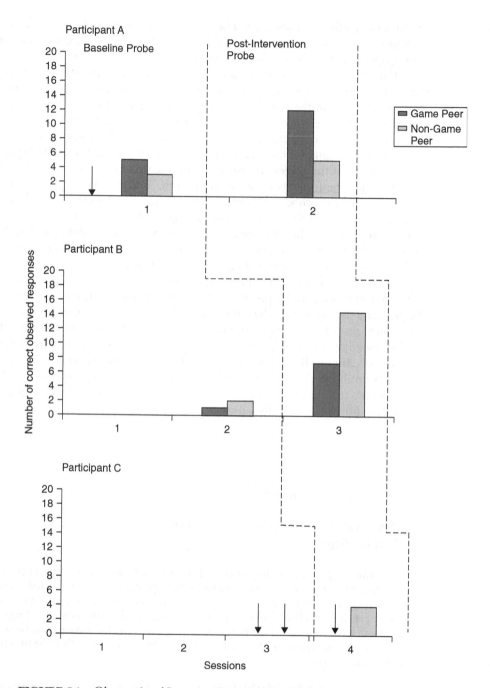

FIGURE 5.1   Observational Learning Pre- and Post-Probes I

From Davies-Lackey, A. (2005). *Yoked peer contingencies and the acquisition of observational learning repertoires.* (Doctoral dissertation, Columbia University, 2005). Abstract from UMI Proquest Digital Dissertations [on-line]. Dissertations Abstracts Item: AAT 3159730.

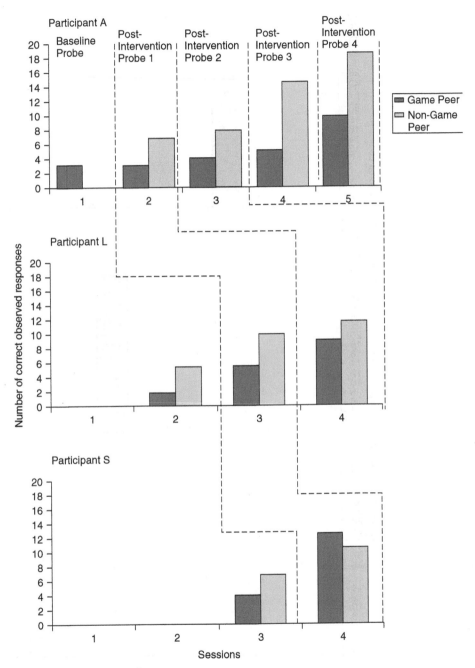

FIGURE 5.1   *(continued)*

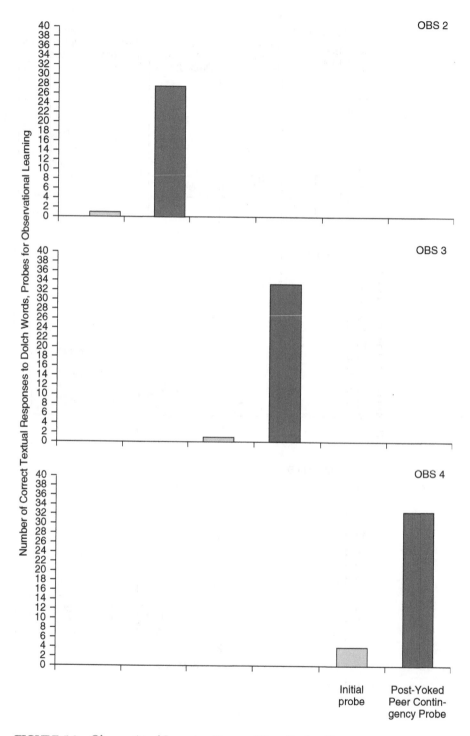

FIGURE 5.2 Observational Learning Pre- and Post-Probes II

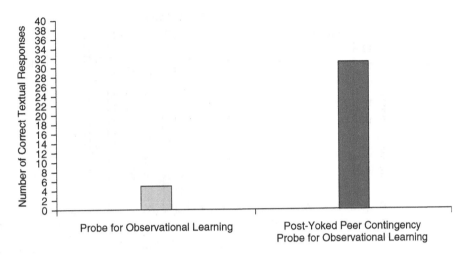

FIGURE 5.2 (*continued*)

Joint Yoked-Contingency and Peer-Monitoring Protocol

This involves both the yoked-contingency game and peer monitoring during which the target student records the peer's responses. If the target student is not a fluent writer, they can use red cubes to indicate that their peer has made an incorrect response and green cubes to indicate a correct response (you may use other substitutes). If the student writes reasonably well, have them mark a plus (+) for a correct response or a minus (−) for an incorrect response on a suitable form that is observable by both students (i.e., a white board or a data collection form). After the peer receives a learn unit, the target student must indicate whether the response was incorrect or correct by recording the data. To move up the path, the target student must accurately

---

RESEARCH BOX **5.2**

Monitoring to Establish Observational Learning

In two experiments, this study tested the effects of a joint yoked-contingency and peer monitoring tactic on the acquisition of untaught tact and textual responses for 5- and 6-year-old students diagnosed with developmental disabilities. Results showed that participants gained observational learning responses to untaught stimuli after learning to monitor their peers' correct and incorrect responses.

From Pereira-Delgado, J. (2005). *Effects of teaching peer-monitoring on the acquisition of observational learning.* (Doctoral dissertation, Columbia University, 2005). Abstract from UMI Proquest Digital Dissertations [on-line]. Dissertations Abstracts Item: AAT 3174775.

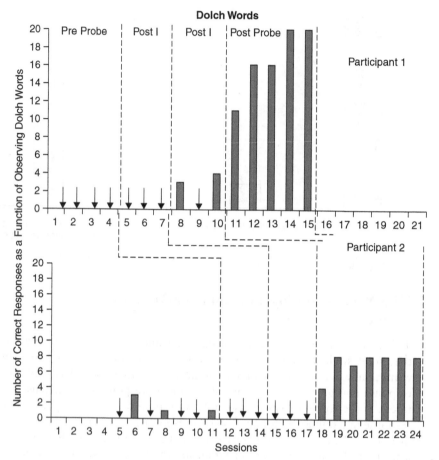

FIGURE 5.3   Monitoring to Establish Observational Learning

From Pereira-Delgado, J. (2005). *Effects of teaching peer-monitoring on the acquisition of observational learning.* (Doctoral dissertation, Columbia University, 2005). Abstract from UMI Proquest Digital Dissertations [on-line]. Dissertations Abstracts Item: AAT 3174775.

monitor their peer's response and also emit the correct response. If that happens, the students advance their figure; if not, the teacher advances her character.

Teach two consecutive sets in which the team or yoked pair wins. This may require teaching several sets to the yoked pair. After they win, return to another Set 1 stimulus probe as described earlier. If the repertoire has still not emerged, a new analysis of the source of the problem needs to be done using the procedures outlined in Chapters 2 and 7. Ensure that all learn unit components or another related tactic are in place, and review the sub-component verbal capabilities of the student. That is, consider that there may be deficits in prerequisite verbal development repertoires (see Chapters 3 and 4).

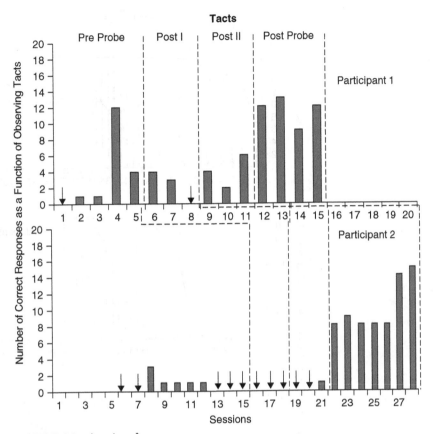

FIGURE 5.3   (*continued*)

As students acquire observational learning repertoires for the tact responses of their peers, they need to be assessed and possibly instructed on other types of observational repertoires, including textual responses such as copying and reading; tacts for smells, tastes, and listening; and writing responses for their tacts. Use the same procedures described here to develop observational learning capabilities for these other repertoires; probe for their presence first so that you have reliable information. If these capabilities are missing, they must be induced or they may very likely lead to problems with more advanced verbal capabilities such as reading comprehension or learning from lectures.

Intraverbal Capabilities and Social Interaction

In his original theory, B. F. Skinner (1957) distinguished between verbal operants that are controlled by verbal antecedents and have point-to-point correspondence with their controlling stimulus (echoics), and verbal operants that are controlled by verbal

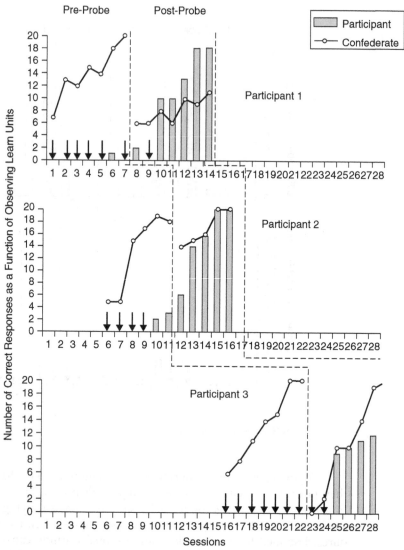

FIGURE 5.3   (*continued*)

antecedents but *do not have* point-to-point correspondence with their controlling stimulus. The latter verbal operant is an intraverbal and is the focus of the current section of this chapter. In Chapter 4, procedures to teach basic intraverbals through multiple exemplar instruction—called impure tacts—were described. Impure tacts are intraverbal responses under multiple control of both a physical and a verbal antecedent stimulus. In those descriptions, speaker responses to multiple control tacts were limited to a single response (i.e., a speaker asks, "What color is this?" and a listener says, "It's red.").

> **TEXTBOX 5.3**
>
> **Making the Yoked-Contingency Game Board**
>
> Create the game board for yoked-peer contingencies by making 20 spaces for game pieces in a column for you and in a column for the pair of students. Use a cartoon figure such as the Incredible Hulk to represent you and let the children select a hero such as Shrek or Spiderman to represent them. Figures should be placed at the beginning of each path. Place a picture of a preferred reinforcer at the end of each path. Move the students' game piece up one space whenever the target student responds correctly. Move your game piece up one space whenever the target student responds incorrectly.
>
> For the monitoring procedure, use the same game board, but the student must indicate the accuracy of their peer's responses and emit the correct tact in order to move the game piece. If the target student can write fluently, give them a data collection form or a dry erase board where they can record correct responses with pluses and incorrect responses with minuses. If they cannot write fluently, give them two cups and a pile of red cubes and green cubes. They should drop red cubes into a cup for incorrect responses and green cubes into a cup for correct responses.

In this portion of the chapter, we discuss advanced intraverbals. Unlike the **sequelics** or intraverbals discussed in Chapter 4, advanced intraverbal capabilities provide for much more than single-word or brief responses to a listener. By engaging children in more complex intraverbals, their senses are extended through the spoken words of others; thus they can vicariously experience what others tell them. Complex intraverbals allow them to learn about the weather, who the new person is on the block, what's for dinner, the latest information about others, and even the experiences that others are having. These experiences also provide the means for empathy for others and for taking the perspective of others. There are several advanced intraverbal repertoires; each is briefly described in the next section.

Through **self-talk** intraverbal capabilities, children can engage in speaker-as-own-listener behavior during which they emit both speaker and listener responses to themselves. This capability is a developmental stage for typically-developing children that must be induced when it is missing because it may affect more advanced developmental stages such as "thinking." The **listener reinforcement component of social exchanges** is another intraverbal function that allows children to extend their experiences through the verbal responses of others. The **deictic** function allows children to engage in perspective taking during intraverbals. The **conversational unit** allows children to become truly social as they function as both speakers and listeners during intraverbal exchanges.

Each protocol described in this section was designed to develop intraverbal capabilities when children with language delays participating in our research and school programs lacked them. In cases where the protocols described here do not result in intraverbal capabilities (i.e., faulty intraverbals including vocal forms of stereotypy such as echolalia and palilalia), teaching procedures to correct faulty verbal responses

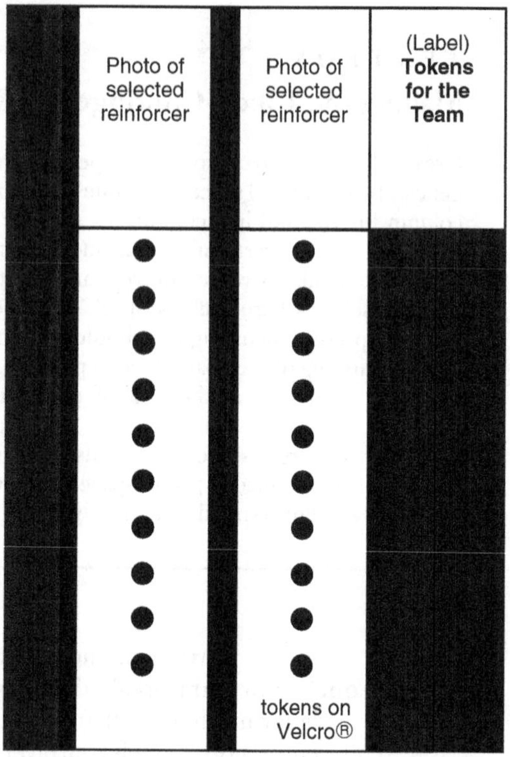

FIGURE 5.4   Yoked-contingency Game Board

From Davies-Lackey, A. (2005). *Yoked peer contingencies and the acquisition of observational learning repertoires.* (Doctoral dissertation, Columbia University, 2005). Abstract from UMI Proquest Digital Dissertations [on-line]. Dissertations Abstracts Item: AAT 3159730.

are presented. However, this section describes protocols to teach the following intraverbal capacities when children do not have faulty intraverbals. Later we describe how to correct the faulty intraverbal. For now we describe the protocols for inducing or expanding

1. Conversational units (capability 6)
2. Self-talk (capability 5)
3. Listener reinforcement for social exchanges (capability 7)
4. Deictic functions (capability 7)
5. Functional responses to replace faulty intraverbals (capability 6)

Conversational Units

Knowing the form and function of conversational units is an important first step when teaching advanced intraverbal responding. **Conversational units** are social exchanges during which two individuals rotate both speaker and listener functions. The presence or absence of conversational units is one of the most critical early indications of truly social behavior. Individuals emit conversational units because of the reinforcement

TEXTBOX **5.4**

Yoked-contingency Protocol

1. Select 20 stimuli (pictures or objects) from local educational standards that neither the target student nor the peer can select by pointing or tacting. Check for their point and tact responses by conducting 20-trial probe sessions during which they do the following after receiving match learn units ("Match [item] to [item]): 1) point to the item and 2) tact the item. If they can tact and point to the stimuli, choose new, unknown items. Arrange materials into sets of four stimuli (20 total stimuli), reserving some sets for probes.
2. Choose one set for a pre-instructional probe. Place the target student next to the peer student. Tell the target student, "We're going to play a game. I am going to teach your friend to match, and I want to see if you can learn the pictures by watching them." Begin by presenting a match learn unit to the peer. Repeat for all four stimuli in the set. Next, present unreinforced and uncorrected probe trials on matching for the same stimulus set to the target student.
3. Repeat the above by presenting the same stimuli in a different order. Continue until there are 20 learn units for the peer and 20 probe trials for the target student. If the target student has less than 80% (16/20) correct responding, then they should receive instruction on observational naming.
4. Before beginning the yoked-contingency procedure, setup the game board (see Textbox 5.3). Explain that if the target student answers correctly, then they can move their game piece; however, if they do not answer correctly, then you, the teacher, can move your game piece. Present the peer with a tact learn unit and contingently reinforce or correct their response. Immediately probe the target student for the tact response. Students may confer independently to help the target student respond. For example, the target student may ask the peer for the answer, if needed. This has helped to induce observational learning. If they respond correctly, let the students move their game piece up one space on the board. If they respond incorrectly, move your game piece up one space and do a bit of gloating. Continue until either you or the students win the game.
5. Present at least one more set even if the student has mastered the sequence because multiple opportunities to engage in observational learning will increase the likelihood that the repertoire emerges. When the target student is emitting responses at the mastery criterion, conduct probes again as in Step 2 using the same stimulus set.
6. Yoked-Contingency Game and Monitoring: Use the yoked-contingency procedure, but to move up the game board, the target student must indicate if the peer's response to the learn unit was incorrect or correct and then emit the correct tact. Continue until the team wins two consecutive games. Conduct post-instructional probes as in Step 5.
7. Repeat for the observation of writing responses, textual responding, and sensory responses.

obtained as both a speaker and a listener. The capacity to be reinforced as a listener is key. For example, a **sequelic** (an intraverbal between individuals) occurs when a speaker says something to a listener and is reinforced by the listener's verbal response. However, if the individual is not reinforced by what others have to say, the exchange often stops at the sequelic. A conversational unit, on the other hand, requires that the first speaker continues the interaction by seeking another verbal response. That is, the response interaction goes beyond the initial sequelic and includes the rotation of speaker and listener responding between two or more individuals. In short, the individual is not only reinforced as a speaker by the mediation of the listener, but, in turn, emits the responses that lead to obtaining reinforcement from listening. When the repertoire of social listening is absent, we need to structure teaching interactions so that the individual can acquire the reinforcing effects of listening. That is, the various types of reinforcement obtained from listening need to be taught just as we find it necessary to teach the basic effects of speaking for some of our children. Figure 5.5 illustrates a conversational unit.

As both tacts and the joint-reinforcing functions of acting as a speaker and listener with others expand exponentially, we need to examine the role of setting events with respect to conversational units. Audience control, listener reinforcement, and speaker reinforcement are all important in the acquisition of conversational units. In addition, the establishing operations associated with carrying on conversations are important. In settings in which the teacher is the primary source of reinforcement, real conversational units are less likely to occur because teachers serve as "translators" for intraverbals for the children they are teaching (Donley & Greer, 1993). For example,

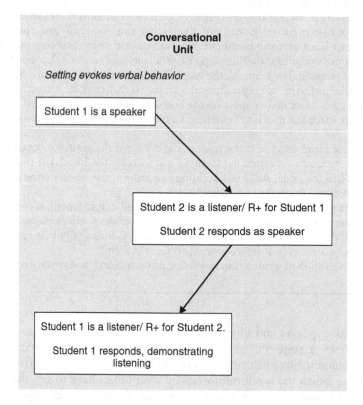

FIGURE 5.5   A Conversational Unit

when an adult or child says, "Hi" to a student and the child does not respond, the teacher typically prompts a response. The child cannot learn the relevant audience control when the teacher does this, the child must come under the control of the person saying, "Hi." Research Box 5.3 shows the research identifying the importance of establishing operations for producing the "need to talk and listen to others." In the study, children who did not engage in conversational units began to do so when the relevant establishing operations were put in place.

RESEARCH BOX 5.3

Conversational Units with Others

This study compared the number of conversational units emitted between adolescents when a teacher was present and when a teacher was absent. Participants were four adolescents with developmental disabilities who emitted conversational units with adults but not with their peers. Results showed that the adolescents emitted more conversational units when the teacher was absent than when she was present. Findings showed that a listening audience can be manipulated as an establishing operation to increase or decrease initiations and responses to conversational units.

From Donley, C., & Greer, R. D. (1993). Setting events controlling social verbal exchanges between students with developmental delays. *Journal of Behavioral Education, 3*, 387–401.

Capability 5: Learning intraverbal functions of self-talk. Self-talk, or the phenomenon of children talking to themselves when engaged in solitary play, is widely acknowledged as a key stage for typically-developing young children (Novak & Pelaez, 2004). While students may be able to emit both mand and tact functions, the more critical function occurs when they can engage in both speaker and listener roles. Speaking aloud to oneself as a child comes under audience control as children mature, and the self-talk "goes underground" (i.e., we stop speaking aloud and "think" instead). However, young children speak aloud and the function is observable, just as beginning readers read aloud, even when they are reading alone. As adults, we talk to ourselves when alone or around people with whom we are close, but we do not speak aloud in most social situations. We talk to ourselves, so to speak, when we think (as in considering alternatives or editing something we write). However, we do so such that it is not audible to others and we do so without involving the vocal apparatus. As adults, we talk aloud to our pets, infants, and even to our computers in certain situations. The presence or absence of certain audiences occasions whether speaker-as-own listener behavior is (or is not) audible to another. At the same time, some children may not acquire that kind of audience control, so they continue to speak aloud. In fact some instances of "palilalia," or repeating one's own sounds, are cases in point. Some individuals with certain developmental disabilities engage in self-talk without respect to the audience that is present. The role of audience control is relevant to most or all instances of self-talk,

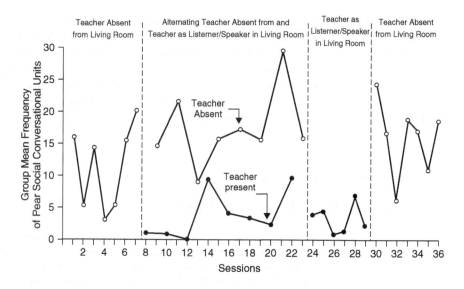

FIGURE 5.6   Establishing Operations for Conversational Units

From Donley, C., & Greer, R. D. (1993). Setting events controlling social verbal exchanges between students with developmental delays. *Journal of Behavioral Education*, *3*, 387–401.

even when we talk to ourselves covertly and respond covertly as a listener. We will address the palilalia issue in the section on repairing faulty vocal verbal behavior.

Children who can engage in conversational units with others are likely to already emit conversational units during self-play. The procedure that we later describe to teach speaker-listener exchanges with others is probably the foundation for occasioning the speaker-as-own listener function. We also build on this function at more advanced stages when we teach individuals to follow the verbal stimuli characterized as algorithms in doing math, following scientific procedures, or simply preparing a recipe. At this point, verbal stimuli take the form of print stimuli that guide verbal and non-verbal behavior. We also construct and then follow our own algorithms in solving problems. Thus, occasioning basic speaker-as-own-listener behavior in early forms of self-talk is a likely necessary stage of development for thinking.

One way to test for the presence or absence of this repertoire is to observe children in free-play areas of the classroom, preferably under solitary play conditions. With preschoolers this is easily detectable because it is rather a common occurrence. With children with language delays, we probe for such incidences as we teach them to engage in conversational units with others. Arranging for the free-play area to have objects that are anthropomorphic in character or figures of popular television or storybooks can create the necessary establishing operations for self-talk as described in the Lodhi and Greer (1989) study (Research Box 5.4). A single unit of self-talk occurs for instance, when a student who is playing with a doll says, "Do you want to play outside? Yes, I want to play outside. Ok, let's go," thus functioning as both a speaker and a listener. During probes, this repertoire is present if the student emits three or more self-talk conversational units during a single 10-minute session.

In some of our work we have induced self-talk conversational units using puppets. In this procedure the teacher has two anthropomorphic (human-like) toys such as puppets or figures. She models conversational units between puppets, and then gives the puppets to a child, thus setting the occasion for the exchange. If the child imitates the conversational unit, the response is not reinforced; rather, children must emit an exchange that differs in some way from that of the teacher. Like generalized imitation, we are trying to establish a generalized self-talk exchange. This instruction may be arranged formally into sessions of 20-learn units where a child's accurate and varied exchanges are recorded as a plus. If a child begins to emit more than one speaker-as-own-listener exchange, wait until the exchanges stop before reinforcing and recording them. If the speaker-as-own-listener exchanges do not occur naturally, the next step is to perform a model of two conversational exchanges followed by the student imitating them for 90% or better across two sessions or 100% for one session. The objective of this program is met when probes of free play show that the child is engaging in self-talk during solitary play.

Computer games may also be used to teach self-talk. Use DVDs or videotapes of preferred cartoons (see Charlop-Christy, Le, & Freeman, 2000). First, stop the tape or disk and prompt tacts of the figures and the actions that they engage in. If necessary, present the tacts in echoic-to-tact fashion (see Chapter 4) until students tact independently without your prompt (a true tact). Next, ask the students to use several tacts of the actions (e.g., describing who did what to whom) until these are also independent tact sequences. Develop new story lines with the figures until the child uses novel story lines. These are reinforced in the same manner as in the puppet scenario, that is, reinforce novel story lines only. As in the self-talk probes with puppets, self-talk conversational units in the free-play area determine whether the child has mastered the objective.

Capability 6: Acquisition of conversational units and related speaker-listener exchanges. Self-talk is a kind of conversational unit, but it is not a truly social exchange because it only involves one person. Although self-talk is an important prerequisite for "thinking," self-editing, and other complex verbal behavior, individuals are not truly social until they can engage in conversational units with others. That is, social behavior occurs when speaker-listener exchanges become social as children have verbal exchanges with others because they are interested in or reinforced by the other person's response. When individuals acquire the **listener reinforcement component of social exchanges** or the capacity to be reinforced by the verbal responses of others, they can engage in conversational units with others.

Social reinforcement verbal behavior is driven by listener behavior or developing a child's interest in what others have to say. This capacity to be reinforced by the speech of others is often missing in children with certain disability labels. Even after such children are proficient speakers and perform at the academic level of their typically-developing peers, the social component of the listener repertoire may be missing in many areas. When this deficit is treated with frequent learn units to teach students to greet others and to make eye contact, the repertoire remains under the control of

TEXTBOX **5.5**

Description of a Self-talk Conversational Unit

A self-talk conversational exchange or unit consists of one puppet responding as a speaker to another puppet. Puppet One (a speaker) speaks to Puppet Two (a listener-speaker) who responds to Puppet One by acting or speaking and then Puppet One responds as a listener. This constitutes a single conversational unit. Each puppet has responded as both a speaker and a listener.

the teacher who functions as a kind of "translator," never allowing the student to really acquire the reinforcement effect of being a listener in which they have contact with various sensory stimuli made possible by a speaker (e.g., a speaker says it's raining outside and the listener benefits by this information).

Several studies and protocols have been developed for teaching children to use scripts as a way to develop conversational skills. However, children do not learn the essential natural controls for verbal episodes with others unless the social control of being reinforced as a listener is acquired. When scripts are used the student essentially functions as a speaker or a listener in sequelic exchanges initiated by the teacher. Thus, emitting relevant questions to obtain reinforcement from listening to others is explicitly taught, while social listener reinforcement is not. In fact, unless children learn the

RESEARCH BOX **5.4**

Self-talk or Speaker-as-Own-Listener Conversational Units

The number of self-talk conversational units emitted by four typically-developing five-year-olds was observed under anthropomorphic and non-anthropomorphic toy conditions. Results showed that children emitted more conversational units with anthropomorphic toys. The closed circle represents the anthropomorphic condition and the open circle the play setting with non-anthropomorphic toys. The study also indicated that the children emitted all of the basic verbal operants identified by Skinner (1957). This study indicated that children engage in conversational units when alone in which they function as both speaker and listener, showing one of the functions of self-talk. Anthropomorphic toys acted as an establishing operation for speaker-as-own-listener exchanges.

From Lodhi, S., & Greer, R. D. (1989). The speaker as listener. *Journal of the Experimental Analysis of Behavior, 51*, 353–359.

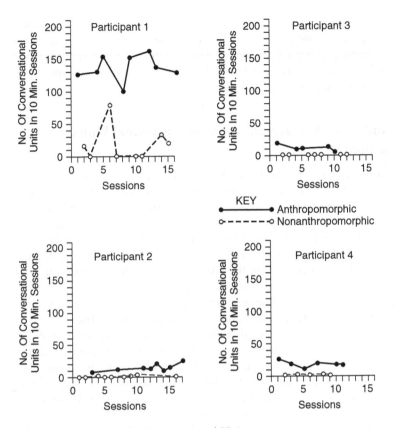

FIGURE 5.7   Self-talk Conversational Units

From Lodhi, S., & Greer, R. D. (1989). The speaker as listener. *Journal of the Experimental Analysis of Behavior, 51*, 353–359.

social reinforcement outcomes of listening incidentally, they have not traditionally received explicit instruction in listener reinforcement. The following protocols, based on the recent research on observational learning we have just described, are designed to induce this capability.

In this section, we describe six games that are designed to increase students' observational learning from a peer. These games increase students' listener capabilities by providing establishing operations for them to function as a listener within a group of two or more students in order to earn points for themselves and for their team. The games are interventions to help students master the long-term objectives for conversational units and for observational learning, specifically: 1) during a post-instructional 10-minute play session with a peer, the student will emit more conversational units (without emitting disapprovals) than during a pre-instructional 10-minute play session; and 2) after observing a peer receive learn units on multiple control responses to target stimuli such as pictures or words, the student will emit 18/20 correct responses to the same target stimuli. The six games include 1) basic peer-yoked contingencies, 2) peer-tutoring with the game board, 3) I spy/20 questions, 4) 20 questions-tacts and textual responding, 5) bingo, and 6) group instruction with the board. Another activity, teaching empathy, is included as well.

Pre- and Post-Assessment for Conversational Units and Sequelics

We begin to teach conversational units by probing for the presence of conversational units and sequelics in a student's repertoire. First, we assess the degree to which the listener function is present in social discourse. Before and after students achieve a criterion on each of these listener reinforcement programs, observe pairs of students in settings with the relevant establishing operations for conversational units. This requires arranging an environment in which competing stimuli eliminate the "need to communicate." This may mean that you need to set up a situation in which only the children can provide a source of reinforcement.

We assess the social conversational repertoire and the presence or absence of reinforcement for listening by conducting probe sessions that are 5-10 minutes in duration. The length of the sessions needs to be standard or constant so that if you probe before instruction for two or three sessions using 5-minute intervals, then you should do the same after instruction to test the effects of instruction on acquisition. The setting for the pre- and post-probes needs to be the same—typically a natural setting for social exchange such as a play area or a waiting area. In some cases you may even do so in settings such as a playground or free-play area.

During the probe sessions, collect data on the frequency or number of occurrences of:

1. Sequelics (speaker and listener exchanges that do not involve rotation of speaker and listener exchanges between the child and other children)
2. Conversational units
3. "Wh" questions
4. Vocal approvals
5. Vocal disapprovals

When games are the independent variable or intervention, record any of the above responses when they occur in the games themselves.

For at least 25% of sessions, an individual with expertise in the science of behavior should conduct observations (in our system, individuals with CABAS® rank; Greer, 2002) using the Teacher Performance Rate and Accuracy (TPRA) Scale as described in Chapter 2 (also see Ross, Singer-Dudek, & Greer, 2005) to obtain response reliability. As in all instruction, plot the data immediately after the sessions. Use the standard decision protocol and any related tactics from Greer (2002) as outlined in Chapter 2 to help the children obtain the criterion on the programs—be careful to label all interventions. Students who are not interested in what others have to say and students with few or no conversational units are candidates for the procedure.

Acquiring the Listener Reinforcement Component of Social Exchanges

General Game Board Description and Set-up

To enhance their reinforcement function, the game boards in this section should only be used for games described herein. The board has two vertical or horizontal paths comprised of several squares with the number two written on each square to indicate points: One path is for the team and one path is for the teacher. There are pictures of treats or preferred activities at the end of each path (use Velcro squares so that the items may be changed). The team's game piece should be a superhero (i.e., Spiderman or Shrek), and the teacher's game piece should be a villain (i.e., the Joker or the Big Bad Wolf). When the team responds correctly, their game piece moves up the path one square and points are awarded. When the team responds incorrectly, then the teacher's game piece moves up the path one square and she receives the points. The game continues until either the teacher's or the team's game piece reaches the end of the path and obtains the treat as the winner. The teacher presents 20 questions that consist of a response opportunity during which a target student (one rotating member of the team) is asked to answer by conferring with a peer. Each member of the team is a target student with their own short-term objectives related to making the response of listening a discriminative source of reinforcement for themselves and eventually for the pair.

Part 1: I spy/20 questions.   Two students are seated next to each other facing the teacher and one student's eyes are covered with a mask (i.e., a Batman mask or that of another action figure). The teacher begins the game by saying, "I spy _____" and then describing an object, staff member, or peer to students ("I spy a tall man with a beard and a tie."). The masked student has a brief opportunity to give the correct response, but if they cannot (we do not want them to be able to supply the answer), then they should ask their peer for the response. If the answer is correct, the team moves up one square on the game board, the teacher reinforces the team's response with praise, and says, "Yeah! Spiderman gets two points." If the answer is incorrect, then the teacher gives a correction consistent with the learn unit to both students, receives the points, and says, "The (character on the game piece) has two points." Avoid scripting questions for the students; instead use time delays to create motivational conditions until the reinforcement conditions of the game take over.

Part 2: 20 Questions: Tact and textual response.   Each stimulus set for this game contains four pictures and their four corresponding printed words (eight total stimuli); each set is used for a single program. Create five sets of four pictures and their printed words; these might include rare animals, flowers or leaves, gemstones, animal breeds, and scientific or social studies curricular materials associated with the child's educa-

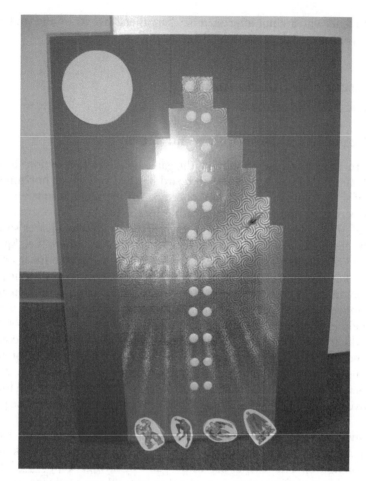

FIGURE 5.8   Game Board Used in Yoked-Peer Contingency

Stolfi, L. (2005). *The induction of observational learning repertoires in preschool children with developmental disabilities as a function of peer-yoked contingencies.* (Doctoral dissertation, Columbia University, 2005). Abstract from: UMI Proquest Digital Dissertations [on-line]. Dissertations Abstracts Item: AAT 3174899.

tional standards. First, probe students' tacts of target pictures and their textual responses to printed words. Next, teach responses to two words from each set; students should not know the name of the picture associated with the words. For example, from a set of four flowers, select two that students cannot identify and teach them to each student (e.g., rose or tulip). These responses will be used later when responding to pictures. For each presentation of a stimulus, rotate the students' roles such that one student is the observer-target student, and then the other student serves as the observer/target student.

The teacher shows one unknown picture (i.e., a rose) to both students, and asks the target student, "What's this?" The target student, who does not know the name of the picture, should ask the peer for help. The teacher should then show the peer the corresponding printed word (i.e., the word *rose*), allow the peer to read it, and again ask the target student, "What's this?" The target student should listen to the peer for the response, after which they should be able to correctly answer the teacher's question. If the target student repeats the peer's correct textual response, then the team's game piece moves up a square and they win points. If the target student does not repeat the peer's correct textual response, then the teacher's game piece moves up one square. As the target student begins to emit the correct response without conferring with the peer, then the team's game pieces move forward, even though the peer was not asked for the answer. When this happens, record the correct response as **+O** (code for an observational learning correct response) on the data collection form. The game continues until the team or teacher wins. Each student's responses as an observer are blocked into 20 response opportunities for graphing and data analysis purposes (i.e., cumulative number of correct responses as an observer). When all of the words for a set are correct during 20 successive response opportunities, then the word set is mastered and the team moves on to the next set. When all of the sets are mastered, individually probe the students on each of the words and pictures to test for observational learning. Additionally, graph cumulative correct responses learned through observation on a separate graph to divide observational learning responses from those governed by functioning as a listener only. Probe for the number of conversational units gained as a function of the intervention. The graphs of observational learning provide us with information on the child's observational learning skills as well as our target conversational units.

Part 3: Bingo. Before each game session, the students chose pictures of reinforcers to place at the top of the game board. During Bingo one student has a bagfull of the Bingo pieces (pictures and letters) and the other student has a Bingo board. The student with the bag pulls out one game piece and tacts the chosen game piece aloud to the other student. The student who has the game board is required to listen and then to respond vocally with either, "Yes, I have (the game piece)," or "No, I don't have (the game piece)." If they do have the game piece, they place a Bingo chip on their game board over the matching picture or letter. The children rotate roles of speaker (in control of the bag of game pieces) and listener (playing the Bingo game board) during the game. If the listener responds correctly (e.g., "Yes" or "No"), the students' character moves up on the yoked-contingency game board. If the listener responds incorrectly (e.g., their answer differs from their game pieces), the teacher's character moves up on the yoked-contingency game board. The team to reach the top of the game board first has access to the reinforcer. During the game, the teacher slightly teases the students, saying that she will reach the top and get the reinforcer first, or that she is catching up to them. If a team reaches the top of the game board before a 20-learn unit session is complete, the reinforcers are delivered and the game is played again later. Data are collected for each student separately as a listener. Bingo continues until each student meets criterion as a listener during the game. Criterion is set at 90% or higher correct responses of 2 consecutive 20 learn unit sessions or 100% mastery of the first 20 learn unit session.

Part 4: Peer tutoring with the game board.   Following mastery of these sets, use the game board so that two peers can teach each other textual responses during alternating tutor/tutee roles, a tactic similar to Classwide Peer Tutoring (Greenwood, 1999). Each student uses a set of five words that they previously mastered; these words will be presented four times each during a 20-learn unit peer-tutoring session. Tutor and tutee roles should alternate between students so that each tutee has a 20-learn unit session. Student 1 tutors Student 2 on one word by saying, "Read the word," or simply by pointing to the word in the book or printed page. Student 2 has three seconds, or initially longer, to respond. The tutor reinforces correct responses with praise and with the team's earned points; the tutor corrects incorrect responses as a teacher does when presenting learn units, and the teacher's game piece moves.

The teacher's game board path has twice as many squares as that of the pupils' because the learn unit is rotated across two students. The game is over when the teacher or team wins. When both students obtain 100% correct responding on blocked 20-learn unit sessions, they have obtained criterion and they move on to a new set of words. Other academic tasks such as math problems may be used at this point if possible. The students must present learn units without the teacher's assistance.

Some students will first need to master the monitoring program for observational learning (described earlier in this chapter) if they cannot tutor accurately. Once students master the tutoring repertoire, it should become a standard part of classrooms for readers and writers where they teach each other spelling, math facts, textual responses, and new tacts. Of course, the game board is faded as natural reinforcement accrues for the students and as the tutors dispense tokens to one another contingent on correct responses without the game board. Classrooms for readers and writers need to have peer tutoring as the major means of delivering high numbers of learn units to children while the teacher observes and conducts the probes for mastery.

Part 5: Group instruction with the game board.   This program is supplemental to the other observational learning games, and should be used only to teach the long-term objective of criterion-level responding in a group, and not the basic observational learning repertoire. Individually probe students in a group or class on words targeted for the game. Next, divide the group into two teams; assign each team to a game board path with a Velcro picture of a preferred reinforcer that the team can win at the end of each path. Then ask Team 1 a question such as "What's this word?" The team talks it over, and then gives the teacher the answer. The team must confer; if someone shouts the answer before the team decides on it, then the other team wins a point. Team 2 then gets a chance to respond. The opportunities rotate from Team 1 to Team 2 until the first team to reach the end of their path wins the game and receives their reinforcers. Probe each team member again on words taught during the game. If the students respond correctly to questions asked of the other team, then record a **+O** for observational learning. The response card tactic for written responses may be used with this protocol (see Heward, 1994).

Part 6: Teaching empathy ("What can you do to help?" program).   In some literature this repertoire is part of what is referred to as having a *theory of mind*. The goal of our program is to teach the student to empathize with someone else. Use reinforcers that are relevant for the particular child. The program does not require the pre- and post-instructional probes of conversational units. You need pictures or video clips of people in need of help such as someone who has lost a favorite toy or an item of clothing, or perhaps a lost dog wearing a nametag with the owner's name on it. Other scenarios include a parent or another child who have a slight injury or cold, are afraid to sleep in their room alone, forgot their lunch, are in a wheelchair and need to be pushed to the library, are having difficulty learning, would like to play with a toy that the target student has, or would like a taste of the target student's treat.

Group these into five scenarios that are presented four times each in a 20-learn unit program. You may add other scenarios that are specific to your particular setting. When natural situations occur, capture them as learn unit opportunities and record students' responses with descriptions on your data collection form. Also, probe the students' responses to the scenarios before teaching. If they can answer the questions without training, they have the repertoire; if not, they are candidates and the probes serve as baseline data.

The long-term objective for this program is for the student to specify (a) that the person in the visual display is in distress and (b) what they might do to help. Have the student use relevant levels of verbal behavior that they have mastered in responding. For example, the student says, "The boy has lost his dog and is worried and sad. I could help him look, ask my parents to help, or tell him not to worry because we will help him." Use textual or echoic responding to teach the target behaviors. Mastery criterion is 90% accuracy for 2 consecutive sessions or 100% accuracy for 1 session.

RESEARCH BOX **5.5**

Social Listener Component of Conversational Exchanges

Two separate experiments were conducted to examine the effects of listener reinforcement games on frequency of students' conversational units. Participants were four 7-to 9-year-old boys and girls with autism. Participants could read and write, but emitted speaker-listener exchanges at low rates. Pre-instructional probes showed that participants had observational learning and self-monitoring in their repertoires, but did not engage in conversational units. Each game in the listener reinforcement instructional protocol was conducted as its own phase (the game *Simon Says* was also played during the second experiment), and the number of conversational units was probed after each one. Results showed that the number of verbal interactions—defined as conversational units, "Wh" questions, and approvals—increased for three of four participants during game and probe sessions.

From Greer, R. D., Reilly-Lawson, T., & Walsh, D. (2006). Teaching the social listener reinforcement component of the speaker-listener exchange stage of verbal behavior. Unpublished manuscript, Teachers College, Columbia University.

Longano, J., Young, K., & Greer, R. D. (2006). The effects of a listener reinforcement procedure on the social repertoires of two students with disabilities. Unpublished manuscript, Teachers College, Columbia University.

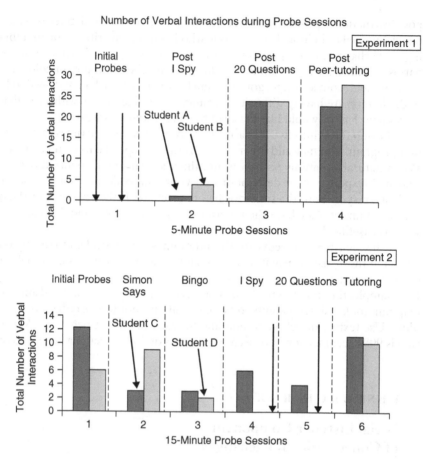

FIGURE 5.9   Social Listener Reinforcement

From Greer, R. D., Reilly-Lawson, T., & Walsh, D. (2006). Teaching the social listener reinforcement component of the speaker-listener exchange stage of verbal behavior. Unpublished manuscript, Teachers College, Columbia University; and from Longano, J., Young, K., & Greer, R. D. (2006). The effects of a listener reinforcement procedure on the social repertoires of two students with disabilities. Unpublished manuscript, Teachers College, Columbia University.

Capability 7: Learning deictic functions or taking the perspective of others.
Hayes, Barnes-Holmes, and Roche (2001) define *deictic relations* as "those that specify a relation in terms of the perspective of the speaker such as left-right; I-you (and all of its correlates, such as "mine"); here-there" (p. 38). Perspective taking is a special type of deictic because it is emitted based on the speaker's location. The only constant variable across perspective-taking deictic relations is the relationship between the speaker and other events or people. For individuals with verbal delays, particularly those with autism and other developmental disabilities, learning and emitting such relations can be challenging; some theorists suggest that this is because of a lack of "theory of mind" or the capacity to see an event from another person's perspective.

Behavior analysts, particularly relational frame theorists, have used multiple exemplar instruction to teach the deictic relations identified in theory of mind. Hayes et al. (2001) describe a study in which a child was given a red and a blue block, and then asked, "If I have a green block and you have a red block, which block do I have? Which block do you have?" Using learn units, this procedure continued until correct responses of "You have a green block. I have a red block" were emitted. The relation was reversed and the student was asked, "If I was you and you were me, which block would you have? I have?" This training continued by building on more deictic relations. They noted that a 7-year-old girl passed the training program, and that a 3.5-year-old boy who failed the theory of mind test passed it later after receiving training in the I-YOU and YOU-I relation. The multiple exemplar instructional protocol in Textbox 5.6 is a preliminary procedure designed for children with verbal delays by Clay (2006) based on Barnes-Holmes, Barnes-Holmes, & Cullinan (2001).

Production Program for Emission of Appropriate Talking

Conduct these protocols first with adults and then with children. Often, children will interact with adults and not with peers, simply because the adults hold the preferred goodies. Developing peer relations in which peers hold the goodies, given some current evidence, is key to building the capability for being reinforced for listening to peers. However, in some cases the intervention may be needed with both adults and peers. Probe assessments with both will allow you to determine the presence or absence of the repertoires.

Two programs are taught simultaneously, each blocked in 20 learn unit sessions—one curricular program for emitting the correct and incorrect verbal behavior, and one for responding with yes/no and plus/minus to positive and negative exemplars of appropriate conversations. Present the LTO's in a sequence as just indicated. Criterion is 90% or better for two successive sessions.

1) Production Program for correct and incorrect verbal behavior: There are two short-term objectives associated with this program. The first requires the student to imitate the appropriate model (zero-second time delay), and the second requires them to emit the behavior in a role-playing context with the teacher. If the zero-second time delay works, then the goal is accomplished with only one short-term objective. If not, then fade out the model/prompts as part of the second short-term objective.

Textbox 5.8 contains five examples of positive and negative exemplars. Present two learn units for each exemplar (10 for positive and 10 for negative exemplars). When the student achieves 9 correct responses out of 10 negative exemplar production opportunities, the production program shifts to 20 learn units for emitting correct exemplars. Exemplars displayed by the teacher must be of varied form, content, and inflection; so must the students' exemplars. We vary these components as part of a general case for the child to attend to the essential components of instruction, which include the function and not the form of appropriate talk.

TEXTBOX 5.6
Deictic Game

Deictic probes: Probe students' responses to 20 questions that require perspective-taking responses (i.e., "I have a cup. What do you have?" or "I am standing here. Where are you standing?"). Obtain responses for each of the following relations: I-YOU, HERE-THERE, NOW-THEN across selection ("Point to what I have") and production responses ("Who has the ball?"). Conduct these probes before and after the deictic game/instruction.

   Game Set-up: Teach missing repertoires by using a game such as Candy Land®. Set-up the game by dividing the game's cards into sets of 12 and labeling each card within a set as follows: GO, STAY, SWITCH, TRADE, VISIT, SPECIAL and GO BACK.

1. GO and SWITCH cards are used to teach I-YOU responses: GO ("I *go* to red" or "You *go* to blue"); SWITCH ("I switch with YOU" or "YOU switch with ME").
2. STAY and VISIT cards are used to teach HERE-THERE responses: STAY ("You stay THERE" or "I stay HERE"); VISIT ("I go THERE to you" or "You come HERE to me").
3. GO BACK cards are used to teach NOW-THEN responses (i.e., if students do not remember where they were before selecting a GO BACK card, they say "NOW I am on blue. Where was I then?" and their peer says "YOU were on red").

   Game/Instruction: The game should then proceed as follows by having the target student: 1) Pick a card from the *I* pile, 2) tact his destination (i.e., "I go to red"), 3) move to the target location on the game board, 4) pick a card from the *YOU* pile, 5) tact the destination of his peer (i.e., "You go to blue").

   Once the peer has followed the target student's directions, they take their turn, choosing first from the *I* pile and then from the *YOU* pile to direct the action of the target student, which allows the target student to function as a listener. Use learn units to repeat this rotation for HERE-THERE and NOW-THEN relations. Each student should have 10 opportunities to respond as a listener and as a speaker. Use echoic corrections and other needed interventions to teach the target vocal responses (see Chapters 2 and 4).

---

   2) Yes/no and plus/minus response program: First, read a rule to the student from Textbox 5.9. Next, provide one positive and one negative exemplar for numbers 1-5 from part 1, and obtain yes or no responses. Note that each time you do one of the 5 responses, use a different topography or different words (teach the general case by multiple exemplars). There are two responses to the general case procedure. The student should emit a yes or no response, but they should also mark a plus or minus using pencil and paper. This will prepare them for the possibility of monitoring others' behavior as a future intervention.

   Rotate the settings inside and outside of the classroom for both programs. Please note that although for data analysis purposes we graph the learn units separately for each program (by the production of the behavior and by the yes/no program), we rotate learn units across the two programs, such that a yes/no response learn unit is followed

---

TEXTBOX **5.7**

Pre-and Post-Instruction Multiple Probe Evaluation

(1) Probe students' interactions with each other before introducing the protocols, (2) teach the students the yes/no and the plus/minus programs described in the next section first; (3) repeat the pre-teaching probes as post-instructional probes, and (4) introduce the observation intervention. The actual training procedures are outlined in the next section for children to interact.

---

by a production learn unit. Thus, you may find that for one teaching session, you end up presenting only 10 learn units for each; nonetheless, graph by 20 learn units.

3) *Role playing:* In this portion, the student should emit correct and incorrect examples of target responses. For the positive exemplar, the student is to emit a correct response. First, role-play an example and say, "This is what you should do." Next, the student should imitate you without your verbal direction to do so (do not say, "You do it." We want the student to begin to beat the teacher. Plot responses as prompted or independent). If the response is incorrect, corrections involve the student doing two imitations of the teacher's performance of the correct response (i.e., "Hiya" "Hi," or "How are you?"). Obtain correct inflections and appropriate eye contact (not necessarily continuous eye contact). Once the student can imitate the teacher to the criterion, drop the modeling and obtain independent responses. You may need to identify rate or latency criteria for responding by timing several adult interactions so that once the student moves to independent responding, they can achieve a rate criterion.

For the negative exemplars, use negative exemplars that the student has used as well as others that you have not heard them use (i.e., "This is what you should not say, '_____,' " followed by "Now you say what you should not say, '_____.'"

Before each opportunity to imitate a negative exemplar, obtain yes/no responses to positive and negative exemplars. Present a positive exemplar and ask, "Is this correct?" Do a negative exemplar and ask, "Is this correct?" Vary the order of positive and negative exemplars.

4) *Evaluation Probe Review:* (1) Probe students with adults and peers before teaching. Use probe trials with natural consequences. (2) Teach both the yes/no and production programs to the criterion with adults. (3) Probe the adult and peer responses again. (4) If the peer responses do not occur, teach the programs with peers to the criterion. By doing this program, we have actually covered many of the rules for speaking appropriately to others, and we need not teach separate programs for looking appropriately, answering questions, and so on. We will need a program for raising hands, but we can simply apply these yes/no production procedures to hand raising. This should be mastered quickly.

TEXTBOX 5.8

Rule/Repertoire—Talk to Others as You Want Them to Talk to You

1. *Definition:* We want others to greet us with a smile and a salutation. This is a tact response done when the student sees someone. (a) DO positive exemplars, "Hi (Hiya, Hey, or Hello) with or without a name," "Good morning," "How are you." "Nice to see you," and so forth. (b) DO NOT DO negative exemplars: Ignoring others, walking by others without greeting them, saying mean things (e.g., "You can't have my toys today," or "I'm not playing with you," "Go away," or staring off in space).

2. *Definition:* We want others to inquire about our lives and well-being. This is an intraverbal response with the goal of having the response function to reinforce another verbal response aside a conversational unit. (a) DO positive exemplars: Did you have a good evening? "Did you play with toys, watch TV, go shopping, play outside, etc. since yesterday at school?" (b) DO NOT DO negative exemplars. What we don't want is for others to ignore us, say something mean (e.g., "Go away." "I don't like you." "Move out of the way." "Don't bother me." "What's wrong with you?" or not ask about our lives or what we did).

3. *Definition:* We want others to say something nice to us, to say something that is true, to offer to share their things such as toys toys/games, or activities. This is a tact function within the conversational unit.
   (a) DO positive exemplars "I like your ____ (items of clothing or something the child is carrying). "I like seeing you." "I'm glad you are in school today." "I missed you yesterday." "Let's play ____ (e.g., jump on trampoline or push the tricycle)." "Want to play with my _____?" "Want to wear my watch until PSI time?"
   (b) DO NOT DO negative exemplars: "I don't like you." "You're ugly, fat, skinny, stupid, not nice, mean, or hateful." "I don't like your ____."

4. *Definition:* We want others to listen to what we say. Speaker reinforced by a listener. (a) DO positive exemplars: Say something about what another has told us. "That's interesting." "What happened next?" "That sounds like fun." "I'd like to do that too." (b) DO NOT DO negative exemplars: We don't want others to not ask about what we said or did and stare into space, talk about themselves only, look uninterested, be falsely interested, or make irrelevant intraverbals or tacts,

5. *Definition:* We want others to answer our questions or help us. This is an intraverbal response and a listener role (i.e., reinforcing the verbal behavior of the questioner). (a) DO Positive exemplars: Respond to "Where are you going?" "What are you doing?" Respond with accurate tacts such as "I'm doing my numbers," PSI, reading, playing with ____, earning tokens, going for my reinforcer." "What do you want to do today?" Responds with accurate tact. What to say when you don't know (e.g., "I'm sorry I don't know." "Let's ask my teacher/mom/dad/friend." (b) DO NOT DO negative exemplars: Respond by ignoring and looking away in space, "Don't bother me." "Go away." Scowls, glares, and whines. "What does it look like, dummy?" "Leave me alone." "I'm busy."

TEXTBOX **5.9**

**Instructional Protocol for Production
of Appropriate Speech**

1. We measure the absence or presence of conversational units with an adult by assessing their frequency under conditions of natural reinforcement. A correct response for a single-response opportunity is a minimum of three conversational units. The student must emit correct responses for 18/20 probe trials (a total of 60 conversational units). We also probe for the presence of conversational units with a peer by placing the student in a 10-minute play session with a peer and counting the frequency of conversational units.
2. Correct responses are conversational units that do not contain disapprovals. During 10-minute probe sessions, also measure the number of "Wh" questions, intraverbals, approvals, and disapprovals that a student emits. Conversational units should also be measured under natural reinforcement conditions.
3. Using the response definitions in Textbox 5.10, teach appropriate talking by using a multiple exemplar procedure. First, state the rule for the student. For example, you might say, "We want others to greet us by smiling and saying, 'Hello.'" Direct the student to repeat the rule.
4. Next, model a positive exemplar of the rule. Ask the student to tell you if that is a good example or a bad example ("Is that what we want others to do?"). They should respond by saying, "Yes" or "No."
5. Lastly, tell the student to show you how they want others to greet them. They should imitate the response you modeled in the last step.
6. Repeat these steps for all five rules, varying the order of positive and negative exemplars. Also, use negative exemplars for production responses. For example, you might say, "We want others to greet us by smiling and saying, 'hello' (model a negative exemplar). Is this what we want others to do?" The student should respond by saying, "No." Finally, tell the student to show you how they *do not* want others to greet them. They should imitate the response you modeled for the negative exemplar.
7. Conduct 10-learn units for each positive exemplar and 10 for each negative exemplar (2 for numbers one through five in Textbox 5.10).
8. Role Play: Use a video or have the student observe your model of correct behaviors with another person. For the first few learn units, you may have to prompt the student to imitate you by saying, "Now you do it." Eventually, the student should perform the correct behavior without your verbal prompt to do so.

Replacing Echolalia and Palilalia
with Functional Verbal Behavior

Fixing Improperly Learned Control
of Echoic Responses

Now that we have described the advanced speaker and listener capabilities and instructional protocols for inducing those capabilities, we want to correct any faulty or nonfunctional forms of vocal responding. These are not verbal capabilities or stages;

rather, they are faulty forms of speaking and frequently they need to be corrected before the advanced verbal capabilities can be induced. They are present only in children who have the parroting repertoire, or children who can vocally duplicate the speech or vocal sounds of others. We believe that these faulty speech patterns are vocal responses that have not come under the appropriate verbal function controls. There are several possible sources for the responding, and thus, several possible solutions based on the potential sources. These include both antecedent and consequence sources for the responses.

When individuals emit echoic responses under conditions that call for intraverbals, the nonfunctional echoic responding is characterized as *echolalia*. Echoic responding is critical to verbal development; however, echoic responding in place of required intraverbal responding thwarts students' progress. There are probably various experiential sources for the problem including the following: (a) an experiential history of having echoic responding reinforced without placing the response into the establishing operations for mands or for tacts, (b) auditory or listener discrimination learning deficits, (c) an inadequate tact repertoire, or (d) combinations thereof. It is likely that they are not true echoics, but parroting responses that are reinforced by sensory consequences, or responses that are emitted because the student does not have the relevant intraverbal or audience control.

Much of the problem may involve the listener side of verbal responding. For instance, for children with this problem, once a response is echoed and a correction is given, the correction is also echoed. Hence, the correction does not correct; rather it simply reinforces the echolalia. The echoic responding is reinforced by further echoic responding. Simply speaking, opportunities for discriminating between accurate and inaccurate intraverbal responses are infrequent. The listener within the skin, so to speak, responds with speaker auditory correspondence. The speaker deficit can be identified as a speaker deficit only if the auditory source of the problem is eliminated. However, before isolating the auditory component, a simpler approach is possible provided the student has a minimal textual repertoire.

Textual Test and Textual Stimulus Prompt Protocol

Textual tactic.   For students who have echoic problems and who have some textual responding, it is possible to use textual responses to shift echolalia to appropriate intraverbal responding. This program is appropriate for students who do not have problems with echolalia during academic literacy instruction (i.e., echoing antecedents when emitting listener responses such as matching or pointing). First teach the student to textually respond and comprehend the following words that are to become intraverbal responses. Print each phrase on an index card.

- "Hi _____ (printed names of teachers and several children in the room, i.e., Renaldo, Mary, Lorenzo, Fussell, Thomas, and Stella)."
- "I am _____ years old"
- "Name of hometown"
- Mother's name

- Telephone number or address
- "I am [grand, fine, good, great]"
- "Not so good"
- Other possible intraverbal responses relevant to the particular setting for the target student

Teach these until the student responds with 100% accuracy to the words in 20-learn unit sessions. At the same time, teach the student to emit the response only when you touch the index card. That is, teach the student to wait for the point before responding. Also teach them to match names of individuals to people in the classroom. The student should textually respond at a rate of 80 to 120 correct words per minute.

While running intraverbal instruction, insert a learn unit using the printed stimulus prompt for intraverbal responding. With the correct printed stimulus for a particular intraverbal response, emit the greeting or question ("How are you?" Hi _____." What's your telephone number?" "What's your mother's name?" "Where do you live?" "How old are you?" etc.), hold the index card in front of the student, and point to the textual stimulus. When the student responds by reading the printed prompt, reinforce with approvals and with other generalized reinforcers. If the student can textually respond without echoing the greeting or question, then she is a candidate for the textual stimulus prompt protocol. If the student continues to echo, do not continue this procedure at present.

Textual stimulus prompt protocol: Continue this procedure but fade the textual print control for response by shifting to your vocal stimulus as the control for accurate intraverbals. Within each 20-learn unit session, fade the textual stimulus. You can do this by covering up portions of the printed stimuli, starting with the end of the phrase. For example, cover the last word in, "I am eight years old (old is covered)." Continue this until only the first word is uncovered. As the student begins responding, cover the stimulus. You may also have the printed phrases on a computer screen and have the student choose the correct response while pointing to the phrase on the screen and reading it. You may first have the student not speak after your greeting or question, but instead have her point to the correct phrase, and then read it. Next have her read without pointing. Fade the words on the computer screen until your vocal stimulus results in accurate responding. After mastery of 90% or better for two sessions or 100% for one session, use the textual prompt for subsequent instances of echolalia as a correction. In this way the correction is under print control and avoids the confounding vocal stimulus control for inaccurate intraverbals.

In cases where this procedure is successful, the problem is probably tied to a particular history of echoing greetings or small talk. In cases where children cannot read, or the textual stimulus prompt protocol is not successful, the problem may lie in auditory discrimination. In Chapter 3, we described the protocol for inducing auditory matching to develop the discrimination of words for listener or echoic responding. For the student with echolalia who has not mastered the auditory-matching protocol, return to that protocol and teach the repertoire. Begin at the level at which you believe the student is capable of responding, such as words versus other words, or words versus sounds. If the student has already mastered the auditory-matching protocol, or after you teach them to master the repertoire, do the following.

RESEARCH BOX **5.6**

Textual Stimulus Prompt for Echolalia during Intraverbals

To decrease echolalic responses during intraverbals, researchers compared effects of a textual and echoic stimulus to prompt a listener's response to a speaker's antecedent for two children with autism. Results showed that the use of a textual stimulus decreased echolalia and maintained correct responding more than an echoic prompt.

From Greer, R. D., & Bruno, V. P. (1997). A pilot study comparing two different types of prompting on intraverbal responding and reduction of echolalia. Unpublished manuscript, Teachers College, Columbia University.

Auditory Matching to Correct Faulty Echoic Responding

Pre- and post-instruction evaluation probes.   First arrange the BigMack® or other auditory devices in the conformation described in Chapter 3. That is, place two buttons in front of the student and one in front of the teacher. Place a picture near each button (i.e., a sample stimulus placed in front of the teacher's button and the exemplar or matching picture and a non-exemplar or non-matching picture in front of the other button). We teach the student to respond to *different*, non-matching stimuli by pressing the button behind the non-matching picture after we say, "Point to the one *not like* mine." As the student begins to master indicating the one that is not like yours, fade your verbal antecedent so that you push a button representing a stimulus and the student presses the button behind the non-matching stimulus. This is a repertoire that can also be taught first as matching instruction so that the student responds to the two different vocal commands of "Match _____," and "Match not _____." You would then add the pointing response to the matching response as in the listener component of naming (e.g., "Point to the _____," or "Point to the NOT _____.") This can be taught during and after listener emersion.

After the student can point to stimuli that are different than a visual sample, we can introduce sounds. Refer to Chapter 3 for a description of the matching procedure to arrange sets of stimuli as well as teaching and measurement procedures. Present sounds until the student can point to sounds that are not like the exemplar produced by the teacher's button. Once the student has mastered pointing to non-exemplar sounds, use words until they demonstrate mastery by pushing the button that produces the word that is different from the exemplar. If this goes quickly, proceed to the next

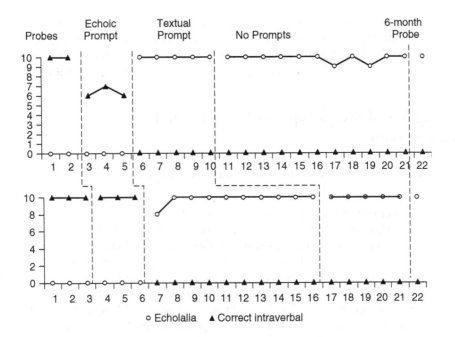

FIGURE 5.10   Textual Stimulus Prompt for Echolalia during Intraverbals

From Greer, R. D., & Bruno, V. P. (1997). A pilot study comparing two different types of prompting on intraverbal responding and reduction of echolalia. Unpublished manuscript, Teachers College, Columbia University.

step; if not, present enough sets for the student to master the task in one or two sessions. When this repertoire is mastered, move on to the next step.

Record appropriate intraverbal responses to greetings or questions described earlier in the textual prompt protocol. The teacher's buttons should have a vocal greeting or question. The student should have the teacher's phrase on one button (an exact echoic), and the correct intraverbal response on the other button. For the student's buttons, say the phrase or greeting, and then record in advance the student's echoic, correct, and incorrect intraverbal responses. Use these recordings for the student's responses. The objective is for the student to push buttons that are intraverbal rather than echoic responses. You can use learn units alone or zero-second time delay procedures to teach the correct selection of the intraverbal response. Arrange the questions and greetings into sets of 5 phrases as described in the auditory-matching program in Chapter 3. Teach at least two sets. After mastery of the two sets, probe again for intraverbals as you did in the pre-instructional evaluation. If the responses are significantly more accurate but not at 90% to 100% accuracy, teach other sets until post-instructional probes show mastery.

If the student is still having difficulty, have them master sets in which they choose the correct button, after which you vocally present the phrase or greeting, and they respond with the correct intraverbal. If corrections are needed, have the student first push the button and then repeat what it says. When the student has developed the intraverbal repertoire but occasionally reverts to echolalia, use the buttons immediately after the incidence for a few learn units. This procedure should induce accurate intraverbal responding and eliminate the echolalia. If this does not occur, use the analytic algorithm described in Chapter 2 to identify the source of the learning problem.

Replacing Vocal Stereotypy with Functional Verbal Behavior

Assessing the Function of Vocal Stereotypy

In cases in which the student emits repetitive speech in free play or between learn units for other instructional programs, there may be at least three functions for the behavior. In this case, the repertoire is referred to in the psychiatric literature as *palilalia*. That is, the repetitive responses are not direct echoes of what was heard, but are repetitive responses derived from earlier speech sources. The three functions we have identified to date describe the vocalizations as 1) parroting stereotypical responses; 2) responses to evoke social generalized reinforcers; that is, the child needs tacts to obtain social reinforcement; and 3) incipient or full-blown incidences of self-talk. In the first and second instances, a tact replacement protocol may be successful. In the third case, the responses may be desirable, but need to be brought under audience control at some point. All of these are, of course, reinforced responses, but the reinforcement source or the establishing operation functions need to be identified to use them toward the development of useful functional verbal behavior.

Parroting stereotypical responses.   One way to identify whether repetitive speech has a stereotypical function is to test out the function. In cases of stereotypy the reinforcement is automatic, that is, the kinesthetic consequence reinforces the response. Thus, the sensory stimulation reinforces the repetitive vocal behavior much like the sensation of rocking, spinning, finger flicking, or touching one's hair reinforces those behaviors. In this case, the actual sound reinforces the response, as in babies babbling. Infants spend a great deal of their day engaging in stereotypy that gains operant control for other reinforcers over time. Vocal sounds move from parroting to echoic-to-mand or echoic-to-tact functions. Phrases become intraverbals for self-talk and fantasy play or singing. Rocking moves to a rocking chair or a swing. Movement of legs moves to locomotion and so on. In other words, the behaviors, so to speak, find new conditioned reinforcers, or perhaps new reinforcers select out the behaviors. In the case of the student with palilalia, we may want to find out if the function is reinforcement by kinesthetic or auditory sources.

One way to determine this is to test for auditory reinforcement, and if this is not the case, the function is likely to be kinesthetic. We can determine a kinesthetic function by arranging a test of the auditory reinforcement of vocal responding (Hugh-Pennie, 2006). Using the procedures outlined for assessing and conditioning reinforcement for voices (see Chapter 3), observe the child in free play (also see Chapter 6 for assessing reinforcement control of book stimuli where the same procedure is described). In the free or solitary play setting, conduct continuous, 5-second partial interval observations of instances of palalia (5-minute sessions contain 60 five-second intervals; see Chapter 3 for the recording procedures when observing in free-play settings). This allows determination of the frequency of intervals containing the response class. Use partial-interval recording to score any incidence of palilalia that occurs. Additionally, in the free-play setting, record incidences of the child emitting palilalia with a computer or audio device until you have 5 continuous minutes of recorded repetitive speech by the student.

Once you have enough measures of palilalia in free play to establish reliability or the stability of the behavior (with high interobserver agreement), begin your assessment by comparing two phases in which palilalia and recorded speech are measured. In one phase, each time the child begins an incidence of palilalia, play the tape until they stop emitting it. Once steady state responding/stability of the data occur, introduce the next phase by turning on the audio device when the child enters the play area, and turning it off when they emit palilalia or after three seconds of no palilalia. Compare the frequency of palilalia for this condition to the previous condition. If there is little or no difference between baseline phases and the two recording device phases, the reinforcement function is likely to be kinesthetic and not auditory stimulation from the child's voice. If, however, turning on the device increases instances of palilalia and turning it off decreases it, then the function of the reinforcement is likely to be auditory in nature. You may want to do the same procedure using music (e.g., a phase of turning it on after palilalia and a phase of turning it off after palilalia). In the Hugh-Pennie (2006) application, turning the tape player on or off, either voice or music, acted to decrease or eliminate palilalia. In the latter case, starting or ceasing the sound functioned to eliminate palilalia, suggesting that the change in sound acted to teach the children to stop palilalia or to make the response covert, and perhaps appropriately so.

While we could turn off the tape player in the play setting to decrease palilalia, continuously emitting palilalia across settings such that others, and the speaker, must listen to it all day is not conducive to harmonious relations! Currently, the most likely effective intervention is to do the tact replacement protocol that we describe next, regardless of whether the function is kinesthetic or auditory. We want to shift from automatic to generalized reinforcement from social sources. If this is difficult—that is, responses are not typically reinforced by adult attention or by other generalized reinforcers such as tokens—they may need to be conditioned first (see the conditioning procedure in Chapters 3 and 6). If social generalized reinforcers function as such for the child, we can shift the response to obtain reinforcement by emitting tacts.

Tact Protocol to Replace Palilalia

Seat the child at a table where they can color, build blocks, or engage in similar activities; or seat them on the floor in a free-play area where they can play with toys. The student receives learn unit instruction for the activity. Begin the baseline by saying, "It's time to (name of an activity)," and start timing the session. If palilalia is emitted,

TEXTBOX 5.10

Determining Functions of Palilalia

1. In a free-play setting, use an audio-recording device to record a sample of the student's palilalia for 5 minutes. Measure the frequency of palilalia by using partial-interval recording when reviewing the tape. That is, if the student emits palilalia during any part of a 5-second interval, record a plus on the data collection sheet. If palilalia is reliably occurring for at least 80% of the 5-second intervals (48/60 interval), then the procedure should be used. Isolate several samples on the audiotape so that there are two or three 1-minute samples of palilalia being continuously emitted.

2. During the first condition, place the child in the free-play area for a 5-minute period. Play the taped palilalia within the child's hearing whenever they begin to emit it. Continue to play the tape until the child stops emitting palilalia. Use 5-second, partial-interval recording; repeat the sessions until the data show steady state responding for palilalia.

3. Return to baseline conditions; the palilalia tape should not be played contingent on occurrences of palilalia.

4. When palilalia is at baseline levels again, begin the second condition by placing the child in the free-play area for a 5-minute period and recording occurrences of palilalia as in the first condition. Play the taped palilalia when the child enters the play area. The tape should be played continuously. Only turn it off when palilalia is emitted and when no palilalia has been emitted for 3 consecutive seconds.

5. Compare the number of intervals during which palilalia was emitted under both conditions (Steps 2 and 4). If playing the taped palilalia increased its occurrence (Condition 1) and turning it off decreased it (Condition 2), then the reinforcement for palilalia was likely auditory. That is, hearing palilalia reinforced the student. However, if there was no difference between the baseline phases and the two conditions where the tape was played, then it is less likely to have an auditory function and is, perhaps, kinesthetic.

---

ignore the behavior. If correct tacts are emitted, deliver verbal praise to the student. If correct mands occur, deliver the requested item to the student.

During the intervention, when the participant emits palilalia, immediately say a tact associated with the activity in which the student is engaged without stopping them from engaging in the activity. For example, if the student says, "Little wolf, little wolf, let me in" while coloring or during instruction, immediately say, "I am coloring" or point to an object (e.g., a book) and say, "That's a book" while the student continues to color. If the student echoes the teacher's tact, deliver vocal praise such as "That's right. That's a book." If the student does not echo the tact but stops emitting palilalia, do not continue to say the tact; allow the activity or instruction to continue. When responding is stable across sessions, return to the initial pre-intervention conditions in which incidences of palilalia are ignored. If palilalia decreases significantly but is still present, then reinsert the intervention, returning to pre- and post-interventions baseline conditions until palilalia is absent and tacts and mands increase significantly.

TEXTBOX **5.11**

Tact Replacement Protocol for Palilalia

1. Place the child at a table with materials used to color or build blocks. They can also be placed in free-play area with toys.
2. Use typical learn unit instruction by saying, "It's time to (name of activity)" and let the child engage in the activity. Time the session.
3. This is the baseline phase, so palilalia should be ignored while correct tacts and mands should be consequated.
4. During the intervention, place the child at the table as in baseline. Start the session and begin to time it.
5. When the child emits palilalia, immediately tact the activity in which the student is engaged such as "I am coloring" or "That's a book." The activity should not be stopped.
6. If the student echoes the teacher's tact, give vocal praise such as "That's right. That's a book." If the student does not echo the tact, present the tact again. Let the activity or instruction continue.
7. When responding is stable across sessions, return to the initial baseline conditions where palilalia was ignored. If it has decreased but is still present, then use the intervention again until palilalia is absent and tacts and mands increase.

This intervention may need to occur several times before success is achieved. If the responding decreases but is not eliminated, introduce several toy-, activity-, or book-conditioning programs as described in Chapters 3 and 6. When the response has both kinesthetic (automatic) and generalized reinforcement functions, it is important to expand the generalized reinforcers to replace the kinesthetic reinforcement function. In the latter case, the problem is a paucity of generalized conditioned reinforcers as well as a function of obtaining generalized reinforcement.

RESEARCH BOX **5.7**

Tact Operant to Decrease Palilalia

To decrease occurrences of palilalia during free play and instruction, researchers examined the effects of presenting a tact opportunity when a student emitted palilalia. Participants were six preschool-age children diagnosed with autism that emitted high rates of palilalia during the baseline. Results showed that the use of a contingent tact opportunity decreased the frequency of palilalia for all participants.

From Karmali, I., Greer, R. D., Nuzzolo-Gomez, R., Ross, D. E., & Rivera-Valdes, C. L. (2005). Reducing palilalia by presenting tact corrections to young children with autism. *The Analysis of Verbal Behavior, 21*, 145–153.

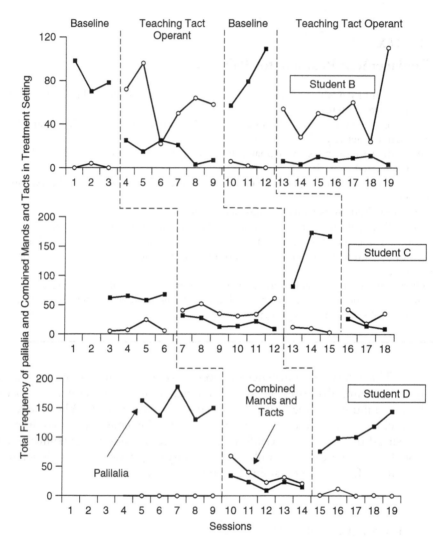

FIGURE 5.11   Tact Replacement Protocol

From Karmali, I., Greer, R. D., Nuzzolo-Gomez, R., Ross, D. E., & Rivera-Valdes, C. L. (2005). Reducing palilalia by presenting tact corrections to young children with autism. *Analysis of Verbal Behavior, 21,* 145–153.

In this chapter, we described the protocols to advance the speaker-listener repertoires and new capabilities. In addition, we described tested tactics to replace faulty vocal verbal behavior. Review the sequence of interventions to induce basic and advanced speaker and listener capabilities shown in Figure 5.12. This sequence should guide your efforts. In Chapter 6, we introduce print into the verbal repertoire. This process involves joining the naming capability with the stimulus control of print as

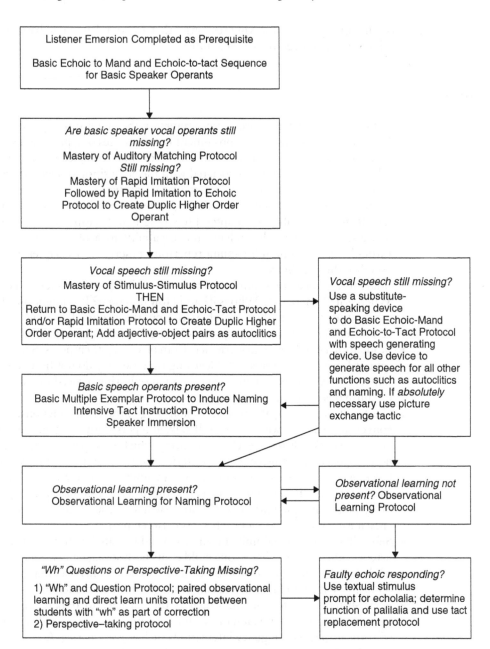

FIGURE 5.12 Sequence of Interventions to Induce Basic and Advanced Speaker Capabilities

well as other prerequisite observing responses that are foundational to basic print control and to more advanced verbal capabilities.

Summary

- While the mand repertoire is important for the acquisition of initial speaker behavior, tacts become more prominent in later stages of typical verbal development because they provide the foundation for more complex verbal repertoires. There are four capabilities associated with the acquisition of tacts: *direct instruction, naming, "wh" questions,* and *observational learning.*
- Individuals initially acquire tacts through *direct instruction.* We use the intensive tact protocol described in Chapter 4 to strengthen this capability if it is missing. We also need to teach students the capability to acquire tacts incidentally through *naming.* The full naming repertoire described in Chapter 4 is used to establish this capability.
- Students also need to acquire tacts through "Wh" questions such as What is it? When is it? Where is it? Who is it? and How do I do it? It is important that after asking the question, they are able to emit the acquired speaker or listener response. The "wh" questions protocol is used to teach this capability.
- Students need to be able to learn tacts from observing their peers. Some children cannot learn from observational learning because they do not have it as a capability. The yoked-peer contingency and monitoring procedures are used to establish observational learning.
- We build on tact capabilities by establishing intraverbal functions, including conversational units with others, self-talk, and perspective taking. *Conversational units* are speaker-listener exchanges during which each participant functions as both a speaker and a listener. The criterion for the presence of this repertoire is three or more conversational units with an adult and with a peer. They can be taught through specific protocols such as the *production emission of appropriate talk* or by presenting establishing operations such as the absence of an adult's presence during speaker-listener exchanges between peers.
- Self-talk conversational units occur when individuals function as speakers and listeners during play. That is, one child emits both speaker and listener responses while playing with *anthropomorphic* toys such as dolls. This is an important developmental stage for children, and can be taught through modeling.
- Social-listener reinforcement, which is the capacity to obtain reinforcement from listening to other, is important for conversational units, and can be taught with yoked-peer contingency interactions such as *peer tutoring, I spy,* and *20 questions.* A yoked-peer contingency involves the use of two peers who work together to obtain reinforcement.
- Faulty vocal responses (echolalia) emitted during intraverbals can be reduced or eliminated by teaching appropriate responses. *Textual stimuli* and *audio feedback* are possible interventions. They can also be reduced by using the auditory-matching protocol to teach same- and different-matching responses.

- Palilalia emitted during instruction and free play can be decreased by first identifying its function (auditory or kinesthetic), and then by replacing it with tacts.

ENDNOTES

1. See Pinker (1999), Premack (2004), and Premack & Premack (2003) for examples of literature arguing that generative verbal behavior is a function of genetically evolved "deep structures or modules." Clearly the structural capacity for generative verbal behavior needs to be present; however, it is increasingly evident that it can, and at times by necessity must, be directly taught through intensive instruction.

2. See Hart & Risley (1995) for a description of these children and the related research. The work reported in their text represents one of the most sustained and thorough investigations of the role of environmental or incidental teaching interactions on the acquisition of vocabulary by young children. Children from professional families received two-thirds more language interactions than those from working-class families; thus the children from low-income families entered school with significant deficits in vocabulary, and we suspect that most of those deficits were deficits in tacts. Although the capabilities we describe herein were not identified at the time, we suspect that children with fewer language experiences are also likely to have fewer verbal capabilities. The capabilities in turn then determine how much each child takes from her language experiences at the time. It would not be surprising to find that the types of multiple exemplar experiences that lead to the induction of generative verbal behavior, as we discussed, also varied between the populations that Hart and Risley described.

Reading and Writing: Print-Governed and Print-Governing Verbal Behavior

A primitive but clear cut example of the modus operandi of automatic reinforcement [as it occurs in reading] is provided by the beginning reader who must hear himself pronounce a word *[emphasis added]—perhaps several times—before reacting to it with behavior he has already acquired as a listener.*

Skinner, 1957, p. 66

Scope and Purpose of the Print Control Chapter

Reading opens the door to new ways to expand children's tact, mand, and autoclitic repertoires. "Seeing and saying print," or what Skinner called textual responding, is a critical aspect of reading. However, reading is much more involved because one must match vocal sounds to words and pictures, see and say print, and then listen to what one speaks/reads (Sidman, 1986). However, as we shall describe, *once children have certain capabilities*, such as naming, they need only learn some of these repertoires, and others emerge without direct instruction. In fact, naming (see Chapter 4) appears to play a key role in what is often termed *reading comprehension* (Greer, Stolfi, Chavez-Brown, & Rivera-Valdes, 2005; Lee Park, 2005).

The purpose of Chapter 6 is to provide research-based, verbal behavior analytic protocols for teaching rudimentary reading and writing functions and capabilities. In verbal behavior analysis, reading and writing are extensions of elementary verbal operants and higher order operants described throughout this text. Reading and writing functions describe how a reader benefits from writing and how a writer affects a reader. Reading and writing involve higher order operants that are controlled by print. We will describe protocols for teaching reading and writing and for inducing these repertoires when they are missing.

The purpose of this chapter is not to provide a curricular sequence for teaching reading. There are tested curricular material for doing this such as those from HeadSprout® (Layng, Twyman, & Stikeleather, 2004) Reading Mastery® Rainbow Edition (Engelmann & Bruner, 1995), Saxon® Phonics and Spelling (Saxon Publishers, 2002), and Edmark® Print Reading Series (River Deep, 2005). However, we do suggest when, where, and how to introduce these curricula as well as how to incorporate function and motivation derived from verbal behavior. We also do not outline the structural or grammatical components of writing; there are readily available educational standards and curricula for this purpose that can be modified by inserting learn unit instruction and other behavior analytic tactics. However, we do describe the foundational capabilities that underlie the learning of reading and writing functions.

Moreover, because this text is devoted to the acquisition of foundational components of verbal behavior, we only introduce the first stages of reading and writing. To those who are new to instructing children with native disabilities, it may seem curious that we even broach reading and writing in a text for teaching children with severe language delays, but we have found time after time that once children acquire speaker-as-own-listener repertoires using the procedures outlined in Chapters 2–5, it is not difficult to bring print stimulus control into their repertoire. In addition, the acquisition of rudimentary reading can be helpful in solving vocal problems such as echolalia, as we described in Chapter 5. We have taught these repertoires and induce these capabilities to hundreds of children from as young as 18 months to as old as 16 years, many of whom are identified as language delayed (Greer, Keohane, & Healy, 2002).

While this text is obviously directed toward building missing verbal capabilities for children with native disabilities, *its contents are equally relevant for children with language delays due to a lack of verbal function experiences.* For the latter group, missing verbal capabilities are typically first identified when their regular schooling does not result in successful reading and writing skills. Unfortunately, this often does not happen until many children are in the fourth grade in the United States, or in the third class in Ireland and England. Providing these children with capabilities identified in verbal behavior analysis will be useful in developing their reader and writer repertoires. In fact, we believe that typically developing children should begin reading instruction between 18 and 36 months of age, once they learn the necessary speaker-as-own-listener repertoires and they have what we describe later as conditioned reinforcement for observing print stimuli.

Our research suggests that the verbal capabilities we identify in this text are real developmental fractures; however, *the development is not a function of age but experience*, along with the necessary structural capacities, of course. For example, we condition books as reinforcers for observing responses because when children learn to enjoy books at an early stage, then reading becomes a preferred activity. It is simply not enough to read fluently; one must love to read! The evidence for book conditioning as a prerequisite is found in both behavior analytic and non-behavior analytic research (Greer, Dorow, Wachhaus, & White, 1973; Greer & Polirstok, 1982; Neuman, 1999; Tsai & Greer, 2006). An operational definition of "reading readiness" is identified in the verbal behavior literature as conditioned reinforcement of textual stimuli for observation of print (Dinsmoor, 1983; Holland, 1958; Tsai & Greer, 2006). The evidence shows that the latter objective is teachable, and if in place, children can and should learn to read much earlier than kindergarten.

Reading requires several components involving listener, speaker, and speaker-as-own-listener repertoires. When we learn to read, we add the control of print stimuli to our verbal repertoire. First, we *see and say* the printed word, and as we say the word, we hear ourselves as a speaker. Next, the consonant-vowel sounds of printed and auditory stimuli must "stand for" some object or event for us in our listener role, not because the event is the same as the word, but because a verbal community associates or arbitrarily relates the word sounds to its corresponding stimuli for the object and for the printed word. In one very basic form of reading and reading comprehension, a printed stimulus is matched to its picture, yet matching the printed word to its auditory stimulus is key for more sophisticated reading (see Lee Park, 2005 for an experiment examining the relationship between naming and reading comprehension). Of course, some individuals who are deaf from birth or who have not acquired the auditory components of reading may read by "matching signs to print and stimulus events." The latter type of reading is similar to the effect that is engendered by international road signs or by the deciphering of hieroglyphics. However, as we described in Chapters 1 and 3, there are important benefits of the auditory forms of language; and if children are not deaf, the spoken topography has certain major advantages in reading and writing (see Robinson, 1995 on the importance of audition to writing and reading). However, for the Deaf, the joint control of a sign across pictures and writing functions in similar ways to the vocal component in naming for those who speak (see Lowenkron and his colleague's work on joint stimulus control) (Lowenkron, 1989, 1991, 1996, 1997; Lowenkron & Colvin, 1992, 1995).

Skinner (1957) outlined two major functions of reading and writing—the **technical** and **aesthetic** functions. The technical function requires that the writer affects the behavior of a reader in a very precise way. For example, a surgeon describes how to conduct a delicate operation, or a cook describes how to precisely prepare a recipe, or a child leaves a note for Mom to bring home a preferred food from the grocery store. The aesthetic function requires that the writer affects the emotions of the reader and both preciseness and impreciseness may be part of producing the effect

---

TEXTBOX **6.1**

Conditioning Books as Reinforcers

When book stimuli are conditioned reinforcers for children to select and observe during free time, they learn to textually, respond, of see and say the printed word. When books are conditioned reinforcers for children, they have a *capability* that can be operationally defined as reading readiness (Dinsmoor, 1983; Tsai & Greer, 2006).

---

sought. While the aesthetic function is equally as important as the technical function, in this text we do not describe the aesthetic function since we only deal with rudimentary reading and writing. However, verbal behavior analysis has basic research findings that are relevant for addressing the aesthetic function (Matthews, 2005; Meincke, Keohane, Gifaldi, & Greer, 2003). That repertoire calls for higher order operants that belong to a future text on establishing advanced repertoires of verbal behavior. At present, it seems clear that basic technical reading and writing is the foundation for aesthetic functions.

In reading, as in the case of basic listener literacy, the auditory properties of the vowel-consonant sounds of textual responding should evoke responses that the reader's verbal community associates with the sounds. For example, if a recipe directs a reader to "add three cups of flour," we know the reader "comprehends" the text by their response to it, just as we know that a listener can follow a direction by their response. In reading, print and related stimuli acquire joint control over speaker and listener responses; at more advanced levels of early reading, readers begin to *say and hear* within their own skin, so to speak (Lee Park, 2005; Lodhi & Greer, 1989).

In the early stages of reading, as teachers we must observe the student *see and say* the print to confirm correspondence; Skinner referred to this as *textual responding* (i.e., seeing the text and saying the word). This is a critical step in the process of reading; some call it decoding, but print is decoded no more than we "decode" from speaker to listener behavior. Rather, a print stimulus evokes consonant-vowel combinations that correspond with stimuli and events to which the relevant listener or speaker functions are added. In listener functions associated with reading, consonant-vowel sounds direct an individual to emit certain responses, as in the case of following a recipe, assembling an object, or following directions to a particular location. The reader is responding as if the print were a speaker providing directions and the listener is the speaker also, as described by Skinner in the opening quotation for this chapter.

Clearly the individual must have listener literacy for the particular words they will read; otherwise the sounds are simply nonsense (Greer, Chavez-Brown, et al., 2005). For example, one can learn how to pronounce and textually respond to words in another language as precisely as a native speaker might. However, if basic listener literacy for the words is not in the reader's repertoire, then there will be no correspondence between reading and doing. Some problems with reading can be traced to a lack of textual response repertoires, which are attributed to problems with *emitting the sounds for the text*, or alternately, *lacking spoken sounds in one's repertoire*—both need to be in place. Provided both are in place, the person who is reading must respond to the sounds as a literate listener. That is, the sounds of the words must evoke a stimulus or set of actions, just as they would if the reader were listening to another speaker. Of course as we expand our reader repertoires, the context of other words can provide the required listener literacy. Individuals can learn the "meaning" of print stimuli by the context. Indeed, this is a major way to acquire new forms for tact and mand functions without direct instruction.

This function also raises another important issue—that we use our listener and speaker repertoires both for reading functions and for expanding our speaker and listener repertoires by using the acquired words. Students can have many reading responses, but still not learn new speaking vocabularies from reading if they lack particular capabilities (this is an area calling for more research). That is, when students have sufficient capabilities to begin learning to read, they must build a basic see-say-listen-do or see-say-listen-see (the stimulus or event) repertoire. The building of this repertoire allows the reader to expand their senses from the written record without the presence of the stimulus, provided that they have listener literacy for the words. In other words, the individual responds to print as if a speaker were present. In writing and reading, the speaker-writer need not be present because the listener-reader controls access to them. Thus, in order to ensure that a listener-reader accesses the speaker-writer's responses, the relevant establishing operations for *needing to read* must be present. We believe that the first step in doing this is for *print stimuli to acquire stimulus control over observing* to the extent that looking at books becomes a preferred activity for children even before those print have any see-say control.

The basis for conditioning print stimuli is a series of studies showing that textual responding is acquired faster when print stimuli are conditioned as reinforcers before word discrimination instruction, and when children are conditioned to "choose" to look at books in free time (Tsai & Greer, 2005). The process of conditioning print stimuli occurs incidentally for most children when parents read stories to them and point to pictures in books. Pairing adult attention—an incidentally and readily acquired conditioned reinforcer for most children—with books, acts to condition book-related stimuli as a reinforcer. Once this stimulus control is acquired, attending to print and teaching the textual response is much easier. It is analogous to the effect of infants acquiring conditioned reinforcement for adult voices. Doing so facilitates the acquisition of early speaker behaviors such as parroting, echoics, and mands and tacts as described in Chapters 3 and 4. Similarly, conditioning book-related stimuli facilitates the acquisition or learning rate of textual responding (Tsai & Greer, 2006).

Rather than leave the process of conditioning print stimuli as reinforcers for observing responses to chance or sporadic exposure, we systematically condition books in our schools for children with and without disabilities. The procedure that we use is the first of our *reader capabilities*. Thus, the acquisition of print stimulus control over observing responses is the foundation on which we build other reader repertoires. The following protocol may be implemented even while children are acquiring basic listener and speaker capabilities.

Book-conditioning Protocol

The book-conditioning procedure is used to implement conditioned or learned reinforcement for observing book-related stimuli. Skinner (1957) defined "observing behavior" (p. 416) as behavior involving observing responses—in this case, visual observing and/or manipulation of the book as objects. Skinner's notion was applied to the objective of the book-conditioning procedure in order to enhance children's observing responses with books (see also Holland, 1958). The current procedure was derived from research designed to condition preferences for previously non-preferred music stimuli for preschool and elementary school students. In these music-conditioning studies, the observing response was listening (listener observation), defined as the duration of choosing and listening to a selection as measured with laboratory instrumentation (also see Chapter 3 for the voice-conditioning procedure). In the book-conditioning procedure, the target stimulus control for visual observing is choosing books and attending to book-related stimuli (e.g., pictures and text) when the child is in a free-play area. In the procedure, book observation or looking at books, is defined as manipulating books by touching, looking, turning pages, tacting, or pointing to pictures/textual stimuli, and emitting textual responses to print stimuli. While formal learn units are not provided for the latter response of textually responding to print stimuli, it is included because some children incidentally acquire textual responses to contents in target books as a function of conditioning book-observing responses. Obviously the printed text needs to be in the language that the child will learn to read.

This protocol, and most of the protocols for conditioning stimuli as reinforcement for observing responses, has three components. First, the child is observed in a free-play area or under free operant conditions for the presence or absence of the observing responses of interest—in this case observing book-related stimuli. If the child does not choose or look at books extensively under these conditions, then they are a candidate for the conditioning procedures. Second, we conduct stimulus-stimulus pairings using train and test trials until a specific criterion is met. Third, after the train/test trial criterion is met, we again observe the child in the free-play setting. If they meet the free play setting criterion, the conditioning objective is met. If not, then we return to the train/test procedure with increased pairing and testing times, and again observe in the free-play setting. This continues until the child has acquired the conditioned reinforcement for choosing books over toys and for observing the books in a prolonged fashion. The details of this protocol are described in the next section.

Stimulus-Stimulus Pairing Training/Test Trials for Conditioning Stimuli as Reinforcers for Observing

As described in the protocol for conditioning voices as reinforcers for listening in Chapter 3, 20 pairs of training/testing trials are presented during each session of book conditioning. Each pair of trials consists of two components—one stimulus-stimulus training trial and one testing trial. The duration of each training/testing trial is

5 seconds initially; this amount of time is gradually increased by 5-second intervals if children do not meet criterion during free play probe sessions as described later. Note that if the child is not meeting the 5-second train/test trial criterion, it is likely that there are prerequisites missing. *Find and fix those prerequisites, rather than decreasing the interval to less than 5 seconds.* During each 5-second training trial, reinforcement is delivered or paired with any book-observing behavior emitted by the child. One instance of "pairing" consists of simultaneously delivering edibles and positive verbal comments about the child looking at books (e.g., "Good, I like the way you're looking at the books," or "Nice job pointing to the pictures!") when they are emitting correct book-observation responses. Either two or three verbal approvals and edible or token reinforcers are delivered during a training trial. For each training interval, alternate training trials containing two verbal approvals and edible reinforcers with training trials containing three verbal approvals and edible reinforcers. If the child displays any behavior other than observation of books, stop the timer and begin the interval again. This process continues until the child looks at the book for the entire 5-second interval (e.g., a continuous 5-second interval). After correct book-observing responses for an entire 5-second interval and only after the correct response duration, the testing trial begins.

A testing trial immediately follows each training trial. Testing trials consist of an opportunity to look at books for the same interval of time as the training trial (i.e., 5 seconds). During the testing trials, no approving comments or edibles are delivered. A correct response to the test trials is recorded as a plus (+) and defined as the child observing, touching, looking, turning pages, selecting new books, pointing to pictures/textual stimuli, tacting pictures, or emitting textual responses to the text for the for the entire time interval. Tacts or textual responses need not necessarily occur. An incorrect response, recorded as a minus (−), occurs when the child emits any behaviors other than observing books (e.g., stops looking at books, talks about irrelevant issues to the teacher, or emits stereotypy). When an incorrect response is emitted, a testing trial is terminated without any consequation, and the next training trial begins once the child is directed to attend to the book.

To summarize, once a testing trial is done and the results are recorded, a new training trial begins; this process continues until 20 training and 20 testing trials are completed. Criterion for each book-conditioning phase is 19 correct responses or better out of a total of 20 testing trial opportunities for two consecutive conditioning sessions. Once the child achieves criterion for the conditioning phase, two 5-minute free-play probes are conducted the following day (described next). The conditioning session and the subsequent free-play probe sessions for each child are separated by at least one day. If a child does not meet criterion on the free-play probes, training and testing intervals increase from the initial 5-second time periods to 10 seconds; this continues until criterion is achieved. To summarize, if the child does not meet the free-play criterion for looking at books, but they have achieved criterion in the training setting, the duration of the training/testing trial conditions is increased in 5-second intervals (i.e., 5, 10, 15, 20, 25, or 30 seconds) until the free-play criterion is met.

Probes for Conditioned Reinforcement
for Observing Books

Students are observed in a free-play area where books, toys, games and other play items are available. We usually provide a stack of several children's books for the child to look at. Sessions consist of 5 minutes of continuous 5-second whole intervals. At the end of a 5-second interval, responding is recorded and a new 5-second interval begins. Use an automatic timer or a pre-recorded tape that beeps to cue the observer at the beginning and at the end of an interval. To avoid missing any portion of the interval, the response must be recorded while simultaneously looking at the student. Students must emit book-observing responses for the entire 5-second interval. If they do so, that interval is recorded as a plus; if they look away for any purpose other than to reach for another book, the interval is recorded as a minus. Students should be looking at or selecting books in the free-play setting for the entire interval as a measure of the reinforcement control of book stimuli over observing responses. Rotate locations of items in the free-play setting for each session (target stimuli and other free-play stimuli) to avoid a location bias. Free-play sessions are typically 5 minutes in duration, and may be lengthened but not shortened. Other children may or may not be in the area, *but the setting events (e.g., the presence or absence of other children) that exist for the first observation must be maintained throughout all other free-play observations.* Criterion for meeting the test of conditioned reinforcement is observation and selection of books for 90% of the intervals for two consecutive 5-minute free-play sessions. If children do not meet criterion, return to the conditioning procedure and add another 5 seconds. However, as the training and testing trials are lengthened, *the number of reinforcements per training trial remains at 2 or 3 reinforcement pairings.* Continue expanding the intervals until the child meets criterion. In some cases, prerequisites may need to be taught or alternate tactics used. See Chapter 2 for the analytic repertoires used to determine what should be done when the student is not progressing, and Chapter 7 for the developmental sequence.

Word-Picture Discrimination and Matching

Once books are established as conditioned reinforcers for observing print-related stimuli and for choosing them during free play, children are ready to discriminate between words and pictures and to textually respond to simple words. Select several simple children's books that have uncluttered pictures and only a few words on each page. The books should attract the child's attention, such as those that they choose to look at during free play. Choose books with simple words and select the nouns as target words. For example, if the books are about animals, select animal names. Pictures and their corresponding words should be on the same page. For each page, select a target word and a target picture. It is best if the words and pictures are repeated throughout the book so that there are several learn units with the picture-word pairs.

TEXTBOX 6.2

Book Conditioning Protocol

1. Select target books and edible reinforcers to be paired for the conditioning procedure. Use an audible indicator of 5-second intervals such as another person in the classroom or a pre-recorded tape. Each conditioning session is 5 minutes (60 five-second intervals).
2. The first 5-second interval is a training interval. When the interval begins, prompt the child (if needed) to look at the book and turn the pages. As they look at the book, give them verbal praise (i.e., "Good, I like the way you're looking at the books" or "Nice job pointing to the pictures!"). Deliver edibles in conjunction with verbal approvals. For the first interval, deliver three verbal approvals and edible reinforcers.
3. If the child displays any behavior other than looking at books, stop the timer and begin the interval again. Repeatedly do so each time the child stops looking at books until they perform correctly for the entire 5-second interval.
4. The second 5-second interval is a test interval. When the interval begins, closely observe the child's attention to the book. No praise or edibles are delivered. Record a plus for this interval if the student observes or touches the book, turns pages, points to or tacts pictures, and textually responds or points to textual stimuli for the entire 5 seconds.
5. Record a minus for the test interval if the student emits any behavior other than observing the books (e.g., stops looking at books and talks to the teacher or emits stereotypy). Terminate the test interval without consequation and begin the next interval when the child attends to the book (use prompting if needed).
6. Immediately after a completed test trial, begin a new training trial. This process continues until 20 train/test trials (intervals) are completed.
7. Mastery criterion is 19/20 correct responses for two consecutive sessions or for some children 100% for one session. After mastering criterion for book conditioning, conduct a 5-minute probe in the play area of the classroom by observing the child with several books and other play items. If they do not choose to look at books for one 5-minute session, return to the book-conditioning procedure, but increase the length of each train/test interval by 5 seconds (i.e., use 10-second intervals instead of 5-second intervals). Continue to extend the time until the child looks at the books for one 5-minute session in the play area.

Construct a simple frame or use pieces of construction paper to block off all of words except the target word. You may have to use highlights to provide visual prompts at first, but if the child is successful without them, do not use them. Cover all of the words *except the target word* on the page. Select five word-picture combinations to be presented four times each during a 20-learn unit session. Begin with learn units to teach the word-picture discrimination. When the child is attending to the target word or picture, say, "Point to the word for (printed word *dog* or another target stimulus)." Wait three seconds for a response. Reinforce correct responses with praise and edibles or tokens. Correct the errors by presenting the antecedent again and having the child emit the correct response (some prompting may be needed), but do not reinforce their response. For the next learn unit, say, "Point to the picture for (dog or another target stimulus)." Wait three seconds for a response, and contingently correct

---

RESEARCH BOX **6.1**

Conditioning Books as Reinforcers

Tsai and Greer examined the effects of conditioning books as reinforcers on four typically developing preschool children. Children were matched based on the number of learn units to criterion for acquiring textual responses, and then observing responses for either toys or books were conditioned for each member of a pair, with books eventually conditioned for all participants. Results showed that all four children required fewer learn units to master textual responses after books were conditioned as reinforcers, those who received the book conditioning first performed best, three of the four children maintained a preference for books during 33%–100% of free-play probes one month after the study ended, and there were no maintenance effects on accuracy of textual responding.

Tsai, H., & Greer, R. D. (2006). Conditioned preference for books and the acquisition of textual responding by pre-school children. *Journal of Early Intensive Behavioral Intervention. 3.1*, 35–60. http://www.behavior-analyst-online.org

---

or reinforce it. Repeat for each word-picture pair, rotating the sequence of presentation between words and pictures. The procedure is then repeated for a speaker response. The following script describes how to rotate between listener or selection responses, and speaker or production responses, during this program.

Tactics for Teaching Word-Picture and Matching Discrimination

 1. Selection responses (listener): a) *Point to the picture of the dog.* Complete the learn unit. b) *Point to the word for dog.* Complete the learn unit. c) Go to the next page with the dog picture and the word. d) Rotate the order of picture and word learn units or counterbalance them. e) *Point to the word for dog.* Complete the learn unit. f) *Point to the picture of the dog.* Complete the learn unit. g) Go to another page with a different word-picture combination. h) *Point to the cat.* Complete the learn unit. i) *Point to the word for cat.* Complete the learn unit. j) Go to the next page with the cat picture and the word. k) Rotate the order of picture and word learn units or counterbalance them. l) Continue to do this until each of the 5 pictures and words has been presented enough times to constitute 20-learn unit sessions—10 words and 10 pictures. Continue these sessions until the student masters the responses at 90% for two successive sessions or 100% for one session.

 2. Selection and Saying Responses. Now you are ready to obtain textual responses. At this point all of the words except the target word are covered. Continue to use the same book and learn unit items. The script for the presentations should be similar to the following: a) Point to the word and say, "*Read the word*". Complete the learn unit.

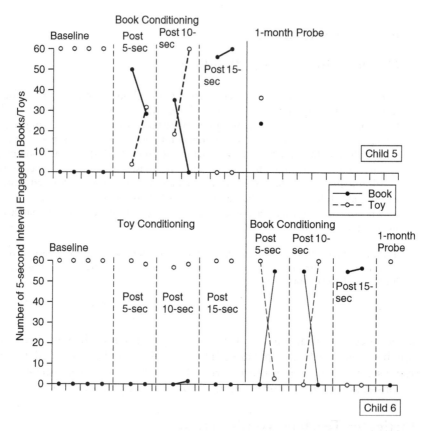

FIGURE 6.1   Free-choice Responses after Conditioning Books

b) *"Find the picture for the word."* Complete the learn unit. c) Go to the next page with the dog picture and the word. Rotate the order as follows. d) *"Point to the dog."* Complete the learn unit. e) Point to the word and say, *"Read the word."* f) Go to the next pair of word-picture combinations, rotating the picture and word order of presentations. g) Continue these sessions until the student masters the responses at 90% for two successive sessions or 100% for one session.

Using the Edmark® Reading Series

The Edmark® reading curriculum is a well-programmed and tested procedure for teaching early reading skills to children experiencing learning problems. It is a whole-word reading program that we use to expand the word-discrimination repertoire described earlier. It also provides children with the prerequisites needed to learn from more abstract phonetic programs (for children without verbal delays, we begin with

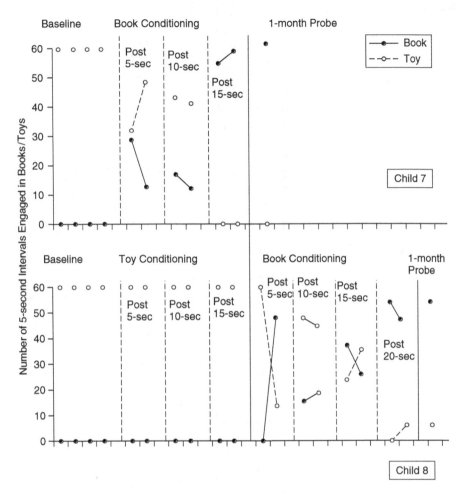

FIGURE 6.1 (*continued*)

phonetic curricula because they often already have the prerequisites). You can begin Edmark® once children master book conditioning and the word-picture discrimination program, or the two programs can be used simultaneously since Edmark introduces printed symbols before words. If children master the word-picture program quickly, they may not need to complete the Edmark® series, and can proceed to a phonetic program such as *Reading Mastery®*.

To teach reading, initially the Edmark® print series use systematically progressive teaching frames or steps to rotate instruction across listener (pointing) and speaker (textual) responses. A frame in this programmed instruction is to be treated as a learn unit. Beginning with lesson one of book one, present the instructional frames per the Edmark curricular guidelines, and provide contingent reinforcement and cor-

FIGURE 6.2 Learn Units to Criterion for Textual Responding after Book Conditioning

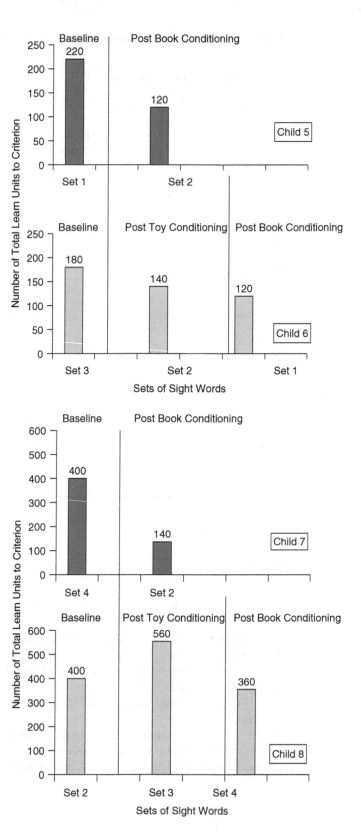

FIGURE 6.3   Picture of Book Conditioning Effects

rections after each frame in order to ensure that learn units are presented. Also, time each lesson in order to obtain a rate of responding, which will be used once a lesson is mastered. Graph the *percentage* of correct responses for each lesson (we do not graph number correct because the number of frames varies across lessons). Mastery criterion is 90% accuracy for each lesson. When a lesson is mastered, set a long-term rate objective of at least 30 correct responses per minute or approximately one correct response every two seconds (modify for children with poor physical coordination whose pointing is not fluent). To teach rates, divide a lesson into smaller sets of five frames, and reinforce responses that are emitted to each set at a targeted rate (i.e., in a lesson with 30 frames, there would be six small sets of frames and the student would need to respond to each small set within 10 seconds). If they meet the rate criterion for each small set (i.e., five correct responses within 10 seconds for the previous example), reinforce their response. Each small set constitutes a single learn unit, and should be recorded with a plus or minus. Achieving the terminal rate may take several lessons, and short-term objectives with slower rates may need to be inserted. Maintain separate graphs for rate and mastery, with the mastery graph showing the percentage correct,

TEXTBOX **6.3**

Word-Picture/Matching Discrimination

1. Select several simple children's books with uncluttered pictures and a few words on each page. The book should have simple, common words, and should attract the child's attention, preferably books that they independently select during play.
2. Select nouns to teach such as animals, food, or vehicles. For example, if the books are about animals, target the animal names (i.e., pig, horse, or cow). Target words and pictures should be on the same page. Construct a simple frame or use pieces of construction paper to block off all of the words except the target word. Select 5–10 target word and picture combinations for each page, preferably words and pictures that are repeated throughout the book. Each word-picture combination should be presented at least twice during a session (2 learn units for each word-picture combination).
3. Turn to the first word-picture combination. First, tell the child to "Point to the *picture* for dog." Wait 3 seconds for a response. Contingently correct or reinforce the response. Next, tell the child to "Point to the *word* for dog." Wait 3 seconds for a response. Contingently correct or reinforce the response.
4. Continue to alternately present picture and textual learn units, ensuring that target stimuli are salient by covering all non-target word-picture pairs on a page or placing only one word-picture pair on each page. When students respond at the mastery criterion, proceed to the next level of responding.
5. Begin the next level of responding by teaching both selection (listener) and production (speaker) responses. Using the same materials targeted for the prior responses, cover all words on a page except for target words.
6. First, point to a word and say, "Read the word." Wait 3 seconds for a response. Contingently correct or reinforce the response. Next, say, "Find the picture for the word." Wait 3 seconds for a response. Contingently correct or reinforce it.
7. Continue to alternate point and textual response learn units until the student achieves mastery criterion for this objective.

---

and the rate graph showing the number per minute of correct and incorrect responses. Identify short-term objectives and new lessons by phase change lines and labels. Use closed triangles to indicate criterion achieved. Refer to Chapters 2 and 7 for more specific procedures on graphing and on graduating response requirements for learn units.

Initially, students will move through the lessons at mastery criterion faster than they will for rate criterion. The importance of providing rate instruction cannot be overemphasized, since the rate of textual responding is critical to the listener literacy component of reading. Students must read fast enough to "hear the story," so to speak. If the rate is not reinforced with Edmark® lessons, the comprehension responses that are required later in the curriculum may become visually dependent. That is, students can only master lessons by matching pictures with words. Thus, when they begin reading material that requires them to "listen to what was read," they will not have the prerequisite repertoire (see the following section for a description of a solution to this problem). However, simultaneously conducting rate and mastery decreases the likelihood that such problems will arise. The existing evidence suggests that *listener literacy is key to comprehension* (Lee Park, 2005). Thus, we need to ensure that the listener literacy component of textually responding is acquired and enhanced. This capability becomes even more important as we teach students phonetic reading.

Reading Comprehension from Hearing One's Own Textual Responses

Using 20-trial sessions, probe students' matching responses on Edmark® picture/phrase cards under three conditions: 1) using the Edmark® series guidelines (the standard procedures for using Edmark picture/phrase cards), 2) with the student's recorded voice reading the phrase cards but with no print stimuli available during responding, and 3) with the teacher's recorded voice reading the phrase cards and with no print stimuli available during responding. Picture/phrase cards are the more advanced lessons that require the student to read a passage and to place items on a board as a measure of reading comprehension (word to picture matching). Stability needs to be achieved in three or more probe sessions using different lessons of the same difficulty level. That is, conduct enough probes to ensure that the student does or does not have a listener-reading comprehension problem. Counterbalance the probe presentation order so that it will not affect the results.

First, the student reads the phrase on the card and completes the comprehension responses with the words present. Second, before the probe, the student reads into a recording device and then completes comprehension responses based on their recorded reading; they should not be able to access the print stimuli (alternately, cover the sentence as soon as the student reads it so that they cannot use the print to answer the questions). Finally, the student listens to the teacher's pre-recorded reading of a phrase and responds to comprehension questions based on the recording; no printed words are available. This latter probe is done to make sure that the problem is not a lack of literacy for the spoken words. After a stable baseline is attained and the student demonstrates that they are not under the listener control of their textual responses, the student is a candidate for the reading listener protocol described in the next section.

If you do not have the Edmark® series you can improvise on these procedures for teaching word-picture discrimination. In this case, use words and pictures in books similar to those used in the word-picture discrimination protocol just described.

Multiple Exemplar Instruction Auditory and Visual Components of Reading Responses

In this program, responding is rotated across each of the conditions just described during a single session until 10 learn units have been presented for each condition. That is, you will use one item from the picture/phrase cards from Edmark® to present a learn unit in Condition 1 (print only, no recording), another item to present a learn

TEXTBOX **6.4**

Probing Reading Comprehension

1. Use the "Picture/Phrase Card" Lessons from the Edmark® reading curriculum (print version) for this program. Each lesson includes about eight small cards containing phrases such as "The boy drives the car" and "The girls eat apples," and a board (about the size of two connected 8 1/2 × 10 pieces of paper) with pictures that match each of the cards, and a distracter. For the adaptation of the picture/phrase card lessons described here, you will also need an audio-recording device (i.e., a digital dicta-recording device).

2. Conduct the first probe by measuring the number of times the student correctly matches the phrase card to its corresponding picture. Conduct this probe in the same manner as the Edmark® picture/phrase card lesson outlined in the program's *Teacher's Guide*. Do not reinforce or correct the student's responses.

3. Before the second probe, have the student read phrase cards from a lesson into the audio-recording device. Conduct the probe by having the student listen as they read a phrase on the pre-recording, after which they should select the corresponding picture with no textual stimulus available to them. Alternatively, the student can read the card and then the teacher can cover it so that the textual stimulus is unavailable during the matching response. The student must respond to the prerecorded words of their own textual responses played back to them without access to the print.

4. Before the third probe, you should read the phrase cards from a lesson into the audio-recording device. Conduct the probe by having the student listen as you read a phrase on the pre-recording, after which they should select the corresponding picture with no textual stimulus available to them. Alternatively, you could read the card and ensure that the textual stimulus is unavailable to the student during the matching response. This is done to ensure that the problem is not a lack of literacy for the spoken words.

5. For probe measures, counterbalance the order of presentations for each type of probe (i.e., no pre-recording, teacher's pre-recording or student's pre-recording). Use different lessons of the same difficulty level across probe types. After stable baseline responding is attained under each condition, proceed to the reading-listener protocol described in Step 1 of the Reader-Listener Protocol.

---

unit in Condition 2 (the student listens to their own vocal reading of the text, no print), and another item to present a learn unit in Condition 3 (the student listens to their teacher's vocal recording, no print). Present all of the items under each condition, but in an unpredictable sequence that will not allow a student to obtain an answer from the immediately preceding learn unit. All learn units are presented individually, but in close conjunction with one another. Continue presenting instruction until a session ends (10 learn units for each condition, when all target items have been presented); mastery is 100% accurate responding for one session or 90% accurate responding for two sessions. When a mastery criterion is achieved, probe students in the manner described earlier. If a criterion is not achieved, conduct other sets of multiple exemplar instruction until responses to the probes show that students can respond correctly to

---

TEXTBOX **6.5**

Reader-Listener Comprehension Instructional Sequence

1. Select Edmark® picture/phrase card lessons that were not used during the probes. Use 20-learn unit sessions during which learn units are rotated across each condition described in the probe measures (text only, teacher's voice without text, and student's voice without text). Mastery criterion is 90% accuracy for each condition.

2. For instruction, we use multiple exemplar instruction during which learn units are rotated across both pre-recorded (voice) and text conditions. Specifically, using the same instructional procedures as the probes, present one learn unit with a textual stimulus (Condition 1), a different item for a learn unit with the student's pre-recorded voice (Condition 2), and a different item for a learn unit with the teacher's pre-recorded voice (Condition 3). Continue these learn units, rotating the order of presentation so that it is unpredictable.

3. Every phrase card is presented under each condition. The instructional sequence for presenting each of these learn units is identical to the probe conditions just described, but the student's responses are contingently reinforced and corrected.

4. This procedure can be modified by using tactics such as zero-second time delay. If students do not achieve mastery criterion on post-instructional probes, omit the textual condition and use the voice conditions only until the student can respond at both a mastery (90% accuracy) and rate criterion.

5. Continue to present multiple exemplar instruction until mastery criterion is achieved for each condition and across all stimuli in a picture/phrase card lesson. Conduct post-instructional probes with the items and measures used in pre-instructional probes.

---

untaught items. If necessary, students may achieve mastery a criterion under each condition, and then return to the multiple exemplar instructional procedure described here. After meeting probe criteria, the student is ready to acquire phonetic textual responding.

Adding Print Stimuli to the Joint Control over Speaker and Listener Responding in the Naming Capability

Learning to read requires adding the print and comprehension components of reading to the joint stimulus control of the speaker, listener, and speaker-as-own-listener classes of responding (see Figure 6.4 showing the types of naming and joining of print to the naming capability). While students may have naming for listener and speaker functions, it does not necessarily follow that they can use "naming" in the reader function (Lee Park, 2005). In many cases, the sequence of instruction, which we described

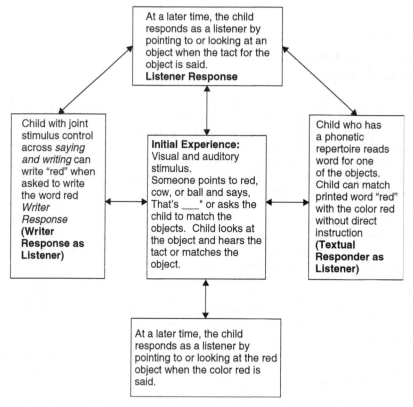

FIGURE 6.4 Joint Stimulus Control When Naming Joins Print Control for Reading and Writing

in the previous sections, will result in print joining the naming relation. Lee Park (2005) found that even though preschool children in her experiment could textually respond, match printed words with corresponding pictures, and match exemplar pictures with matching pictures, they could not match the picture with the spoken word. However, after multiple exemplar instruction with a separate subset of stimuli, print joined naming and the children could match all of the different stimuli. Thus, for some students who are having difficulty with acquiring listener comprehension, it may be advantageous to provide multiple exemplar instruction .

This procedure is to be used with students who have acquired naming. Readers must learn to see the printed word, match it to print, and then listen to what they are speaking and match what they hear. It is useful to use multiple exemplar instruction to ensure that this occurs. In this procedure, have the student respond to the following using learn units and words in different type fonts or script. Type the print stimuli on index cards, or alternately use children's books in which there are a few words on each page and the picture of the word with other items in the picture. For the former, use small or suitably size cards containing the print stimuli so that the student can match them to words on the page.

Before beginning, ensure that students can match target pictures with copies of them. If you use a book, you can have the student point to their picture, and then "point to the one like it." Probe for matching responses to pictures associated with all target words from each word group. If they match all of the pictures, proceed with the next section; if not, teach picture matching to 100% accuracy for each of the four pictures, presented five times during a 20-learn unit session.

When this repertoire is present, proceed through the following sequence by having the student match and point to words and pictures given rotated non-exemplars of the stimuli: 1) Match the printed word with the target word by putting the printed word on top of the target word or pointing to the target word after seeing it; 2) match the word to the picture for the word (i.e., the printed word for dog to a picture of the dog); 3) point to the picture after the teacher says the word for the picture; 4) point to the word after the teacher says the word, given two non-exemplar words; and 5) say the word while touching it. Do this in such a manner that each of these responses are rotated for 4 different words totaling to 20-learn units for a single session. For each presentation rotate the words. That is, the learn unit for matching pictures for one word is followed by matching a printed word to another word, followed by matching another word to a picture.

Once the student has mastered this, teach them to first textually respond to the print, and then to point to the correct picture located in an array of pictures. The student must correctly respond to both the print and picture stimuli to achieve a plus (+). Each word-picture pair is presented 5 times for a 20-learn unit session. Do this until the student achieves 100% accuracy for one session. Next the student must respond to all of the words at 50 accurate word-pictures per minute. This means that they must respond to each set of four word-picture combinations in eight seconds. Each word picture unit constitutes a single learn unit.

When the student can respond to 10 learn units at the target rate criterion, they have met criterion for these words. You should teach several word sets at different stages in the sequence at any given time. Continue adding and teaching word sets until the student has a basic phonetic repertoire as described next. If the student has phonetic responding, and they still have comprehension problems, use the phonetically learned words with relevant pictures and repeat this sequence until comprehension is present. When the student has mastered several sets of words, we can be fairly confident that print has entered the speaker-as-own-listener class of responding and that the student has the necessary skills and capabilities for reading. Once the student has a phonetic reading repertoire, and print control has joined the naming capability, sounding out a novel word can result in immediately having comprehension if the stimulus is part of the naming repertoire. For example, if "zebra" is in the naming repertoire of a child, but they have never encountered the printed word for "zebra," they will immediately comprehend what they read when they sound out the components of the word (i.e., child sounds out ZEE-BRA), and the child can match the picture of zebra as a listener to their own textual response. Also, once the child acquires joint stimulus control across saying and writing, which we describe later in this chapter, simply sounding out the word results in reading comprehension and a writer response (i.e., they can write the word *zebra* without direct instruction).

Phonetic Reading for Textual Responding: Acquiring the Topography

There are a few tested curricula for teaching phonetic textual responding identified earlier in this chapter. While most of these are designed for group instruction, they may be conducted individually or with pairs of students. If students have acquired good observational learning capabilities as described in Chapter 5, group instruction may even be the most effective and efficient way to teach it. If they respond well with computers, consider using the HeadSprout® reading curriculum. Although in the latter case you will have to monitor the children to ensure that they are emitting the textual responses and provide corrections as needed. Each of the commands and sequences in the material can be presented and graphed as responses to learn units. However, since the numbers of learn units vary from lesson to lesson, you will need to use percentage graphs. Reading series should provide children with the 38 basic sets of phonograms that prepare them to use abstract pronunciation with untaught words. If tested curricula are not available, use an available phonetic curriculum, and arrange learn units and long-term and short-term objectives. The Morningside Academy® has published excellent materials that provide extensive material to use as supplements in teaching vowel-consonant blends. The contribution of research-based material is that it systematically programs the acquisition of abstraction for vowel-consonant combinations such that children will learn to textually respond to novel arrangements blends without direct instruction. These materials can be used by employing learn unit protocols, learn unit measurement, and the decision protocol such that the child's individual progress directs instruction along with the curricular materials. Of course, there are words in the English language that are not pronounced phonetically—these exceptions must also be taught.

As students learn to sound out words they have never before encountered, they become independent textual responders. However, the words they sound out should be in their listener repertoire, or else they must acquire the repertoire to induce the "meaning" of the word from context. If one has no listener or speaker history with a duck-billed platypus (either pictures or actual observation), the textual response will not result in "comprehension." However, other "meanings" can be learned from context. Future research may identify the controlling variables for this repertoire.

Using the Auditory-Matching Protocol in Solving Phonetic Reading Difficulties

If students are having difficulty with phonetic discriminations such as reversals of letters, as in b and d reversals, you can use the auditory-matching protocol and device described in detail in Chapter 3. Modify the procedure in the following way: First, identify basic vowel sounds and print examples of them on index cards (or better yet, use published material). For example, one card has the long *A* sound printed on it (sound card) and two simple words containing a long *A* sound are printed on other cards (word cards). The student has two sound buttons, one that produces the correct vowel sound and one that is a non-exemplar. Present the sound card to the student and press the two buttons in succession (alternating the order). The student then presses the button that has the matching sound. Once the student matches the sound accurately, they are also to pronounce the words on the word cards. If this proceeds with success, conduct the procedure with vowel-consonant blends (sets of phonograms) until they accurately match and pronounce the sounds and words containing them.

If the student has difficulty, proceed to the next step. Record vowel sounds on the buttons; arrange them in sets of five. Push your button to produce a target vowel sound and then have the student push their own two buttons, one that produces the target vowel sound and one that produces a non-exemplar vowel sound. Begin with sounds that are phonetically similar (i.e., a short *A* and a long *E*), but if the student has difficulty, use dissimilar vowel or consonant sounds. Successively program instruction so that the student progresses from very different sounds to very similar sounds in the scheme outlined in Chapter 3 for auditory matching. Each set of approximations is a single short-term objective. Once the student can discriminate closely related vowel sounds, have them match and echo the sounds until they master the pronunciation. Once this is done, they should master saying the vowel sound while seeing the print. If necessary, repeat the procedure with vowel-consonant blends.

TEXTBOX **6.6**

Solving Phonetic Reading Difficulties with the Auditory-Matching Protocol

1. On index cards, write basic vowel sounds and words that contain them. For example, one card may have a long *A* sound and two words that contain the long *A* sound. As in the auditory, matching protocol, the student should have two sound-producing buttons—one that produces the target vowel sound and one that is a non-exemplar.
2. Present an index card with sound symbols and words printed on it that correspond to the vowel sound on one of the sound-producing buttons. Press both of the student's buttons and wait three seconds for the student to choose the button with the matching sound. Contingently reinforce or correct.
3. Immediately after the learn unit just described the student should pronounce the word or words on the page. Contingently reinforce or correct their response. After the student meets criterion at this level, then add vowel consonant blends until the student matches and pronounces them accurately.

Motivational Functions of Reading and Writing

Establishing the "Need to Read"

An important objective of reading instruction is that children learn the "need to read." By "need to read" we mean that the child reads because doing so provides them with something they want. How can we do this? One way, of course, is by providing prosthetic reinforcement in the form of edibles or tokens. Still other ways involve having the child read in order to find preferred items. For example, preferred items or tokens can be located under a container with a corresponding word on top (including several "distracter" containers with different words). As students read the words, they can obtain the item.

As the student acquires a minimal reading repertoire, they can read directions for finding hidden items in the room. Another student or teacher writes directions for finding a hidden object. In this procedure you can have teams of students compete for prizes on the game reinforcement board that we described in Chapter 5. That is, the reader and writer are yoked for reinforcement. When the reader successfully finds the object or does what the written instructions say, both the writer and reader win; if the reader does not follow the instructions within the appropriate number of attempts (based on the childrens' reader repertoires), the teacher's game piece moves up the board. Each attempt with a rewrite or success constitutes a response to a learn unit.

The reinforcement for reading aesthetic material such as fiction and poetry resides in the listener reinforcement that accrues from the emotional effects of having the listener's senses extended. The listener can experience the thrill of danger, intrigue, or the emotional effects involving relationships. While it is beyond the scope of our discussion of beginning reading, it is likely that experiences in listening to stories, preferably with positive reinforcement pairings, will condition the type of stimu-

---

TEXTBOX 6.7

Establishing the "Need to Read"

Tactic 1

In three containers, hide two non-preferred and one preferred items. On each container, affix an index card that contains the corresponding word. For example, on each of three identical containers, the words *cookie*, *bag*, and *tape* would be placed. Tell the student to find the cookie and wait three seconds for them to begin to read the words and locate the cookie. Contingently correct and reinforce.

Tactic 2

Hide preferred objects in the classroom. Give the students a set of simple directions that they should follow to find the objects. This can be conducted as a team game during which the yoked-contingency game board described in Chapter 5 is used.

TEXTBOX **6.8**

Teaching Sequences for the Topography of Writing

Children need to learn the motor skills of forming letters and words as the basis for subsequently acquiring the functions of writing. Often this takes a prolonged period of time; using the computer to type allows the function to be taught while the topogra- phy of writing is being learned. Simultane- ously, teach textual responses, transcription, and dictation in a multiple exemplar fashion such that the foundation is established for the transformation of stimulus function across saying and writing.

lus control. Also, as the "words" themselves have multiple response relations, the aes- thetic response is extended. For example, the word *snake*, not only has a "picture" matching component, but for most people there is a concomitant learned respondent (see Staats, 1968, for the seminal research on this relation; see also Hayes, Barnes- Holmes, & Roche, 2001, for subsequent and more recent treatments by relational frame theorists). In a manner of speaking, the aesthetic effects of "words" appear to be the various respondent-learning histories encountered by the individual. Metaphoric expressions that function as extended tacts also play a critical role in the aesthetic effect (Matthews, 2005; Meincke, Keohane, Gifaldi, & Greer, 2003).

Establishing the Topography of Writing

Establishing the topography of writing requires extensive instruction in copying let- ters, numbers, lines, and circles. One effective procedure is to have children trace let- ters comprised of dotted lines. That is, provide page(s) of dot outlines of the letters of the alphabet and the child's name (choose them from a web page for elementary grade teachers). Fade the dots by increasing the distance between them and by decreasing the number of dots. The child should also have exemplars to copy, and not just to trace since the goal is for them to copy or **transcribe** (Skinner, 1957). When children have mastered some of the topographies of tracing and copying letters, teach them to write letters from dictation. Subsequently, use words that they can read, copy, and write from dictation. Alternate transcription and dictation in a multiple exemplar instruc- tion fashion so that the child learns the relationship between seeing and writing, and between hearing and writing. This develops the capability to **hear-write** and **see- write** as a higher order operant. See Figure 6.4 showing the relationship between naming, textually responding, and writing.

Once this is established, have the child write words for their mands as prescribed in the section on teaching the "need to write." When this is established, they can write tacts, and when the tacts are accurate, they can write mands and receive the specified items. If the process of teaching the topography is proceeding slowly, have the chil- dren type on the computer. This is probably useful for all students regardless of their

RESEARCH BOX 6.2

Multiple Exemplar Instruction and Novel Verbal Responses

This study tested the effects of multiple exemplar instruction on the acquisition of joint stimulus control of dictated words for both written and vocal spelling responses to sight words by eight kindergartners with language delays or autism. Results showed that all of the participants acquired more untaught spelling responses for novel stimuli than they did during single exemplar instruction. The procedure provides joint stimulus control of a spoken word across speaking and writing.

From Greer, R. D., Yuan, L., & Gautreaux, G. (2005). Novel dictation and intraverbal responses as a function of a multiple exemplar instructional history. *Analysis of Verbal Behavior, 21*, 99–116.

writing progress, but for those for whom the topography of writing is proceeding slowly, teach typing so that the function of writing can be quickly taught. This is done to rapidly lead the student to the functional effect of writing.

After students learn to copy words by typing, then you arrange the contingencies such that writing has a functional effect. In this process, write a short question that the student must respond to by typing. For example, the child can type answers to questions such as "What is your name?" "What is your sister's name?" "What did you come

TEXTBOX 6.9

Establishing the "Topography of Writing"

1. Create several handwriting worksheets containing letters comprised of dotted lines that are progressively faded across worksheets. The student's handwriting becomes more independent as fewer dotted lines are available to trace.
2. After the child can write the letters without dotted lines, use similar worksheets (without faded lines) so that the student can copy letters.
3. After the child can copy letters to criterion, have them write letters and words that you dictate. Follow this with writing words for their mands as described in the section on teaching the "need to write." When they can mand by writing, they should write tacts, and then receive a reinforcer because they manded it through writing.
4. For students who have difficulties with writing, typing may be more useful. The student should copy words by typing (without a function) before they type mands and tacts. Well-designed computer programs can be used to teach touch-typing to more advanced students.
5. To teach functional writing through typing, have the child type answers to simple questions such as "What is your name?" and "What is your sister's name? What is your favorite toy?" After typing the correct answer to the question, the student can mand a reinforcer by typing.

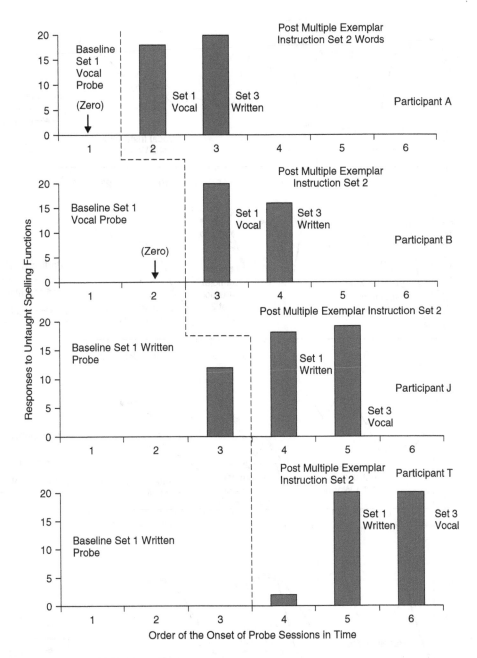

FIGURE 6.5   Multiple Exemplar Instruction and Spelling

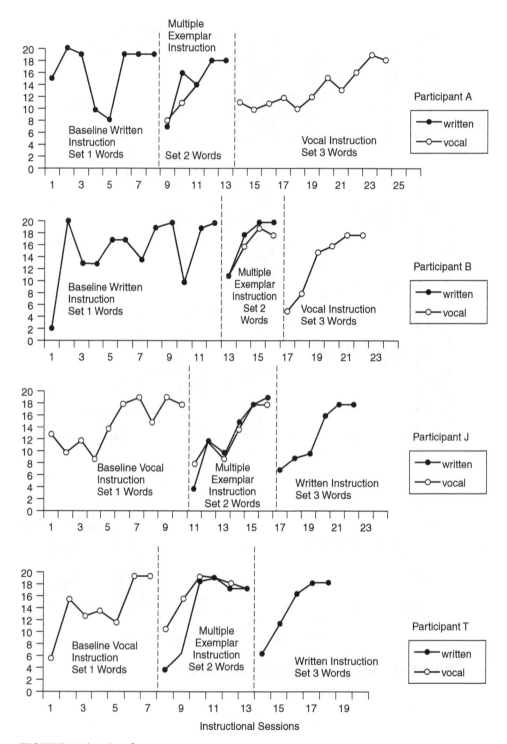

FIGURE 6.5 (*continued*)

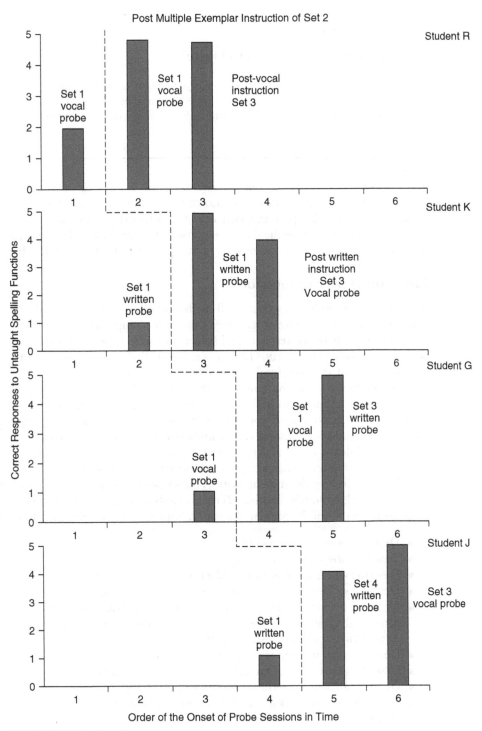

FIGURE 6.5 (*continued*)

> TEXTBOX **6.10**
>
> ## Establishing the "Need to Write"
>
> Children need to learn the verbal behavior function of writing under the appropriate establishing operations if they are to learn the natural motivational conditions for effective writing. Writers need to learn that the function of writing is to affect the behavior of the reader.

to school in?" and "What is your favorite toy, animal, color, game, or place to go?" Subsequently, they can mand their reinforcers by typing the answers and writing their mands. Provide word-typing experiences in the same manner as teaching echoics (see Chapter 4), but in this case the duplic response is written. More advanced students can then be introduced to well-designed computer programs for teaching touch-typing.

Protocol: Writer Immersion

As the student gains better writing skills with a pencil, use the functional writing exercises described in the typing program. At this point arrange periods of the day when all communication between teachers and students as well as between students and their peers occurs in written form. This procedure, called **writer immersion,** leads to improvements in the structural and functional components of writing. Ensure adequate reinforcement for the effects of the writing. A peer should read the written response and attempt to do it. The procedure continues until the peer accomplishes the task, at which point *both* students win a point. Use the yoked-contingency game board (see Chapter 5). Responses and editing corrections are arranged as learn units in sessions of 20-learn units, and the achievement of the objective of each assignment constitutes a short-term goal. Other exercises that assist the acquisition of the "need to write" include having the student write 1) directions for how to get from one place in the school or classroom to another, 2) their mands and tacts, or 3) their favorite jokes for peers to read until the peer laughs at it. Additional topics include the following:

- Describe how to make a sandwich
- Describe how to start the computer
- Describe where a student can find a toy
- Describe someone in the room without using their name
- Describe an animal, insect, flower, or mode of transportation without using name of the item until a peer accurately identifies it (use the yoked-contingency game board to enhance establishing operations)
- Describe a toy without using its name until the peer identifies it
- Describe the seasons of the year without using the names of the seasons
- Describe an activity in the classroom without using the name of the activity
- Describe the contents of a children's book without using the title until the peer identifies the book

RESEARCH BOX 6.3

Writer Immersion

Reilly Lawson and Greer (2006) implemented writer immersion with seven ninth-grade students in a program for children with behavior disorders. Writers edited their papers until a reader could accurately draw the picture described in their writing. The dependent variables were the number of accurate structural responses of a writer and the number of components that were accurately drawn by a reader. Results showed that writer immersion and self-editing increased both functional and structural accuracy during two experiments. See also Jadlowski (2000) and Madho (1997).

These are only a few of the many possible exercises. The nature of the classroom and level of children's verbal behavior determine the complexity or simplicity of the task. It is important that students rotate the reading and writing functions. Current evidence indicates that the process of responding as a reader or editor acts to improve the writing effectiveness of students. Thus, by providing yoked contingencies during which reader and writer functions are rotated, the basis for eventually effective **self-editing** is provided.

In this chapter, we described the basic protocols and teaching tactics to teach print control and the joining of print control to the naming repertoire. We also described how children write to control the behavior of readers through writing and the joining of reader and writer responses to the naming capability. These are the functional goals of teaching reading and writing. The structural goals are present in standard reading curricula, and these need to be taught simultaneously with the teaching of the functions of reading and writing. The information in this chapter concerns only the foundations of reading and writing. However, we suspect that many, if not most, problems that students have with reading or writing at more advanced stages are related to the lack of these foundational components. We identified and described tested teaching protocols to induce capabilities with beginning readers or to induce them in children for whom those are missing. In addition, we identified and described basic teaching tactics that can be used to teach the components of reading and writing.

At this point in the text, we have described the range of antecedent stimulus and reinforcement control that constitutes the foundation of complex verbal behavior—the behavior of the speaker, the listener, and the interlocking relation within and outside of the skin. These multiple relations include verbal and non-verbal antecedent control. They also include the multiple verbal responses ranging from those of the speaker to those of the writer related to the various antecedent and consequences for these responses—verbal and non-verbal consequences across listener and speaker functions. We also identified the interaction of these antecedent, responses, and consequences involved in the process of acquiring and using self-editing and the solving of problems governed by the verbal behavior of others or emitting verbal behavior to

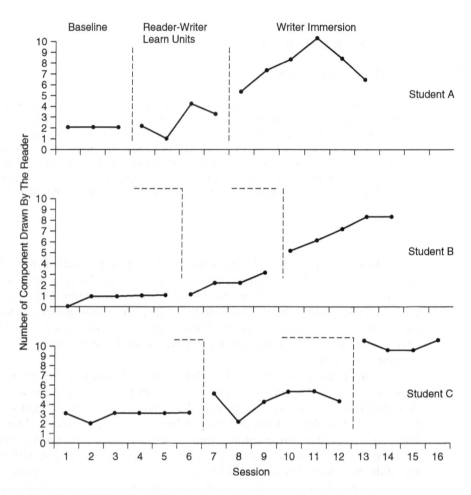

FIGURE 6.6   Writer Immersion

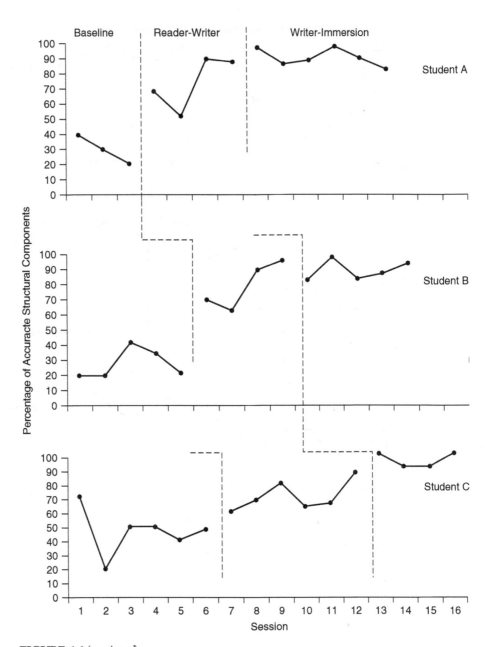

FIGURE 6.6 (*continued*)

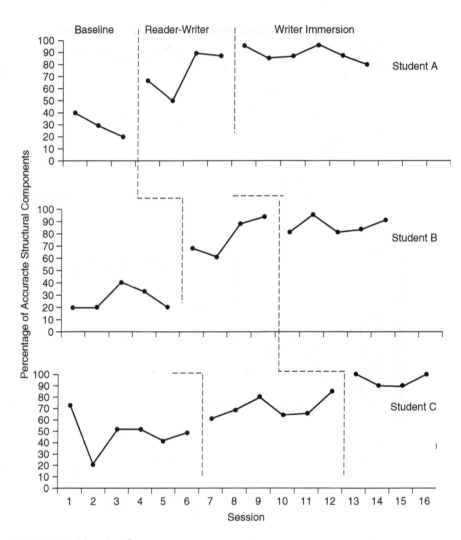

FIGURE 6.6 (*continued*)

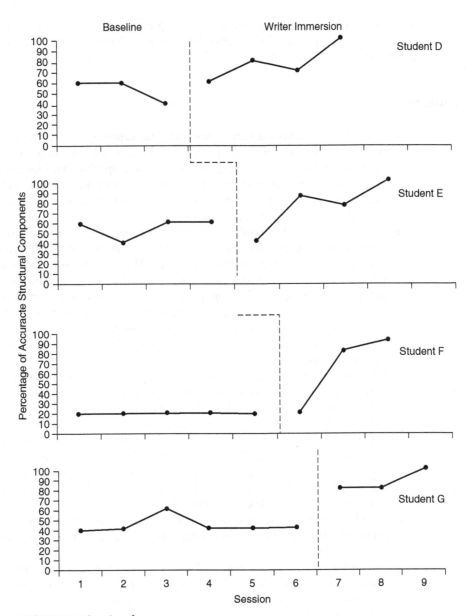

FIGURE 6.6 (*continued*)

assist the reader in solving problems. In Chapter 7, we provide an overview of the developmental sequence, the evidence base for why that sequence is important, and comments on scientific validity.

Summary

- This chapter identified verbal functions and capabilities associated with rudimentary reading and writing, and provided research-based protocols for teaching them. Writing and reading are extensions of speaking and listening in that readers respond to print stimuli in the same way that listeners respond to auditory stimuli. However, effective reading and writing involves the joining of print control to the basic naming capability.
- Conditioning book stimuli is important because children learn to textually respond at an accelerated pace as a function of book stimuli acquiring conditioned reinforcement control for observing. When books are conditioned reinforcers for observing, children have a capability that can be operationally defined as "reading readiness." The conditioning procedure involves training trials during which two or three stimulus-stimulus pairings are presented, followed by a test trial during which no pairing occurs. Observations in free-play areas are used before and after the conditioning interventions to determine the acquisition of the capability.
- Word-picture matching and discrimination is used to teach relationships and differences between pictures and words and between the initial discrimination between pictures and words. Identify simple children's books and use nouns with corresponding pictures to teach this repertoire.
- The role of the listener within the skin of the textual responder is key and often that relationship requires the special instruction described in the joining of print stimuli to the naming capability. Moreover, the listener response is sometimes missing or weak, and we described protocols to ensure that the textual responder is a listener to her own textual responses.
- We identified the motivational functions of reading and writing and we provided procedures for including the necessary establishing operations in the teaching of reading and writing.
- The utility of both whole word and phonetic responding is apparent in first the discrimination of words from non-words via whole word procedures and in the subsequent acquisition of phonemic responding as the abstraction needed for textual responding.
- When children have difficulty with the listener aspects of phonemic responding, the auditory-matching protocol can be adapted to assist in the building of this repertoire.
- We described and identified procedures for inducing and teaching the joining of both reading and writing repertoires to the naming capability.
- Writing requires the joint control of speech over saying and writing and we described how this capability can be induced.

- Edmark®, Reading Mastery®, and Saxon® are examples of commercial reading curricula for teaching early whole word and phonetic-reading repertoires. Learn units and the decision protocol are important tools to use with these and with other curricula that provide the structural components of reading. The motivational conditions for reading need to be incorporated with the teaching of the structural components if the "need to read" is to be acquired.

- Use the *writer immersion* program to teach the "need to write." During this program, students modify their technical writing pieces based on the response of a reader; if the reader can follow the writer's directions or tact an item they describe, the written piece is functional. Providing this functional component of writing to the structural objectives is key to the teaching of effective writing.

- The topography of writing is established by using tracing or copying. However, the functional effects may be taught via typing when the topography of writing is slow in coming.

Identifying and Inducing Verbal Developmental Capabilities

So far as I am concerned, science does not establish truth or falsity: it seeks the most effective way of dealing with subject matter.

Skinner, 1986, p. 241

Regard no practice as immutable. Change and be ready to change again. Accept no eternal verity. Experiment.

Skinner 1979, 1984, p. 346

Problems in Verbal Development, Current Solutions, and a Trajectory for More Solutions

In the first section of this chapter, we briefly outline capabilities that some children lack or do not acquire in their verbal development. These deficits in verbal capabilities underlie many of the major obstacles professionals have encountered in developing verbal behavior in children who were missing some or all of the verbal capabilities. We identify protocols and sequences of protocols for each of the missing capabilities as they relate to the sequence of capabilities identified as obstacles to verbal development. The protocols are described in detail elsewhere in the book; here we provide an overview. The first 12 problems and capability objectives concern the building of the basic listener and speaker capabilities; the next five concern the joining of speaker and listener repertoires, and the final two concern the joining of print to the speaker as own listener capabilities. In the second section of this chapter, we outline verbal developmental capabilities and their interrelation. We also relate specific protocols to the verbal developmental capabilities in order to show the trajectory of the capabilities and the protocols to induce them. In the third section of the chapter, we discuss scientific methodology and its relationship to practice as well as some suggestions for further research.

Foundations of Speaker and Listener Capabilities

In the process of dealing with missing verbal repertoires, research and practice based on verbal behavior accrued because children had certain deficits. Developing procedures to overcome these deficits led to the identification of these verbal capabilities and protocols that led to solutions. The following constitutes a brief outline of the verbal developmental problems presented by some children we have taught; and a reference to the protocols, capabilities, and their sequences that are used to establish speaker and listener functions. *Once each capability is mastered, provide and teach curricular objectives that are feasible to teach the student at this stage of development.* For example, when visual tracking and the capacity for sameness are present, then teach matching responses for various curricula.

1) When Attention to the Teacher Is Missing

The student needs to be under pre-listener instructional control. When the child is a pre-listener and is not under the instructional control of the presence of the teacher, major interventions are needed. Teach the pre-listener emersion programs to mastery or the attending repertoires that are needed by the child (Chapter 3). Once the instructional control is present, teach curricular instructional goals that can also contribute to the acquisition of pre-listener control such as conditioned reinforcement programs for voices, toys, books, and puzzles. The students can also be taught to stay in the play area as described in Chapter 3 in this text and in Chapter 5 of *Designing*

Teaching Strategies: An Applied Behavior Analysis Systems Approach (Greer, 2002). Until the teacher has *pre-listener instructional control*, little can be accomplished. By pre-listener instructional control, we mean that the student responds to a teacher as a source of reinforcement and will follow instructions by *responding to visual or sequential prompts*, but the consonant/phonetic component units of the speech of others do not necessarily control responding in the absence of visual or sequential cues. At this point it does little good, and may do harm, to teach more advanced curricular objectives until the student has mastered this basic capability. First, you have to have the student's attention. One must, so to speak, hold the tokens as a necessary condition for presenting learn units. Review the details described in Chapter 3.

Do not conduct instruction for other capabilities until the student meets the requirements for pre-listener instructional control. In many cases, the pre-listener instructional control can be taught in a full day or week of instruction, although some children may require more instructional time. You can teach curricular goals that do not require more advanced capabilities just as described. It is best if the attending repertoire and relevant instructional goals are taught across multiple teachers in order to evoke control across all teachers rather than with a single teacher. It is the use of *procedures* accurately across instructors, and not the presence of a particular instructor that must teach the student. The presence of reinforcement operations needs to occur across teachers such that the presence of reinforcers evokes attention. Once attention to the teacher is present, probe for attention to instructional stimuli by either doing the visual-tracking procedure or doing matching instruction to determine if attention to instructional stimuli is present. If attention to instructional stimuli is missing, then conduct the following protocol to induce it.

2) When Attention to Instructional Stimuli Is Missing

While the student needs to learn to attend to visual stimuli so that they can *master matching instruction*, they first need to be under pre-listener instructional control. Once established, teach visual tracking to induce stimulus control for observing stimuli on the desktop (see Chapter 3). You will need to teach visual tracking first if the student does not match stimuli readily. You may want to institute the listener emersion protocol to induce basic listener literacy at this point, but do not include visual matching or point-to instruction until the tracking program is mastered and has resulted in rapid mastery of matching programs. If you have doubts about the student's capability for sameness across the different senses as evidenced by difficulty in matching stimuli, do the sensory-matching protocol. *Do not do the next procedure until attention to visual instructional stimuli is present.* Also, if the student matches visual and auditory stimuli and is acquiring speaker operants quickly, the next protocol may not be needed.

3) When the Capacity for Sameness Is Missing— Do the Sensory-Matching Protocol

Probe for this repertoire and if it is missing (Chapter 3), then teach the sensory-matching protocol that is designed to ensure that the child has cross-modal or inter-model sameness by matching (i.e., the student responds to sameness for scents, textures, sounds, and visual stimuli). Continue reinforcement conditioning for observing responses to books, games or other stimuli, matching, and even listener emersion, provided that objectives are being met. If objectives in the listener emersion protocol are not being met, then wait until the student masters sensory matching followed by acquiring the capability to be reinforced by voices that will be described next. If the child does not orient to the teacher, then use the conditioned reinforcement for voices protocol before doing the auditory-matching protocol.

4) When the Capability to Be Reinforced for Attention to Adult Voices Is Missing

If this is missing, before going to the auditory-matching protocol, condition reinforcement for observing adult speech using the voice-conditioning protocol (see Chapter 3). Once the voice-conditioning protocol is present, proceed to the auditory matching protocol.

5) When the Capability for Emitting Speaker Verbal Operants Is Missing

As soon as the child is under the instructional control of the teacher, regardless of the presence or absence of basic listener literacy, begin teaching the verbal speaker operants described in detail in Chapter 4. This includes the development of the echoic-to-mand and echoic-to tact-capabilities with related autoclitics and any needed protocols to induce these capabilities as detailed in Chapter 4. If the child is making no progress, suspend instruction on speaker behavior until the listener emersion protocol is mastered and then do the auditory-matching protocol. If the student is making slow but steady progress, continue the speaker instruction but also do the listener emersion protocol. If the child's learning of speaker behavior accelerates significantly after the listener emersion protocol, you may not need to conduct auditory matching. If the progress is the same as before acquisition of listener emersion, conduct the auditory-matching protocol as you continue the speaker instruction.

6) When the Capability to Match Consonant/Vowel Combinations of Spoken Words Is Missing or Speech Is Faulty—Do the Auditory-Matching Protocol

The student needs to acquire the listener capability to match the spoken words of others (appropriate echoics). If the student was not mastering the listener emersion protocol, use the auditory-matching protocol and then return to the listener emersion protocol. If echoic responding was missing prior to the mastery of auditory matching, probe afterward to see if echoic responding has emerged. If echoics were not exact, that is, the elocution or enunciation was approximate or unrelated to the vocal antecedent for the echoic, then probe for the presence of the auditory-matching capability. The auditory-matching protocol has four possible outcomes: (a) the emersion of the capability to now learn basic listener literacy (i.e., mastery of listener emersion), (b) improvement in point-to-point echoic forms, (c) emergence of approximations of echoics, or (d) emergence of vocal sounds that are not approximations but are first instances of vocal sounds in response to vocal antecedents. The outcomes of this protocol determine what is to be done next. That is, the emergence of clarity in speech or emergence of first instances of echoics, approximations, or non-approximate vocalizations suggests the steps that must be taken for speaker responding. When problems with echoics or clarity of the forms occur, use the auditory procedure as a listener-to-speaker intervention for those specific speech sounds undergoing problems. That is, if the child says *pan* for *pen*, use the auditory device with words of close proximity. Similarly, if the child omits endings in speech or textual responding, teach her to match the spoken word sounds as a listener until she discriminates between words with and without endings. Once this is mastered, probe for basic listener literacy (listener emersion) if the student has not already mastered it (see Chapter 3). Do curricular programs that the child can make progress in as you work through the capabilities described in the next section, but do not present instruction that is dependent on basic listener literacy until that listener repertoire is mastered.

7) When Basic Listener Literacy Is Missing

You should do the listener emersion protocol as soon as the child is under instructional control (see Step 1). You might have to suspend the listener emersion program because of deficits that were just described. If these are mastered and the child still needs to acquire basic listener literacy, return to the listener emersion protocol until that repertoire is present. When that repertoire is present, we are ready to induce the listener component of naming. After each of these repertoires is in place, then probe for the listener component of naming. Once the listener and early stages of the speaker capabilities are present, expand the curricula that you teach so that you are using all of the child's existing capabilities (see Chapter 3).

8) When There Are Few Tacts in Repertoire: Expand the Tact Repertoire

As soon as the speaker capabilities emerge, expand the teaching of tacts significantly. Remember, until the child has naming and a basic reading repertoire, the only way that you can expand the child's vocabulary is by teaching tacts directly (see Chapter 5 for the intensive tact protocol).

9) When The Listener Capability of Naming Is Missing: Implement the Multiple Exemplar Protocol for the Listener Component of Naming

If probes for the listener-to-speaker repertoire show that this capability is not present, do the procedures for teaching the listener component of naming. Also, if the child is making progress with echoics-to-mands and echoic-to-tacts, probe for the full naming repertoire which includes the listener and speaker components. If the full naming capability is not present and the student has echoic-to-mands, echoic-to-tacts, and the listener component of naming, then do the protocol for inducing naming. Alternately, if the basic speaker operants are present and the listener component is missing, then skip Step 9 and move directly to Step 10, which is the induction of naming. *Note:* If the basic speaker operants are missing, expand the naming protocol by teaching observational learning of the listener component of naming. First probe for the observational learning of the listener component of naming, and if it is not present, then conduct that protocol or Step 8 (see Chapter 3).

10) When Capability for Observational Learning of the Listener Half of Naming Is Missing

Once the student has the listener component of naming, but not the speaker half, you can introduce the protocol for inducing observational learning of the listener component of naming. If the student has full naming, then proceed to Step 11 or to the section on joining speaker and listener capabilities. Once this is present and the student has both the basic verbal operants and naming, probe for the capability of observational learning for full naming. If that is not present, proceed to the joining of the speaker and listener responding (see Chapter 5).

11) When the Capability of Observational Learning of Tacts Is Missing

If full naming is in the child's repertoire and the capability for learning tacts by observation is not present, then do the protocol for teaching observational learning of tacts (see Chapter 5).

12) Fixing Faulty Echoic and Intraverbal Repertoires

If the child's echolalia remains a problem but she has mastered the auditory-matching protocol, then use the auditory discrimination procedure to teach her how to match appropriate intraverbals. If the problem with echolalia interferes with some of these steps, you may need to do one of the procedures described in a subsequent section before moving the child through the verbal capabilities. Teach the auditory intraverbal matching protocol as a listener and then probe for the presence or absence of the intraverbal. If echolalia is still present, do the procedure involving the listener intraverbal followed by the child echoing the correct listener response; fade by pushing the teacher's button until the student produces the correct intraverbal instead of the faulty echoic response. When this is mastered, instead of using the button to produce the greeting or question, the teacher initiates the question vocally and the student responds by pushing the button that produces the appropriate intraverbal or the not-echoic button. If palilalia is the problem, do the protocols for fixing palilalia as described in Chapter 5.

Joining Speaker and Listener Capabilities

1) Speaker-as-Own-Listener

First, probe the child for conversational units, tacts, and self-talk conversational units in solitary free-play settings. If these are not present, do the speaker-as-own-listener protocols as needed until these are present (Chapter 5). Continue all other instructional programs to teach those local educational standards and curricula that the child has the necessary verbal capabilities to learn, including objectives for academic literacy, self-management, problem-solving, and enlarging the community of conditioned reinforcers for observation and activity.

When the child has these listener repertoires and they culminate in observational learning of full naming, we want to join the listener and speaker repertoires. The following protocols are designed as steps to develop these verbal capabilities. First, probe for independent pure and intraverbal tacts as well as for sequelics and conversational units. Even if they are present, we will want to expand the emission of these verbal repertoires.

2) How to Expand Tacts Before Naming Is Present and to Continue Rapid Expansion of the Tact Repertoire

If the student does not have a fluent naming, and reading repertoires at or above grade level, then continue to do the intensive tact protocol. Once this is in place and the student's tact repertoire is expanding, probe for the observational learning of tacts. If this is not occurring with 90% to 100% accuracy, do the protocol for inducing the observational learning of tacts (see Chapter 5).

3) Observational Learning of Tacts and the "Wh" Repertoire

If observational learning of tacts is not fluent, do this protocol alone or in conjunction with the "wh" question protocol. Begin by probing for acquisition of the "wh" repertoire and then teach both the "wh" protocol and the observational learning of tacts (see Chapter 5).

4) Expanding Observational Learning of Tacts and the Observational Learning Capability

Once the student has completed the observational learning of tacts and the "wh" protocol, we want to devote periods of the day to group individualized instruction designed to expand observational learning so that the student alternates between direct and indirect contact with learn units. There should be a period of the day devoted solely to this type of instruction. Begin with two students with comparable repertoires and, as the students' repertoires and the teacher's skills warrant, expand the number of students involved. Separately or in combination, use tact, textual, or math instructional programs that are new for each of the children. Each child will receive direct learn units on a particular set of programs alternated with another child receiving direct learn units. That is, one child receives a learn unit on his program while the other child observes. Then, immediately after the first child receives the learn unit, probe the observing child to see if she has learned the correct response from observation. Reinforce each child for the correct response—the child receiving the learn unit and the child receiving the probe. If the child receiving the direct learn unit requires a correction, they should respond with, "What is it?" followed by the teacher responding with a correction that they repeat while attending to the stimulus. No reinforcement follows, but the observing student receives a probe trial, and if she responds correctly, reinforce her. Also, reinforce the team with a token on the game token board. If the observing student is incorrect, do not perform a correction; rather, put a token on the game board with a bit of gloating. Then return to the observing child and present a learn unit from that child's program followed by an observational probe response for the observing child. Children should receive the relevant consequence for their responses. If the observing student is correct, dispense a point for the team and if she is incorrect, a point for the teacher on the token game board. Continue this procedure until each child has received several 20-learn unit sessions on sets of five tacts or other instructional stimuli, and until each child has received corresponding observational probes. Our goal is for the students to begin to master programs as both a receiver of direct learn units and an observer of others receiving learn units. If the students are not fluent observers, check to ensure that observational learning is fluent. If not, then teach the observational learning protocol part of students until you can run these programs and both students can learn in this context.

This procedure will prepare our students to learn in mainstream setting. It will also occasion reinforcement for listening and may induce or expand both conversational units and the capability to be reinforced as a listener. You can also build on this capability by doing the social listener reinforcement procedure; but it is very likely that if you can obtain observational learning in the mainstream setting, then the goals of the social listening reinforcement program will accrue. Other capabilities that still need to be taught may include the speaker-as-own-listener capability; however, children who can learn observationally in this setting are likely to have the speaker-as-own-listener repertoire.

5) Inducing Observational Learning If It Is Missing

One of the most important ways that individuals learn is through observation and imitation. We distinguish between imitation and observational learning because they are two different repertoires. Imitation occurs when one does what someone else does, as in the "do this" programs that we described earlier. That is, the act of imitating is reinforced by the effect of doing the imitation. The more advanced version of imitation is generalized imitation where the child imitates actions you have not taught her directly—imitation has become a higher order class of responding. Observational learning differs from imitation in that in observational learning, one learns a new operant by observing the consequences received by others. Observational learning

TEXTBOX **7.1**

Summary of Expanding Observational Learning of Tacts and the Observational Learning Capability

1. Pair students with similar repertoires including observational learning capabilities.
2. Each student has a set of instructional programs (spelling, tacts, math, and textual responses).
3. Some of the programs for each student will involve direct learn units and others are to be programs that each student is to learn by observation only.
4. Students should master both the direct instruction and the observational instruction consistent with the Decision Protocol (see Chapter 2). If the student is not mastering the observational learning programs consistent with the Decision Protocol, remove this student from this procedure and do the procedure to induce observational learning. Once the observational learning repertoire is mastered, return to this procedure. Different types of observational learning may need to be taught. These include, but are not limited to auditory observational learning or naming; learning that combines text, print, or three dimensional objects; responses that

involve observation of multiple antecedent stimuli; and other student's responses.
5. When the pair of students is achieving instructional objectives consistent with the Decision Protocol, add an additional student (i.e., three students are involved).
6. As the students achieve increasing numbers of educational objectives via observational learning, add additional students.
7. Continue adding students until several students are involved. At this point if the student has writing repertoires, you may use the response card procedure in which students write their response, wait for the correct response, and are reinforced or perform written corrections.

The goal of this sequence is to prepare the students to learn by observation. This is critical if they are to do well in mainstream settings. Moreover, all children stand to benefit by acquiring advanced observational-learning capabilities. Once children have advanced-learning capabilities and can provide their own learn units, they are independent learners.

takes at least two different forms. The first is learning a new operant because one observes another person respond accurately and then obtain a consequence that functions as a reinforcer for the observer. For example, the model, the one observed, answers a question and receives an item that is preferred by the observer. The observer then emits the same response, which is now part of a newly acquired operant and is reinforced by the preferred item. This is an important capability and a major educational achievement. Much of the learning that occurs in mainstream education must occur through observational learning because the numbers of learn units available in mainstream settings are minimal. Still another form of observational learning involves learning responses by observing others as they receive corrections; that is, when the target child responds correctly, she does so because she observed another student receive a correction.

In Chapters 3 and 5 we described how to induce observational learning for the listener component of tacting. Within those procedures we also described how to induce or enhance observational learning (see Greer, Singer-Dudek, & Gautreaux, (2006) for an overview of this research and a list of research references).

Joining Print to Speaker as Own-Listener Capabilities

When you are ready to join print to speaker-as-own-listener repertoires, follow the procedures and protocols in Chapter 6. These involve the procedures described for reading and writing.

The sequence for using all of the protocols described in this text was based on applications of the research for advancing children's verbal capabilities. The exact sequencing of these protocols requires the teacher to strategically analyze the progress of her students and identify various possible sources for lack of capabilities. As such, it is useful to view the sequence of interventions in terms of an overall developmental scheme. Over several years the evidence led us to propose the following developmental stages. While the overall scheme calls for a great deal of additional research, we have found it to be useful in our practice. In addition, the scheme holds promise for identifying further capabilities and protocols and even for eliminating capabilities and reconstructing the developmental trajectory.

Stages of Verbal Development

Throughout this text we emphasized two important goals of teaching functional communication: 1) teaching important educational goals and (2) advancing verbal development. Instruction needs to be tied to local and international educational goals across the range of curricula that our children need to master—this is particularly important for those children with disability labels. Each instructional session and each objective needs to be tied to real educational goals. We should teach the range of educational needs including academic literacy, an enlarged community of reinforcers, self-management, and problem-solving as verbal mediation. Moreover, the educational goals can be taught when the verbal functions that we have described in this text are present. In most cases, these educational goals can be obtained from the state's national departments of education or similar sources, and then converted to functional repertoires, as described in earlier chapters. However, the degree to which it is possible to teach children certain educational goals *is governed by the child's existing verbal development*. This leads us to the second and unique contribution of verbal behavior analysis—the means to advance children's verbal development so that instruction in more advanced educational standards becomes possible.

Some say that the stages of verbal development that we have identified constitute a verbal development theory. However, it is not a theory of verbal development in the traditional sense. We did not develop a hypothesis for verbal development, nor did we start out to develop a theory of verbal development. Ours is not a hypothetical-deductive theory. Rather, in the process of researching how to induce new verbal-learning capabilities in children, the evidence showed the way to a sequence. Once that sequence was revealed, it provided an evidence-based guide for what to do with children who were at particular stages, and how to achieve more advanced stages. Thus, the verbal development scheme that we identified was inductively driven, that is, the data suggested the developmental sequence. Future research will expand, modify, and revise that scheme. For now, we have a path that works and that provides new questions that can be investigated. The scheme identifies critical verbal and learning developmental cusps and how we can achieve those with children who are missing them as well as suggesting questions that need to be answered.

The capacity or potential for verbal development is *determined in all humans by the neurological structures* that exist for our species. In cases where verbal development is limited or thwarted by the lack of experiences and by the lack of the developmental capability to benefit from experiences, verbal behavior analysis has extended our possibilities for maximizing verbal development. This means that what was previously viewed as generative or productive verbal behavior can be induced for children who do not have it, and can compensate for what was initially seen as missing structural neurology. While structural limitations are real barriers, this recent work shows that some of these barriers are not as limiting as previously thought. This is not to say that we can overcome all barriers, but that we can overcome many more than we could before. Our goal as educational behavior analysts is not to "heal" a diagnosis; rather, we set out to find ways to provide extraordinary means to teach children so that they can overcome structural or environmental deficits. However, this has led to outcomes that show the importance of environmental and neurological interrelations. In a manner of speaking, "kids say the darnedest things" not just because of cognitive "hard wire" but also because of particular experiences (Greer & Yuan, 2006). Hearing aids allow individuals with hearing impairments to hear, individuals with eyeglasses to see more clearly, and children with language-learning disabilities to learn missing verbal capabilities because of intensive environmental interventions.

At this point, we describe our current verbal development trajectory, which was derived from existing evidence that identified those experiences that led to the evolution of some critical verbal functions. Figure 7.1 outlines these verbal developmental capabilities that we have identified to date. They provide the trajectory or sequence that should drive verbal behavior interventions. Despite possible limitations of our existing trajectory, it appears to be the first data-driven developmental scheme for verbal behavior. Following our belief that any data-based approach should displace non-data driven schemes, it constitutes the best workable approach to date.

The capabilities that we identified in Figure 7.1 for the evolution of verbal behavior grew out of our research and reading of various scientific literatures concerning the evolution of language in the species and some of the research on language development by non-behavior analytic developmental psychologists. Table 7.1 describes the research-based protocols that we have identified to date that have proven effective in inducing missing capabilities with many, but not all, of the children we have worked with. This table serves as an outline of the sequence of protocols as they relate to the overall verbal development of children that we described in detail in earlier chapters and reviewed earlier in this chapter. It should guide your sequence of interventions for bringing about missing capabilities until such time that new evidence is found.

While future research will modify and expand this sequence, for now the sequence suggests directions for how we proceed in teaching individual children and provides taxonomies for further research. Each child will require modifications in

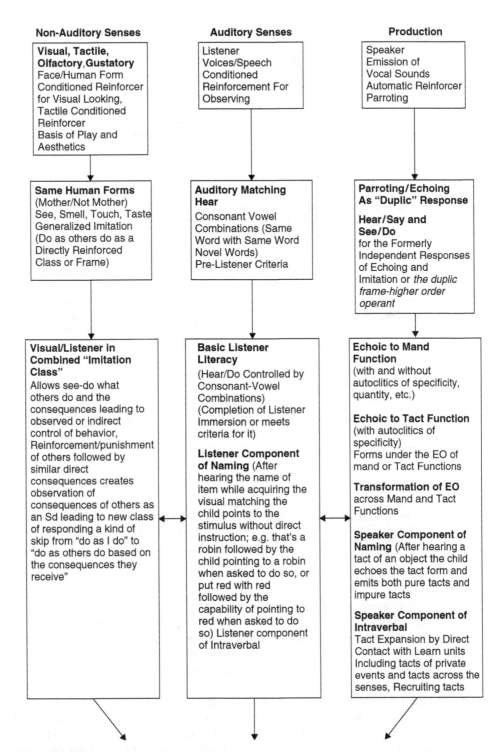

FIGURE 7.1 Development of Verbal Function Capabilities

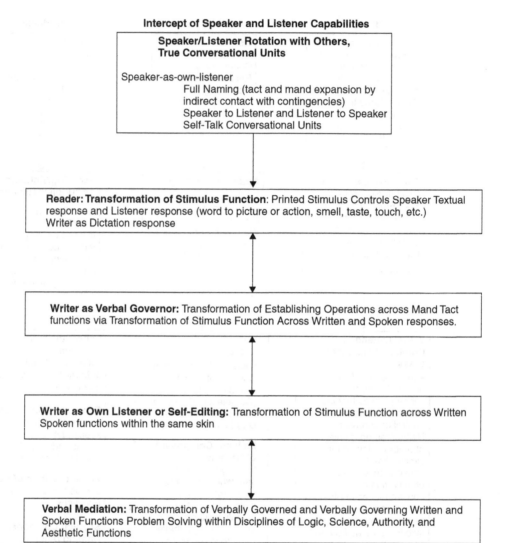

FIGURE 7.1 *(continued)*

instructional tactics for teaching the component repertoires that result in the new capabilities. That is both the challenge and promise of expertise in verbal behavior analysis. Instructional expertise tied to an increased knowledge of the wherewithal to induce verbal development enhances the educational and developmental prognoses for our children. We believe that what has been learned about verbal behavior from children with severe language delays provides the means to radically improve these children's prognoses. The work also suggests that all children can gain from this. That is, it is very likely that many children not labeled as having delays or disabilities also encounter learning problems attributable to missing capabilities that do not allow them to benefit from the incidental experiences that children typically receive. These

TABLE 7.1   Verbal and Related Capabilities and the Protocols for Inducing Capabilities*

Visual, Tactile, Olfactory, Gustatory Senses	The Auditory Sense and the Emergence of the Listener and Selection Responses	The Emergence of the Speaker and Production Responses
Development of non-listener observing: Differentiating the world by the separate senses: Face/Human form conditioned reinforcer for visual looking, orienting to voices, conditioned tactile reinforcers, olfactory and gustatory relations. At some point these acquire a same-ness originating from the pairings. *Some of this can be brought on by protocols, such as visual tracking and the capacity for sameness across senses.*	**Development of observational listening:** Listener Voices/Speech Conditioned Reinforcement for observational listening paired with the visual orienting and olfactory and gustatory experiences. *Some of this can be brought on by protocols such as conditioning voices.*	**The production responses:** Emission of Vocal Sounds as Automatic Reinforcer These are simply *emitted* by most infants, just as is the continuous movement of other motor capacities. *They can be induced for some children through the experiences that produce the* duplic *frame, see the next step*
Further development of non-listener observing: Same Human Forms (Mother/Not Mother) Seeing and other senses connected with touching and mouthing (early relating of observing or selection with production from Carmen Luciano's paper on see-touch) a) Observation by one sense develops joint control over other senses, see-touch, smell-see-touch, etc coordinated. *Some of this can be brought on by protocols such as visual tracking, capacity for sameness across senses.*	**Further development of observational listening:** Auditory Matching, word sounds with word sounds, non-word sounds with non-word sounds of like frequency-timbre-volume. Consonant Vowel Combinations (Same Word with Same Word for Novel Words). Pre-Listener Criteria. *Some of this can be brought on by the Chavez-Brown & Greer (2003) protocol.*	**The production responses begin to be related to the observing or selecting responses of observational listening.** Parroting/Echoing as "Duplic" Response for the Formerly Independent Responses of Echoing and Imitation. Imitation from see touch to see-do joined to hear say. Early higher order operant connecting selecting/observing and production. *Some of this can be brought on by the Ross & Greer (2003) and Tsiouri & Greer (2003) Protocol and or the Sundberg, Michael, Partington, & Sundberg (1996) pairing protocol.*

(continued)

TABLE 7.1 *(continued)*

Visual, Tactile, Olfactory, Gustatory Senses	The Auditory Sense and the Emergence of the Listener and Selection Responses	The Emergence of the Speaker and Production Responses
b) See others and do a resulting in Generalized Imitation. (Do as others do as a Directly Reinforced Class or Frame). *Generalized imitation taught via multiple exemplars to form a frame or higher order operant.*		
Development of the indirect control of consequences for observationally induced behavior: Visual/Listener in Combined "Imitation Class" Allows see-here what others do as an extension of generalized imitation and the consequences leading to observed or indirect control of behavior. Reinforcement/punishment of others followed by similar direct consequences creates observation of consequences of others as an Sd leading to new class of responding a kind of skip from "do as I do" to "do as others do based on the consequences that the child observes other receive." This makes it possible to come under the control of indirect contingencies, that is, seeing consequences for others enters the same frame as generalized imitation.	**Further development of the observational listener capability resulting in correspondence between hear and do:** Basic Listener Literacy (Hear/Do Controlled by Consonant-Vowel Combinations) Auditory Instructional Control *Completion of Listener Immersion brings this capability on when it is missing.*	**Productions affects the behavior of others:** Echoic to Mand Function (with autoclitics of specificity, quantity, etc.) Echoic to Tact Function (with autoclitics of specificity, etc.) Forms under the EO of mand or Tact Functions. Production controls a listener who mediates between the verbal and the nonverbal world for the speaker. Forms learned as mands are independent of forms learned as tacts, the establishing operation is tied to particular forms. *Protocol for echoic to mand and echoic to tact* Expansion of tact repertoire and acquisition of the "need to know" as a conditioned establishing operations using "wh" questions, tacts of private events, and tacts across the senses.

TABLE 7.1   *(continued)*

Visual, Tactile, Olfactory, Gustatory Senses	The Auditory Sense and the Emergence of the Listener and Selection Responses	The Emergence of the Speaker and Production Responses
Pre-Listener Immersion Protocol for obtaining instructional control that is not driven by auditory stimuli (presence of individual with reinforcers results in non-auditory instructional control)		
Further development of observational learning: Child acquires new operants and higher order operants from indirect contact with the contingencies. *Some of this can be brought on by monitoring and yoked contingency protocols for inducing and expanding observational learning capabilities.* New tacts acquired from observing consequences with others, reading from observation and naming as described in adjacent column.	**Further development of the observational listener capability resulting in correspondence between hearing and saying:** Listener Component of Naming (After hearing the name of item while acquiring the visual matching the child points to the stimulus without direct instruction; e.g., That's a robin, followed by the child pointing to a robin when asked to do so, or putting red with red followed by the capability of pointing to red when asked to do so) *Protocol for MEI for matching to listener responding* Listener component of Intraverbal Listener Sequelic as Intraverbal, Impure Tact Sequelic as Multiple Control Listener response (e.g., "what color," with spoken listener response "red") *Intraverbal protocols*	**Joining of the different speaker functions and speaker listener functions.** A) Transformation of EO across Mand and Tact Functions. The emission of the form comes under the control of the relevant establishing operations the single form is jointly controlled by different establishing operations; the form is no longer tied to a specific establishing operation. *Nuzzolo-Gomez & Greer (2004) Protocol for Transformation of EO control across mand and tact functions* B) Speaker Component of Naming joined with the listener component of naming. (After hearing a tact of an object the child echoes the tact form and emits both pure tacts and impure tacts). *Greer, Stolfi, Chavez-Brown, & Rivera-Valdez (2005) Protocol for inducing full naming* Speaker Component of Intraverbal Tact expansion protocol continued *Protocol for the "Wh" so that the student learns to recruit tacts and acquires the conditioned establishing operation for "need to know"*

(continued)

TABLE 7.1   *(continued)*

Visual, Tactile, Olfactory, Gustatory Senses	The Auditory Sense and the Emergence of the Listener and Selection Responses	The Emergence of the Speaker and Production Responses
⟶	**Speaker and Listener Joined** Speaker/Listener Rotation with others, True Conversational Units	⟵
Merging of Capabilities	*Sequelic intraverbal protocols and conversational unit protocol*	Merging of Capabilities
⟶	Speaker-as-own-listener: Transformation of Stimulus Control across Speaker and Listener as well as other sensory observational capabilities Enhanced listener reinforcement in conversational units Social reinforcement for listening protocol Perspective of others enhanced *What can I do to help perspective-taking protocols and protocols for acquiring reinforcement as a listener when not acquired in above sequence?*	⟵

children's failure to benefit from certain verbal experiences at particular points in their instructional histories shows up at advanced stages as problems that result in disability labels. Children with problems in reading may have certain difficulties because of inadequate mastery of earlier stages of verbal development. That is, certain listener components may be missing—such as not hearing what is read as a listener or not learning the functions of writing—these, in turn, may be tied to missing production capabilites. Clearly, observational learning can be enhanced in children for whom this repertoire is not present or fluent, and this allows the child to learn even if learn units are not directly received by them. Moreover, listener repertoires that are missing can be induced and this can improve reading skills. Thus, the trajectory of verbal develop-

TABLE 7.1 *(continued)*

Visual, Tactile, Olfactory, Gustatory Senses	The Auditory Sense and the Emergence of the Listener and Selection Responses	The Emergence of the Speaker and Production Responses
	Print Stimuli Joins Frames **Extension of above to print stimulus control:** Reader: Conditioned reinforcement for print and book stimuli, *Conditioning protocol,* *Transformation of Stimulus Function Protocol* Printed Stimulus Controls speaker textual response and listener response	**Production of Print Stimuli Joins Frames** **Extension of Production from above to and adjacent to formation of print:** Writer as verbal governor: Mand tact functions via written responses.
	Protocols for teaching textual responding	**Extension of above and Extension of production from above and selection from the adjacent column to:** Writer as Own Listener or Self-editing Transformation of Stimulus Function Across written spoken functions within the same skin *Writer immersion protocol for technical writing*
	(word-to-picture or action, smell, taste, touch, etc.) Writer as dictation response Printed stimulus controls written and vocal responses jointly *Protocol for joint stimulus control of dictated words to written and spoken responses*	Metaphoric production *Meincke protocol for transformation of stimulus control from literal to metaphorical*

The protocols, which are italicized, are described here and in previous chapters.

ment may suggest sources for enhancing *all* children's verbal development. While much more research is needed, the current trajectory suggests new and promising sources to compensate for deficiencies in verbal development that underlie children's difficulties with advanced educational objectives.

The critical component of providing what we know to our children rests on the repertoires of those who teach them. The expert verbal behavior analyst must draw on all of the existing tactics in behavior analysis, those concerned with the management of previously learned behaviors as well as those concerned with the induction of new verbal operants and higher order operants. The key to this is the use of decisions about the data and using relevant tactics for all children who come to the table with different structural and environmental histories. Several years ago, research identified a decision algorithm that is useful for maximizing children's progress; we refer to this as the *decision protocol* and it was described in Chapter 2 (Keohane & Greer, 2005). It provides the analytic repertoires to solve new learning problems as they are encountered. These procedures will stand you in good stead as you contribute to our efforts to develop an even more sophisticated verbal behavior analysis. Good verbal behavior analysis will soon make the work that we have summarized in this text out-of-date. If we can contribute to this, the text will have served its function. In the mean time, if you use the work we have described competently, you will save a few more children.

A Note on Scientific Evidence

We opened the final chapter of this text with a quotation from B. F. Skinner on science and the importance of experimenting. In our practice, the value of science resides in its usefulness for *identifying what works*. The core of verbal behavior analysis that we describe is the use of scientific practice as a basis of where to begin, how to determine if a protocol works in an individual case, and how to go about identifying alternatives when best-known practices do not work. The scientific method is the most effective way to determine relationships that our species has identified. In our case, the relationships are between humans and their environment—an environment that incorporates verbal stimuli along with non-verbal stimuli. The particular brand of science that we have found most useful in pedagogy is a science of the behavior of the individual—behavior analysis.

Like all sciences, the science of the behavior of the individual draws on the basic logic of science. John Stuart Mills parsimoniously described this logic (Mills, 1950). Reduced to its most basic foundation by Mills, science consists of five different methods—the Method of Agreement, the Method of Concomitant Variance, the Method of Difference, the Joint Method, and the Method of Residues. A first level (Method of Agreement) indicates the occurrence of agreement between phenomena—uncommon agreement between events. The second level (Method of Concomitant Variance) identifies the degree of relationship between two or more events. For example, when an intervention shows that a behavior changed after a baseline, but there was no return to the baseline, there is only a correlation or concomitant relation between the treatment and a change in behavior. A third level (Method of Difference) introduces experimentation. For example, when you recover baseline level of measurement during a return to baseline, a method of difference analysis has occurred; each time you replicate the differences between baseline and treatment, it increases the experimenter's confidence that the relationship is a functional one. However, the tactics vary for implementing the Method of Difference when developing new operants or higher order operants because once an operant or higher order operant has been taught or induced, the former state of pre-intervention cannot be recaptured. In research of teaching and learning, within-subject experimentation is replaced with between-subject experimentation; thus, multiple baseline designs or pre-post-time lagged multiple probe designs are used. Numerous examples of these are found in the Research Boxes throughout the text. Indeed, experimental-control *group* designs employ this logic.

Experimentation isolates a functional relation and allows the most rigorous identification of relations between events. While the occurrence of agreement between events captures our attention and curiosity, many of those coincidences are just that—coincidences. For instance, the relationship between vaccinations and the apparent agreement with increased incidences of certain disabilities is seductive. However, like all coincidences (i.e., "red clouds at night, sailor's delight"), basing one's actions on such observations (i.e., deciding not to take an umbrella the next day) is not the wisest way to decide a course of action when means that are more rigorous are available. With the Method of Concomitant Variance, one can determine the degree of agreement between several events; for instance, rain is forecast based on the degree of agreement between certain weather conditions and the probability of rain. Years of determining such relationships can be very helpful in setting courses of action. Yet, we still do not know whether the rain is a function of those conditions until we perform experiments between those relationships using the Method of Difference. Combining the Method of Difference and the Method of Concomitant Variance provides us with even greater predictability; but in all sciences, there is much left over that remains part of the puzzle. These are the residual questions in science.

The Method of Residues tells us that improved courses of action are found in studying what remains as yet, untested relations. Setting a course of action based on what we know now is always subject to change—change accomplished by further experimentation. These methods of science are applicable both at the individual level and at the level of groups, that is, the methods are the same whether applied to individuals or groups. Most of the natural sciences began, and many continue, with applications at the individual level. When the target is a group, group applications are best; when the target is an individual, then individual applications are best. We believe that effective teaching is concerned with individual variance, and a science of principles and tactics of individual variances has strong advantages.

Given these provisos, how is one to set a course of action? In our case, we need to determine what and how to intervene to teach new verbal operants and induce new verbal capabilities. A prime consideration must be to follow non-scientific prescriptions or to follow scientific prescriptions? Given our experience with children and adults, we choose the scientific path for those we care for, and for those to whom we are professionally responsible; but as the levels of the scientific methods indicate, there are different levels of believability. Still, even the weakest level of scientific evidence takes precedence over non-scientific predictions.

The method of logic is also one of our species' contributions to setting courses of action. That is, is a solution rational and does it make sense? Still another way we operate is by appealing to authority—as in asking, "What did others do?" Despite the improvements of the Methods of Authority and Logic over superstition or the inertia of doing what we have always done (method of a priori), a scientific course of action seems preferable when that evidence is available. Behavior is not always rational, nor does it make sense in many instances. The world is not flat; sunlight that we see today did not originate today; and bread did not heal infection in wounds even though it was applied to those wounded in the U.S. Civil War (although the mold on the bread did heal—shades of method of agreement). Thus, given the option of choosing between courses of action based on varying levels of evidence, logic, or tradition, it might be prudent to follow the scientific evidence to date.

When dealing with the absence of verbal behavior in children or adults, it was not the logic that motivated us to become basic scientists and scientific practitioners, nor will the logic of science convince you—and it shouldn't. We came to this realization based on numerous experiences with working directly with children using scientific procedures—it simply worked best. We expect that those experiences will determine the readers' courses of action also.

Some propose that experiments that incorporate "group clinical trials" with a large sample of a given population are the best way to determine valid findings—the so-called gold standard. That is true in questions about populations. However, what are these populations? In many cases, the populations are not natural fractures like those of the heritability of traits of peas. Often in social science, these "populations" are psychological constructs like "locus of control." Psychological constructs that are used to identify populations are sometimes faulty. Are populations of learning disabilities, locus of control, or measures of intelligence quotients real natural fractures, or are they arbitrary social constructs? So one must consider what it is that is being subjected to scrutiny when populations are the source of experimentation.

In our study of procedures to teach new verbal operants and to induce new verbal capabilities, the presence of individual differences has been omnipresent. The variability within the human species appears to be greater than that of any species and individual differences call for a science that deals directly with those differences. We have found that real effective education is individualized instruction, whether that individualization is done with groups or one-on-one; but individualized instruction alone is not the answer. Thousands of experiments across many species and thousands of experiments with humans have shown that the basic principles of behavior apply broadly. Moreover, once the predictability of these principles combines with various ways to individualize their application, a real science of human behavior accrues. Next, when our science developed means to test the reliability of applications, outcomes improved considerably (i.e., presence of learn units and accuracy in decisions). When these levels are combined with the use of continuous measurement in applications to a specific child who is being taught, the benefits are obvious. Multiple levels of science are more rigorous than the application of only one or two, particularly at the level of the individual.

Rigorous experiments at the level of individuals with similar capabilities provide the strongest science for individualized instruction. Given the choices available—findings from studies with large groups or findings from rigorous single-case experimental studies—we choose the findings of single-case experiments for applications to individuals. Typically, single-case experiments involve repeated and long-term analyses using procedures that implement the Method of Difference and the Joint Method (i.e., multiple baselines and probes, reversal designs and, alternating treatment designs). This is particularly the case for pedagogy. A science of teaching must be a science of individualized instruction based on the most related basic science—the science of the behavior of the individual. Thus, we are confident that the procedures we have described in this text are valid at this stage in our understanding. They are, given what we know today, some of the best courses of initial action. Moreover when the practitioner uses scientific practices of verbal behavior analysis at the individual level, she has the means to seek alternative solutions if the procedures we describe do not work. If we use the procedures for teaching someone to read based on group or prior single-case experiments and do not use behavior analysis teaching practices, those who do not learn to read (i.e., those who do not respond in the same manner as the group) will remain illiterate. However, if we apply scientific practices to the teaching of each individual child, not all is lost.

Verbal behavior analysis is a growing subject field within behavior analysis (more than 100 experiments). Nevertheless, there is much work that remains to be done. The verbal capabilities that we have proposed grew out of Skinner's theory, the research of other verbal behavior analysts, and our own work with children who were missing those capabilities. We do not know if this verbal development scheme applies to children without verbal deficits, although in several cases we have found this to be viable (e.g., typically developing two-year-olds; see Gilic, 2005). We need, and intend, to further investigate the broad population possibilities for the verbal development stages. Nevertheless, given the evidence that we now have, we believe that the protocols we described are the best current approaches to verbal developmental deficits that we have identified. However, "Regard no practice as immutable. Change and be ready to change again. Accept no eternal verity. Experiment" (Skinner 1979, 1984, p. 346). Armed with the tools we describe, we can all continue the quest in every individual case.

Some Suggested Areas for Future Research

- Is observational learning a prerequisite for naming or is naming a more advanced form of observational learning? Our most recent, and as yet unpublished, research suggests that learning involving the observation of contingencies received by others is easier to acquire than naming. Some work suggests that acquiring observational learning may be a step toward the acquisition of naming.
- The difficulty with reading comprehension found in typically-developing children who are deaf from birth is one of the most compelling reasons for vocal verbal behavior. However, some researchers in deaf education are working on a phoneme-based sign language systems that may alleviate the phonogram problems with sign language and with subsequent reading comprehension difficulties.
- Some children who we have taught to use electronic-speaking devices began to emit vocal verbal behavior and others became very proficient at using these devices. Will usage of these devices promote listener repertoires and reading comprehension?
- At present, it appears that there are different types of observational learning capabilities. Observational learning of tacts differs from observational learning of textual responses, to name just two possibilities. Will observational learning differences mirror the basic verbal operants? That is, do the differences in learning the different types of speaker and listener repertoires extend to differences in observational learning?
- Acquisition of naming with three-dimensional objects appears to differ from acquisition of naming for two-dimensional or textual stimuli. That is, our work with typically-developing children shows to date that 2-year-olds can acquire naming with three-dimensional objects after multiple exemplar experiences. Yet, 54 of 58 typically-developing first-grade children did not have full naming for

pictures at the beginning of first grade (Greer & O'Sullivan, 2006). Most, but not all, had full naming for pictures at the end of the year. There appears to be a relationship between the presence of naming and success in first grade. We are in the process of testing the emergence of this repertoire with first grade children and its relationship to school success.

- Observational learning is as critical as naming. Once we have the capability in place, how do we expand the observational learning repertoire? Currently we are developing an observational system of learning that maximizes opportunities for observational learning. Our current investigations suggest that we can significantly increase observational learning capabilities, hence, exponentially expanding the effects of teaching.

- We believe that at some point certain of the capabilities need to be tested for components of mutual and combinatorial entailment per the relational frame theory.

- The research by Lowenkron (1997) appears to be closely related to some of our research on joint stimulus control. It is likely that the basic stimulus control of the echoic is fundamental to more advanced types of joint stimulus control.

- The deictic protocol that we described in Chapter 5 is in its infancy and we are currently conducting studies that incorporate the standard developmental psychology tests for theory of mind. Regardless of the validity of theory of mind, perspective taking is an important capability that may benefit form studying it as a listener reinforcement deficit.

- The relation of categorization of stimuli and verbal behavior is a pressing issue in our science. Some work suggests that categorization is preverbal and to some extent, that suggestion is feasible—hummingbirds identifying flower species, for example. However, certain types of categorization may hinge on the presence of certain verbal capabilities, as in the case of math categorizations, or at a basic level, the categorization of sameness across senses. Is sameness across senses the first higher order operant that makes verbal behavior possible?

- Multiple exemplar instruction for transformation of stimulus function, as in saying and writing or transformation of establishing operation functions, has proved very beneficial to many of the children that we have worked with. However, many more possibilities need to be investigated. For instance, is transformation of stimulus function an impediment or benefit to becoming bilingual?

- While multiple exemplar experiences have been found to be key in the development of many productive types of verbal behavior, there are other influences on the development of capabilities. Conditioned reinforcement for observing is another key factor predicting the emergence of certain capabilities as is the isolation of certain stimulus control as in the provision of conditions under which only vowel-consonant speech control results in reinforcement. We suspect there are more that are yet to be identified.

- Obtaining the capacity to be reinforced by listening is key to progress in social behavior as well as observational learning, particularly for many children diagnosed with autism. Our yoked-contingency procedures hold promise, but are there other procedures? It does not appear that script protocols for verbal exchanges are working in that regard, but perhaps this is because the key establishing operation for listener reinforcement is not built into the use of these procedures. Perhaps there are ways to incorporate key establishing operations such as providing the "need to converse" (see Donley & Greer, 1993).

■ More work needs to be done on the relationship, between conditioned observing of books and rates of learning to read. Conditioned reinforcement for stimuli is a real phenomenon and appears to replace stereotypy as well as to improve learning rates. We need to know how listening to stories or getting "hooked" on reading a story is related to conditioned reinforcement. Computer technology now makes this possible, provided adequate programs can be written.

■ The possibilities for teaching reading based on the expanded and intensive use of multiple-exemplar training holds promise for teaching children to read much more quickly. What is the range of exemplars needed for the emission of all derived relations in each set of phonograms and what are the prerequisite verbal capabilities that affect the range of exemplars needed? Can phonetic reading be taught much more rapidly if certain verbal capabilities are put in place? How many major reading problems can be traced to certain prerequisite verbal capabilities?

■ Is the phenomenon identified as *adduction* a result of multiple-exemplar experiences and not just rate of performance? For example, the emergence of first instances of vocal echoics in Ross & Greer (2003) might be seen as an incidence of adduction, where fast-rate performance, under deprivation of a known reinforcer, rotates between see, hear, say responses. How much of this effect was due to rate or to the rapid alteration of response types? This is a cross-modal and cross-senses relationship as are many of the verbal capabilities.

■ One of our doctoral students is working on the effects of having children with autism tutor each other on the numbers of conversational units. Perhaps this can also induce listener reinforcement.

These and many other questions and genuine puzzles surround the study of verbal behavior. Other verbal behavior analysts have proposed additional programs of research in verbal behavior including Jack Michael and Mark-Sundberg. Clearly, future research will need to deal with basic conceptual issues. However, what is interesting about the verbal behavior analysis research with children with language deficits, is that it has been driven by applied needs, and this work has serendipitously led to conceptual breakthroughs as well. We believe that there is much more to be learned from being driven by particular children's needs for verbal capabilities and the continuous reflection on Skinner's work, especially if you are trying to find out what works.

Skinner's text remains a continuous source for new perspectives on learning problems that we encounter. We have read the text many times and we have taught courses in verbal behavior for some time, one of us for over 20 years. Our experiments led to other questions about prerequisites and relationships between senses and motor responses; each new finding was suggested or implied in Skinner's text. The outcome of verbal behavior research will simply drive future research. Hopefully, this text will contribute to building more verbal behavior analysts and they will, in turn, add to it in ways that we cannot currently envision. Verbal behavior may prove to be one of the most important educational contributions of the twentieth century. In fact, we think Skinner was right when he said that verbal behavior was his most important work!

APPENDIX A

A Description of the Comprehensive Application of Behavior Analysis to Schooling (CABAS®) Model

The CABAS® model is a tested behavior-analytic systems approach to schooling that applies principles of behavior and other scientific findings to all members of the school community (students, parents, teachers, administrators, and psychologists) and is continuously modified based on the students' outcomes and an ongoing research program. Experimental research done by both professionals in the system and independent evaluators report four to seven times greater learning after CABAS is implemented than in baseline or control conditions. In the CABAS system, all instruction is measured; all instructional procedures are derived from scientifically tested procedures that are, in turn, individualized for each learner; and scientific procedures are used as part of the implementation of the procedures. In addition, scientific procedures are used in applying all instructional tactics and strategies to each individual case. Initiated in 1981, the model has been used in schools for children and adolescents with and without disabilities in the United States, Italy, England, and Ireland.

CABAS® accredits schools that meet the standards for measurable effective schools that are research and demonstration centers. Tuition for all students in CABAS schools is publicly funded. CABAS also certifies nine levels of expertise in teaching as applied behavior analysis, in which the expertise demonstrated has been functionally tied to effective instruction. CABAS was developed to demonstrate that it is possible to have learner-driven schools that are based entirely on teaching as a science for individualized instruction across the entire curriculum. Essentially, we set out to design schools around what individual children need in order to learn what they are capable of learning based entirely on the use of scientific procedures. We also set out to maintain real-world schools that contribute to the cutting edge of basic and applied behavior analysis and a science of schooling. The schools also serve as university training sites for masters and PhD level students and post-doctoral fellows. The research agenda is based on programs of research for the advancement of effective individualized instruction. The collaboration between CABAS schools and Columbia University has contributed to extensive research programs in components of effective schooling, verbal behavior analysis, and observational learning. The objective of CABAS schools is to provide research, demonstration, and training sites for developing procedures and systems that can be used by other behavior analysts and schools. CABAS was not established to be a competitive method; rather, it was established as a vehicle to provide scientifically tested procedures for all to use.

Our current aspiration is the development of a research and demonstration center to bridge the learning gap between low-income and middle-class/upper-middle-class students by an intensive application of CABAS procedures to cadres of 2-year-olds from underprivileged communities (see www.cabas.com). CABAS holds an intellectual trademark to control use of its name as a means of controlling quality. While CABAS is not a nonprofit corporation, we are not driven by profit motives. Rather, we are self-supporting research, advanced professional training, and demonstration centers designed to maintain the wherewithal to expand the science of schooling driven by the needs of children rather than a politically driven research agenda. This allows us to follow the leads of our research findings rather than the particular research agenda of governmental funding agencies or the particular research agenda of currently popular funding efforts. While the great majority of the components of CABAS come from the science of the behavior of the individual, we draw procedures from any science that serves the goals cited above.

APPENDIX B

Sample Data Collection Forms

Sample Data Collection Form for Multiple Exemplar Instruction
(R = Response type; fill in specific response types)

	R1	R2	R3	R4	R1	R2	R3	R4
1.								
2.								
3.								
4.								
5.								
6.								
7.								
8.								
9.								
10.								
11.								
12.								
13.								
14.								
15.								
16.								
17.								
18.								
19.								
20.								
Total Correct								
Date								
Instructors Initials								

Sample Data Collection Form for Mand/Tact Instruction

	E	M	T	E	M	T	E	M	T	E	M	T	E	M	T	E	M	T	E	M	T
1.																					
2.																					
3.																					
4.																					
5.																					
6.																					
7.																					
8.																					
9.																					
10.																					
11.																					
12.																					
13.																					
14.																					
15.																					
16.																					
17.																					
18.																					
19.																					
20.																					
Total Correct																					
Date																					
Instructors Initials																					

E = Echoic; M = Mand; T = Tact

Sample Data Collection Form for Conditioning Stimuli as Reinforcers

Interval	# of Pairings	Train	Test	Train	Test	Train	Test	Train	Test
1	2								
2	3								
3	2								
4	3								
5	2								
6	3								
7	2								
8	3								
9	2								
10	3								
11	2								
12	3								
13	2								
14	3								
15	2								
16	3								
17	2								
18	3								
19	2								
20	3								
21	2								
22	3								
23	2								
24	3								
25	2								
Total Correct									
Date									
Initials									

APPENDIX C

Sample Training Graphs

Sample Mand and Tact Training Graph

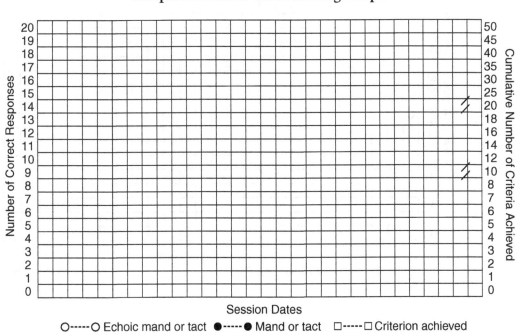

Session Dates

O-----O Echoic mand or tact   ●-----● Mand or tact   □-----□ Criterion achieved

Sample Mand and Tact Generalization Graph

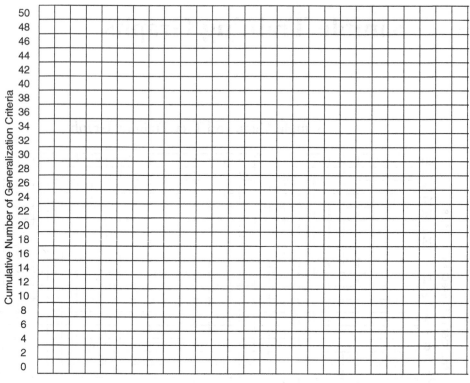

Multiple Exemplar Training Graph

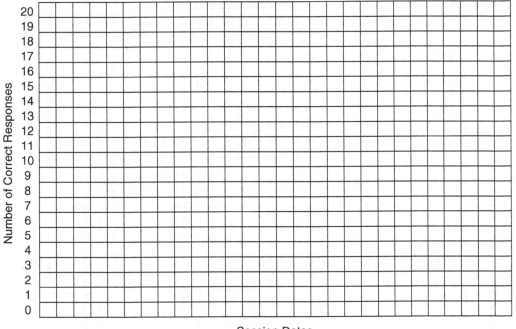

Multiple Exemplar Instruction (MEI) Probe Graph

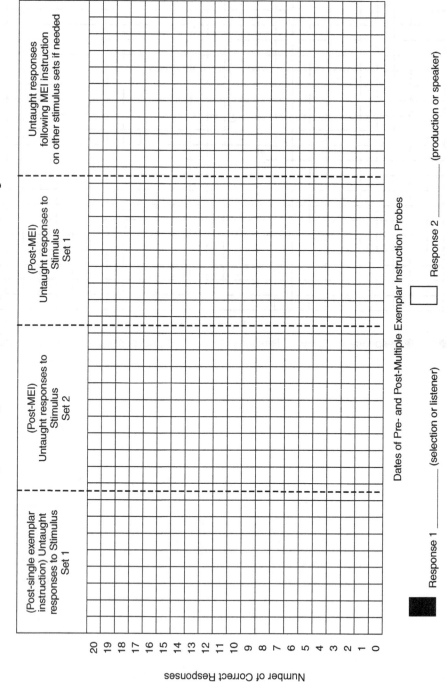

Number of Correct Responses

Dates of Pre- and Post-Multiple Exemplar Instruction Probes

Response 1 _____ (selection or listener)   Response 2 _____ (production or speaker)

Conditioning Graph

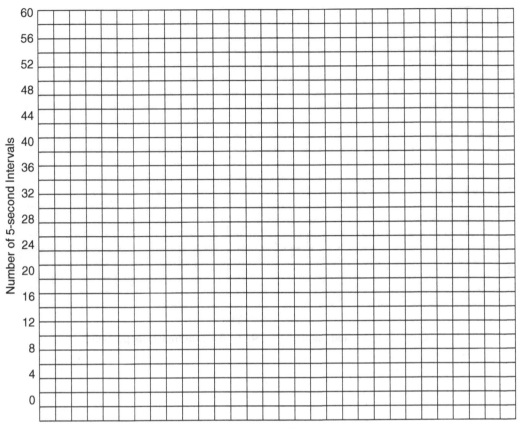

Session Dates

○----○ Observing responses for target stimuli (looking, listening, touching)

●——● Passivity or stereotypy

General Graph for Prompted and Unprompted Responses

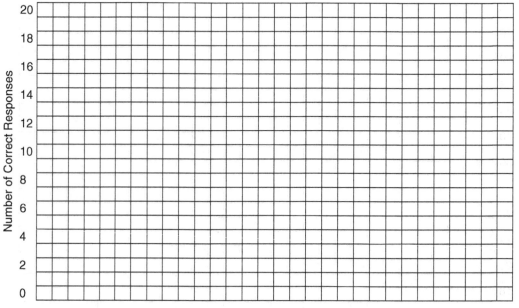

Session Dates

O----- O Prompted responses   ●----- ● Unprompted responses

GLOSSARY

academic engaged time A measure of the amount of time during an instructional period that students are engaged in activities associated with responding to curricular materials and teacher questions such as reading aloud, asking questions, or responding to questions in written or spoken topographies. Educational research literature in the 1980s identified correlations between standardized test scores of academic achievement and observations of periods of time that students were engaged in responding to academic material. Since it is a topographical and not a functional measure, engaged time may involve activities not related to actual teaching and learning. Learn units, on the other hand, not only measure engagement within time, but they measure both student and teacher performance that are functional predictors of learning. Engaged time that does not include learn units (i.e., teacher presentations and student responses are not consequated) is not a reliable predictor of learning (see Albers & Greer, 1991).

acoustic properties of speech Include vowel-consonant or phonemic combinations of vocal speech that listeners discriminate when responding to commands and speakers emit to affect the behavior of listeners. Other acoustic properties include characteristics of the initial articulation, the loudness or volume, voice timbre, and frequency or Hertz ranges of voices.

active responding Also called *active student responding*. Active student responses are measurable responses made by students to instructionally related antecedents (see Heward, 1994). Without active responding during learn units and correction procedures, students are less likely to acquire a target response. Students must respond or have the opportunity to respond to learn unit presentations in order for a learn unit to occur (see McDonough & Greer, 1999).

antecedent The first component of a three-term contingency (antecedent-behavior-consequence relation) that becomes a discriminative stimulus (S^d) as a function of consequences associated with it. In learn unit presentations, antecedents should be unambiguous with only their essential or salient characteristics presented, and teachers should have students attend to the antecedent before presenting it. In the learn unit an antecedent is a potential S^d (see Chapter 2). Of course there are other antecedents to responses, including establishing operations, conditional stimuli, and setting events, and instructional histories but some of these are distant antecedents. The immediate antecedent and conditional stimuli are, however, proximate antecedents to the potential S^d.

aphasia Partial or complete deficit in verbal responses, including listening, speaking, reading, and writing.

applied behavior analysis A branch of the science of behavior devoted to producing socially significant improvements and establishing new behavior-environment relation or higher order operants for human behavior through the systematic application of principles, practices, and research findings derived from both basic and applied analysis of behavior. Its essential components include 1) continuous and repeated measurement as part of continual contact with behavioral outcomes; 2) identification of functional or concomitant relations between behavior and research-based instructional tactics, protocols, or systematic interventions; and 3) systematic analysis of learning or performance problems when interventions are unsuccessful.

auditory matching A probable prerequisite skill to listener and speaker behavior during which a listener discriminates between positive and negative exemplars of different words and sounds by matching the sample sound to the positive exemplar. In the instructional protocol described in Chapter 3, a sound-producing apparatus is used to teach students this capability. The capability of auditory matching may be fundamental to the development of parroting or echoic responses since speakers must match the components of what is heard to what they say. The instructional protocol is designed to teach the auditory-matching capability, which helps develop echoic responding and facilitates basic listener literacy.

auditory properties of speech See *acoustic properties of speech*.

auditory stimulus control   A listener is under auditory stimulus control when the acoustic properties of speech are the sole stimuli that exert control over their response (true auditory stimulus control). When a listener responds to visual cues that accompany auditory commands, an early form of auditory stimulus control is established. However, a listener under true auditory stimulus control can respond to the vowel-consonant properties of commands without relying on additional cues. Of course other non-speech sounds can control responding but we use the term herein to refer to the control of the auditory properties of speech. See Chapter 3 and *acoustic properties of speech*.

autoclitic   Adjective/adverb form that functions for the speaker in ways that modify the effects of mand and tact operants on listeners by specifying, quantifying, affirming, and negating them (i.e., *blue* ball). Autoclitics also function to avoid punishing consequences from audiences, as in the word *please* in a mand, for example, or when a speaker attributes a controversial issue to another person by saying, "Some argue that——," therefore removing possible audience punishment for the speaker. See Chapter 4 for an in-depth description.

automatic reinforcement   The occurrence of a form of behavior (verbal behavior in this case) that is shaped and strengthened as speakers hear themselves repeat it or experience the kinesthetic responses of speaking; it is not initially shaped or strengthened by a history of having one's duplicative vocal sounds resulting in verbal functional effects on another listener as are echoics that lead to verbal functions (i.e., mands and tacts). *Stimulus-stimulus pairing* is a procedure used to induce automatic reinforcement during which an existing reinforcer for behavior is paired with a spoken sound. A non-vocal example of automatic reinforcement is *stereotypy*. The term *automatic reinforcement* refers to behavior emitted for no other apparent function than the emission of the behavior per se, and the inference is that the behavior itself functions to reinforce repetition. Another conspicuous incident of automatic reinforcement occurs when one sings to oneself.

baseline   Repeated observational or teaching sessions during which one measures the occurrence of a behavior before or after the application of interventions. In learning studies, baseline-level responding cannot be recovered, whereas, in studies of the controls of existing behavior, introducing and removing certain conditions leads to behavior that fluctuates consistently with the conditions or interventions. Raising one's hand can be increased or decreased by introducing and removing reinforcement for the response. However, learning to mand or tact should not reverse if the relevant conditions under which the mand was learned are in place (unless one repeats the procedures to the extent that the child is sated). Baselines in learning research or teaching refer to the pre-intervention or pre-teaching accuracy of responding.

basic attention programs   Instructional control programs that teach responses to five commands given by a teacher: sit, look at me, sit still, do this (imitation), and do this (generalized imitation). This protocol may or may not teach initial auditory discrimination, although it should teach the student to come under the reinforcement control of the teacher, even if the discriminative stimuli are visual or sequential. For some students the programs do establish auditory-controlled attention responses to the teacher that are needed for future instruction. Other students will need to be taught the control of vowel-consonant components by the procedures outlined in the listener emersion protocol. Also referred to as *pre-listener programs*.

behavior beneath the skin   Behaviors, such as electronic brain impulses or pain, that are unobservable by a verbal community; they are only detectable to the person behaving or through an MRI or other instrumentation. Covertly talking to oneself is also a behavior beneath the skin. When one textually responds without speaking aloud or moving one's lips, one is engaging in behavior beneath the skin. The fact that such behavior is not public does not obviate its existence. The scientific problem is in the lack of public verification. However, public verification of covert behavior may not be as important as the public effects of overt behavior on outcomes. Covert behavior does not call for a "mediating" construct or agency such as thoughts, locus of control, intelligence, and expressive behavior (as in a homunculus that is being expressed by expressive speech).

behavioral cusp (behavioral developmental cusp). "A cusp is a change [*in the capability of the child*] that (1) is often difficult, tedious, subtle, or otherwise problematic to accomplish, yet (2) if not made, means little or no further development is possible in its realm (and perhaps in several realms); but (3) once it is made, a significant set of subsequent developments suddenly becomes easy or otherwise highly probable which (4) brings the developing organism into contact with other cusps crucial to further, more complex, or more refined development in a thereby steadily expanding, steadily more interactive realm." (Rosales-Ruiz & Baer, 1996, p. 166) [The italics in brackets were inserted in the quotation.]

behavior outside of the skin Behaviors such as speaking or writing that are detectable to a verbal community or someone other than the person behaving.

capability "An undeveloped faculty or property; a condition, physical or otherwise, capable of being converted or turned to use" (Oxford English Dictionary, 2nd edition, Volume II, pp. 855–856). *Verbal capabilities* are developmental stages that are acquired incidentally or induced. Certain verbal capabilities are *higher order operants*; once acquired, they permit learning of classes of operants, which allows one to progress through the verbal developmental scale. When a capability is not present, acquisition of certain operants is not possible. For example, when children without physical vocal apparatus deficits cannot echo the speech of others, they are missing the verbal capability to echo, and thus need to learn vocal verbal functions. Similarly, children who do not have *naming* cannot acquire speaker or listener vocabulary without direct instruction. Each capability has a repertoire, which identifies the extent or range of operants within a given capability. If a capability is not present, development and expansion of a repertoire is not possible. While there are likely many yet unidentified capabilities, the research-based protocols described in this text and in the research literature can be used to induce some capabilities for children who are missing them. A verbal developmental capability is also a behavioral developmental cusp. See *behavioral cusp*.

capacity for sameness The ability to identify attributes of sameness for stimuli across the senses. We speculate that the notion that matching stimuli in one sensory experience can be related as the same to matching stimuli in another sense is an arbitrary relation that may be the basis for origins of verbal behavior. That is, when infants match their mother's face to the smell, taste, and face of their mother, that relation occasions the prerequisites for matching "MUM" as a listener and as a speaker. It is likely that children acquire this capa-

bility early on in a very basic step similar to the process whereby they later learn to discriminate between printed words, pictures, or figures. See *sensory matching*.

captured learn units Learn units occurring in non-instructional environments. The terms *incidental learning* and *milieu teaching* are also used to describe captured learn units. They are typically evoked by setting events in those environments, and are subsequently "captured" or measured and reinforced by a listener (usually a teacher). In this way, they are analogous to responses described in incidental teaching. When collecting data on mands and tacts, captured learn units represent "generalization" of target responses once they are emitted twice in non-instructional settings. In instructional settings, massed 20-learn unit presentations are used instead to teach verbal repertoires because they result in more learning opportunities and ensure the likelihood that a repertoire is acquired. However, a repertoire is not truly acquired until students can emit it in natural environments where the *essential stimulus and motivational control* can evoke a response.

community of reinforcers A variety of conditioned reinforcers (for behaviors they reinforce, or unrelated behaviors, e.g., generalized reinforcers) that act to reinforce certain behaviors. For students with socially inappropriate behaviors that may be reinforced by their conditioned effects, we teach a community of reinforcers that includes reading, writing, and playing with toys, such that conditioned activities will compete with or replace destructive behaviors. The conditioning protocol in Chapters 3 and 6 is one method that we use to enlarge the community of reinforcers for early speakers and for individuals with stereotypy. One may also describe the community of reinforcers as one's preferred activities and events and the responses of observing, or otherwise behaving that ensues from the behavior.

Comprehensive Application of Behavior Analysis to Schooling (CABAS®) A tested behavior analytic, systems approach to schooling that applies principles of behavior and other scientific findings to all members of the school community (students, parents, teachers, administrators, and psychologists). The model is continuously modified based on student outcomes and on an ongoing research program. In the CABAS® system, all instruction is measured. All instructional procedures are derived from scientifically tested procedures that are individualized for each learner, using scientific procedures as part of their implementation. In addition, scientific procedures are used to apply all instructional tactics and strategies to individual learning problems. Experimental research conducted by professionals in the system and independent evaluators report four to seven times greater learning after the model was implemented than in baseline or control conditions. Initiated in 1981, CABAS® has been used in schools for children and adolescents with and without disabilities in the United States, Italy, England, and Ireland. See Appendix A for a detailed description of the CABAS® model.

conditioned establishing operation   See *establishing operation.*

conditioned reinforcers   Items that become reinforcers because they are paired with other reinforcing items either incidentally or through systematic instruction. For example, when books do not function as reinforcers for observing responses for a student, books are paired with edibles and praise until the books become reinforcers for observing. *Generalized conditioned reinforcers* are items such as tokens or money that become reinforcing through pairing, but can function as reinforcers for a number of different responses. When a preferred activity is a conditioned reinforcer for an activity, the opportunity to engage in that activity can itself function as a generalized reinforcer. For example, the opportunity to mand may function as a generalized reinforcer for the tact response.

conversational unit   A research-identified verbal relation comprised of interlocking intraverbals between at least two people during which each person functions as both a listener and a speaker in a rotated episode. Skinner (1957) referred to this as a *verbal episode.* Listener-speaker responses are rotated across each person such that each person is reinforced as a speaker and as a listener and each affects the behavior of the other. See Chapter 5 for a description and flowchart. Conversational units are also involved in self-talk, in which the roles of speaker and listener occur within the skin of a single individual. *Conversational units differ from the interlocking verbal operants that constitute learn units,* in that the conversational unit requires shifts in listener and speaker reinforcement control between individuals or within the skin of a single individual. In the learn unit, the essential control is maintained by the teacher or teaching device until the student has acquired the operant being taught or the higher order operant capability being induced.

corrections   Operations presented contingent on an incorrect response by a student. They involve presenting the antecedent again, allowing a student to observe the correct response, and then having the student perform it without receiving reinforcement. Corrections are key to both direct and observed learn units as identified in research on programmed instruction, computer-based instruction, peer and cross-age tutoring, and teacher-mediated instruction.

cumulative graph   A graph on which sequentially plotted points represent the cumulative addition of the previous sessions' data to the current data. For example, for one session, a student may have responded correctly four times, and a data point representing 4 would be plotted. In the second session, a student may have responded correctly 8 times. However, a data point representing 12, not 8, is graphed for that day because the first and second days are added together and then plotted. We frequently use cumulative displays to represent the numbers of criteria achieved by a student, classroom, or school.

data paths   Lines that connect data points on a visual display of data. We use broken lines to connect open circles, and unbroken lines to connect closed circles and triangles. Data paths are not connected across *phase change lines.* In the Decision Protocol (see Chapter 2), *the trend is determined by data paths and not by data points.* Specifically, the slope of three data paths determines the progress of a student and the need for an instructional intervention. We use the paths because it is the count of the slope of the path between each data point that actually identifies the trend. Other texts frequently refer to the trend of data points. Of course both the path and the point are involved in a trend; however, in the scientific algorithm used in the tested decision protocol one must count the trend of each path separately. See also *decision protocol.*

data points   Markers used on graphic displays of data to represent numbers. For example, in our description of graphic displays, open circles are used to plot prompted responses (echoic and zero-second time delay), closed circles are used to plot unprompted responses (mands and tacts), and closed triangles are used to plot mastery criterion when they are attained.

deprivation   A condition that occurs when an item (preferred or non-preferred) has not been accessible to a learner for a period of time. It is one necessary condition for mands. Deprivation of generalized reinforcement, such as attention, can also affect tacts or conversational units. It also affects non-speaker instruction because when an item is *satiated* for a student, it no longer functions as a reinforcer. Deprivations must be countable events, not inferences. See also *establishing operation*.

decision protocol, decision algorithm, or decision tree   A research-based algorithm that delineates the steps for analyzing and solving instructional problems. It presumes that learn units are in place during instruction, and analyzes learning problems based on the *learn unit context*. The learn unit context (which differs from but incorporates the learn unit) includes setting events and establishing operations, a student's instructional history, a teacher's behavior or conditions of the operant chamber, and the components of the student's potential operant or higher order operant. Using information from the learn unit context, one takes the following measurable sequential steps when analyzing learning problems: 1) a choice point for a decision, 2) a strategic question about the likely source of the problem within the learn unit context, 3) identification of a viable research-based tactic to solve the problem, 4) reliable implementation of the scientific tactic, and 5) subsequent tests for the effects of the tactic, resulting in success or identifying another viable tactic.

echoic   A verbal operant function during which a speaker emits a vocal response with point-to-point correspondence to the vocal stimulus of another person. It differs from imitation because the speaker matches the auditory stimulus produced by another person, and not the unobservable musculature components used to produce speech. Echoics are also distinguished from *parroting* in that the echoic response has the potential to be reinforced by a listener as a mand or tact, while parroting is automatically reinforced. Sign language and picture exchange systems can substitute for mand and tact functions, but they are not echoic functions because they involve see-do and not hear-say relations. We argue that both echoic and parroting responses eventually enter into an early *relational frame* that allows the joining of see-do and hear-say in a *duplic* relational frame or higher order verbal operant. Others argue that behavior is not truly verbal until the level of the relational frame involved in naming is achieved (Barnes-Holmes, Barnes-Holmes, & Cullinan, 2001).

echoic-to-mand   A speaker behavior of the echoic form that has or is presented pedagogically in the mand function. That is, the emission of the echoic response is reinforced because the student receives the target stimulus that is specified by the spoken word or words under the relevant deprivation conditions. Echoic-to-mand teaching procedures are used to establish the independent mand function. Signs or pictures may be substituted as response topographies in mand conditions. Alternately, one may use an electronic speaking device for mand functions.

echoic-to-tact   A pedagogical tactic from verbal behavior analysis that is designed to induce a tact function and to expand the numbers of tact operants, particularly for children who have not yet acquired the *naming* capability for acquiring tacts incidentally. Tact verbal operants are reinforced by generalized reinforcement and occur under non-verbal stimulus control. Echoic-to-tact teaching procedures are used to establish the independent tact function. Initially, the teacher states the tact for a stimulus in the presence of the stimulus and the student attends to the stimulus under conditions in which the generalized reinforcer is, at least momentarily, contingent on the emission of the tact response. Once the echoic is established in two or three learn unit presentations, the teacher shifts the control from the teachers saying the "name" of the object, to the object solely as the antecedent event at which point the tact is said to be independent. One may simulate an echoic-to-tact function by using signs or pictures in which imitation of the sign use of a picture leads to tact consequences. Similarly, one may use a match-to-sample procedure with pictures to simulate a tact function. In both of the latter cases however, the processes simulate the echoic to tact function, since these latter responses are not spoken. Alternately, one may use an electronic speaking device for tact functions. Regardless of the topography used, all of the other components for inducing tacts need to be in place (i.e., presence of the stimulus, control of a generalized reinforcer, and the imitation to independent responding sequence). When non-spoken topographies are used, the sequence is an imitation-to-tact sequence rather than an echoic-to-tact sequence.

echolalia   Inappropriate immediate repetition of a proximate verbal antecedent. An instance of echolalia occurs when a child is asked, "What's your name?" and responds by repeating, "What's your name?" instead of stating her name. It is different from palilalia because it is controlled by faulty listener control instead of by auditory or kinesthetic reinforcement. The protocols described in Chapter 5 can be used to replace echolalia with functional responses.

electronic speaking device A substitute for vocal speech by an individual who does not have spoken verbal behavior in which the "speaker" uses mechanical speaking devices that she manipulates (i.e., by pressing a button) for verbal operant functions. The use of this procedure is more closely related to speaking since the student hears the vocal sounds for the function. In some cases we have found that using the electronic speaking device has served to evoke spoken words. In still other cases we have developed reading comprehension using the speaker device.

elementary verbal operants See *function*.

environmental interventions See *tactic*.

environmentally disenfranchised Students who require specialized instructional practices due to language and learning delays associated with missing experiences rather than with native disabilities. The evidence suggests that verbal operants or higher order operants (speaker, listener, or textual) may be missing as a result of a lack of early experiences even though the child does not have native disabilities.

establishing operation Conditions, such as deprivation or aversive conditions, which act to alter the momentary effectiveness of a reinforcer. They may be unconditioned or conditioned, and different establishing operations are associated with different verbal operants (i.e., mands and tacts have different establishing operations). They are learned together with a three-term contingency, and effective instruction—both verbal and nonverbal—incorporates them as part of instruction. Once an establishing operation is learned with a three-term contingency, the operant will be emitted under related environmental conditions when they are present. Findings from research on establishing operations can be applied by teachers to create motivational conditions such that they need not wait for them to occur naturally. See Michael (1982, 1984, 1993) and Chapter 4 for a discussion on establishing operations and verbal functions. In more recent papers Michael has suggested the term *abolishing operations* for establishing operations that act to decrease the reinforcement effects of consequences, as well as changes in terminology based on Michael's (1975) clarification of reinforcement.

faultless instructional presentations Presenting antecedent stimuli that are unambiguous and that communicate the salient components of a target stimulus. Also referred to as *flawless* antecedent presentations.

fluency The term *fluency* has acquired a technical definition in behavior analysis. The term, as used in Precision Teaching, refers to the achievement of a combined rate and accuracy criterion. For example, an indication of fluency might be textually responding at 120 words per minute to material at grade 3 reading level. Some suggest that fluency objectives should differ for different students based on their performance history. There is a theory associated with fluency that maintains that learning to fluency results in better maintenance among other benefits. The related research literature has reported mixed findings. See Andronis, Layng, & Goldiamond (1997); Covington (2006); Dougherty & Johnston (1996); Johnson & Layng (1992, 1994, 1996, 2000); Lindsley (1992); Singer-Dudek & Greer (2005); and Young, West, Howard, & Whitney (1986). In verbal behavior analysis, fast-rate instruction has been used in Ross & Greer (2003), Tsiouri & Greer (2003), and in Greer, Chavez-Brown et al. (2005). The latter studies involved procedures to induce vocal verbal behavior described in Chapter 4 and as part of the listener emersion procedure described in Chapter 3.

form The topography of an instance of verbal behavior that is used in each of the verbal functions. Form refers to the topography of communication that students use in verbal functions (i.e., speech, sign, pictures, or electronic-speaking device). Also, a form may be a particular part of speech such as an adjective or adverb; however, when those forms have particular functions they become verbal operants such as autoclitics or intraverbals.

full naming See *naming*.

function We determine verbal function by the effect that an instance of verbal behavior has on a listener as a mediator who then "benefits" the speaker—the speaker uses the listener to mediate the environment. Also, function affects the listener component of verbal behavior in that the function of listening acts to extend the senses of the listener. Function may be obtained with numerous topographies or forms such as signs, pictures, smoke signals, drumbeats, Braille, or Morse code.

general case The presentation of a positive exemplar of a stimulus with a range of rotated negative exemplars such that irrelevant attributes of the salient component of target stimuli are contrasted with the salient attributes. General case instruction begins with the subtlest discriminations between negative and positive exemplars that the individual can successfully discriminate; this is modified as required by a learner. The use of positive and negative exemplars of stimuli during matching and pointing instruction is an example of general case teaching. The generic name for general case instruction is multiple exemplar instruction. The term *general case* was originated in the Direct Instruction curriculum.

generalized reinforcer A reinforcer, such as a token or praise, or consequence that is not specific to a particular behavior; that acquires its effectiveness through pairing with a conditioned or unconditioned positive or negative reinforcer; and can be used to reinforce many different behaviors. Money, praise, or the opportunity to mand may act as a generalized conditioned reinforcer. The acquisition of attention from others is a key component of acquiring the tact repertoire, and a key component of extending the sensory experiences for the listener.

gestural topographies Pointing or other gestures that can function as precursors to vocal speech or more complex gestural topographies, or can substitute for vocal speech if it is not forthcoming. Various sophisticated systems of signing or simple gestures such as pointing are examples of gestural topographies of verbal behavior. Spoken forms of verbal behavior are often emitted along with related topographies, as when a speaker points emphatically to attain closer attention from a listener, or when speakers roll their eyes during speech as a type of autoclitic (i.e., "I am saying this, but I don't really believe it").

hear-write Refers to transcription and to other writer functions involving hearing an auditory stimulus as a listener, and then producing a written response as a writer.

higher order operants Higher order operants are overarching operants that are occasioned, for example, by multiple-exemplar experiences that join two or more operant relations into a single overarching operant. Overarching operants occur when previously independent responses to a stim-ulus, such as the independence of listener and speaker responses to a stimulus, come to jointly control both listener and speaker responding. Generalized imitation is also an example of a higher order operant in that children respond to novel behavior of a model even when not reinforced. Other examples include the joining of see-do to hear-say, naming, transformation of stimulus control across saying and writing, metaphoric responses, and transformation of establishing operations across mand and tact functions.

impure mand A mand that occurs under verbal antecedent control together with establishing operations: such as the emission of a mand following the question, "What do you want?" The mand is under the control of both deprivation of the item and a verbal antecedent.

impure (intraverbal) tact A tact that occurs under multiple control (verbal and physical) antecedents such as asking the question, "What is this?" when pointing to a stimulus.

incidental language training Instruction in which the establishing operations (EOs) that occur throughout the day are captured as a means of incorporating the establishing operation. Also, one may construct the environment to increase incidental moments; for example, placing toys or treats on a shelf out of reach but within sight of a child or placing these items in a covered box. Other procedures have been identified to incorporate EOs into massed learn unit instructions. See *momentary deprivation, interrupted chain, rapid momentum, speaker immersion, listener immersion, reader immersion,* and *writer immersion.* All EOs are natural, but one can manipulate those natural conditions. Systematic efforts must be used to ensure that both captured and massed learn unit instruction include the critical EO.

induction of capabilities Refers to the teaching protocols that are used to produce verbal capabilities or verbal developmental cusps for learners. The term *induction* is used because the teaching protocols are not designed, and usually not used, if the repertoire can be taught directly. In most cases, capabilities are induced when direct instruction in a repertoire is ineffective. Thus, teaching the necessary prerequisite skills produces the capability without necessarily teaching it directly. For example, when students do not have vocal verbal capabilities, we find that teaching prerequisite repertoires associated with listener responding (namely, matching) results in the induction of vocal verbal capabilities or, for some students, far less instruction to acquire vocal verbal behavior.

instructional control Refers to the attention behaviors or attending responses of a student that are needed to teach; specifically, sitting still, making eye contact, sitting when told or indicated to do so, imitation of motor actions, and generalized imitation of motor actions. Until students have this basic instructional control, instruction in other repertoires will likely be ineffective. In his book *Verbal Behavior*, Skinner referred to instructional control as the control of verbal stimuli for a listener who had basic listener literacy. In this text, we distinguish between listener control derived from the spoken vowel-consonant combinations of a speaker and non-vocal control.

interrupted chain An establishing operation tactic developed by Sundberg (1993) and Michael (1982) in which an item is needed to complete a chain of responses. For example, a piece or pieces of a puzzle is/are withheld such that a child has to request the piece(s) to complete the puzzle; or an ingredient needed to construct a sandwich or other construction is withheld such that a child needs to mand the ingredient. This is particularly useful in creating the relevant establishing operations for developing transformation of establishing operations across mand and tacts. That is, an item that a child would not request or mand can be used in an interrupted chain as an establishing operation for the mand function (Nuzzolo & Greer, 2004).

intersperse Derived from the tactic *interspersal of known items*, the term *intersperse* refers to rotating mastered operants with new antecedents for potential operants during instruction. We frequently use this tactic to maintain a student's attention during probe sessions when incorrect responses are likely to occur, thus reducing the amount of reinforcement and ensuring that a student is discriminating auditory commands. Mastered operants that are interspersed with learn units are not learn units; they are interspersed simply to ensure that some responses are reinforced. Hence they are used as an establishing operation to maintain the student's motivation for attending.

intraverbal Verbal responses that are controlled by a verbal antecedent as in greetings; the two responses do not have point-to-point correspon-

dence with one another. Intraverbals may occur between individuals (e.g., "How are you?" "I'm fine."), or they may be composed of verbal behavior controlling verbal behavior for the same individual, such as counting, saying the verses of a memorized poem, reciting the pledge of allegiance, praying, or singing.

joint stimulus control Occurs when a single stimulus controls two or more topographically dissimilar behaviors such as the joint control of responding to a dictated word in either spoken or written form or responding to a stimulus as both listener and speaker; also includes the control of the echoic response across a tact or a listener response, the control of textually responding to a word across matching comprehension, and responding as a listener and responding as a writer as when print stimuli are joined with the naming capability. See also Lowenkron (1997) for another but related usage of the term *joint stimulus control*.

language A given community's agreed-upon verbal topographies. In verbal behavior analysis, language is not a compendium of behavior function; rather it is a lexicon of words defined by other words in a given verbal community. Verbal functions are arbitrarily applicable relations between topographies of behavior and environmental stimuli that are mediated by listeners or speakers. Across communities, any number of "codes" could have particular communicative functions. Language defines words by using other words that are used within a particular verbal community. Verbal behavior defines the function of language for an individual under particular conditions. Language requires referents to other words (e.g., dictionaries or lexicons); verbal behavior requires reference to the functional effects of a speaker on the listener.

learn unit Research-identified basic measures of teaching comprised of interlocking three-term contingencies, at least two for a teacher or teaching device and one potential three-term contingency for the learner. Learn units measure the behavior of a teacher, teaching device, or experimenter; responses to learn units are measures of a student or experimental participant. The components of learn units are (a) instructional presentations by a teacher, experimenter, automated operant chamber presentation, or teaching device in which the antecedent stimulus presentation is unambiguous, the participant is attending to the antecedent stimulus, and the experimenter-teacher is not providing unwitting prompts; (b) the participant has an opportunity to respond (i.e., a 3-second intraresponse period); (c) correct responses are followed by reinforcement derived from an individual's instructional history; and (d) incorrect responses are followed by a correction operation. Generally, correction operations must include all of the following: a) the teacher provides the answer, b) the stimulus is presented again, and c) at that point, the student provides the correct answer. Corrected responses of the student are not reinforced. Although not identified as such, Skinner used the components of the learn unit in what he described as programmed instruction *frames* (Skinner, 1968). Converging findings from basic and applied research on academic engaged time, opportunity-to-respond, computer-based-instruction, and an extensive literature on the learn unit shows that it is necessary, if not sufficient, for teaching new operants. Currently, it is one of the most powerful predictors of educational outcomes in classrooms. Children can learn from either direct or indirect contact with learn units, as when they observe others receiving learn units.

learn unit context   The setting events or establishing operations, instructional histories, or existing repertoires of both the student and the teacher. When a learn unit is present and a student is having difficulty learning, the probable sources for the learning problem reside in the contextual fields surrounding the learn unit. Setting events include the conditioned and unconditioned establishing operations and conditional stimuli. The instructional history or ontogeny includes the student's existing operants and higher order operants (particularly those in their verbal repertoires), and their community of reinforcers. The student and teacher's phylogeny or traumatic injury histories, in turn, affect these. There are numerous tactics in the applied literature that may be applied to solving the problem once the possible sources are identified. Frequently the problems reside in instructional histories where missing operants or higher order operants or capabilities are missing. An experimentally tested algorithm has proven successful in using the context to solve learning problems and to identify sources of poor experimental effects in basic experiments. See the description of the algorithm in Chapter 2.

learn units to criterion   The mean numbers of learn units required by a student to obtain mastery criterion for an instructional repertoire. This is typically a measure of instructional effectiveness, and fewer learn units to criterion should be required as teachers become more skilled at presenting learn units and identifying and implementing appropriate research-based tactics or verbal developmental protocols.

listener   Listeners are governed by the verbal behavior of others as they respond to vocal sounds and other verbal topographies; individuals with basic listener literacy have a measure of independence and can be warned, instructed, comforted, and praised as a result of the topography of behavior of a speaker. Children with listener literacy do not require the close supervision required of pre-listeners. The function of listening extends the senses of the listener provided by the behavior of speakers (e.g., "Bring an umbrella when you come; it's raining here.")

listener behavior   Responding to another person's speaker behavior. This is a capability associated with listener literacy. See *listener literacy.*

listener component of naming   When a child hears the name of a stimulus (smell, taste, appearance, or kinesthetic touch) and sees, smells, tastes, or feels the stimulus, the student can emit a point-to-response or listener's response (i.e., observing response) for the same set of stimuli without direct instruction. This learned relation between looking at a stimulus, hearing someone else tact it, and a listener's responses can emerge without direct instruction and is a necessary component for the full naming repertoire. It allows the child to build her listener vocabulary without direct instruction. A child may acquire the listener component of naming without having the speaker component.

listener literacy   Refers to the capability to respond fluently and discriminatively to the auditory properties of speech. Individuals without *basic listener literacy* may rely on cues from a teacher or other setting events to respond to auditory commands. We identify the origin of listener literacy at the point at which the vocal phonemes of a speaker can reliably control at least two different responses of a listener. This discriminative responding demonstrates that the listener's responses are controlled by speaker responses—first instances of such control.

mand   A verbal operant that occurs under conditions of deprivation or aversive control and is reinforced by receiving the target stimulus or the removal of a stimulus. The mand specifies its reinforcer. Mands are critical to the individual, but they are probably less frequent in normal discourse than are tacts. Pure mands are verbal operants that are not preceded by verbal stimuli. The item may be present (e.g., "Bread, please!"; Skinner, 1957, p. 37) or not present (e.g., "Let's go for ice cream."). When the item is present, it is important to ensure that the establishing operations are those for mands rather than tacts.

massed learn units   Presenting all learn units from a particular repertoire in a single session. This typically refers to sessions of 20-learn units that only target one repertoire. Students who need additional learning opportunities benefit from massed learn unit presentations. Massed learn units are differentiated from *captured* learn units, which are initiated by a student in a non-instructional environment, and then measured and reinforced by a teacher. Captured learn units are similar to those described in incidental teaching.

mastery criterion   The degree to which a response must be emitted accurately before it is considered acquired or mastered. This includes the reinforcement conditions that should ultimately maintain a repertoire. For many probe and instructional repertoires, *standard mastery criterion* is 90% correct responding for two consecutive sessions, or 100% correct responding for one session. However, mastery criterion is also individualized depending on the target repertoire and a learner's instructional history, which is based on the number of learn units to criterion they usually require. See Chapter 2 for details.

matching   or   match-to-sample   responding   Occurs when one acts as a listener, or emits other observing responses, involving two positive exemplars (one sample and one target) and at least one negative exemplar. The student discriminates between the examples by placing or pointing to identical stimuli or stimuli that are arbitrarily related. One may match via any of the senses. The term *match-to-sample* is the more formal term and describes what happens when an individual matches a particular response to the same stimulus between or among a sample of stimuli that include the target stimulus and a non-exemplar or non-exemplars.

momentary deprivation   a condition whereby access to a reinforcer used in reinforcement operations is denied for a brief period to provide an establishing operation. The period of deprivation may be only a few seconds or minutes. The amount of deprivation varies according to the motivational conditions needed to enhance the consequence as a reinforcer for a particular behavior.

multiple control   Involves antecedents, target or existing S^ds, in a verbal operant comprised of verbal and non-verbal stimuli (i.e., "Point to red."), and different verbal stimuli (i.e., "Read the word.") that gain control over a response during instruction or conversation. Multiple controls also include the establishing operations and conditional stimuli preceding and following the verbal response.

multiple exemplar instruction   The term *multiple exemplars* in teaching and research is used in two types of applications. The first (also called general case teaching) is related to the teaching of abstractions or essential stimulus control as in the control of abstract properties such as colors, shapes, parts of speech, and properties of mathematics (i.e., mammals, phonetic reading, chairs, tables, and dresses). In this case, students respond to presentations of abstractions in which the irrelevant aspects of a stimulus or conglomerate of stimuli are rotated across positive exemplars. For example, in teaching children to sound out words from the "at" family of phonetic textual responding, printed "at" words (i.e., cat, fat, and sat) are presented with altering font types and sizes and different first letters. In addition, negative exemplars, sometimes called foils, are presented (cut, sun, and veg) with positive exemplars, and the student identifies the correct stimulus.

The second type involves bringing responses that were initially independent under joint stimulus control. This is done by rotating different responses to a single stimulus (i.e., writing, spelling, and textually responding to a single word) such that learners acquire the capability of learning multiple responses from instruction in only one (e.g., after learning to spell a word vocally, a student can write it without direct instruction). For example, one type of multiple-exemplar instruction involves rotating match, point, pure tact, and impure tact responses to the same set of stimuli, resulting in untaught responses to novel stimuli. In still another instance, using multiple-exemplar instruction across establishing operations for mands and tacts results in the emergence of untaught responses within each verbal function.

naming A phenomenon through which students acquire tacts and listener responses without direct instruction. That is, after hearing someone say a tact (or viewing someone providing a sign or picture) of a stimulus during listener instruction (match or point), the student can say (sign, generate an electronic spoken response, or produce a picture for) the stimulus without receiving learn units for doing so. The student learns the echoic, the tact (pure and impure), and the listener response to a stimulus without direct instruction. Simply hearing an adult tact and then observing the stimulus results in a child responding to the stimulus as both a listener of speaker. Typically developing children and children with language delays have acquired naming following multiple-exemplar instruction in several experiments and applications in teaching settings. Thus, the child acquires new tacts or other verbal operants incidentally. Until a child has naming, verbal operants are acquired by learn unit instruction. Once naming is in place and conditions are in place to exercise the new capability, verbal operant forms multiply at rapid rates. Full naming involves a bidirectional relationship between the speaker-listener capabilities of the individual—learning a listener operant results in a speaker operant. When a child with naming learns to match stimuli while hearing the verbal tag, speaker and listener responses emerge without direct instruction.

native disabilities Children with intellectual native disabilities are those who have diagnosed disabilities of known or unknown etiology, usually physiological or neurological, which have genetic or traumatic injury sources. Regardless of whether the etiology is known, behavior analytic treatment procedures are not selected or differentiated based on diagnosis, but rather on the individual's level of verbal behavior.

natural fractures Phenomena that occur as a result of true natural events. They are distinguished from social or psychological constructs. DNA are natural fractures as are the properties of chemical compounds, the phenomenon of gravity. In behavior, operants are natural fractures. Psychological constructs are often based on arbitrary scales like intelligence scores or measures of locus of control. When a speaker affects the behavior of a listener, this constitutes a natural fracture.

natural reinforcer Those that occur as an effect of the behavior that is reinforced. Natural reinforcers that are unconditioned include, for example, food, liquid, novelty, salt, and sugar. Many conditioned reinforcers are incidentally conditioned as a typical course of events and they too are natural. The effects of touch, praise, music as reinforcement for various behaviors, to name a few examples, are conditioned reinforcers. These are incidentally acquired and they may be positive or negative reinforcers, although in most cases those listed function as positive reinforcers. Natural reinforcement for the mand is obtainment of the item specified, not praise. The natural reinforcer for tacts are conditioned generalized reinforcers, frequently of a social nature. Academic or educational reinforcers can be praise or obtaining a correct response, and although these may seem prosthetic they are natural to an academic environment. That is, since the long-term natural reinforcers for, say, reading are slow in coming, thus prosthetic reinforcers like praise and attention may be said to be natural to the academic setting. It also may be argued that praise and correct answers are a form of verbal reinforcement. It is possible that the capacity to be reinforced by a range of prosthetic reinforcers may be one of the unique capabilities of humans.

naturalistic language intervention Any language function intervention that uses the relevant establishing operation that is tied to the natural reinforcing effect of the consequence can be characterized as natural. Also known as *naturalistic language training*.

ontogenetic The developmental, experiential, and learning history of an individual. More so than phylogeny, the concern of behavior analysis and behavioral selection is the ontogenetic development of an individual through environment-behavior relations. See *phylogenic*.

operant Antecedent-behavior-consequence contingencies including the relevant contexts, particularly the establishing operations, tied to the operant. Operant responses are selected out by their consequences. The same behavior may have many antecedents and consequences and each of these has different operant functions. See *verbal operants*.

opportunity-to-respond Involves the presentation of an antecedent followed by a period for the student to emit a response. The evidence shows that the number of opportunities-to-respond in school and at home is highly correlated with the academic achievement of students (see Hart & Risley, 1995). This was first identified in research conducted by Hall, Greenwood, and Delquadri in the late 1970s. This research, along with the opportunity-to-respond, made up the sequence of findings that led to the identification of the learn unit, which by definition must include an opportunity-to-respond.

palilalia A vocal response characterized in psychiatric literature as repetitive nonsensical speech. It is the repetition of previously heard speech, but the source is not immediate, as in the case of echolalia. This type of vocal responding appears to have no relation to current environmental sources. While in some cases it may function as a form of stereotypy, in other cases it may possibly represent speaker-as-own-listener responses. More research is needed on the possible functions of such behavior, including its possible developmental function.

parroting A point-to-point vocal response in which students emit a vocal sound or word under the control of automatic reinforcement. It appears to be occasioned by stimulus-stimulus pairings in which the pairing of positive reinforcement with spoken sounds leads to conditioned automatic reinforcement. Providing that certain conditions are in place, parroting may lead to echoic operants. It appears to be an early joining between see-do and hear-say in a duplic relational frame.

performance behaviors or performance Previously learned operant behaviors associated with events in the environment or actions taken by teachers or parents. For example, certain events act to increase or decrease the probability that a child will wear a seat belt or complete their chores. Given the conditions under which these behaviors were learned, the behavior will be present or absent. Performance behaviors, unlike the learning of operants, are reversible depending on the presence or absence of reinforcement and setting events.

phase change lines Broken lines drawn on visual displays to represent the introduction of a different condition (i.e., a tactic or a new short-term objective). A description of the condition is represented by a *condition* or *phase label*.

phylogenic A biological term that refers to the development of a species. In behavior analysis, it represents the influence of structural physiological variables for a particular learner. While the science of behavior is concerned with the influence of environment over a learner's behavior, it also maintains that phylogenic variables interact with *ontogenetic* variables to develop the behavioral repertoires of an individual.

picture topographies Drawings, photographs, forms, or figures that symbolize actual stimuli in the environment and are used in place of vocal speech for verbal functions. They may be used in mand functions as in a picture exchange system, or they may be used for tact functions given the relevant consequences and antecedent conditions.

point-to-point correspondence Topographies that have formal similarity, or are exact duplications, of the behavior of a model.

point-to response A listener response during which a student points to discriminate between stimuli upon hearing a teacher say, "Point to ——" (e.g., as a response to a teacher tact of a stimulus).

pre-listener Individuals who cannot be governed by the vocal verbal behavior of others. As a result, they are highly dependent on others to meet their needs, and they have little progress in verbal and cognitive repertoires until they achieve listener status. Pre-listeners may or may not have match-to-sample responses, capacity for sameness across senses, and voices and faces may or may not be conditioned stimuli for observing.

private events Behavior within or beneath the skin. Private events are identified when a speaker tells a listener about emotions, hunger, pain, or other events that are not observable to listener. They are learned by correspondence with external events.

probes Probes are measures of untaught relations or tests of collateral relations, generalized stimulus control, or other operants or higher order operants that either emerge or are brought about as a function of certain experiences. Typically there is no reinforcement or correction consequence to probe responses (e.g., probes for naming), although in the case of certain operants (e.g., mands) reinforcement is delivered for correct responses but corrections for incorrect responses are not given.

prosthetic reinforcer The use of a reinforcing item within a contingency such that its use is not a natural result of the behavior. In verbal behavior analysis, prosthetic reinforcers are used for some programs until behaviors can be brought under natural or generalized reinforcement control. See natural reinforcer.

pure mands Mands that occur under non-verbal antecedent control. They are differentiated from impure mands that occur under verbal antecedent control (i.e., "What do you want?"). The latter are multiply controlled by both verbal and non-verbal events; otherwise they have all of the characteristics of pure mands. See *tact.*

pure tacts Tacts that occur under the control of a physical stimulus, but not under verbal stimulus control. They are reinforced by attention or other forms of generalized reinforcement, such as the opportunity to mand. See *mand.*

rapid motor imitation A component used in the tactic for joining see-do to hear-say. It is used and described in Ross & Greer (2003) and Tsiouri & Greer (2003) to induce first instances of vocal mands and tacts. See Chapter 4 for a complete description.

reader A stage of verbal development at which a student can respond to textual stimuli and match print to pictures or action. The student can read and do, or read and have his or her emotions affected. Readers can surmount the restrictions of time and distance that are associated with vocal stimuli. Reading involves several different but related responses including textually responding (i.e., see the printed word and say the word), pointing to the printed word when heard, matching the printed word to a picture or action, and vice versa. Once an individual is a reader and has naming, the actual hearing of their textual responses constitutes the comprehension of the word, provided that the reader has the relevant tact.

reader immersion An establishing operation in which all classroom reinforcement is contingent on reading responses. It is implicit in writer immersion. See Chapter 6 for a detailed description.

reinforcement Presentations of reinforcers (generalized, natural, or prosthetic) follow a student responding to a learn unit presentation in the process of acquiring a new operant or higher order operant. Reinforcement operations also can be used to manage performance or control the rate and emission of previously acquired operants. A reinforcement operation performed by a teacher may not, in fact, act to reinforce the behavior or instructional response. Thus, we distinguish between an actual reinforcer for a given response and a reinforcement operation. Reinforcers typically are related to behaviors, while preferred items may or may not serve a reinforcement function for a particular response. See *community of reinforcers.*

relational frames Theoretical constructs developed by the originators of Relational Frame Theory (RFT) to explain the possible source of certain higher order operants and complex cognitive behavior consistent with the epistemological tenets of radical behaviorism and behavioral selection (Hayes, Barnes-Holmes, & Roche, 2001). That is, relational frames provide environmental, experiential sources for the development of complex cognitive behavior. Hayes, Barnes-Holmes, & Roche (2001) stated, "Relational frame theory (RFT) is a behavior analytic approach to human language and cognition" (p. 41). RFT treats relational responding as a generalized overarching or higher order operant, and appeals to a history of multiple exemplar instruction as a possible source for the development of the transformation of establishing operations. The research in RFT has contributed many empirical demonstrations of cognitive constructs as purely behavior-environment relations. The various patterns of derived relational responding possess three properties: mutual entailment, combinatorial entailment, and transformation of stimulus function (Hayes, 1991, 1994; Hayes, Barnes-Holmes, & Roche, 2001). Relational Frame Theorists were the first to propose that higher order operants or relational frames of various types were theoretically traceable to certain multiple exemplar experiences rather than to psychological mental constructs or instinctual theories. Frames such as the ones that result in stimulus equivalence are not purely instinctual; rather they are products of certain instructive experiences. Recent research in verbal behavior analysis has provided substantial evidence that constructs such as generative language are functionally related to multiple-exemplar instruction. Multiple-exemplar instruction has led to the induction of various higher order verbal operants and capabilities such as those previously seen as untaught usages of tense, suffixes, production or selection responses, joint stimulus control over different behaviors, cross-modal transfer, and establishing operation control over different verbal behavior topographies. The theory contributed to advances in verbal behavior analysis, particularly with regard to the role of the listener in an expansion of verbal behavior theory. Arguably, RFT expanded the contributions of stimulus equivalence to verbal behavior by extending emergent relations to the constructs of verbal behavior. While emergent relations were identified in stimulus equivalence

(SE) research as a particular type of relational frame, the SE relations themselves were not necessarily verbal. Extrapolation of the notion to incorporate a broader range of frames led to identifying and researching arbitrarily applicable verbal frames as higher order verbal operants. This has proven immensely important to the expansion of verbal behavior analysis in terms of explaining complex verbal behavior and inducing missing higher order operants in children with and without native disabilities. See Hayes, Barnes-Holmes, & Roche (2001) for a thorough treatment of relational frame theory and the relevant extensive research base.

repertoire   A class or category of operants that was learned by an individual and is likely to be emitted given the learned setting events and antecedents. We test for the presence or absence of repertoires in the natural setting. If students can perform them under the natural antecedent and consequence conditions, the behavior is said to be in their repertoire. A cluster of behaviors becomes a repertoire; a cluster of repertoires constitutes the range of responses within a *capability*. See *capability*.

respondent behavior   Unlearned behavior that is elicited by either conditioned or unconditioned stimuli. Unconditioned stimuli such as a loud noise when paired with a neutral stimulus, such as a light, can result in the neutral stimulus acquiring conditioned stimulus control. If the noise elicits a startle response, the light elicits the startle response. Words for stimuli, such as *snakes*, can become conditioned stimuli that elicit an emotional response from a reader. The respondent control of words plays an important role in the emotional responses involved in reading and when writing to affect the emotional responses of a reader (see Donahoe & Palmer 2004; Hayes, Barnes-Holmes, & Roche, 2001; Staats, 1968).

response topography   In this text, response topography has two meanings. First, it refers to the *form* or shape of a particular response (see *form*). However, it also refers to the response type that a speaker uses, including pictorial, gestural, sign, vocal, or electronically produced topographies of responding.

say and do correspondence   The relation between the verbal and non-verbal behavior of an individual. An individual who follows the directions of another or herself has say and do correspondence.

science of behavior   See *applied behavior analysis*.

science of verbal behavior   See *verbal behavior analysis*.

see-write   A copying function during which an individual looks at a printed stimulus, and then writes it. A part of the writer repertoire referred to by Skinner as *transcription*.

self-editing or writer-as-own-reader   A stage of verbal development at which a student has the ability to read their own writing from the perspective of the eventual audience without immediate responses from the target audience or teacher. The writer "hears" the overt or covert spoken textual response as the intended audience would hear the spoken text. The writer can affect the behavior of the intended audience without recourse to other editorial assistance.

self-talk conversational units   An important developmental milestone in which children emit conversational units by behaving as both speaker and listener in play (i.e., a child playing with toys). That is, the child acts as both speaker and listener. Young typically developing children talk aloud to themselves in free-play settings, and developmental psychologists have studied the topography of self-talk extensively. Cognitive psychologists regard the emission of self-talk as a key milestone in children's development. Skinner (1957) described the process whereby self-talk becomes covert as a function of audiences as children grow older. From a radical behavioral perspective self-talk is the basis of much of what is typically seen as "thinking." In one experiment, five-year-old children who engaged in self-talk during free play with anthropomorphic toys used mands, tacts, sequelics, and conversational units (Lodhi & Greer, 1989). We believe that inducing self-talk conversational units is a key to the acquisition of other higher order operants such as self-editing and may well be related to naming.

self-talk to govern other behavior (say-do correspondence)   Also called say-do responses. Children emit an instance of verbal behavior that indicates their future behavior (say) and then they perform the behavior (do). In the literature this is also referred to a *verbal correspondence* or *correspondence between saying and doing*.

sense modality   One or more of the five senses through which a response is emitted. Also verbal responses are said to have *point-to-point correspondence* and formal similarity when they are identical to a controlling verbal stimulus, and when they are in the same sense modality (i.e., writing, speech, and sign).

sensory matching for sameness across senses (protocol): A very early pre-listener protocol to induce the basic capacity for sameness. The capacity for sameness may be basic to the subsequent acquisition of discriminations. The capacity for sameness across senses may be a very fundamental abstraction on which subsequent verbal functions are built. In the sensory-matching protocol, students match a target stimulus to a positive exemplar rotated across auditory, gustatory (taste), olfactory (smell), tactile (touch), and visual senses. Inducing this repertoire has improved the learning rate of children who were having difficulty with visual or auditory matching. See Chapter 3 for a detailed description.

sequelic Individual responds as a listener and speaker to intraverbals that may or may not have mand or tact functions. The sequelic is one part of a conversational unit. An individual responds to a speaker by speaking, but does not continue the verbal episode after the listener responds. See *intraverbal*.

setting events Events that precede a response and, in some cases, occasion behavior along with the antecedent. In some cases, setting events are unwanted, as in unintentional cues from a teacher that prompt a student's response. In that case, the student is not relying on the target antecedent, but rather on events that accompany it (see the listener function in Chapter 3). In other cases, responses to setting events are desired, as in establishing operations when teaching mands. Students should respond to setting events conditions of deprivation as well as to the presence of a stimulus, thus increasing the likelihood that in the absence of a stimulus, the mand will still be emitted when a condition of deprivation is present.

sign topographies The use of sign language to emit verbal operants. American Sign Language is one type of sophisticated sign language. Signs are substituted for spoken responses for children who have difficulty acquiring spoken speaker repertoires.

simultaneous stimulus prompts See *zero-second time delay*.

single-subject designs Experimental procedures to test the effects of an independent variable on a dependent variable with individuals. Such designs employ the basic logic of experimental design. Typically, several individuals are studied. The effects of the independent variable may be replicated across or within individuals or both. The questions and methods of experimentation differ depending on whether one is studying the acquisition of (a) new operants, (b) higher order operants, or (c) the modification of performance. In experiments on the acquisition of new operants the tactic leads to mastery and is not reversible. The visual display demonstrates the acquisition rate, and the acquisition is not reversible. Hence, the experimental method calls for between-subject designs that control for maturation and history (e.g., multiple baseline designs). In studies of the acquisition of higher order operants or new capabilities, the same between-subjects design is necessary, but with some differences. In the study of capabilities, probes before and after interventions demonstrate the acquisition of the higher order operant—in pre-intervention probes the capability is absent and in post-intervention probes the capability is present. Measures of the acquisition of the target repertoire in the intervention serve as an indication that the newly taught repertoire is mastered (e.g., mastery of responses to multiple-exemplar instruction for a subset of stimuli). If the intervention leads to the emission of the formerly lacking capability, the acquisition is demonstrated to be a function of the acquisition of the repertoire taught as the intervention. In the study of existing operants, changes in the environment lead to changes in the behavior and these changes may be reversed by removing the environmental intervention. When a behavior is reversible, it is a performance behavior and reversal or within-subject designs are possible.

speaker When someone can govern the behavior of others by using various topographies of verbal behavior, including vocal speech, signs, pictures, or electronic vocal transducers, they are functioning as a speaker.

speaker-as-own-listener A verbal development stage at which individuals can function as a listener to their own verbal behavior (e.g., "First I do this; then I do this.") Naming is a type of speaker-as-own-listener behavior, as is engaging in self-talk conversational units within one's own skin.

speaker component of naming A student who can hear the name for a stimulus during instruction (as a listener) and then use it as a speaker has the speaker component of naming.

speaker immersion A tactic that places the child under conditions in which they must use speaker behavior on a continuous basis. The child is immersed in establishing operation conditions that require the use of speaker behavior (vocal or substitute speaker responses. Similar conditions are found in language immersion methods for teaching a second language. See Ross, Nuzzolo, Stolfi, Leonard, & Valdes (2006) and Chapter 4 for a description.

speaker-listener exchanges   Sequelics and conversational units with others or with oneself. Individuals can respond as both a listener and as speaker. See *conversational unit.*

tact   A verbal operant that occurs under non-verbal stimulus control (i.e., an object or a picture) and is reinforced by generalized reinforcement. The relevant establishing operation is deprivation of generalized reinforcement. Pure tacts occur under non-verbal antecedent control, and impure tacts occur under verbal antecedent control and non-verbal antecedent control.

tactic   An operation or set of procedures derived from strategies and principles of the science of behavior, and used as an intervention to teach a particular repertoire to a student. Tactics, as used in this text, refers only to tactics that have a research basis.

Teacher Performance Rate and Accuracy (TPRA) Scale   A measure of the teacher's instructional behaviors on a teaching device that assesses the accuracy and rate of learn unit presentations. (see Chapter 2).

teaching interventions   See *tactic.*

textual responding   Skinner (1957) described *textual behavior* as a verbal operant under the control of printed, verbal stimuli. Textual responding is a reader function during which the consonant-vowel phonemes associated with a printed stimulus evoke a speaker's responses. It is only one component of reading.

topography   The shape or form of an instance of verbal behavior. See *form.*

transcription   A writer function during which one sees a word and writes it, as when a child copies a word that a teacher has written on the blackboard. It is distinguished from dictation, which consists of writing a word after hearing the auditory stimulus.

transformation of establishing operation functions   Represents a point in verbal development in which a child can learn a form of language, spoken or other topography, in a tact function and use the form as mand without instruction or vice versa. Initially, and for children with developmen-

tal delays, learning a form in one function does not result in its usage in the other function (e.g., "milk" as a mand and "milk" as a tact are independent). However, children can develop transformation of establishing operations as a function of receiving multiple-exemplar instruction across the relevant establishing operations for each function. Thereafter, when a word topography or related autoclitic is learned in one form, they can use the same form in the "untaught" function without direct instruction in it (see Chapter 4).

transformation of stimulus function   This capability occurs when a single stimulus can control two different verbal response forms or topographies. Spelling a word by saying the letters is a different behavior than writing the letters. Similarly, summarizing what another says in written or vocal verbal behaviors is different. Initially, these are different and require instruction as independent operants. However, if a child has acquired transformation of stimulus functions across saying and writing, then they may emit either response after learning only a single response class to a stimulus. The stimulus jointly controls both responses when only a single one is learned. Multiple-exemplar experiences with a subset of stimuli can induce transformation of stimulus function. When the transformation of stimulus function is present across two or more responses, a single stimulus results in a higher order operant or frame.

trend determination   In the Decision Protocol, after four data points/three data paths, the presence of an ascending trend indicates that present instructional procedures should continue; the presence of a descending trend or the absence of a trend indicates a decision opportunity to analyze the source of the learning problem. In experiments, trend and stability are determined by visual examination. Convincing changes in trends that result in stability or mastery are the basis on which judgments of the effects of independent variables/teaching procedures on dependent variables/students' responses are made. Trends may be gradual, steep, variable, or stable. The angle of data paths determines a trend. Counts of the direction of data paths determine whether the data are ascending, descending, or flat/stable.

verbal   Refers to usages of language, not the particular form or topography of language used. Verbal does not mean *vocal.* Instead, it refers to the form of communication (speech, electronic, sign, or pictures) that a speaker uses in verbal operants. Verbal and vocal have come to be used interchangeably in certain communities; however,

Skinner's usage and our usage maintain the distinction between verbal and vocal. The term *oral language* is also used in some quarters to refer to vocal. However, a click language may be oral but not involve the vocal apparatus; thus, we prefer the term *vocal.*

verbal behavior analysis A subfield of the science of behavior that is devoted to identifying functional verbal repertoires and researching teaching procedures to produce them when they are missing. These may be the identification of initial capabilities such as the shift of parroting to echoing the expansion of forms of the capability, or the expansion of mand operants. The research may contribute to both the identification of verbal operant functions as in the testing of the constructs of Skinner's verbal behavior, or to the identification of procedures to teach them. Verbal behavior not only extends the basic principles of behavior to communication, but its extensions are increasingly identified as principles in their own right—essentially extensions of the basic principles. For example, while conversational units, the phenomenon of naming, and the variables that result in naming or conversational units are themselves uniquely principles of verbal behavior that may be simulated in non-verbal organisms, the verbal principles are essentially about human behavior.

Analysis of Verbal Behavior is a journal devoted exclusively to research in verbal behavior; some research papers have also been published in a number of behavior analysis journals listed in the References and Bibliography of this text. In Chapter 1, the history of early applications of behavior analysis to language, and its relation to applications of Skinner's theory of verbal behavior, is described.

verbal behavior A term coined by Skinner (1957) in his text *Verbal Behavior* in which he presented a functional account of communication during which instances of verbalizations, vocal or otherwise, were identified by their effect on a listener. In verbal behavior analysis, the theory has been extended to incorporate listener functions as well as speaker functions.

verbal capabilities See *capability.*

verbal community Refers to the language of a culture or group. Different cultures and groups associate particular behaviors with specific verbal topographies and as such, usually reinforce particular forms for speaker or listener functions. For example, in some verbal communities culture, the words *por favor* function as an autoclitic for mands, thus enhancing the speaker's influence over a listener's behavior. An English-speaking verbal community would not usually reinforce words spoken in another language. Thus, verbal functions emitted by individuals who cannot communicate within the language of a particular verbal community are less likely to be naturally reinforced and maintained. This is also the rationale for vocal verbal behavior over non-vocal verbal behavior, whenever possible; the broader verbal community of most students is more likely to reinforce verbal functions emitted in vocal form.

verbal functions See *function.*

verbally governed behavior Also called rule-governed behavior, verbally governed refers to behavior controlled by verbal contingencies instead of non-verbal contingencies. See *verbal mediation for problem solving.*

verbal mediation for problem solving Describes the emission of a sequence of verbally governed responses using verbal algorithms such as the Decision Protocol (see Chapter 2). Teachers do so when they apply the science of teaching to locate and solve a student's learning problems. This function is also evident when students learn algorithms for performing problem-solving responses such as following verbal directions to complete double-digit addition, performing an experiment, or locating primary sources. This function is an extension of basic verbally or rule-governed responses, progressing from *say and do* to *first I do this, then the next step, the next,* and so on.

verbal operants Include the basic six speaker verbal operants identified by Skinner and by the listener operant response. See *verbal behavior* and *verbal behavior analysis.*

visual tracking The capacity to track visual stimuli is a developmental stage (Novak & Pelaez, 2004). It is also a likely prerequisite for attending to a speaker, thus facilitating the acquisition of early listener behavior. The *conditioning visual-tracking* protocol described in Chapter 3 is designed to induce the visual-tracking capability or developmental stage by pairing preferred stimuli with a tracking procedure (see Chapter 3).

vocal topographies Speech is one form or topography of communication; there are numerous advantages for teaching the vocal topography when that is possible. Vocal topographies are particular advantageous in the development of higher order verbal operants or verbal relational frames. Pictures, signs, or speech-generating electronic devices can be substituted for verbal operants and the development of some verbal higher order operants. See Chapter 1 for the pros and cons of teaching alterative topographies.

vocal verbal behavior The functions and not the forms of verbal behavior are the focus of both the theory of verbal behavior and verbal behavior analysis. As such, *verbal* does not mean vocal, but refers to a verbal function regardless of its response form—vocal, gestural, pictorial, or electronically produced by a selection response. *Vocal verbal behavior* refers to speech forms. When physiologically possible, vocal verbal behavior is the preferred response form for speaker behavior because of the many advantages it has over other possible response forms (see Chapters 1, 2, and 7).

writer A verbal developmental stage at which a person can affect the behavior of a reader such that a reader (as a kind of listener) need not be present in the same time or location as the writer. There are two categories: technical writing and aesthetic writing. In technical writing, the writer specifies what the reader is to do, from following a recipe or a complex algorithm for preparing slides, to identifying chromosomes or genetic codes. In technical writing the writer must be precise and the reader and writer must have the same tact repertoires. In aesthetic writing, the writer sets out to affect the emotions of the reader. Extended tacts such as metaphors are particularly useful in affecting the emotions of the reader. Students must learn both repertoires and their relevant audience control.

writer-as-own-reader See *self-editing or writer-as-own-reader.*

writer immersion An establishing operation during which all communication between teacher and student requires the use of writing. No talking or signing is allowed, and responses to writing are made in writing. One of the key components is that writers must edit their own writing until it affects the behavior of those who reply in written form. See Reilly-Lawson & Greer (2006) and Chapter 6.

writer immersion protocol An instructional protocol during which all communication between teacher and student is written. During immersion settings, the functional effects of the student's writing are measured by the reader's response. That is, if the reader can follow the writer's directions or tact a stimulus as described, then the writing is functionally accurate. Topographical writing responses are also measured.

yoked contingencies The term *yoked contingencies* is loosely based on animal yokes, which create conditions where a couple or pair must work together. In this text, yoked contingencies refer to conditions in which children must work or learn together in order for both to receive reinforcement. They are similar to group contingencies in which three or more members of a group must collaborate or cooperate to obtain reinforcement. As described in Chapter 5, we use the yoked-contingency protocol to induce the capability of observational learning.

zero-second time delay Also called simultaneous stimulus prompt, the zero-second time delay tactic refers to the amount of time between an antecedent and a prompt to emit a correct response. The amount of time increases from zero or no seconds to two seconds, four seconds, and so on before presenting a prompt. In zero-second time delay, a verbal antecedent stimulus is immediately followed by the teacher emitting the correct response as a prompt for the student to emit the correct response. This prompt is systematically faded by successively longer periods of time in which the student has the opportunity to emit a correct response before the teacher does.

REFERENCES AND A
SELECTED BIBLIOGRAPHY
OF RELATED RESEARCH
AND CONCEPTUAL PAPERS

Ahearn, W. H. (2003). Using simultaneous presentation to increase vegetable consumption in a mildly selective child with autism. *Journal of Applied Behavior Analysis, 36(3)*, 361–365.

Albers, A. E., & Greer, R. D. (1991). Is the three-term contingency trial a predictor of effective instruction? *Journal of Behavioral Education, 1*, 337–354.

Andronis, P. T., Layng, T. V. J., & Goldiamond, I. (1997). Contingency adduction of "symbolic aggression" by pigeons. *Analysis of Verbal Behavior, 14*, 5–17.

Arntzen, E., & Almas, I. K. (2002). Effects of mand-tact versus tact-only training on the acquisition of tacts. *Journal of Applied Behavior Analysis, 35*, 419–422.

Baer, D. M. (1964). Reinforcement control of generalized imitation in young children. *Journal of Experimental Child Psychology, 1*, 37–49.

Baer, D. M., Peterson, R. F., & Sherman, J. A. (1967). The development of imitation in young children. *Journal of Experimental Analysis of Behavior, 10*, 405–416.

Bahadourian, A. J., Tam, K. Y., Greer, R. D., & Rousseau, M. K. (2006). The effects of learn units on student performance in two college courses. *International Journal of Behavioral and Consultation Therapy*, 246–265. Retrieved June 12, 2006, from http://www.ijbct.com.

Barbera, M. L., & Kubina, R. M. (2005). Using transfer procedures to teach tacts to a child with autism. *Analysis of Verbal Behavior, 21*, 155–161.

Barnes-Holmes, D., Barnes-Holmes, Y., & Cullinan, V. (2001). Relational frame theory and Skinner's *Verbal Behavior. Behavior Analyst, 23*, 69–84.

Barnes-Holmes, Y., Barnes-Holmes, D., & Roche, B. (2001). The development of self- and perspective-taking: A relational frame analysis. *Behavioral Development Bulletin, 1*, 42–45.

Barnes, D., McCullagh, P. D., & Keenan, M. (1990). Equivalence class formation in non-hearing impaired children and hearing impaired children. *Analysis of Verbal Behavior, 8*, 19–30.

Becker, B. J. (1989). The effect of mands and tacts on conversational units and other verbal operants. (Doctoral dissertation, 1989, Columbia University). Abstract from UMI Proquest Digital Dissertations [on-line]. Dissertations Abstracts Item: AAT 8913097.

Bijou, S. W. (1996). Reflections on some early events related to behavior analysis of child development. *The Behavior Analyst, 19*, 49–60.

Birnbrauer, J. S., Hopkins, N. R., & Kauffman, J. M. (1981). The effects of vicarious prompting on attentive behavior of children with behavior disorders. *Child Behavior Therapy, 3*, 27–41.

Bloom, B. (1986). Automaticity: The hands and feet of genius. *Educational Leadership, 43(5)*: 70–77.

Bloomfield, L. (1961). *Language*. Chicago: University of Chicago Press.

Bondy, A., & Frost, L. (2001). The picture exchange communication system. *Behavior Modification, 25(5)*, 725–744.

Bosch, S., & Fuqua, R. W. (2001). Behavioral cusps: A model for selecting target behaviors. *Journal of Applied Behavior Analysis, 34(1)*, 123–125.

Bourret, J., Vollmer, T. R., & Rapp, J. T. (2004). Evaluation of a vocal mand assessment and vocal mand training procedures. *Journal of Applied Behavior Analysis, 37(2)*, 129–144.

Braam, C., & Malott, R. W. (1990). "I'll do it when the snow melts": The effects of deadlines and delayed outcomes on rule-governed behavior in preschool children. *Analysis of Verbal Behavior, 8*, 67–76.

Brady, N. C., Saunders, K. J., & Spradlin, J. E. (1994). A conceptual analysis of request teaching procedures for individuals with severely limited verbal repertoires. *Analysis of Verbal Behavior, 12*, 43–52.

Brasolotto, A. G., de Rose, J. C., Stoddard, L. T., & de Souza, D. G. (1993). Stimulus control analysis of language disorders: A study of substitution between voiced and unvoiced consonants. *Analysis of Verbal Behavior, 11*, 31–42.

Bruner, E., Engelmann, S., Hanner, S., Osborn, J., Osborn, J., & Zoerf, L. (1995). *Reading mastery rainbow edition*. Desoto, TX: SRA/McGraw Hill.

Burgeois, M. S. (1990). Enhancing conversation skills in patients with Alzheimer's disease using a prosthetic memory aid. *Journal of Applied Behavior Analysis, 23,* 29–42.

Bushel, Jr., D., & Baer, D. M. (1994). Measurably superior instruction means close continual contact with the relevant outcome data. Revolutionary! In R. Gardner et al. (Eds.), *Behavior analysis in education: Focus on measurably superior instruction.* Pacific Groves, CA: Brooks/Cole.

Carr, E. G., & Durand, V. M. (1985). Reducing behavior problems through functional communication training. *Journal of Applied Behavior Analysis, 18,* 111–126.

Carr, J., & Firth, A. (2005). The verbal behavior approach to early and intensive behavioral intervention for autism: A call for additional empirical support. *Journal of Early and Intensive Behavioral Intervention, 2,* 18–27.

Carroll, R. J., & Hesse, B. E. (1987). The effect of alternating mand and tact training on the acquisition of tacts. *Analysis of Verbal Behavior, 5,* 55–65.

Catania, A. C. (1998). *Learning,* 4th edition. Englewood Cliffs, NJ: Prentice-Hall.

Catania, A. C. (1993). Coming to terms with establishing operations. *Behavior Analyst, 16(2),* 219–224.

Catania, A. C. (2007). *Learning,* interim 4th edition. Cornwall-on-Hudson, NY: Sloan Publishing.

Catania, A. C., Horne, P., & Lowe, C. F. (1989). Transfer of function across members of an equivalence class. *Analysis of Verbal Behavior, 7,* 99–110.

Catania, A. C., & Matthews, B. A. (1982). Instructed versus shaped human verbal behavior: Interactions with nonverbal responding. *Journal of the Experimental Analysis of Behavior, 38,* 233–248.

Catania, A. C., Mathews, B. A., & Shimoff, E. H. (1990). Properties of rule-governed behavior and their implications. In D. E. Blackman & H. Lejeune (Eds.), *Behavior analysis in theory and practice* (pp. 215–230). Hillside, NJ: Erlbaum.

Chase, P. N., Bjarnadottir, G. S. (1992). Instruction variability: Some features of a problem-solving repertoire. In S. C. Hayes & L. J. Hayes (Eds.), *Understanding verbal relations* (pp. 181–196). Reno, NV: Context Press.

Chase, P. N., Johnson, T. R., & Sulzer-Azaroff, B. (1985). Verbal relations within instruction: Are there subclasses of the intraverbal? *Journal of the Experimental Analysis of Behavior, 43,* 301–313.

Charlop-Christy, M. H., Carpenter, M., Le, L., LeBlanc, L. A., & Kellet, K. (2002). Using the picture exchange communication system (PECS) with children with autism: Assessment of pecs acquisition, speech, social-communicative behavior, and problem behavior. *Journal of Applied Behavior Analysis, 35,* 213–231.

Charlop-Christy, M. H., Le, L., & Freeman, K. A. (2000). A comparison of video modeling with in vivo modeling for teaching children with autism. *Journal of Autism and Developmental Disorders, 30,* 537–552.

Charlop, M. H., & Milstein, J. P. (1989). Teaching autistic children conversational speech using video modeling. *Journal of Applied Behavior Analysis, 22,* 275–285.

Chavez-Brown, M. (2005). The effects of the acquisition of a generalized auditory word match-to-sample repertoire on the echoic repertoire under mand and tact conditions. (Doctoral dissertation, Columbia University, 2005). Abstract from UMI Proquest Digital Dissertations [on-line]. Dissertations Abstracts Item: AAT 3159725.

Chavez-Brown, M., & Greer, R. D. (2003, July) The effect of auditory matching on echoic responding. Paper presented at the First European Association for Behavior Analysis, Parma, Italy.

Chomsky, N. (1959). A review of B. F. Skinner's *Verbal Behavior. Language 35,* 26–58.

Chomsky, N., & Place, U. (2000). The Chomsky-Place correspondence 1993-1994, edited with an introduction and suggested readings by Ted Schoneberger. *Analysis of Verbal Behavior, 17,* 7–38.

Chu, H. C. (1998). A comparison of verbal-behavior and social-skills approaches for development of social interaction skills and concurrent reduction of aberrant behaviors of children with developmental disabilities in the context of matching theory. (Doctoral dissertation, Columbia University, 1998). Abstract from UMI Proquest Digital Dissertations [on-line]. Dissertations Abstracts Item: AAT 9838900.

Clay, K. (2006). Multiple exemplar instruction and the emergence of deictic relations for children with developmental delays. Unpublished manuscript. Teachers College, Columbia University.

Coates, B., & Hartup, W. (1969). Age and verbalization in observational learning. *Developmental Psychology, 1,* 556–562.

Cooper, J. O., Heron, T. E., & Heward, H. L. (1987). *Applied behavior analysis.* Upper Saddle River, NJ: Prentice-Hall.

Corson, J. A. (1967). Observational learning of a lever pressing response. *Psychonomic Science, 7,* 197–198.

Covington, T. M. (2006.) Effects of rate-based training on comprehension and maintenance of textual responding in beginning readers. (Doctoral Dissertation, Columbia University, 2006). Abstract from: UMI Proquest Digital Dissertations [on-line]. Dissertation Abstracts Item: AAT 3203746

Cullinan, V., Barnes-Holmes, D., & Smeets, P. M. (2001). A precursor to the relational evaluation procedure: Searching for the contextual cues that control equivalence responding. *Journal of Experimental Analysis of Behavior, 76*, 339–349.

Culotta, E., & Hanson, B. (2004). First words. *Science, 303*, 1315.

Daly, N. A. (1987). Recognition of words from their spellings: Integration of multiple knowledge sources. Unpublished master's thesis, Massachusetts Institute of Technology. Available on-line at http://hdl.handle.net/1721.1/14791

Daly, E. J., & Martens, B. K. (1994). A comparison of three interventions for increasing oral reading performance: Application of the instructional hierarchy. *Journal of Applied Behavior Analysis, 27*, 459–469.

Darcheville, J. C., Madelain, L., Buquet, C., Charlier, J., & Miossec, Y. (1999). Operant conditioning of the visual smooth pursuit in young infants. *Behavioural Processes, 46*, 131–139.

Dattilo, J., & Camarata, S. (1991). Facilitating conversation through self-initiated augmentative communication treatment. *Journal of Applied Behavior Analysis, 24*, 369–378.

Danforth, J. S. (2001). Altering the function of commands presented to boys with oppositional and hyperactive behavior. *Analysis of Verbal Behavior, 18*, 31–50.

Davies-Lackey, A. (2005). Yoked peer contingencies and the acquisition of observational learning repertoires. (Doctoral dissertation, Columbia University, 2005). Abstract from UMI Proquest Digital Dissertations [on-line]. Dissertations Abstracts Item: AAT 3159730.

Davis, C. A., Brady, M. P., Williams, R. E., & Hamilton, R. (1992). Effects of high-probability requests on the acquisition and generalization of responses to requests in young children with behavior disorders. *Journal of Applied Behavior Analysis, 25(4)*, 905–916.

Deacon, T. (1997). *The symbolic species: The co-evolution of language and the brain.* New York: Norton.

Deguchi, H. (1984). Observational learning from a radical-behavioristic viewpoint. *Behavior Analyst, 7(2)*, 83–95.

Delquadri, J., Greenwood, C. R., Whorton, D., Carta, J. J., & Hall, R. V. (1986). Classwide peer tutoring. *Exceptional Children, 52(6)*, 535–542.

Devin-Sheehan, L., Feldman, R. S., & Allen, V. L. (1976). Research on children tutoring children: A critical review. *Review of Educational Research, 46*, 355–385.

Dewey, J. (1910). *Educational essays.* London: Blackie & Son.

Dewey, J. (1916). *Democracy and education: An introduction to the philosophy of education.* New York: Macmillan.

Dinsmoor, J. A. (1983). Observing and conditioned reinforcement. *Behavioral and Brain Sciences, 6*, 693–728.

Donahoe, J. W., & Palmer, D. C. (2004). *Learning and complex human behavior,* Richmond, VA: Ledgetop Corporation.

Donley, C. R., & Greer, R. D. (1993). Setting events controlling social verbal exchanges between students with developmental delays. *Journal of Behavioral Education, 3(4)*, 387–401.

Dougherty, K. M. & Johnston, J. M. (1996). Overlearning, fluency, and automaticity. *Behavior Analyst, 19*, 289–292.

Drabman, R. S., & Lahey, B. B. (1974). Feedback in classroom behavior modification: Effects on the target and her classmates. *Journal of Applied Behavior Analysis, 7*, 591–598.

Drasgow, E., Halle, J. W., & Ostrosky, M. M. (1998). Effects of differential reinforcement on the generalization of a replacement mand in three children with severe language delays. *Journal of Applied Behavior Analysis, 31*, 357–374.

Drash, P. W., High, R. L., & Tudor, R. M. (1999). Using mand training to establish an echoic repertoire in young children with autism. *Analysis of Verbal Behavior, 16*, 29–44.

Durand, V. M., & Crimmins, D. B. (1987). Assessment and treatment of psychotic speech in an autistic child. *Journal of Autism and Developmental Disorders, 17*, 17–28.

Esch, B. E., Carr, J. E., & Michael, J. (2005). Evaluating stimulus-stimulus pairing and direct reinforcement in the establishment of an echoic repertoire of children diagnosed with autism. *Analysis of Verbal Behavior, 21*, 43–58.

Edmark® Reading Program: Level 1 Print Version. (2005). Cedar Falls, IA: River Deep.

Emurian, H. H. (2004). A programmed instruction tutoring system for Java™: consideration of learning performance and software self-efficacy. *Computers in Human Behavior, 20, 423–459.*

Engelmann, S., & Bruner, E. C. (1995). *Reading Mastery I Fast Cycle Rainbow Edition.* Columbus, OH: SRA/McGraw-Hill.

Engelmann, S., & Carnine, D. (1991). *Theory of instruction: Principles and applications.* Eugene, Oregon: ADI Press.

Farmer-Dougan, V. (1994). Increasing requests by adults with developmental disabilities using incidental teaching by peers. *Journal of Applied Behavior Analysis, 27(3)*, 533–544.

Finkel, A. S., & Williams, R. L. (2001). A comparison of textual and echoic prompts on the acquisition of intraverbal behavior in a six-year old boy with autism. *Analysis of Verbal Behavior, 18*, 61–70.

Fiorile, C. A., & Greer, R. D. (2006). *The induction of naming in children with no echoic-to-tact responses as a function of multiple exemplar instruction.* Manuscript submitted for publication.

Foxx, R. M., Faw, G. D., McMorrow, M. J., Kyle, M. S., & Bittle, R. G. (1988). Replacing maladaptive speech with verbal labeling responses: An analysis of generalized responding. *Journal of Applied Behavior Analysis, 21(4)*, 411–417.

Gardner III, R., Sainato, D. M., Cooper, J. O., Heron, T. E., Heward, W. L., Eshleman, J., & Grossi, T. A. (Eds.). (1994). *Behavior analysis in education: Focus on measurably superior instruction.* Monterey, CA: Brooks/Cole.

Gautreaux, G. (2005). The effects of monitoring training on the acquisition of an observational learning repertoire under peer tutoring conditions, generalization and collateral effects. (Doctoral dissertation, Columbia University, 2005). Abstract from UMI Proquest Digital Dissertations [on-line]. Dissertations Abstracts Item: AAT 3174795.

Gautreaux, G., Keohane, D. D., & Greer, R. D. (2003, July). *Transformation of production and selection functions in geometry as a function of multiple exemplar instruction.* Paper presented at the First Congress of the European Association for Behavior Analysis, Parma, Italy.

Gifaldi, H., Greer, R. D., & Pereira, J. A. (2003, July). *Effects of writer immersion on functional writing by middle school students.* Paper presented at the First Congress of the European Association for Behavior Analysis, Parma, Italy.

Gilic, L. (2005). Development of naming in two-year-old children. (Doctoral dissertation, Columbia University, 2005). Abstract from UMI Proquest Digital Dissertations [on-line]. Dissertations Abstract Item: AAT 3188740.

Goldiamond, I., & Dyrud J. E. (1966). Reading as operant behavior. In J. Money and G. Schiffman (Eds.), *The disabled reader: Education of the dyslexic child* (pp. 93–115). Baltimore: Johns Hopkins University Press.

Greenfield, P. M. (1997). Culture as process: Empirical methods for cultural psychology. In J. W. Berry, Y. Poortinga, & J. Pandey (Eds.), *Handbook of cross-cultural psychology: Vol. 1: Theory and method.* Boston: Allyn & Bacon.

Greenspoon, J. (1955). The reinforcing effects of two spoken sounds on the frequency of two responses. *American Journal of Psychology, 68*, 409–416.

Greenwood, C. R. (1999). Reflections on a research career: Perspective on 35 years of research at the Juniper Gardens Children's Project. *Exceptional Children, 66*, 7–21.

Greenwood, C. R., Hart, B., Walker, D. I., & Risley, T. (1994). The opportunity to respond and academic performance revisited: A behavioral theory of developmental retardation. In R. Gardener, III et al. (Eds.), *Behavior analysis in education: Focus on measurably superior instruction.* Pacific Groves, CA: Brooks/Cole.

Greenwood, C. R., Horton, B. T., & Utley, C. A. (2002). Academic engagement: Current perspectives in research and practice. *School Psychology Review, 31(3)*, 328–349.

Greer, R. D. (1983). Contingencies of the science and technology of teaching and pre behavioristic research practices in education. *Educational Researcher, 12*, 3–14.

Greer, R. D. (1986). A manual of teaching operations for verbal behavior. Unpublished manuscript, Yonkers, NY: CABAS® and The Fred S. Keller School.

Greer, R. D. (1991). Teaching practices to save America's schools: The legacy of B. F. Skinner. *Journal of Behavioral Education, 1*, 159–164.

Greer, R. D. (1994a). A systems analysis of the behaviors of schooling. *Journal of Behavioral Education, 4*, 255–264.

Greer, R. D. (1994b). The measure of a teacher. In R. Gardner III, D. M. Sainato, J. O. Cooper, T. E. Heron, W. L. Heward, J. W. Eshleman, & T. A. Grossi (Eds.), *Behavior analysis in education: Focus on measurably superior instruction* (pp. 161–171). Pacific Groves, CA: Brooks/Cole.

Greer, R. D. (1996a). Acting to save our schools (1984–1994). In J. Cautela & W. Ishaq (Eds.), *Contemporary issues in behavior therapy: Improving the human condition,* (137–157). New York: Plenum. Press.

Greer, R. D. (1996b). The educational crisis. In M. S. Mattaini & B. A. Thyer (Eds.), *Finding solutions to social problems: Behavioral strategies for change* (pp. 113–146). Washington DC: America Psychological Association.

Greer, R. D. (2002). *Designing teaching strategies: An applied behavior analysis systems approach.* New York: Academic.

Greer, R. D. (2005). Opinion: The two subject matters of behavior analysis and early intervention. *Journal of Early and Intensive Behavioral Interventions, 1 (2), 239–245.* http://www.behavior-analyst-online.org.

Greer, R. D., Becker, B. J., Saxe, C. D., & Mirabella, R. F. (1985). Conditioning histories and setting stimuli controlling engagement in stereotypy or toy play. *Analysis and Intervention with Developmental Disabilities, 5, 269–284.*

Greer, R. D., & Bruno, V. (1997, May). Effects of textual and echoic prompts on intraverbal responding and reduction of echolalia in young children with autism. Poster session presented at the annual international conference of the Association for Behavior Analysis, Chicago.

Greer, R. D., Chavez-Brown, M., Nirgudkar, A. S., Stolfi, L., & Rivera-Valdes, C. L. (2005). Acquisition of fluent listener responses and the educational advancement of young children with autism and severe language delays. *European Journal of Behavior Analysis, 6(2), 88–126.*

Greer, R. D., Dorow, L., Wachhaus, G., & White, E. (1973). Adult approval and students music selection behavior. *Journal of Research in Music Education, 21, 345–354.*

Greer, R. D., & Keohane, D. D. (2005). The evolutions of verbal behavior in children. *Behavioral Development Bulletin, 1, 31–47.* Reprinted in 2006 in the *Journal of Speech and Language Pathology: Applied Behavior Analysis, Volume 1(2).* http://www.behavior-analyst-today.com.

Greer, R. D., & Keohane, D. D. (in press). CABAS®: Comprehensive Application of Behavior Analysis to Schooling. In Handleman, J. (Ed.), *Pre-school education programs for children with autism, 3rd* Edition. Austin, TX: PRO ED.

Greer, R. D., Keohane, D. D., & Healy, O. (2002). Quality and applied behavior analysis. *Behavior Analyst Today, 3 (2), 120–132.* http://www.behavior-analyst-today.org

Greer, R. D., Keohane, D. D., Meincke, K., Gautreaux, G., Pereira, J. A., Chavez-Brown, M., & Yuan, L. (2004). Key instructional components of effective peer teaching for tutors, tutees and peer observers. In D. J. Moran & R. W. Malott (Eds.), *Evidence-based educational methods* (pp. 295–334). New York: Elsevier/Academic Press.

Greer, R. D. & McCorkle, N. P. (2003). *CABAS® curriculum and inventory of repertoires for children from pre-school through kindergarten,* 3rd edition. Yonkers, NY: CABAS®/Fred S. Keller School. (Publication for use in CABAS® schools only).

Greer, R. D., McCorkle. N. P., & Williams, G. (1989). A sustained analysis of the behaviors of schooling. *Behavioral Residential Treatment, 4, 113–141.*

Greer, R. D., & McDonough, S. (1999). Is the learn unit the fundamental measure of pedagogy? *Behavior Analyst, 20, 5–16.*

Greer, R. D., Nirgudkar, A., & Park, H. (2003, June). *The effect of multiple exemplar instruction on the transformation of mand and tact functions.* Paper presented at the annual international conference of the Association for Behavior Analysis, San Francisco.

Greer, R. D., & O'Sullivan, D. (2006). *Preliminary report of naming for 2-dimensional stimuli in typically developing first graders.* Unpublished report, Columbia University, Teachers College.

Greer, R. D., & Polirstok, S. R. (1982). Collateral gains and short term maintenance in reading and on-task responses by inner city adolescents as a function of their use of social reinforcement while tutoring. *Journal of Applied Behavior Analysis, 15, 123–139.*

Greer, R. D., Reilly-Lawson, T., & Walsh, D. (2006). *Teaching the social listener reinforcement component of the speaker-listener exchange stage of verbal behavior.* Unpublished manuscript, Teachers College, Columbia University.

Greer, R. D., & Ross, D. E. (2004). Verbal behavior analysis: A program of research in the induction and expansion of complex verbal behavior. *Journal of Early Intensive Behavioral Intervention, 1(2).* 141–165. http://www.jeibi.com/JEIBI-1-2.pdf.

Greer, R. D., Singer-Dudek, J, & Gautreaux, G. (2006). Observational learning. *International Journal of Psychology, 42 (6),* pp. 486–499.

Greer, R. D., Stolfi, L., Chavez-Brown, M., & Rivera-Valdez, C. (2005). The emergence of the listener to speaker component of naming in children as a function of multiple exemplar instruction. *Analysis of Verbal Behavior, 21, 123–134.*

Greer, R. D., Stolfi, L., & Pistoljevic, N. (2006). *Acquisition of naming for 2-dimensional stimuli in preschoolers: A comparison of multiple- and single-exemplar instruction.* Paper submitted for publication.

Greer, R. D., Weigand, K., & Kracher, E. (2006, May). *Yoked peer contingency game to teach observational learning repertoires and effects on naming.* Paper presented at the annual international conference of the Association for Behavior Analysis, Atlanta, GA.

Greer, R. D., & Yuan, L. (2006). *Kids say the darnedest things.* Paper submitted for publication.

Greer, R. D., Yuan, L., & Gautreaux, G. (2005). Novel dictation and intraverbal responses as a function of a multiple exemplar instructional history. *Analysis of Verbal Behavior, 21,* 99–116.

Guess, D., Keogh, W., & Sailor, W. (1978). Generalization of speech and language behavior. In R. Schiefelbusch (Ed.), *Bases of language intervention.* Baltimore: University Park Press.

Guess, D., Sailor, W., & Baer, D. M. (1976). *Functional speech and language training for the severely handicapped.* Lawerence, KS: H & H Enterprises.

Halle, J. W., Marshall, A. M., & Spradlin, J. E. (1979). Time delay: A technique to increase language use and facilitate generalization in retarded children. *Journal of Applied Behavior Analysis, 12(3),* 431–439.

Hall, G., & Sundberg, M. L. (1987). Teaching mands by manipulating conditioned establishing operations. *The Analysis of Verbal Behavior, 5,* 41–54.

Halvey, C., & Rehfeldt, R. A. (2005). Expanding vocal requesting repertoires via relational responding in adults with severe developmental disabilities. *The Analysis of Verbal Behavior, 21,* 13–25.

Hanratty, S., & Greer, R. D. (2001, May). *Comparison of two performance criteria on long-term maintenance of sight words.* Poster presented at the annual international conference of the Association for Behavior Analysis, Washington, DC.

Harapiak, S. M., Martin, G. L., & Yu, D. (1999). Hierarchical ordering of auditory discriminations and the assessment of basic learning abilities test. *Journal on Developmental Disabilities, 6,* 32–50.

Hart, B. M., & Risley, T. R. (1975). Incidental teaching of language in the preschool. *Journal of Applied Behavior Analysis, 8,* 411–420.

Hart B. M., & Risely, T. R. (1995). *Meaningful differences in the everyday life of America's children.* Baltimore: Paul Brookes.

Hart, B. M., & Rogers-Warren, A. (1978). A milieu approach to teaching language. In R. Schiefelbusch (Ed.), *Language intervention strategies* (pp. 193–235). Baltimore: University Park Press.

Hayes, S., Barnes-Homes, D., & Roche, B. (2001). *Relational frame theory: A Post-Skinnerian account of human language and cognition.* New York: Kluwer/Academic Plenum.

Hayes, S., Fox, E., Gifford, E. V., Wilson, K. G., & Barnes-Holmes, D. (2001). Derived relational responding as learned behavior. In S. Hayes, D. Barnes-Holmes, & B. Roche (Eds.). In *Relational frame theory: A Post-Skinnerian account of human language and cognition* (pp. 21–50). New York: Kluwer/Academic Plenum.

Hayes, S. C., & Hayes, L. J. (1992). Mixing metaphors: Skinner, Chomsky, and the analysis of verbal events. *Behavior and Social Issues, 2(1),* 43–46.

Henry, L. M., & Horne, P. J. (2000). Partial remediation of speaker and listener behaviors in people with severe dementia. *Journal of Applied Behavior Analysis, 33,* 631–634.

Hesse, B. E. (1993). The establishing operation revisited. *Behavior Analyst, 16(2),* 215–218.

Heward, W. L. (1994). Three "low-tech" strategies for increasing the frequency of active student response during group instruction. In R. Gardner III., D. M., Sainato, J. O., Cooper, T. E., Heron, W. L., Heward, J. W., Eshleman, & T. A., Grossi (Eds.), *Behavior analysis in education: Focus on measurably superior instruction* (pp. 283–316). Pacific Groves, CA: Brooks/Cole.

Hodges, P., & Schwethelm, B. (1984). A comparison of the effectiveness of graphic symbol and manual sign training with profoundly retarded children. *Applied Psycholinguistics, 5(3),* 223–253.

Hogin, S. E. (1996). Essential contingencies in correction procedures for increased learning in the context of the learn unit. (Doctoral dissertation, Columbia University, 1996). Abstract from UMI Proquest Digital Dissertations [on-line]. Dissertations Abstracts Item: AAT 9631721.

Holland, J. G. (1958). Human vigilance. *Science, 128,* 61–67.

Holland, J. G., & Skinner, B. F. (1961). *The analysis of behavior: A program for self instruction.* New York: McGraw Hill.

Horne, P. J., & Lowe, C. F. (1996). On the origins of naming and other symbolic behavior. *Journal of the Experimental Analysis of Behavior, 65,* 185–241.

Horne, P. J., Lowe, C. F., & Randle, V. R. L. (2004). Naming and categorization in young children II: Listener behavior training. *Journal of the Experimental Analysis of Behavior, 81,* 267–288.

Howard, J. S., & Rice, D. (1988). Establishing a generalized autoclitic repertoire in preschool children. *Analysis of Verbal Behavior, 6,* 45–60.

Ingham, P., & Greer, R. D. (1992). Changes in student and teacher responses in observed and generalized settings as function of supervisor observations of teachers. *Journal of Applied Behavior Analysis, 25,* 153–164.

Jodlowski, S. M. (2000). The effects of a teacher editor, peer editing, and serving as a peer editor on elementary students' self-editing behavior. (Doctoral dissertation, Columbia University, 2000). Abstract from UMI Proquest Digital Dissertations [on-line]. Dissertations Abstracts Item: AAT 9970212.

Johnson, K. R., & Layng, T. V. J. (1992). Breaking the structuralist barrier: Literacy and numeracy with fluency. *American Psychologist, 47,* 1475–1490.

Johnson, K. R., & Layng, T. V. J. (1994). The Morningside model of generative instruction. In R. Gardner, D. M. Sainato, J. O. Cooper, T. E. Heron, W. L. Heward, J. W. Eshleman, & T. A. Grossi (Eds.), *Behavior analysis in education: Focus on measurably superior instruction* (pp. 173–197). Pacific Grove, CA: Brooks/Cole.

Johnson, K. R., & Layng, T. V. J. (1996). On terms and procedures: Fluency. *Behavior Analyst, 19,* 281–288.

Karchmer, M. A., & Mitchell, R. E. (2003). Demographic and achievement characteristics of deaf and hard-of-hearing students. In M. Marschark & P. E. Spencer (Eds.), *Deaf studies, language, and education.* Oxford: Oxford University Press.

Karmali, I. L. (2000). Reducing palilalia and echolalia by teaching the tact operant to young children with autism. (Doctoral dissertation, Columbia University, 2000). Abstract from UMI Proquest Digital Dissertations [on-line]. Dissertations Abstracts Item: AAT 9976731.

Karmali, I., Greer, R. D., Nuzzolo-Gomez, R., Ross, D. E., & Rivera-Valdes, C. L. (2005). Reducing palilalia by presenting tact corrections to young children with autism. *Analysis of Verbal Behavior, 21,* 145–153.

Kazdin, A. E. (1978). *History of behavior modification: Experimental foundations of contemporary research.* Baltimore: University Park Press.

Keller, F. S. (1968). Good-bye teacher . . . *Journal of Applied Behavior Analysis, 5,* 79–89.

Keller, F. S., & Schonfeld, N. (1950). *Principles of psychology.* New York: Appleton Century-Crofts.

Kelly, R. L. (1997) A functional analysis of the effects of mastery and fluency on maintenance. (Doctoral dissertation, Columbia University, 1997). Abstract from UMI Proquest Digital Dissertations [on-line]. Dissertations Abstracts Item: AAT 9616720.

Kelly, R. L., & Greer, R. D. (1997, May). *Rate mastery and the long-term maintenance of sight words.* Paper presented at the annual international conference of the Association for Behavior Analysis, Chicago.

Kennedy, C. H., Itkonen, T., & Lindquist, K. (1994). Nodality effects during equivalence class formation: An extension to sight-word reading and concept development. *Journal of Applied Behavior Analysis, 27,* 673–683.

Keohane, D. D. (1997). A functional relationship between teachers' use of scientific rule governed strategies and student learning. (Doctoral dissertation, Columbia University, 1997). Abstract from UMI Proquest Digital Dissertations [on-line]. Dissertations Abstracts Item: AAT 9723806.

Keohane, D. D., & Greer, R. D. (2005). Teachers' use of a verbally governed algorithm and student learning. *International Journal of Behavioral and Consultation Therapy, 1,* 249–268.

Keohane, D. D., Greer, R. D., & Ackerman, S. A. (2006a, May). *Effects of teaching sameness across the senses on acquisition of instructional objectives by pre-listeners and listeners and emergent speakers.* Paper presented as part of a symposium at the annual international Association for Behavior Analysis, Atlanta.

Keohane, D. D., Greer, R. D., & Ackerman, S. A. (2006b, May). *The effect of conditioning visual tracking on the acquisition of instructional objectives by pre-listeners and pre-speakers.* Paper presented as part of a symposium at the annual international Association for Behavior Analysis, Atlanta.

Knapp, T. J. (1990). Verbal behavior and the history of linguistics. *Analysis of Verbal Behavior, 8,* 151–153.

Lamarre, J., & Holland, J. (1985). The functional independence of mands and tacts. *Journal of the Experimental Analysis of Behavior, 43,* 5–19.

Lamm, N., & Greer, R. D. (1991). A systematic replication of CABAS in Italy. *Journal of Behavioral Education, 1,* 427–444.

Layng, T. V. J., Twyman, J. S., & Stikeleather, G. (2004). Selected for success: How Headsprout Reading Basics™ teaches beginning reading. In D. J. Moran & R. W. Malott (Eds.), *Evidence-based educational methods* (pp. 171–195). New York: Elsevier/Academic Press.

Laraway, S., Snycerski, S., Michael, J., & Poling, A. (2003). Motivating operations and terms to describe them: Some further refinements. *Journal of Applied Behavior Analysis, 36(3),* 407–414.

Leakey, R., & Lewin, R. (1992). *Origins reconsidered.* London: ABACUS.

Lee Park, H. S. (2005). Multiple exemplar instruction and transformation of stimulus function from auditory-visual matching to visual-visual matching. (Doctoral dissertation, Columbia University, 2005). Abstract from UMI Proquest Digital Dissertations [on-line]. Dissertations Abstracts Item: AAT 3174834.

Lee, V. L. (1984). Some notes on the subject matter of Skinner's verbal behavior. *Behaviorism, 12(1),* 29–40.

Lee, V. L., & Pegler, A. M. (1982). Effects on spelling of training children to learn. *Journal of Experimental Analysis of Behavior, 37,* 311–322.

Leigland, S. (1996). An experimental analysis of ongoing verbal behavior: Reinforcement, verbal operants, and superstitious behavior. *Analysis of Verbal Behavior, 13,* 79–104.

Lerman, D. C., Parten, M., Addison, L. R., Vorndran, C. M., Volkert, V. M., & Kodak, T. (2005). A methodology for assessing the functions of emerging speech in children with developmental disabilities. *Journal of Applied Behavior Analysis, 38,* 303–316.

Lindsley, O. R. (1992). Precision teaching: Discoveries and effects. *Journal of Applied Behavior Analysis, 25,* 51–57.

Lodhi, S., & Greer, R. D. (1989). The speaker as listener. *Journal of the Experimental Analysis of Behavior, 51,* 353–360.

Longano, J. & Greer, R. D. (2006). The effects of a stimulus-stimulus pairing procedure on the acquisition of conditioned reinforcement for observing and manipulating stimuli by young children with autism. *Journal of Early and Intensive Behavior Interventions, 3.1,* 135–150. Retrieved February 22, 2006, from http://www.behavior-analyst-online.org

Longano, J., Young, K., & Greer, R. D. (2006). *The effects of a listener reinforcement procedure on the social repertoires of two students with disabilities.* Unpublished manuscript, Teachers College, Columbia University.

Lovaas, O. I. (1964). Cue properties of words: The control of operant responding by rate and content of verbal operants. *Child Development, 35,* 245–256.

Lovaas, O. I. (1977). *The autistic child: Language development through behavior modification.* New York: Irvington Publishers.

Lowe, C. F., Horne, P. J., Harris, D. S., & Randle, V. R. L. (2002). Naming and categorization in young children: Vocal tact training. *Journal of the Experimental Analysis of Behavior, 78,* 527–549.

Lowe, C. F., Horne, P. J., & Hughes, J. C. (2005). Naming and categorization in young children: III Vocal tact training and transfer of function. *Journal of Experimental Analysis of Behavior, 83(1),* 47–65.

Lowenkron, B. (1984). Coding responses and the generalization of matching to sample in children. *Journal of the Experimental Analysis of Behavior, 42,* 1–18.

Lowenkron, B. (1988). Generalization of delayed identity matching in retarded children. *Journal of the Experimental Analysis of Behavior, 50,* 163–172.

Lowenkron, B. (1989). Instructional control of generalized relational matching to sample in children. *Journal of the Experimental Analysis of Behavior, 52,* 293–309.

Lowenkron, B. (1991). Joint control and the generalization of selection-based verbal behavior. *Analysis of Verbal Behavior, 9,* 121–126.

Lowenkron, B. (1996). Joint control and word-object bi-directionality. *Journal of the Experimental Analysis of Behavior, 65,* 252–255.

Lowenkron, B. (1997). The role of naming in the development of joint control. *Journal of the Experimental Analysis of Behavior, 68,* 244–247.

Lowenkron, B., & Colvin, V. (1992). Joint control and generalized identity nonidentity matching: Saying when something is not. *Analysis of Verbal Behavior, 10,* 1–10.

Lowenkron, B., & Colvin, V. (1995). Generalized instructional control and the production of broadly applicable relational responding. *Analysis of Verbal Behavior, 12,* 13–29.

Luciano, M. C. (1986). Acquisition, maintenance, and generalization of productive intraverbal behavior through transfer of stimulus control procedures. *Applied Research in Mental Retardation, 7(1),* 1–20.

Luciano, C., Barnes-Holmes, Y., & Barnes-Holmes, D. (2002). Establishing reports of saying and doing and discriminations of say-do relations. *Research in Developmental Disabilities, 23,* 406–421.

Luke, N. M. (2003). Analysis of poetic literature using B.F. Skinner's theoretical framework from verbal behavior. *Analysis of Verbal Behavior, 19,* 107–114.

MacCorquodale, K. (1970). On Chomsky's review of Skinner's *Verbal Behavior. Journal of the Experimental Analysis of Behavior, 13,* 83–99.

Madho, V. (1997). The effects of the responses of a reader on the writing effectiveness of children with developmental delays. (Doctoral dissertation, Columbia University, 1997). Abstract from UMI Proquest Digital Dissertations [on-line]. Dissertations Abstracts Item: AAT9809740.

Madsen, C. H., Jr., Becker, W. C., & Thomas, D. R. (1968). Rules, praise, and ignoring: Elements of elementary classroom control. *Journal of Applied Behavior Analysis, 1,* 139–150.

Malott, R. W. (1992). Language, rule-governed behavior, and cognitivism: On Moerk's integration of Skinner and Chomsky's approaches to language. *Behavior and Social Issues, 2(1),* 33–42.

Malott, R. W. (2003). Behavior analysis and linguistic productivity. *Analysis of Verbal Behavior, 19,* 11–18.

Malott, R. W., & Garcia, M. E. (1991). Role of private events in rule-governed behavior. In L. J. Hayes & P. N. Chase (Eds.), *Dialogues on verbal behavior* (pp.237–258). Reno, NV: Context Press.

Marion, C., Vause, T., Harapiak, S., Martin, G. L., Yu, D. C, Sakko, G., & Walters, K. L. (2003). The hierarchical relationship between several visual and auditory discriminations and three verbal operants among individuals with developmental disabilities. *The Analysis of Verbal Behavior, 19,* 91–106.

Marquez, G. G. (2003). *One hundred years of solitude.* New York: Harper-Collins.

Marsico, M. J. (1998). Textual stimulus control of independent math performance and generalization to reading. (Doctoral dissertation, Columbia University, 1998). Abstract from UMI Proquest Digital Dissertations [on-line]. Dissertations Abstracts Item: AAT 9822227.

Martinez, R. (1996). *Single alternative environments: The matching theory and aberrant behavior.* (Doctoral dissertation, Columbia University, 1996). Abstract from UMI Proquest Digital Dissertations [on-line]. Dissertations Abstracts Item: AAT 9631746.

Matthews, B. A., Shimoff, E., & Catania, A. C. (1977). Uninstructed human responding: Sensitivity to ratio and interval responding. *Journal of the Experimental Analysis of Behavior, 27,* 543–465.

Matthews, B. A., Shimoff, E., & Catania, A. C. (1987). Saying and doing: A contingency-space analysis. *Journal of Applied Behavior Analysis, 20,* 69–74.

Matos, M. A., & de Lourdes R. da F. Passos, M. (2006). Linguistics sources of Skinner's *Verbal Behavior. Behavior Analyst, 29,* 89–108.

McCauley, R. (1987). The role of cognitive explanations in psychology. *Behaviorism, 15(1),* 27–40.

McGee, G. G., Krantz, P. J., Mason, D., & McClannahan, L. E. (1983). A modified incidental-teaching procedure for autistic youth: Acquisition and generalization of receptive object labels. *Journal of Applied Behavior Analysis, 16(3),* 329–338.

McGee, G. G., Krantz, P. J., & McClannahan, L. E. (1985). The facilitative effects of incidental teaching on preposition use by autistic children. *Journal of Applied Behavior Analysis, 18,* 17–31.

McGuiness, D. (2004). *Early reading instruction: What science really tells us about how to teach reading.* Cambridge, MA: MIT Press.

McLeish, J., & Martin, J. (1975). Verbal behavior: A review and experimental analysis. *Journal of General Psychology, 93,* 3–66.

Mead, G. H. (1909). Social psychology as counterpart to physiological psychology. *Psychological Bulletin, 6,* 401–408.

Matthews, K. M. (2005). Induction of metaphorical responses in middle school students as a function of multiple exemplar instruction. (Doctoral dissertation, Columbia University, 2005). Abstract

from: UMI Proquest Digital Dissertations [on-line]. Dissertations Abstracts Item: AAT 3174851.

Meincke, K. M., Keohane, D. D., Gifaldi, H., & Greer, R. D. (2003, July). *Novel production of metaphors as a function of multiple-exemplar instruction.* Paper presented at the First Congress of the European Association for Behavior Analysis, Parma, Italy.

Meltzoff, A. N., & Moore, M. K. (1983). Newborn infants imitate adult facial gestures. *Child Development, 54:* 702–709.

Meyers, W. A. (1970). Observational learning in monkeys. *Journal of the Experimental Analysis of Behavior, 14,* 225–235.

Michael, J. (1982). Skinner's elementary verbal relations: Some new categories. *Analysis of Verbal Behavior, 1,* 1–3.

Michael, J. (1984). Verbal behavior. *Journal of the Experimental Analysis of Behavior, 42,* 363–376.

Michael, J. (1993a). *Concepts and principles of behavior analysis.* Kalamazoo, MI: Western Michigan University.

Michael, J. (1993b). Establishing operations. *Behavior Analyst, 16,* 191–206.

Miguel, C. F., Carr, J. E., & Michael, J. (2001/2002). The effects of a stimulus-stimulus pairing procedure on the verbal behavior of children diagnosed with autism. *Analysis of Verbal Behavior, 18,* 3–14.

Mills, J. S. (1950). A system of logic. In E. Wagel (Ed.), *John Stuart Mill's philosophy of scientific method* (pp. 20–105). New York: Harper.

Moxley, R. A. (1984). Graphic discriminations for radical functional behaviorism. *Behaviorism, 12(2),* 81–96.

Moxley, R. A. (2001). The selectionist meaning of C. S. Pierce and B. F. Skinner. *Analysis of Verbal Behavior, 18,* 71–92.

Moxley, R. A. (2003). Some early similarities and later differences between Bertrand Russell and B. F. Skinner. *Behavior Analyst, 26(1),* 111–130.

Moxley, R. A. (2004). Advanced behavioral applications in schools: A review of R. Douglas Greer's designing teaching strategies: An applied behavior analysis systems approach. *Analysis of Verbal Behavior, 20,* 135–140.

Moxley, R. A. (2005). Ernst Mach and B. F. Skinner: Their similarities with two traditions for verbal behavior. *Behavior Analyst, 28(1),* 29–48.

Murphy, C., Barnes-Holmes, D., & Barnes-Holmes, Y. (2005). Derived manding in children with autism: Synthesizing Skinner's verbal behavior with relational frame theory. *Journal of Applied Behavior Analysis, 38,* 445–462.

Neuman, S. B. (1999). Books make a difference: A study of access to literacy. *Reading Research Quarterly, 34*, 286–311.

Newman, B., Buffington, D. M., & Hemmes, N. S. (1995). The effects of schedules of reinforcement on instruction following. *Psychological Record, 45*, 663–684.

Nirgudkar, A. S. (2005). The relative effects of the acquisition of naming and the multiple exemplar establishing operation experience on the acquisition of the transformation of establishing operations across mands and tacts. (Doctoral dissertation, Columbia University, 2005). Abstract from UMI Proquest Digital Dissertations [on-line]. Dissertations Abstracts Item: AAT 3159751.

Northup, J., George, T., Jones, K., Broussard, C., & Vollmer, T. R. (1996). A comparison of reinforcer assessment methods: The utility of verbal and pictorial choice procedures. *Journal of Applied Behavior Analysis, 29(2)*, 201–212.

Novak, G., & Pelaez, M. (2004). *Child and adolescent development: A behavioral systems approach.* Thousand Oaks, CA: Sage.

Nuzzolo-Gomez, R. (2000). *The use of an electronic device to mediate speech.* Unpublished manuscript, Columbia University, Teachers College.

Nuzzolo-Gomez, R. (2002). The effects of direct and observed supervisor learn units on the scientific tacts and instructional effects of teachers. (Doctoral dissertation, Columbia University, 2002). Abstract from UMI Proquest Digital Dissertations [on-line]. Dissertations Abstracts Item: AAT 3048206.

Nuzzolo-Gomez, R., & Greer, R. D. (2004). Emergence of untaught mands or tacts with novel adjective-object pairs as a function of instructional history. *The Analysis of Verbal Behavior, 24*, 30–47.

Nuzzolo-Gomez, R., Leonard, M. A., Ortiz, E., Rivera-Valdes, C. L., & Greer, R. D. (2002). Teaching children with autism to prefer books or toys over stereotypy and passivity. *Journal of Positive Behavior Interventions, 4*, 80–87.

Osborne, J. G., & Heath, J. (2003). Predicting taxonomic and thematic relational responding. *The Analysis of Verbal Behavior, 19*, 55–89.

Palmer, D. C. (2000). Chomsky's nativism reconsidered. *The Analysis of Verbal Behavior, 17*, 39–56.

Palmer, D. C., & Donahoe, J. W. (1992). Essentialism and selectionism in cognitive science and behavior analysis. *American Psychologist, 47(11)*, 1344–1358.

Paniagua, F. A., & Baer, D. M. (1982). The analysis of correspondence training as a chain reinforceable at any point. *Child Development, 53*, 786–98.

Partington, J. W., & Bailey, J. S. (1993). Teaching intraverbal behavior to preschool children. *The Analysis of Verbal Behavior, 11*, 9–18.

Partington, J. W., Sundberg, M. L., Newhouse, L., & Spengler, S. M. (1994). Overcoming an autistic child's failure to acquire a tact repertoire. *Journal of Applied Behavior Analysis 27*, 733–734.

Pereira-Delgado, J. (2005). Effects of teaching peer-monitoring on the acquisition of observational learning. (Doctoral dissertation, Columbia University, 2005). Abstract from UMI Proquest Digital Dissertations [on-line]. Dissertations Abstracts Item: AAT 3174775.

Petursdottir, A. I., Carr, J. E., Michaels, J. (2005). Emergence of mands and tacts among preschool children. *The Analysis of Verbal Behavior, 21*, 59–74.

Pinker, S. (1999). *Words and rules.* New York: Perennial.

Pistoljevic, N., & Greer, R. D. (2006). The effects of daily intensive tact instruction on preschool students' emission of pure tacts and mands in noninstructional setting. *Journal of Early and Intensive Behavioral Interventions, 3.1*, 103–120. http://www.behavior-analyst-online.org.

Place, U. T. (1982). Skinner's verbal behavior III–How to improve parts I and II. *Behaviorism, 10(2)*, 1–20.

Place, U. T. (1983). Skinner's verbal behavior IV–How to improve part IV-Skinner's account of syntax. *Behaviorism, 11(2)*, 163–186.

Place, U. T. (1985a). Three senses of the word "tact." *Behaviorism, 13(1)*, 63–74.

Place, U. T. (1985b). Three senses of the word "tact": A reply to professor Skinner. *Behaviorism, 13(2)*, 155–156.

Place, U. T. (1991). Conversation analysis and the analysis of verbal behavior. In L. J. Hayes & P. N. Chase (Eds.), *Dialogues on verbal behavior* (pp. 85–118). Reno, NV: Context Press.

Place, U. T. (1995/1996). Symbolic process and stimulus equivalence. *Behavior and Philosophy, 22(3)/24(1)*, 13–30.

Polirstok, S. R., & Greer, R. D. (1986). A replication of collateral effects and a component analysis of a successful tutoring package for inner-city adolescents. *Education and Treatment of Children, 9*, 101–121.

Poulson, C. L., Kymissis, E., Reeve, K. F., Andreatos, M., & Reeve, L. (1991). Generalized vocal imitation in infant vocal conditioning. *Journal of the Experimental Analysis of Behavior, 51, 267–279.*

Premack, D. (1976). *Intelligence in ape and man.* Hillsdale, NJ: Erlbaum Associates.

Premack, D. (2004, January 16). Is language key to human intelligence? *Science, 303,* 318–320.

Premack, D., & Premack, A. (2003). *Original intelligence.* New York: McGraw-Hill.

Rehfeldt, R. A., & Root, S. L. (2005). Establishing derived requesting skills in adults with severe developmental disabilities. *Journal of Applied Behavior Analysis, 38,* 101–105.

Reilly-Lawson, T., & Greer, R. D. (2006). Teaching the function of writing to middle school students with academic delays. *Journal of Early and Intensive Behavioral Interventions, 3.1,* 151–169. http://www.behavior-analyst-online.org

Reese, H. W. (1992a). Rules as nonverbal entities. In S. C. Hayes & L. J. Hayes (Eds.), *Understanding verbal relations* (pp. 121–134). Reno, NV: Context Press.

Reese, H. W. (1992b). Problem solving by algorithms and heuristics. In S. C. Hayes & L. J. Hayes (Eds.), *Understanding verbal relations* (pp. 153–180). Reno, NV: Context Press.

Reitman, D. (1996). A review of H. D. Schlinger, a behavior analytic view of child development. New York: Plenum (1995). *Research in Developmental Disabilities, 17,* 413–415.

Ribes-Iñesta, E. (2000). Instructions, rules, and abstraction: A misconstrued relation. *Behavior and Philosophy, 28,* 41–55.

Robinson, A. (1995). *The story of writing: Alphabets, hieroglyphs and pictograms.* London: Thames & Hudson Ltd.

Rogers-Warren, A. R., & Baer, D. M. (1976). Correspondence between saying and doing: Teaching children to share and praise. *Journal of Applied Behavior Analysis, 9,* 335–354.

Rosales-Ruiz, J., & Baer, D. M. (1996). A behavior-analytic view of development. In S. Bijou & E. Ribes (Eds.), *New Directions in Behavior Development.* Nevada: Context Press.

Rosales-Ruiz, J., & Baer, D. M. (1997). Behavioral cusps: A developmental and pragmatic concept for behavior analysis. *Journal of Applied Behavior Analysis, 30(3),* 533–544.

Ross, D. E. (1995, May). *Verbal immersion to increase speaker behavior.* Poster presentation at the annual international conference for the Association for Behavior Analysis, Washington, DC.

Ross, D. E. (1998). Generalized imitation and the mand: Inducing first instances of vocal verbal behavior in young children with autism. (Doctoral dissertation, Columbia University, 1998). Abstract from UMI Proquest Digital Dissertations [online]. Dissertations Abstracts Item: AAT 9834364.

Ross, D. E., & Greer, R. D. (2003). Generalized imitation and the mand: Inducing first instances of speech in young children with autism. *Research in Developmental Disabilities, 24,* 58–74.

Ross, D. E., Nuzzolo, R., Stolfi, L., & Natarelli, S. (2006). Effects of speaker immersion on independent speaker behavior of preschool children with verbal delays. *Journal of Early and Intensive Behavior Interventions, 3. 1,* 135–150. Retrieved February 22, 2006, from http://www.behavior-analyst-online.org

Ross, D. E., Singer-Dudek, J., & Greer, R. D. (2005). The teacher performance rate and accuracy scale (TPRA): Training as evaluation. *Education and Training in Developmental Disabilities, 40(4),* 411–423.

Saxon Phonics and Spelling Program. (2002). Orlando, FL: Saxon Publishing.

Salzinger, K. (2003). On the verbal behavior of relational frame theory: A post-Skinnerian account of human language and cognition. *Analysis of Verbal Behavior, 19,* 7–10.

Sarakoff, R. A., Taylor, B. A., & Poulson, C. L. (2001). Teaching children with autism to engage in conversation exchanges: Script fading with embedded textual stimuli. *Journal of Applied Behavior Analysis, 34,* 81–84.

Savage-Rumbaugh, E. S. (1984). Verbal behavior at a procedural level in the chimpanzee. *Journal of the Experimental Analysis of Behavior, 43,* 5–19.

Scharff, J. L. (1982). Skinner's concept of the operant: From necessitarian to probabilistic causality. *Behaviorism, 10(1),* 45–54.

Schauffler, G., & Greer, R. D. (2006). The effects of intensive tact instruction on audience-accurate tacts and conversational units. *Journal of Early and Intensive Behavioral Interventions, 3.1,* 120–132. http://www.behavior-analyst-online.org

Schnaitter, R. (1984). Skinner on the "mental" and the "physical." *Behaviorism, 12(1),* 1–14.

Schnaitter, R. (1987). Behaviorism is not cognitive and cognitivism is not behavioral. *Behaviorism, 15(1),* 1–12.

Schreck, P. (1979). *Acorn magic readers.* England: Macmillan Publishers.

Schwartz, B. S. (1994). A comparison of establishing operations for teaching mands to children with language delays. (Doctoral dissertation, Columbia University, 1994). Abstract from UMI

Proquest Digital Dissertations [on-line]. Dissertations Abstracts Item: AAT 9424540.

Selinski, J., Greer, R. D., & Lodhi, S. (1991). A functional analysis of the comprehensive application of behavior analysis to schooling. *Journal of Applied Behavior Analysis, 24*, 108–118.

Shafer, E. (1999). A review of Sundberg and Partington's teaching language to children with autism or other developmental disabilities. *The Analysis of Verbal Behavior, 16*, 45–48.

Sidman, M. (1986). Functional analysis of emergent classes. In T. Thompson & M. Zeiler (Eds.), *Analysis and integration of behavioral units* (213–245). Hillsdale, NJ: Lawrence Erlbaum.

Sidman, M. (1992). Equivalence relations: Some basic considerations. In S. C. Hayes & L. J. Hayes (Eds.), *Understanding verbal relations* (pp.15–28). Reno, NV: Context Press.

Sigafoos, J., Doss, S., & Reichle, J. (1989). Developing mand and tact repertoires in persons with severe developmental disabilities using graphic symbols. *Research in Developmental Disabilities, 11*, 165–176.

Sigafoos, J., Reichle, J., Doss, S., Hall, K., & Pettit, L. (1990). "Spontaneous" transfer of stimulus control from tact to mand contingencies. *Research in Developmental Disabilities, 11*, 165–176.

Simic, J., & Bucher, B. (1980). Development of spontaneous manding in language deficient children. *Journal of Applied Behavior Analysis, 13*, 523–528.

Simpson, J. A., Werner, E. S. (Eds.). (1989). *Oxford English dictionary* (2nd edition, vols. 1–20). New York: Oxford University Press.

Singer, J. L. (2000). A comparison of rate, contingency-shaped, and verbally governed responding to component skills and the effects on the mastery and maintenance of composite mathematical operations. (Doctoral dissertation, Columbia University, 2000). Abstract from UMI Proquest Digital Dissertations [on-line]. Dissertations Abstracts Item: AAT 9970281.

Singer-Dudek, J., & Greer, R. D. (2005). A long-term analysis of the relationship between fluency and the training and maintenance of complex math skills. *Psychological Record, 55*, 361–376.

Skinner, B. F. (1938). *The behavior of organisms: An experimental analysis*. New York: Appleton-Century, 1938.

Skinner, B. F. (1957, 1992). *Verbal Behavior*. Acton, MA: Copley Publishing Group and the B. F. Skinner Foundation.

Skinner, B. F. (1968). *A science and technology of teaching*. New York: Appleton-Century-Crofts.

Skinner, B. F. (1969). *Contingencies of reinforcement*. New York: Appleton-Century-Crofts.

Skinner, B. F. (1979). *The shaping of a behaviorist*. New York: Knopf.

Skinner, B. F. (1984a). Some consequences of selection. *Behavioral and Brain Sciences, 7(4)*, 502.

Skinner, B. F. (1984b). Theoretical contingencies. *Behavioral and Brain Sciences, 7(4)*, 541.

Skinner, B. F. (1984c). Coming to terms with private events. *Behavioral and Brain Sciences, 7(4)*, 572.

Skinner, B. F. (1984d). Contingencies and rules. *Behavioral and Brain Sciences, 7(4)*, 607.

Skinner, B. F. (1984e). Phylogenic and ontogenic environments. *Behavioral and Brain Sciences, 7(4)*, 701.

Skinner, B. F. (1985). Reply to Place. *Behaviorism, 13(1)*, 75–76.

Skinner, B. F. (1986). Some thoughts about the future. *Journal of the Experimental Analysis of Behavior, 45*, 229–35.

Skinner, B. F. (1989). The behavior of the listener. In S. C. Hayes (Ed.), *Rule-governed Behavior: Cognition, contingencies and instructional control* (85–96). New York: Plenum.

Smith, R., Michael, J., & Sundberg, M. L. (1996). Automatic reinforcement and automatic punishment in infant vocal behavior. *The Analysis of Verbal Behavior, 13*, 39–48.

Smith, T. L. (1983). Skinner's environmentalism: The analogy with natural selection. *Behaviorism, 11(2)*, 133–154.

Spradlin, J. E. (1985). Studying the effects of the audience on verbal behavior. *The Analysis of Verbal Behavior, 3*, 6–10.

Spradlin, J. E. (2003). Alternative theories of the origin of derived stimulus relations. *Analysis of Verbal Behavior, 19*, 3–6.

Staats, A. W. (1968). *Learning, language, and cognition: Theory, research, and method for the study of human behavior and its development*. New York: Holt.

Stafford, M. W., Sundberg, M. L., & Braam, S. J. (1988). A preliminary investigation of the consequences that define the mand and the tact. *The Analysis of Verbal Behavior, 6*, 61–71.

Steele, D. L., Hates, S. C., & Brownstein, A. J. (1990). Reinforcement, stereotypy, and rule discovery. *The Analysis of Verbal Behavior, 8*, 57–66

Stolfi, L. (2005). The induction of observational learning repertoires in preschool children with developmental disabilities as a function of peer-yoked contingencies. (Doctoral dissertation, Columbia University, 2005). Abstract from UMI Proquest Digital Dissertations [on-line]. Dissertations Abstracts Item: AAT 3174899.

Sulzer-Azaroff, B. Drabman, R., Greer, R. D., Hall, R. V., Iwata, B., & O'Leary, S. (Eds.). (1988).

Behavior analysis in education from the Journal of Applied Behavior Analysis, 1968–1987. Lawrence, KS: Society for the Experimental Analysis of Behavior.

Sundberg, C. T., & Sundberg, M. L. (1990). Comparing topography-based verbal behavior with stimulus selection-based verbal behavior. *The Analysis of Verbal Behavior, 8*, 31–41.

Sundberg, M. L. (1985). Teaching verbal behavior to pigeons. *The Analysis of Verbal Behavior, 3(1)*, 11–17.

Sundberg, M. L. (1991). 301 research topics from Skinner's book *Verbal behavior. The Analysis of Verbal Behavior, 9*, 81–96.

Sundberg, M. L. (1993). The application of establishing operations. *Behavior Analyst, 16(2)*, 211–214.

Sundberg, M. L. (1993). Selecting a response form for nonverbal persons: Facilitated communication, pointing systems, or sign language? *The Analysis of Verbal Behavior, 11*, 99–116.

Sundberg, M. L. (1998). Realizing the potential of Skinner's analysis of verbal behavior. *Behavior Analyst, 15*, 143–147.

Sundberg, M. L., Loeb, M., Hale, L., & Eigenheer, P. (2001). Continuing establishing operations to teach mands for information. *The Analysis of Verbal Behavior, 18*, 15–30.

Sundberg, M. L., Michael, J., Partington, J. W., & Sundberg, C. A. (1996). The role of automatic reinforcement in early language acquisition. *The Analysis of Verbal Behavior, 13*, 21–37.

Sundberg, M. L., & Partington, J. W. (1998). *Teaching language to children with autism or other developmental disabilities.* Pleasant Hill, CA: Behavior Analysts.

Sundberg, M. L., San Juan, B., Dawdy, M, & Argüelles, M. (1990). The acquisition of tacts, mands, and intraverbals by individuals with traumatic brain injury. *The Analysis of Verbal Behavior, 8*, 83–100.

Taylor, B. A., & Harris, S. L. (1995). Teaching children with autism to seek information: Acquisition of novel information and generalization of responding. *Journal of Applied Behavior Analysis, 28*, 3–14.

Thorndike, E. L. (1901). Mental life of monkeys. *Psychological Review, Monograph Supplements, 15*. New York: Macmillan.

Thorndike, E. L. (1911). *Animal intelligence: Experimental studies.* New York: Macmillan.

Tiger, J. H., & Hanley, G. P. (2004). Developing stimulus control of preschooler mands: An analysis of schedule-correlated and contingency-specifying stimuli. *Journal of Applied Behavior Analysis, 37*, 517–521.

Tsai, H., & Greer, R. D. (2006). Conditioned preference for books and faster acquisition of textual responses by preschool children. *Journal of Early and Intensive Behavioral Interventions. 3(1)*, 35–60. http://www.behavioranalyst-online.org

Tsiouri, I., & Greer, R. D. (2003). Inducing vocal verbal behavior through rapid motor imitation training in young children with language delays. *Journal of Behavioral Education, 12*, 185–206.

Twyman, J. S. (1996a). An analysis of functional independence within and between secondary verbal operants. (Doctoral dissertation, 1998, Columbia University). Abstract from UMI Proquest Digital Dissertations [on-line]. Dissertations Abstracts Item: AAT 9631793.

Twyman, J. S. (1996b). The functional independence of impure mands and tacts of abstract stimulus properties. *The Analysis of Verbal Behavior, 13*, 1–19.

Valleley, R. J., Shriver, M. D., & Rozema, S. (2005). Using brief experimental assessment of reading interventions for identification and treatment of a vocal habit. *Journal of Applied Behavior Analysis, 38(1)*, 129–133.

Vargas, E. A. (1982b). Intraverbal behavior: The codic, duplic, and sequelic subtypes. *Analysis of Verbal Behavior, 1*, 5–7.

Vargas, E. A. (1982a). Hume's "ought" and "is" statement: A radical behaviorist's perspective. *Behaviorism, 10(1)*, 1–24.

Vargas, E. A. (1988). Event-governed and verbally-governed behavior. *Analysis of Verbal Behavior, 6*, 11–22.

Vargas, E. A. (1991). Verbal behavior and artificial intelligence. In L. J. Hayes & P. N. Chase (Eds.), *Dialogues on verbal behavior* (pp.287–308). Reno, NV: Context Press.

Vargas, E. A. (1993). From behaviorism to selectionism. *Educational Technology, 33*, 46–51.

Vaughan, M. E., & Michael, J. L. (1982). Automatic reinforcement: An important but ignored concept. *Behaviorism, 10(2)*, 101–112.

Warren, S. F., McQuarter, R. J., & Rogers-Warren, A. K. (1984). The effects of mands and models on the speech of unresponsive language delayed preschool children. *Journal of Speech and Hearing Disorders, 49*, 40–51.

Watson, J. B. (1908). Imitation in monkeys. *Psychological Bulletin, 5*, 169–178.

Watson, J. B. (1914). *Behavior-an introduction to comparative psychology.* New York: Holt.

Wenrich, W. W. (1964). The tact relation: An experiment in verbal behavior. *Journal of General Psychology, 71*, 71–73.

Wessells, M. G. (1982). A critique of Skinner's views on the obstructive character of cognitive theories. *Behaviorism, 10(1)*, 65–84.

Winokur, S. (1976). *A primer of verbal behavior: An operant view.* Englewood Cliffs, NJ: Prentice Hall.

Williams, G., & Greer, R. D. (1993). A comparison of verbal-behavior and linguistic communication curricula for training developmentally delayed adolescents to acquire and maintain vocal speech. *Behaviorology, 1*, 31–46.

Wolery, M., Holcombe, A., Billings, S. S., & Vassilaros, M. A. (1993). Effects of simultaneous prompting and instructive feedback. *Early Education and Development, 4*, 20–31.

Wraikat, R., Sundberg, C. T., & Michael, J. (1991). Topography-based and selection- based verbal behavior: A further comparison. *Analysis of Verbal Behavior, 9*, 1–17.

Yamamoto, J., & Mochizuki, A. (1988). Acquisition and functional analysis of manding with autistic students. *Journal of Applied Behavior Analysis, 21(1)*, 57–64.

Yoon, S. Y. (1998). Effects of an adult's vocal sound paired with a reinforcing event on the subsequent acquisition of mand functions. (Doctoral dissertation, Columbia University, 1998). Abstract from UMI Proquest Digital Dissertations [online]. Dissertations Abstracts Item: AAT 9839031.

Yoon, S. Y., & Bennett, G. (2000). Effects of a stimulus-stimulus pairing procedure on conditioning vocal sounds as reinforcers. *Analysis of Verbal Behavior, 17*, 75–88.

Young, J. M., Krantz, P. J., McClannahan, L. E., & Poulson, C. L., (1994) Generalized imitation and response-class formation in children with autism. *Journal of Applied Behavior Analysis 27(4)*, 685–697.

Young, K. R., West, R. P., Howard, V. F., & Whitney, R. (1986). Acquisition, fluency training, generalization, and maintenance of dressing skills of two developmentally disabled children. *Education and Treatment of Children, 9(1)*, 16–29.

INDEX